WORLD FOOTBALL RECORDS

This edition published in 2018

Copyright © Carlton Books Limited 2018

Carlton Books Limited
20 Mortimer Street
London W1T 3JW

A CIP catalogue record for this book is available from
the British Library

10 9 8 7 6 5 4 3 2 1

ISBN: 978-1-78739-160-4

Editor: Martin Corteel
Designers: Darren Jordan & Luke Griffin
Picture research: Paul Langan
Production: Ena Matagic

Printed in Slovenia

**Right: France captain Hugo Lloris shows
off the FIFA World Cup after his country
had won the trophy for a second time
in 2018, beating Croatia 4-2 in the final.**

**Next pages (left to right): Top:
Philippe Coutinho (Brazil): Middle:
Kylian Mbappe (France), Eden Hazard
(Belgium): Bottom: Harry Kane
(England), Luka Modric (Croatia),
Thibaut Courtois (Belgium).**

WORLD FOOTBALL RECORDS

TENTH EDITION

KEIR RADNEDGE

CARLTON BOOKS

CONTENTS

INTRODUCTION

FOOTBALL'S status as a global phenomenon was emphasized by the 2018 FIFA World Cup finals in Russia. Dramatic matches supported by the media and sponsorship explosion of the past three decades fuelled a tournament which attracted three billion viewers to televisions around the planet, almost eight million to the fan fests in Russia and record numbers to FIFA's digital channels.

Technology not only provided winning numbers it also secured an important role out on the pitch with the utilization of a video assistant referee at every game. In 2014, when FIFA decided to pursue goal-line technology, opponents feared the advance of technology. Russia 2018 proved that football had much more to gain from VAR than lose.

Football's global following is continually expanding. The UEFA Champions League is not merely a European tournament. TV broadcasts pack bars and cafes around the planet to watch clubs whose teams are as appreciated worldwide as the national teams who contest the FIFA World Cup.

That explains, out on the pitch, the particular factor which mesmerizes fans: football's mixture of both team tradition and individual expertise. This has been represented in outstanding fashion by the goal-scoring achievements for both countries and clubs of Argentina's Lionel Messi and Portugal's Cristiano Ronaldo.

One of the most intriguing questions for the game's worldwide audience concerns the identity of the next generation of superstars? Will French World Cup-winner Kylian Mbappe lead the way, or are there other teenage talents about to explode on the game?

All the many aspects of this grand football landscape feature in this latest, 10th edition of *World Football Records*. Here are the achievements and stars, old and new, from all of football's major international tournaments for men and women at senior and junior levels ... and maybe tomorrow's superstars as well.

Keir Radnedge
London, July 2018

FIFA's Fan Fests drew huge crowds to all of the sites. As well as the matches being shown on giant screens, there was plenty of entertainment for those who attended the events.

PART 1:
THE COUNTRIES

FOOTBALL'S popularity is evident across all levels of society through all the world's continents and nations. It knows no boundaries of politics or religion or race – and at its heart is a simple structure that has worked effectively for well over a century.

At the head of the global football pyramid is FIFA, the world federation. Supporting FIFA's work are the six regional geographical federations representing Africa, Asia, Europe, Oceania, South America, plus the Caribbean, Central and North America.

Empowering the regions in turn are the national associations of 211 countries – and thus FIFA can boast more countries in membership than even the United Nations.

The member associations are pivotal. They field the national teams who have built sporting history through their many and varied achievements in international competitions such as the FIFA World Cup. They also oversee the growth of football in their countries, from professional leagues to grassroots.

Representative teams from England and Scotland played out the first formal international football matches in the late 19th century, thus laying the foundation for the four British home nations' unique independent status within a world football family otherwise comprised of nation states. The original British home championship was the first competition for national teams but its demise, through fixtures pressure, has left the Copa America in South America as the oldest survivor. This is contested every four years with the next edition just around the footballing corner in Brazil in June and July of 2019.

Later came the FIFA World Cup in 1930 as well as the regional continental championships. Such traditional events may yet be supplemented by the exciting prospect of a global nations league. The competitive structure of the world game is always evolving. Football is indeed a game of perpetual motion.

The Opening Ceremony at every FIFA World Cup is greatly anticipated and the show put on by the Russian hosts in Moscow in June 2018 did not disappoint, being a combination of colour, history and pageantry.

EUROPE

Europe's footballing pre-eminence was underlined in 2017–18. Spain's Real Madrid won the FIFA Club World Cup for the second consecutive year and then France triumphed at the FIFA World Cup which was staged in Europe, in Russia. In addition, all four semi-finalists were from the home continent. Europe had been the original cradle of the modern game and sources more than 90 per cent of world football's modern wealth. UEFA, the European football federation, claims more full FIFA members (55) than any other regional governing body.

Hundreds of thousands of ecstatic French football fans line the Avenue des Champs-Elysees as they celebrate the nation's second victory in the FIFA World Cup, after beating Croatia 4-2 in the 2018 final.

ENGLAND

England is where football began; the country where the game was first developed, which saw the creation of the game's first Football Association and the first organized league, and which now plays host to the richest domestic league in the world. But England have not had it all their own way on the international scene. Far from it. A solitary FIFA World Cup win apart, as hosts in 1966, the Three Lions have struggled to shake off the "underachievers" tag in big tournaments – but a run to the 2018 semi-finals reignited optimism.

IF THE CAP FITS

England's players in the historic first game against Scotland all wore **cricket-style caps** while the Scots wore hoods. England's "fashion statement" prompted the use of the term "cap" to refer to any international appearance. The tradition of awarding a cap to British international footballers still survives today.

NEW SOUTHGATE, NEW HOPE

England enjoyed their best FIFA World Cup performance since 1990 in Russia in 2018. Their manager was **Gareth Southgate**, the successor to Sam Allardyce, who had lasted just one match – a last-minute 1-0 qualifier win in Slovakia in September 2016. A defender or midfielder, Southgate had missed the decisive penalty in the 1996 UEFA European Championship semi-final against Germany. But he earned redemption in summer 2018 as his side – and his waistcoat – won nationwide acclaim. England enjoyed their biggest victory at a FIFA World Cup when beating Panama 6-1 in their second first-round match and went on to finish fourth, losing 2-1 to Croatia after extra-time in their semi-final and then 2-0 to Belgium in the third-place play-off. Southgate's squad was the second-youngest in Russia and became the first England team to win a FIFA World Cup penalty shoot-out, at the fourth time of asking. They beat Colombia 4-3 in the second round following a 1-1 draw. Everton goalkeeper Jordan Pickford was the hero, saving from Carlos Bacca, before Eric Dier struck the decisive penalty.

RUNAWAY SUCCESS

England have hit double figures five times: beating Ireland 13-0 and 13-2 in 1882 and 1899, thrashing Austria 11-1 in 1908, crushing Portugal 10-0 in Lisbon in 1947 and then the United States 10-0 in 1964 in New York. The ten goals were scored by Roger Hunt (four), Fred Pickering (three), Terry Paine (two) and **Bobby Charlton**.

IN THE BEGINNING

The day it all began ... 30 November 1872, when England played their first official international match, against Scotland, at Hamilton Crescent, Partick. The result was a 0-0 draw in front of a then massive crowd of 4,000, who each paid an admission fee of one shilling (5p). In fact, teams representing England and Scotland had played five times before, but most of the Scottish players had been based in England and the matches are considered unofficial. England's team for the first official game was selected by Charles Alcock, the secretary of the Football Association. His one regret was that, because of injury, he could not pick himself to play. In contrast, the first rugby union international between England and Scotland had been played in 1871, but England's first Test cricket match was not played until March 1877, against Australia in Melbourne.

FIRST DEFEAT

Hungary's 6-3 win at Wembley in 1953 was the first time England had lost at home to continental opposition. Their first home defeat by non-British opposition came against the Republic of Ireland, who beat them 2-0 at Goodison Park, Liverpool, in 1949.

HAVE A BASH, ASH

Left-back **Ashley Cole** is one of only nine England footballers to win 100 caps but is the only outfield player to reach the mark without ever having scored a goal – next on the list is Gary Neville (85 caps). He overtook Kenny Sansom as England's most-capped full-back when he represented his country for the 87th time, against Denmark in February 2011, and made his 100th appearance against Brazil at Wembley in February 2013. Cole's 98th international, against Italy in the Euro 2012 quarter-final, ended unhappily, as he missed England's final penalty in the shoot-out. But Cole did set another record that day: his 22nd finals match is the most by an England player. After 107 apperances, Cole announced his retirement from international football after being omitted from England's 2014 FIFA World Cup squad. In the club game he boasts more FA Cup winner's medals than any other

ENGLAND'S BIGGEST WINS

1882	Ireland 0 England 13
1899	England 13 Ireland 2
1908	Austria 1 England 11
1964	United States 0 England 10
1947	Portugal 0 England 10
1982	England 9 Luxembourg 0
1960	Luxembourg 0 England 9
1895	England 9 Ireland 0
1927	Belgium 1 England 9
1896	Wales 1 England 9
1890	Ireland 1 England 9

ENGLAND'S BIGGEST DEFEATS

1954	Hungary 7 England 1
1878	Scotland 7 England 2
1881	England 1 Scotland 6
1958	Yugoslavia 5 England 0
1964	Brazil 5 England 1
1928	England 1 Scotland 5
1882	Scotland 5 England 1
1953	England 3 Hungary 6
1963	France 5 England 2
1931	France 5 England 2

NAUGHTY BOYS

Raheem Sterling's red card against Ecuador in June 2014 was the 15th for an England player in a full international. Alan Mullery was England's first player to be dismissed, against Yugoslavia in June 1968. David Beckham and Wayne Rooney have both been sent off twice. Paul Scholes was the only England player to be sent off at the old Wembley Stadium, against Sweden in June 1999.

FRANK'S A LOT, STEVIE G FORCE

A 15-year era encompassing what some dubbed England's "golden generation" ended in 2014 when midfield mainstays **Steven Gerrard** and **Frank Lampard** retired from international football. Gerrard bowed out as the country's third most-capped player, scoring 21 goals in 114 appearances. He was captain at the 2010 and 2014 tournaments, as well as the 2012 UEFA European Championship. The Liverpool legend, who joined LA Galaxy in summer 2015, is the only player to score in an FA Cup final, a League Cup final, a Uefa Cup final and a UEFA Champions League final. Lampard, who joined New York City FC in 2014, is England's most prolific penalty-scorer, amounting for nine of his 29 England goals in 106 appearances.

SENIOR MOMENT

Goalkeeper David James became the oldest player ever to make his FIFA World Cup finals debut, aged 39 years and 321 days, when he appeared for England at the 2010 competition in South Africa. He kept a clean sheet in a goalless Group C draw against Algeria.

HEAD FOR GOAL

Robust and commanding centre-backs had the honour of scoring both the last England goal at the old Wembley stadium, closed down in 2000, and the first in the new version, which was finally opened in 2007. Tony Adams scored England's second in a 2-0 win over Ukraine in May 2000 – Germany's Dietmar Hamann hit the only goal of the final international at the old Wembley, four months later – and captain John Terry headed his side ahead in the new stadium's showpiece June 2007 friendly against Brazil, which ended 1-1. Terry shares the honour of scoring the most England goals (six) by a defender with 1966 FIFA World Cup winner Jack Charlton.

BLANKS OF ENGLAND

A goalless draw against Algeria in Cape Town in June 2010 made England the first country to finish 10 different FIFA World Cup matches 0-0. Their first was against Brazil in 1958, while the tally also includes both second-round group games in 1982 against eventual runners-up West Germany and hosts Spain. An 11th goalless draw followed against Costa Rica at Belo Horizonte in 2014. England's 1-1 second round draw with Colombia in 2018 saw them join Italy as the FIFA World Cup record-holders for most drawn matches with 21.

THE LONG AND THE SHORT OF IT

At 6ft 7in, centre-forward Peter Crouch is the tallest player ever to stretch above opposing defences for England – while Fanny Walden, the Tottenham winger who won two caps in 1914 and 1922, was the shortest at 5ft 2in. Sheffield United goalkeeper Billy "Fatty" Foulke became the heaviest England player at 18st when he played against Wales on 29 March 1897.

NEW KING KANE

Centre-forward **Harry Kane** went into the 2018 FIFA World Cup as England's new permanent captain; he ended it as the nation's first Golden Boot winner since Gary Lineker in 1986. His six goals, including a hat-trick in a 6-1 first round victory over Panama – made him only the third England player to score a FIFA World Cup treble, after Sir Geoff Hurst in the 1966 final and Lineker in 1986. Kane's tally included three penalties, two against Poland and another in the second-round victory over Colombia when he also found the net from the spot in England's shoot-out triumph. Kane ended the tournament with19 England goals from 30 appearances. The first strike came just 79 seconds into his international debut as a substitute, a header against Lithuania at Wembley in March 2015. Only two men have scored earlier in their England debuts: Bill Nicholson, against Portugal in 1951, 19 seconds into his only international appearance, and decorated First World War soldier Jack Cock after 30 seconds against Ireland in 1919, in the first of his two matches for England.

WAITING FOR THE CALL

Four England internationals played at the 1966 FIFA World Cup yet missed out on the triumphant final against West Germany – Ian Callaghan, John Connelly, Jimmy Greaves and Terry Paine. Liverpool winger Callaghan would then endure the longest wait between England appearances, when he went 11 years and 49 days between his showing in a 2-0 win over France at that 1966 tournament and his return to international action in a goalless draw with Switzerland in September 1977. The game against the Swiss was his third – and penultimate – outing for England.

TEENAGE PROMISE

Manchester United rookie Marcus Rashford became, at 18 years and 209 days, the youngest England debutant to score, when he found the net just three minutes into his international bow, a friendly against Australia on 27 May 2016. England's youngest debutant is Theo Walcott, who was 17 years and 75 days when facing Hungary in May 2006. Michael Owen – at 18 years and 183 days – became the country's youngest player at a FIFA World Cup when coming on as a substitute against Tunisia in 1998.

BECKHAM'S RECORD

David Beckham played for England for the 109th time when he appeared as a second-half substitute in the 4-0 win over Slovakia in a friendly international on 28 March 2009. That overtook the record number of England games for an outfield player, which had been set by Bobby Moore, England's 1966 FIFA World Cup-winning captain.

Beckham, born on 2 May 1975, in Leytonstone, London, made his first appearance for his country on 1 September 1996, in a FIFA World Cup qualifying match against Moldova. He was appointed full-time England captain in 2001 by the then manager Sven-Goran Eriksson – stepping down after England's quarter-final defeat by Portugal at the 2006 FIFA World Cup. He ended his England career on 115 caps and hung up his boots in May 2013, at the age of 38, having just won the league in a fourth different country with French club Paris Saint-Germain. Beckham's 68 competitive matches record for England was passed by Steven Gerrard against Costa Rica in the 2014 FIFA World Cup. Also retiring from the game in summer 2013 was England's fourth highest scorer **Michael Owen**, who netted a stunning solo goal against Argentina at the 1998 FIFA World Cup – only for Beckham to be sent off in a 2-2 draw before England lost on penalties.

ALEXANDER THE LATE

The oldest player to make his debut for England remains Alexander Morten, who was 41 years and 114 days old when facing Scotland on 8 March 1873 in England's first home game, at The Oval in Kennington, London. He was also captain that day and is still the country's oldest-ever skipper.

THE GOOD SONS

Eighteen-year-old winger Alex Oxlade-Chamberlain became the fifth son of a former England international to earn a cap for his country when he made his debut against Norway in May 2012 – 28 years after the last of his father Mark Chamberlain's eight appearances. Oxlade-Chamberlain became England's youngest scorer in a FIFA World Cup qualifier with his strike against San Marino in October 2013. The earlier pairings were George Eastham Snr (one cap, 1935) and George Eastham Jnr (19, 1963–66); Brian Clough (two, 1959) and Nigel Clough (14, 1989–93); Frank Lampard Snr (two, 1972–80) and **Frank Lampard Jnr** (106, 1999–2014); and Ian Wright (33, 1991–98) and his adopted son Shaun Wright-Phillips (36, 2004–10). The only grandfather and grandson to play for England are Bill Jones, who won two caps in 1950, and Rob Jones, who won eight between 1992 and 1995.

GRAND OLD MAN

Stanley Matthews became England's oldest-ever player when he lined up at outside-right against Denmark on 15 May 1957 at the age of 42 years 104 days. That was 22 years and 229 days after his first appearance. Matthews was also England's oldest marksman. He was 41 years eight months old when he scored against Northern Ireland on 10 October 1956. In stark contrast to Matthews's longest England career, full-back Martin Kelly holds the record for the shortest – a two-minute substitute appearance in a 1-0 friendly win over Norway in 2012.

CAPTAIN SOLO

Claude Ashton, the Corinthians centre-forward, set a record when he captained England on his only international appearance. This was a 0-0 draw against Northern Ireland in Belfast on 24 October 1925.

TOP SCORERS

1	Wayne Rooney	53
2	Bobby Charlton	49
3	Gary Lineker	48
4	Jimmy Greaves	44
5	Michael Owen	40
6	Tom Finney	30
=	Nat Lofthouse	30
=	Alan Shearer	30
9	Frank Lampard	29
=	Vivian Woodward	29

TOP CAPS

1	Peter Shilton	125
2	Wayne Rooney	119
3	David Beckham	115
4	Steven Gerrard	114
5	Bobby Moore	108
6	Ashley Cole	107
7	Bobby Charlton	106
=	Frank Lampard	106
9	Billy Wright	105
10	Bryan Robson	90

CAPTAINS COURAGEOUS

The international careers of Billy Wright and **Bobby Moore**, who both captained England a record 90 times, very nearly overlapped. Wright, from Wolves, played for England between 1946 and 1959 and Moore, from West Ham, between 1962 and 1973, including England's FIFA World Cup win in 1966. Moore remains England's youngest captain, having been 22 years and 47 days old when appointed against Czechoslovakia on 29 May 1963.

SHARED RESPONSIBILITY

Substitutions meant the captain's armband passed between four different players during England's 2-1 friendly win over Serbia and Montenegro on 3 June 2003. Regular captain David Beckham was missing, so Michael Owen led the team out, but was substituted at half-time. England's second-half skippers were Owen's then-Liverpool team-mates Emile Heskey and Jamie Carragher and Manchester United's Philip Neville. The first time three different players have captained England in one FIFA World Cup finals match was against Morocco in 1986, when first-choice skipper Bryan Robson went off injured, his vice-captain Ray Wilkins was then sent off and goalkeeper Peter Shilton took over leadership duties.

HEAD START

Bryan Robson holds the records for fastest England goal in the FIFA World Cup, after 27 seconds of a 3-1 win against France in 1982, and for England at (old) Wembley, netting after 38 seconds in a 2-1 win over Czechoslovakia in 1989. Another Manchester United player, Teddy Sheringham, scored sooner than any other England player has managed after coming on to the field – he scored with his first touch, a header 15 seconds into a substitute appearance, against Greece in a 2002 FIFA World Cup qualifier in October 2001.

GAME OF STONES

No England defender had ever scored more than one FIFA World Cup goal – until Manchester City centre-back **John Stones** managed two in 32 first-half minutes, against Panama in Nizhny Novgorod, Russia, in 2018. He was joined on the scoresheet, two games later, by fellow centre-back **Harry Maguire**, who opened the scoring in a 2-0 quarter-final victory over Sweden. Neither defender had scored for England before the tournament – and Maguire only received his first international call-up in August 2017, turning up with his kit in black bin-bag – earning himself a ticking-off from his mother. Maguire had attended the 2016 UEFA European Championship in France – but as an England fan, with friends.

ROON AT THE TOP

When **Wayne Rooney** scored against Macedonia in September 2003, he became England's youngest goalscorer at the age of 17 years and 317 days – and it has long seemed only a matter of time before he broke Sir Bobby Charlton's England record of 49 strikes. He drew level thanks to a penalty against San Marino in September 2015, then reached his half-century with another spot-kick, against Switzerland, three days later. By this time Rooney was not only Manchester United but also England captain. His 100th cap against Slovenia in November 2014, aged 29 years and 22 days, made him the youngest man to reach a century of caps for England – three years younger than previous record-holder Bobby Moore. Rooney retired from international football in 2017 with 119 caps, 53 goals and 74 tournament games and moved to play in the United States with DC United in 2018.

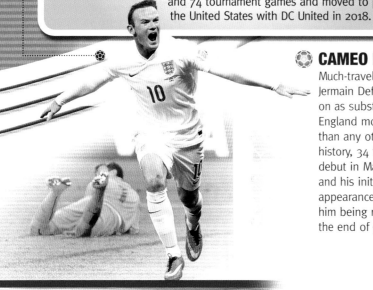

COMING OVER HERE

Argentina were the first non-UK side to play at Wembley – England won 2-1 on 9 May 1951 – while Ferenc Puskas and the "Magical Magyars" of Hungary were the first "foreign", or "continental", side to beat England at home, with their famous 6-3 victory at Wembley in 1953. This humiliation marked Alf Ramsey's last game as an England player. England first tasted defeat to a "foreign" side when they lost 4-3 to Spain in Madrid on 15 May 1929. Two years later England gained their revenge with a 7-1 win at Highbury.

CAMEO ROLE

Much-travelled striker Jermain Defoe has come on as substitute for England more often than any other player in history, 34 times since his debut in March 2004 – and his initial 17 starting appearances all ended in him being replaced before the end of 90 minutes.

ROLL UP, ROLL UP

The highest attendance for an England game came at Hampden Park on 17 April 1937, when 149,547 spectators crushed in to see Scotland's 3-1 victory in the British Home Championships. Only 2,378 turned up in Bologna, Italy, to see San Marino stun England after nine seconds in Graham Taylor's side's 7-1 victory that was not enough to secure qualification to the 1994 FIFA World Cup.

FIRST AND FOREMOST

England's first official international was a 0-0 draw against Scotland in Glasgow on 30 November 1872, though England and Scotland had already played a number of unofficial representative matches against each other prior to that. Given that England's only opponents for four decades were the home nations – and only Scotland for the first seven years, it is not surprising that England's first draw, win and defeat were all against their northern neighbours. After the goalless first game, the second fixture – played at The Oval on 8 March 1873 – proved a more exciting affair, with England winning 4-2. In their third game, back in Glasgow almost exactly a year later, Scotland evened things up with a 2-1 win. These fixtures completed the trio of first wins, defeats and draws for the oldest participants in international football. The Football Association's 150-year anniversary celebrations in 2013 included a Wembley friendly against Scotland, the first time the two sides had met since a two-leg Euro 2000 qualifying play-off in October 1999. Competitive rivalry returned in the FIFA World Cup 2018 qualifiers as England won 3-0 at Wembley and drew 2-2 at Hampden Park.

SPURRED TO GLORY

Right-wing-back Kieran Trippier's goal against Croatia in the 2018 FIFA World Cup semi-final made him the 11th Tottenham Hotspur player to score for England at a major tournament – more than any other English club. Clubmates Harry Kane (six) and Dele Alli (one) also scored in Russia – and they followed in the footsteps of England and Spurs goalscoring legends Jimmy Greaves and **Gary Lineker.** Greaves holds the England record for hat-tricks, with six, while Lineker is England's leading FIFA World Cup goalscorer with 10. Tottenham have also provided the country with more players than any other club. Midfielder Harry Winks became the 78th and latest with his debut away to Lithuania in October 2017.

YOUR COUNTRY NEEDS YOU

The first England teams were selected from open trials of Englishmen who responded to the FA's adverts for players. It was only when these proved too popular and unwieldy that, in 1887, the FA decided that it would be better to manage the process through an International Selection Committee, which continued to pick the team until Sir Alf Ramsey's appointment in 1962.

MANAGERIAL ROLL OF HONOUR

Walter Winterbottom	(1946–62)
Sir Alf Ramsey	(1962–74)
Joe Mercer	(1974)
Don Revie	(1974–77)
Ron Greenwood	(1977–82)
Bobby Robson	(1982–90)
Graham Taylor	(1990–93)
Terry Venables	(1994–96)
Glenn Hoddle	(1996–98)
Howard Wilkinson	(1999–2000)
Kevin Keegan	(1999–2000)
Peter Taylor	(November 2000)
Sven-Goran Eriksson	(2001–06)
Steve McClaren	(2006–07)
Fabio Capello	(2008–2012)
Stuart Pearce	(March 2012)
Roy Hodgson	(2012–2016)
Sam Allardyce	(July–September 2016)
Gareth Southgate	(2016–)

RARE COMEBACK

Liverpool striker Daniel Sturridge's injury-time winner against Wales in an all-British first-round clash in Lille at the 2016 UEFA European Championship, after 2015–16 Premier League Footballer of the Year Jamie Vardy's equalizer, meant it was the first time England had come from behind at half-time to win a match at a major tournament. Sturridge also became only the tenth Englishman to score at both a FIFA World Cup and a UEFA European Championship, having struck against Italy in Brazil two years earlier.

WONDERFUL WALTER

Walter Winterbottom was the England national team's first full-time manager – and remains both the longest-serving (with 138 games in charge) and the youngest-ever England manager, aged just 33 when he took the job in 1946 (initially as a coach and then, from 1947, as manager). The former teacher and Manchester United player led England to four FIFA World Cups.

FRANCE

France – nicknamed "Les Bleus" – are one of the most successful teams in the history of international football. They are one of only three countries to be World and European champions at the same time. They won the FIFA World Cup in 1998 as tournament hosts, routing Brazil 3-0 in the final. Two years later, they staged a sensational, last-gasp recovery to overhaul Italy in the Euro 2000 final. The French equalized in the fifth minute of stoppage time, then went on to win 2-1 on a golden goal. France had previously won the UEFA European Championship in 1984, beating Spain 2-0 in the final in Paris. They also won the 1984 Olympic football gold medal and the FIFA Confederations Cup in 2001 and 2003. Following final defeats, at the 2006 FIFA World Cup and as hosts, UEFA Euro 2016, *Les Bleus* triumphed at the 2018 FIFA World Cup in Russia.

KOPA – FRANCE'S FIRST SUPERSTAR

Raymond Kopa (born on 13 October 1931) was France's first international superstar. Born into a family of Polish immigrants (the family name was Kopaszewski), he was instrumental in Reims's championship successes of the mid-1950s. He later joined Real Madrid and became the first French player to win a European Cup winner's medal. He was the playmaker of the France team that finished third in the 1958 FIFA World Cup finals. His performances for his country that year earned him the European Footballer of the Year award. Kopa's death, aged 85, on 3 March 2017 was met with sadness around the world.

SINNER AND SAINT MICHEL

Michel Platini enjoyed a glittering career both on and off the pitch, rising from a youngster at Nancy to club glory with Saint-Etienne and Juventus and international triumph for France. He scored a tournament record nine goals as his country both hosted and won the 1984 UEFA European Championship before becoming national manager for the 1992 UEFA European Championship and then becoming joint organizing president (along with Ferdinand Sastre) as his nation staged the 1998 FIFA World Cup. He served as president of European football's governing body UEFA from January 2007 until his suspension for misconduct in December 2015.

IN FOR THE KYL

France won their second FIFA World Cup on 15 July 2018 – 20 years and three days after their first. The striking spearhead in 2018 was 19-year-old **Kylian Mbappe**, who scored their last goal in the 4-2 final triumph over Croatia – his fourth of the tournament – he was later named the best young player of tournament. Mbappe is only the second teenager to score in the final of the FIFA World Cup, following Pele against Sweden in 1958 – and the Brazilian legend congratulated him afterwards, posting online: "Welcome to the club." He had opened his FIFA World Cup account with the only goal of France's Group C victory over Peru, becoming the country's youngest scorer at a major tournament – aged just 19 years and 183 days – and was, unsurprisingly the first Frenchman born after their 1998 World Cup triumph to play in a senior tournament. In the second round, Mbappe joined Pele as the only teenagers to score more than one goal in a FIFA World Cup knock-out match, his double helping to see off Argentina 4-3. Mbappe rose through the ranks at AS Monaco but moved to Paris Saint-Germain in summer 2017, initially on a year-long loan but with the promise of a £166m permanent transfer.

GRIEZ LIGHTNING

Atletico Madrid and France striker **Antoine Griezmann** won both the Golden Boot as the six-goal top scorer and Golden Ball for best player at the 2016 UEFA European Championship. Unfortunately for him and France, he did not score in the final which France lost 1-0 to Portugal. Griezmann made amends two years later, however, when his four goals helped France win the 2018 FIFA World Cup. His tally included three penalties, one in the final to give his team a 2-1 lead over Croatia after VAR technology prompted referee Nestor Pituna to award a penalty against Ivan Perisic for handball. Griezmann had also been aided by VAR in France's opening game against Australia, scoring from the spot after referee Andres Cunha used video replays to rule the French forward had been fouled in the area by Joshua Risdon. Griezmann's FIFA World Cup triumph came just weeks after he scored twice in Atletico's 3-0 defeat of Marseille in the UEFA Europa League final.

PERFECT TEN

Eight different players appeared on the scoresheet for France in their largest international victory, a 10-0 defeat of Azerbaijan in Auxerre in September 1995 in a Euro 96 qualifier. **Marcel Desailly** opened the scoring after 13 minutes, before Youri Djorkaeff and Vincent Guerin scored before half-time. After the break Reynald Pedros quickly made it 4-0, before Frank Leboeuf, Christophe Dugarry, Zinedine Zidane all got in on the act. Djorkaeff and Lebeouf completed their doubles before substitute and local Auxerre favourite Christophe Cocard rounded off the scoring with the only goal of his nine-match international career.

FRANCE AND FIFA

France were one of FIFA's founding members in 1904. Frenchman Robert Guerin became the first president of the governing body. Another Frenchman, Jules Rimet, was president from 1921 to 1954. He was the driving force behind the creation of the FIFA World Cup and the first version of football's most coveted trophy was named in his honour.

IT'S A SHAME ABOUT RAY

France's failure to win a match at the 2010 FIFA World Cup meant coach Raymond Domenech equalled but failed to exceed Michel Hidalgo's record of 41 victories in charge of the national side. Domenech did at least end his six-year reign having surpassed Euro 84-winning Hidalgo's tally of matches in the job. Domenech's final game, against South Africa, was his 79th as coach, four more than Hidalgo achieved. Domenech, a tough-tackling defender who was picked for France by Hidalgo, proved eccentric as national coach. He admitted partly judging players by their star signs and responded to being knocked out of the 2008 UEFA European Championship by proposing to his girlfriend on live television.

POGBA POWER

France's triumph at the 2013 FIFA U-20 World Cup in Turkey made them the first country to complete a grand slam of FIFA eleven-a-side international men's titles, having previously won the FIFA World Cup, the FIFA U-17 World Cup and Olympic Games gold medal. The star of the show in 2013 was dynamic midfielder and captain Paul Pogba, who was awarded the Golden Ball as the tournament's best player. He was among the French players who scored from the spot in a 4-1 penalty shoot-out victory against Uruguay in the final, the game having finished goalless after extra-time. Pogba had made his senior France debut in March 2013, in a 3-1 win over Georgia, but he was sent off against Spain in his next appearance, four days. Better was to come, in the summer of 2014, when Pogba was named Best Young Player at the FIFA World Cup. He has enjoyed success at club level too. Pogba spent three teenage years at Manchester United before a 2012 move to Juventus brought him three successive Serie A league titles and a UEFA Champions League runners-up medal in 2015. A return to Manchester United in 2016 – for a world record fee of £89 million – saw him win the domestic EFL Cup (formerly Football League Cup) and the UEFA Europa League in his first season back in Manchester. Pogba was among France's star performers at the 2018 FIFA World Cup and scored their third goal against Croatia in the final.

MICHEL PLATINI (league and national career)

Duration	Team	Appearances	Goals
1972–79	Nancy	181	98
1979–82	Saint-Etienne	104	58
1982–87	Juventus	147	68
1976–87	France	72	41

BITTERSWEET FOR TREZEGUET

Striker David Trezeguet has bittersweet memories of France's clashes with Italy in major finals. He scored the "golden goal" that beat the Italians in extra-time in the Euro 2000 final but, six years later, he was the man who missed as France lost the FIFA World Cup final on penalties. Trezeguet's shot bounced off the bar and failed to cross the line.

DESCHAMPS THE MULTIPLE CHAMP

Didier Deschamps is only the third man to have won the FIFA World Cup both as a player and a manager, after Brazil's Mario Zagallo in 1958 and 1970 and Franz Beckenbauer with West Germany in 1974 and 1990. Like Beckenbauer, Deschamps was his country's captain when first lifting the trophy – as he was when France won the 2000 UEFA European Championship. He retired after winning 103 caps, 55 as captain. Defensive midfielder Deschamps was derided by compatriot Eric Cantona as being a mere "water-carrier", but won trophies at both club and national level. He took over as national head coach in 2012, and led France to the Euro 2016 final, where they lost 1-0 to Portugal. Two years later, France and Deschamps won the 2018 FIFA World Cup and Deschamps passed Raymond Domenech's record of 79 games in charge – the final was his 83rd match as coach.

TOP SCORERS

1	Thierry Henry	51
2	Michel Platini	41
3	David Trezeguet	34
4	Olivier Giroud	31
=	Zinedine Zidane	31
6	Just Fontaine	30
=	Jean-Pierre Papin	30
8	Youri Djorkaeff	28
9	Karim Benzema	27
10	Sylvain Wiltord	26

UNITED FOR ABIDAL

Defender Eric Abidal, a key member of the French teams at the 2006 and 2010 FIFA World Cups, was enjoying his best form for Barcelona when he was diagnosed with liver cancer in March 2011. He was well enough to play in his club's triumphant Champions League final against Manchester United three months later and was allowed to lift the trophy as if he were captain. Even Barcelona's arch rivals Real Madrid donned supportive T-shirts before one of their games. He was told he needed a liver transplant in March 2012 but again returned to action.

TOP CAPS

1	Lilian Thuram	142
2	Thierry Henry	123
3	Marcel Desailly	116
4	Zinedine Zidane	108
5	Patrick Vieira	107
6	Hugo Lloris	104
7	Didier Deschamps	103
8	Laurent Blanc	97
=	Bixente Lizarazu	97
10	Sylvain Wiltord	92

PRESIDENTIAL PARDON

Imperious centre-back Laurent Blanc was known as "Le President" during his playing days and went on to become national coach when he succeeded Raymond Domenech after the 2010 FIFA World Cup. He was unlucky to miss the 1998 FIFA World Cup final after being sent off in the semi-final for pushing Slaven Bilic in the face, though replays showed Bilic had over-reacted. Blanc did enjoy some redemption by being part of the French team that won the UEFA European Championship two years later. He became national coach 12 months after leading Bordeaux to the 2008–09 domestic championship, ending Olympique Lyonnais's run of seven league titles in a row.

SO NEAR AND YET SO VAR

Antoine Griezmann became the first man to have an international goal disallowed through the intervention of a video assistant referee. Griezmann was deemed offside after finding the net against Spain in a friendly at the Stade de France on 28 March 2017, a match Spain won 2-0. The VAR technology, approved for a trial by FIFA's International Board, was first used officially in September 2016 when France defeated Italy 3-1 in another friendly.

PATRICK'S DAY

The first six players to earn 100 caps for France were in the winning squads at the 1998 FIFA World Cup and 2000 UEFA European Championship: Lilian Thuram, Thierry Henry, Marcel Desailly, Zinedine Zidane, Patrick Vieira and Didier Deschamps. Only Vieira and Desailly added the 2001 FIFA Confederations Cup to their medals collection, and Vieira scored the only goal of the final against Japan, one of six the powerful midfielder netted for his country.

HENRY BENCHED

Thierry Henry missed out on an appearance in the 1998 FIFA World Cup final because of Marcel Desailly's red card. Henry, France's leading goalscorer in the finals with three, was a substitute and coach Aime Jacquet planned to use him late in the game. But Desailly's sending-off forced a re-think: Jacquet instead reinforced the midfield, with Arsenal team-mate Patrick Vieira going on instead, so Henry spent the full 90 minutes of the final on the bench. But Henry does have the distinction of being the only Frenchman to play at four different FIFA World Cups (1998, 2002, 2006 and 2010). He passed Michel Platini's all-time goal-scoring record for France with a brace against Lithuania in October 2007.

VICTOR HUGO

Hugo Lloris has worn the captain's armband more than any other Frenchman, lifting the FIFA World Cup trophy on 15 July 2018 in his 104th appearance for his country and his 80th as skipper. Yet it took some time for Lloris – also captain of English club Tottenham Hotspur – to be given the national honour. After Patrice Evra lost the captaincy for his role in France's 2010 FIFA World Cup fiasco, when the players briefly went on strike and Nicolas Anelka was sent home for insulting manager Raymond Domenech, new coach Laurent Blanc tried three captains during qualification for the 2012 UEFA European Championship before turning to Lloris, and he was given the job permanently in February 2012.

THE FULL SET

Five France stars have a full set of top international medals as FIFA World Cup, UEFA European Championship and UEFA Champions League winners. Didier Deschamps, Marcel Desailly, Christian Karembeu, Bixente Lizarazu and Zinedine Zidane all played for France's winning teams in 1998 and 2000. Desailly won the European Cup with Marseille in 1993 and AC Milan the following year. Deschamps won with Marseille in 1993 and Juventus in 1996; Lizarazu did so with Bayern Munich in 2001, Karembeu with Real Madrid in 1998 and 2000, and Zidane with Real Madrid in 2002. While Karembeu ended the 1999–2000 season with UEFA Champions League and UEFA European Championship winners' medals, he was an unused substitute in both finals – making him the only player to have achieved that particular bittersweet double.

LILIAN IN THE PINK

Defender **Lilian Thuram** made his 142nd and final appearance for France in their defeat by Italy at Euro 2008. His international career had spanned nearly 14 years, since his debut against the Czech Republic on 17 August 1994. Thuram was born in Pointe a Pitre, Guadeloupe, on 1 January 1972. He played club football for Monaco, Parma, Juventus and Barcelona before retiring in the summer of 2008 because of a heart problem. He was one of the stars of France's 1998 FIFA World Cup-winning side and scored both goals in their semi-final victory over Croatia – the only international goals of his career. He gained another winner's medal at Euro 2000. He first retired from international football after Euro 2004, but was persuaded by coach Raymond Domenech to return for the 2006 FIFA World Cup campaign and made his second appearance in a FIFA World Cup final. He broke Marcel Desailly's record of 116 caps in the group game against Togo.

ALBERT THE FIRST

Albert Batteux was France's first national coach. Before his appointment in 1955, a selection committee picked the team. Batteux was also one of the most successful managers in French football history, even though he combined it with his club job at Reims. His biggest achievement was guiding France to third place at the 1958 FIFA World Cup finals. The team's two big stars, Raymond Kopa and Just Fontaine, had both played for him at Reims. The only non-Frenchman to be national coach was a Romanian, former Ajax Amsterdam boss, Stefan Kovacs. He was succeeded by Michel Hidalgo after failing to reach either the 1974 FIFA World Cup or the 1976 UEFA European Championship.

JACQUET'S TRIUMPH

Aime Jacquet, who guided France to FIFA World Cup glory in 1998, was one of their most controversial national coaches. He had been attacked for alleged defensive tactics despite France's run to the semi-finals of Euro 96 and a record of only three defeats in four years. A month before the 1998 finals, the sports daily *L'Equipe* claimed he was not capable of building a successful team!

UMTITI BOOM

Barcelona defender **Samuel Umtiti** was thrown in at the deep end at the 2016 UEFA European Championship, in France's 5-2 quarter-final victory against Iceland. He became the first outfield player to make his French international debut at a major tournament since Gabriel De Michele at the 1966 FIFA World Cup. He was firmly established in the starting line-up by the time of the 2018 FIFA World Cup and scored the only goal of the semi-final against Belgium, a thumping header from Antoine Griezmann's corner.

OVAL BALL

Fabien Barthez holds his country's record for most FIFA World Cup finals appearances, 17 between 1998 and 2006. His superstitious ritual during the 1998 tournament which France won as hosts, was to have centre-back Laurent Blanc kiss his bald head before kick-off. Barthez's father Alain Barthez was a rugby union player who won one cap for his country. Current French No.1, Hugo Lloris, passed Barthez's previous record of 87 caps to become France's most-capped goalkeeper in early 2017.

NO TIME FOR FONTAINE

Former striker **Just Fontaine** spent the shortest-ever spell in charge of the France team. He took over on 22 March 1967 and left on 3 June after two defeats in friendlies. More happily, he still holds the record for most goals at a single FIFA World Cup – 13 across all six games he played at the 1958 tournament, including four in France's 6-3 victory over West Germany to finish third. He remains the only Frenchman to score a FIFA World Cup hat-trick.

FRANCE MANAGERS

Albert Batteux	1955–62
Henri Guerin	1962–66
Jose Arribas/Jean Snella	1966
Just Fontaine	1967
Louis Dugauguez	1967–68
Georges Boulogne	1969–73
Stefan Kovacs	1973–75
Michel Hidalgo	1976–84
Henri Michel	1984–88
Michel Platini	1988–92
Gerard Houllier	1992–93
Aime Jacquet	1993–98
Roger Lemerre	1998–2002
Jacques Santini	2002–04
Raymond Domenech	2004–10
Laurent Blanc	2010–12
Didier Deschamps	2012–

GIROUD AWAKENING

Olivier Giroud's goal against Wales in November 2017 was his seventh in seven international starts – a run that included a 5-0 friendly victory over Paraguay in June 2017, when he became the first Frenchman to hit an international hat-trick since winger Dominique Rocheteau in a 6-0 win against Luxembourg 32 years earlier. Just Fontaine struck a record five of France's 22 trebles, though only Eugene Maes against Luxembourg in April 1913 and Thadee Cisowski versus Belgium in November 1956 have managed to score five times in a game. Giroud joined Zinedine Zidane as France's joint fourth top scorer scoring against Colombia and the Republic of Ireland in early 2018. A winner of the Bronze Boot at the 2016 UEFA European Championship, Giroud finished joint second top scorer with three goals and two assists. At the 2018 FIFA World Cup, Giroud played in all seven games and ended with a winner's medal, but he was not credited with a single shot on target despite 13 attempts in the tournament. It prompted comparisons to Stephane Guivarc'h who was France's non-scoring centre-forward when they were world champions in 1998.

WINNING WITH YOUTH

In the early 1990s, France was the first European country to institute a national youth development programme. The best young players were picked to attend the national youth academy at Clairefontaine. They went on to the top clubs' academies across France. The scheme produced a rich harvest of stars. FIFA World Cup winners Didier Deschamps, Marcel Desailly and Christian Karembeu started at Nantes. Lilian Thuram, Thierry Henry, Manu Petit and David Trezeguet began with Monaco and **Zinedine Zidane** and Patrick Vieira graduated from Cannes. Zidane scored the only goal, against Spain, in the January 1998 inaugural match staged at the new national stadium, the 81,000-capacity Stade de France in St Denis, just north of Paris.

BLINK AND YOU'LL MISS HIM

Unfortunate defender Franck Jurietti's international debut proved bittersweet – it lasted just five seconds and he never won another cap. The Bordeaux full-back came on just before the final whistle of France's match against Cyprus in October 2005, amounting to an international career even shorter than fellow defender Bernard Boissier's two minutes against Portugal in April 1975.

EARNING THEIR STRIPES

France are the only country to play at a FIFA World Cup wearing another team's kit. In the 1978 tournament in Argentina, for a first-round match at Mar del Plata, *Les Bleus* were forced to wear the green and white stripes of a local club side, Atletico Kimberley, when they met Hungary. France brought their second, white, kit instead of their normal blue, while Hungary turned up in their second strip, white, too. The quick-change did not seem to affect France, who won the match 3-1.

KANTE CAN DO

Despite being just 1.68m tall, **N'Golo Kante** has proved a midfield powerhouse. He won back-to-back English Premier League titles, with Leicester City in 2016 and Chelsea the following year – the first outfielder to do so with different clubs since compatriot Eric Cantona triumphed with Leeds United in 1992 and Manchester United 12 months later. Kante's magic touch continued as he helped motor France to FIFA World Cup glory in 2018. Yet it was suggested he was too shy to get his hands on the trophy in the post-match celebrations following victory over Croatia, prompting team-mate Blaise Matuidi to force him forwards. The 4-2 win meant France extended to 18 games their record of never losing with Kante and fellow midfielder Paul Pogba in the starting line-up.

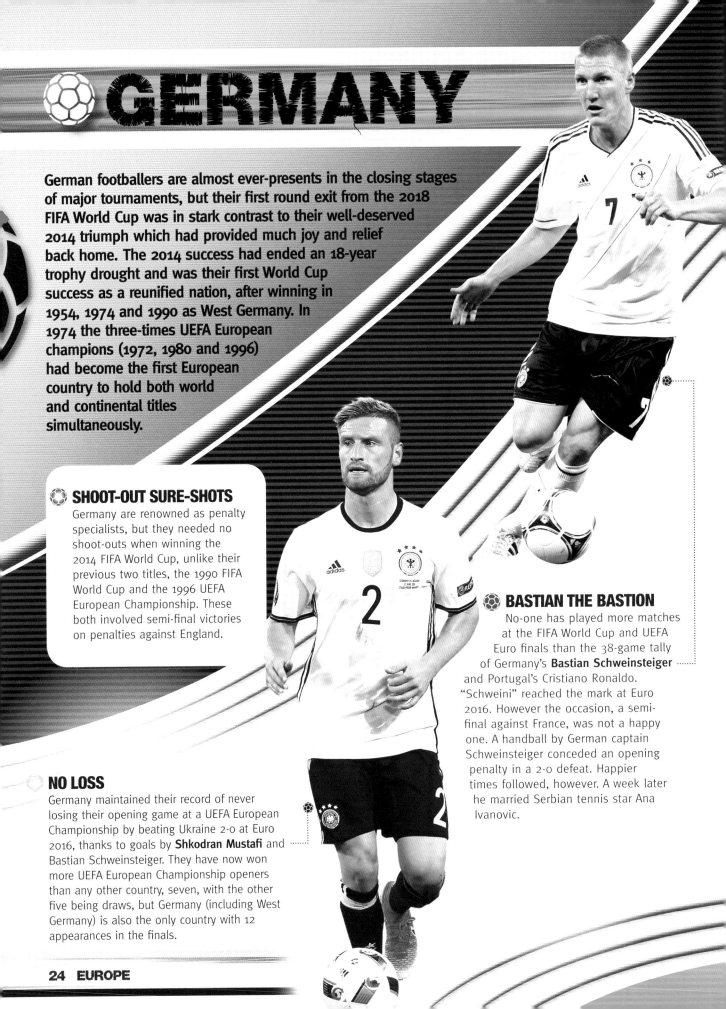

GERMANY

German footballers are almost ever-presents in the closing stages of major tournaments, but their first round exit from the 2018 FIFA World Cup was in stark contrast to their well-deserved 2014 triumph which had provided much joy and relief back home. The 2014 success had ended an 18-year trophy drought and was their first World Cup success as a reunified nation, after winning in 1954, 1974 and 1990 as West Germany. In 1974 the three-times UEFA European champions (1972, 1980 and 1996) had become the first European country to hold both world and continental titles simultaneously.

SHOOT-OUT SURE-SHOTS

Germany are renowned as penalty specialists, but they needed no shoot-outs when winning the 2014 FIFA World Cup, unlike their previous two titles, the 1990 FIFA World Cup and the 1996 UEFA European Championship. These both involved semi-final victories on penalties against England.

BASTIAN THE BASTION

No-one has played more matches at the FIFA World Cup and UEFA Euro finals than the 38-game tally of Germany's **Bastian Schweinsteiger** and Portugal's Cristiano Ronaldo. "Schweini" reached the mark at Euro 2016. However the occasion, a semi-final against France, was not a happy one. A handball by German captain Schweinsteiger conceded an opening penalty in a 2-0 defeat. Happier times followed, however. A week later he married Serbian tennis star Ana Ivanovic.

NO LOSS

Germany maintained their record of never losing their opening game at a UEFA European Championship by beating Ukraine 2-0 at Euro 2016, thanks to goals by **Shkodran Mustafi** and Bastian Schweinsteiger. They have now won more UEFA European Championship openers than any other country, seven, with the other five being draws, but Germany (including West Germany) is also the only country with 12 appearances in the finals.

BOTH SIDES NOW

Eight players appeared for both the old East Germany and then Germany after reunification in October 1990.

Player	East Germany	Germany
Ulf Kirsten	49	51
Matthias Sammer	23	51
Andreas Thom	51	10
Thomas Doll	29	18
Dariusz Wosz	7	17
Olaf Marschall	4	13
Heiko Scholz	7	1
Dirk Schuster	4	3

EAST GERMANY –
TOP APPEARANCES AND GOALS

Appearances

1	Joachim Streich	98
2	Hans-Jurgen Dorner	96
3	Jurgen Croy	86
4	Konrad Weise	78
5	Eberhard Vogel	69

Goals

1	Joachim Streich	53
2	Eberhard Vogel	24
3	Hans-Jurgen Kreische	22
4	Rainer Ernst	20
5	Henning Frenzel	19

UNHAPPY EIGHTY-YEAR FATE

Germany went into the 2018 FIFA World Cup as defending champions – and 2017 FIFA Confederations Cup holders, which they had won in Russia. Yet Joachim Low's side finished bottom of Group F, ensuring their first first-round exit for 80 years – they did not compete in 1950 – and only their second ever. Germany were eliminated in 1938, a straight knock-out tournament, after losing 4-2 to Switzerland in a first-round replay following a 1-1 draw. That German team featured several Austrian players, following the Anschluss (German annexation of Austria) earlier in the year.

HISTORY MAN

East and West Germany met only once at senior national team level. That was on 22 June 1974, in the FIFA World Cup finals. Drawn in the same group, East Germany produced a shock 1-0 win in Hamburg, but both teams advanced. Jurgen Sparwasser, scorer of East Germany's winning goal, defected to West Germany in 1988 – two years before the two countries reunited.

GRAND SAMMER

Matthias Sammer is not only one of eight men to play for both East Germany and the reunified Germany, he also holds the honour of captaining and scoring both goals in East Germany's final game, a 2-0 away win over Belgium on 12 September 1990, 21 days before the official reunification. His powerhouse midfield performances later drove Germany to glory at the 1996 UEFA European Championship, where he was voted the official player of the tournament.

SAMBA SILENCED

Germany's 1-0 win over Argentina in 2014 came in their record eighth FIFA World Cup Final, this coming after they were the first side to reach four consecutive semi-finals. But the 7-1 semi-final humiliation of Brazil may live longest in the memory – and the record books. Germany led 5-0 at half-time in what became the biggest FIFA World Cup semi-final win and the hosts' heaviest defeat. Other FIFA World Cup finals records include: Toni Kroos's two goals in 69 seconds were the fastest brace and Germany were the first team to score four goals in six minutes. Also Thomas Muller's opening goal was Germany's 2,000th.

TOP AND TAIL

Germany ended 2014 top of the FIFA world rankings – the first time they had occupied this position in December since 1993, when the rankings were originally introduced.

GOLDEN WONDER

Germany became the first team to win a major title thanks to the now-discarded golden goal goal system when they beat the Czech Republic in the UEFA Euro 96 final at Wembley. **Oliver Bierhoff**'s equalizer forced extra-time after Patrik Berger scored a penalty for the Czechs. Bierhoff grabbed Germany's winner five minutes into extra-time to end the game and the championship.

MEIN BENDERS

You could have thought you were seeing double when manager Joachim Low made a double substitution with 12 minutes remaining during Germany's 5-3 defeat to Switzerland in May 2012. His two midfield substitutes were twin brothers Lars and Sven Bender. Born on 27 April 1989, they both began their careers with 1860 Munich before Lars (the elder by 12 minutes) moved to Bayer Leverkusen and Sven to Borussia Dortmund. Both were members of Germany's 2008 UEFA U-19 European Championship-winning side, but only Lars was selected for Euro 2012. They were were the second twins to play for Germany after Erwin and Helmut Kramers. Striker Erwin scored three goals in 15 games between 1972 and 1974, while full-back Helmut played eight times without scoring. Erwin was part of the 1972 UEFA European Championship-winning squad, but was overlooked for the triumphant 1974 FIFA World Cup-winning squad, a set-up that included Helmut.

OZIL'S AWARDS

Mesut Ozil – Germany's player of the year 2011–13 and 2015–16 – was almost ever-present as the team won the 2014 FIFA World Cup – and at the end of the final handed his shirt to then-UEFA president Michel Platini. He was man of the match when Germany beat England 4-0 in the 2009 UEFA U21 European Championship final and was among ten nominees for the 2010 FIFA World Cup Golden Ball. Ozil, however, missed Germany's first tournament penalty for 40 years at the 2016 UEFA European Championship. His failure against Slovakia – in a 3-0 win – was the first since Uli Hoeness missed in the 1976 UEFA European Championship final penalty shoot-out.

NO WAY THROUGH

Joachim Low's Germany team went a national record of 11 hours and 19 minutes without conceding a goal, between Antoine Griezmann scoring for France in the 2016 UEFA European Championship semi-final and a 31st-minute equalizer by Azerbaijan's Dimitrij Nazarov on 26 March 2017, in a 2018 FIFA World Cup qualifier, a match Germany went on to win 4-1. The final clean sheet of the run had been kept by Marc-Andre ter Stegen, four days earlier, in a 1-0 friendly victory over England.

"DER BOMBER"

Gerd Muller was the most prolific scorer of the modern era. Neither tall nor graceful, he was quick, strong and had a predator's eye for the net. He also had the temperament to score decisive goals in big games, including the winner in the 1974 FIFA World Cup final, the winner in the semi-final against Poland and two goals in West Germany's 1972 UEFA European Championship final victory over the USSR. He netted 68 goals in 62 appearances for West Germany and remains the leading scorer in the Bundesliga and all-time record scorer for his club, Bayern Munich.

A LAHM CALL

Philipp Lahm surprised many when retiring from international football after the 2014 FIFA World Cup, at the age of only 30. He went out on a high, having just lifted the trophy as German captain at the end of his 113th appearance. Lahm had already made a mark in his two previous finals. He scored the opening goal of the 2006 FIFA World Cup, and played every minute of that tournament. Four years later, he became the youngest man to captain Germany at a FIFA World Cup – and the only action he missed was when given a well-earnest rest for the third-place play-off against Uruguay. In his youth, Lahm was a ballboy at Bayern Munich and he later captained them to 2013 UEFA Champions League glory.

DER KAISER

Franz Beckenbauer is widely regarded as the greatest player in German football history. He has also made a huge mark as a FIFA World Cup-winning coach, administrator and organizer. Beckenbauer (born on 11 September 1945) was a 20-year-old attacking wing-half when West Germany reached the 1966 FIFA World Cup final. He later defined the role of attacking sweeper, first in the 1970 FIFA World Cup finals, and then as West Germany won the 1972 UEFA European Championship and the 1974 FIFA World Cup. When West Germany needed a coach in the mid-1980s, they turned to Beckenbauer, despite his lack of experience. He delivered a FIFA World Cup final appearance in 1986, a Euro 88 semi-final and 1990 FIFA World Cup triumph in his final game in charge. He later became president of Bayern Munich, the club he captained to three consecutive European Cup victories between 1974 and 1976. He also led Germany's successful bid for the 2006 FIFA World Cup finals and headed the organizing committee. His achievements and influence earned him the nickname "Der Kaiser" ("The Emperor").

MAGICAL MATTHAUS

Lothar Matthaus is Germany's most-capped player. He appeared in five FIFA World Cup finals – 1982, 1986, 1990, 1994 and 1998 – a record for an outfield player he shares with Mexico's Rafael Marquez. Versatile Matthaus could operate as a defensive or attacking midfielder or a sweeper. He was a FIFA World Cup winner in 1990, a finalist in 1982 and 1986 and a UEFA European Championship winner in 1980. His record 150 appearances – spread over a 20-year international career – were split 87 for West Germany and 63 for Germany. He also scored 23 goals and was voted top player at the 1990 FIFA World Cup.

TOP CAPS
(West Germany & Germany)

1	Lothar Matthaus	150
2	Miroslav Klose	137
3	Lukas Podolski	130
4	Bastian Schweinsteiger	121
5	Philipp Lahm	113
6	Jurgen Klinsmann	108
7	Jurgen Kohler	105
8	Per Mertesacker	104
9	Franz Beckenbauer	103
10	Thomas Hassler	101

TOP SCORERS
(West Germany & Germany)

1	Miroslav Klose	71
2	Gerd Muller	68
3	Lukas Podolski	49
4	Jurgen Klinsmann	47
=	Rudi Voller	47
6	Karl-Heinz Rummenigge	45
7	Uwe Seeler	43
8	Michael Ballack	42
9	Thomas Muller	38
10	Olivier Bierhoff	37

KLOSE ENCOUNTERS

Miroslav Klose became the third player, after Uwe Seeler and Pele to score in four FIFA World Cup finals. His first goal in 2014, an equalizer against Ghana, put him alongside Ronaldo at the top of the all-time FIFA World Cup scoring charts. And it was against Ronaldo's Brazil that Klose pushed ahead on his own, his 16th finals goal being a typically-opportunistic finish to give Germany a 2-0 semi-final lead. All 16 of Klose's FIFA World Cup goals came from inside the penalty area. He ended the 2014 FIFA World Cup with the scoring record and also a winners' medal. His 24 appearances left him behind only compatriot Lothar Matthaus (25) and Klose's 17 wins were one more than previous record-holder Cafu, of Brazil. Klose retired in 2014 as Germany's all-time leading scorer, with 71 goals in 137 matches – and his team-mates never lost an international in which he found the net.

KOPKE'S UP FOR CUPS

Andreas Kopke was involved – and celebrating – on the sidelines when West Germany won the FIFA World Cup in 1990 and when Germany won in 2014. He was one of Franz Beckenbauer's two back-ups to first-choice goalkeeper Bodo Illgner in 1990 and, 24 years later, he was Joachim Low's goalkeeping coach for No. 1 keeper Manuel Neuer, as well as reserves Ron-Robert Zieler and Roman Weidenfeller. Kopke did at least play throughout Germany's 1996 UEFA European Championship-winning campaign, contributing an especially crucial role in reaching the final when saving a spot-kick by England's Gareth Southgate in their semi-final shoot-out.

YOUNGEST CENTURION LUKAS

Lukas Podolski was briefly Europe's youngest footballer to reach 100 caps when, aged 27 years and 13 days old, he appeared in Germany's third first-round game of the 2012 UEFA European Championship, against Denmark. He marked the occasion by scoring the opener in a 2-1 win. Podolski was born in Gliwice in Poland, but opted to play for Germany – his family having emigrated there when he was two years old. He was voted best young player of the tournament when Germany hosted and finished third at the 2006 FIFA World Cup. He bowed out of international football in March 2017 with the only goal – his 49th – of what he said in advance would be his 130th and final game for Germany, a 1-0 friendly win over England in Dortmund.

KROOS CONTROL

Attacking midfielder Toni Kroos became in 2014 the only man born in East Germany to win the FIFA World Cup. He was born in Greifswald in January 1990, nine months before Germany's reunification. His two goals in the 7-1 semi-final thrashing of hosts Brazil were scored in the 24th and 26th minutes, taking the score from 2-0 to an impregnable 4-0. He also played the full final against Argentina and ended the tournament on FIFA's ten-man Golden Ball shortlist. At the 2018 FIFA World Cup, Kroos scored Germany's latest-ever regulation-time goal – excluding extra-time – to clinch a 2-1 Group F victory over Sweden. It was timed at 94 minutes and 42 seconds.

KEEPING A LOW PROFILE

Joachim Low was, in 2014, the 19th coach to win the FIFA World Cup, but the first German coach to do so without having played for his country. After a respectable career as a midfielder for a number of clubs, including Freiburg, and coaching spells in Germany, Austria and Turkey, Low was appointed as Jurgen Klinsmann's assistant in 2004, before taking the top job after the 2006 FIFA World Cup. He led Germany to the 2008 UEFA European Championship final and the semi-finals of Euro 2012, as well as third-place at the 2010 FIFA World Cup. West Germany's 1954 FIFA World Cup-winning manager Sepp Herberger had won three caps as a player, 1974 boss Helmut Schon made 16 appearances and 1990 coach Franz Beckenbauer won 103 caps and lifted the trophy as captain in 1974. Despite Germany's shock first-round exit at the 2018 FIFA World Cup, Low remained in charge and was looking ahead to future tournaments.

NEUER RECORD

Manuel Neuer has the longest run between conceding international tournament goals for Germany. There were 557 minutes between Brazil's late goal in the 7-1 2014 FIFA World Cup semi-final rout before Italy's Leonardo Bonucci scored in the 2016 UEFA European Championship quarter-final. Germany won 6-5 on penalties, helped by two spot-kick saves by Neuer. The previous best had been Sepp Maier's 481-minute sequence in the 1970s. Neuer – renowned for his ease with the ball at his feet, as a so-called "sweeper keeper" – was appointed Germany captain in September 2016 after Bastian Schweinsteiger retired. In addition to his football talents Neuer has voiced a minor character in the German dubbing for *Pixar* and Disney's 2013 animated film *Monster University*.

GERMANY'S MANAGERS

Otto Nerz	1928–36
Sepp Herberger	1936–64
Helmut Schon	1964–78
Jupp Derwall	1978–84
Franz Beckenbauer	1984–90
Berti Vogts	1990–98
Erich Ribbeck	1998–2000
Rudi Voller	2000–04
Jurgen Klinsmann	2004–06
Joachim Low	2006–

GOAL RUSH

Germany's biggest win was 16-0 against Russia in the 1912 Olympic Games in Stockholm. Karlsruhe's Gottfried Fuchs scored ten of the goals, still a national team record.

BONUS BATTLE

Helmut Schon's 1974 FIFA World Cup winners came close to walking out before the finals started. Schon was prepared to send his squad home in a row over bonuses. A last-minute deal was brokered between Franz Beckenbauer and federation vice-president Hermann Neuberger. The vote among the squad went 11-11, but Beckenbauer persuaded the players to accept the DFB's offer. It was a great decision: they beat Holland 2-1 in the final.

NEW BOYS REUNION

Bayern Munich's **Mario Gotze** was the hero when Germany finally overcame Argentina's resistance in the 2014 FIFA World Cup final. His 113th-minute volley was the first winner hit by a substitute. It seemed apt that Germany's first FIFA World Cup triumph since the reunification of East and West Germany in 1990 was secured by Gotze, set up by Andre Schurrle. They had jointly become the first German football internationals born post-reunification, when making their debuts as 79th-minute substitutes against Sweden in November 2010.

THIRD TIME UNLUCKY AGAIN

Germany became in 2018 the third consecutive FIFA World Cup champions to go out at the group stage. Joachim Low's team lost their opening game 1-0 to Mexico, beat Sweden 2-1, but then lost 2-0 to already-eliminated South Korea. Both goals came in injury-time – the second tapped in by Heung-min Son with German goalkeeper Manuel Neuer in the Korean half seeking an equalizer. Germany thus followed Italy in 2010 and Spain in 2014 in making instant exits. They had qualified for Russia 2018 with a 100 per cent record, winning all ten games while scoring 43 goals and only conceding four.

FRITZ WALTER BETTER

Fritz Walter was the inspirational inside-left and captain when West Germany won their first FIFA World Cup in 1954, coming from two goals down to defeat favourites Hungary 3-2 in the final in Switzerland – a triumph memorialized back home as "The Miracle of Berne". He and brother Ottmar became the first siblings to win a FIFA World Cup together. He played his entire club career for FC Kaiserslautern, whose home ground staged a FIFA World Cup tie between Italy and the USA on 17 June 2006, the fourth anniversary of his death at the age of 81 – and a minute's silence was held for him before kick-off. He was renowned for his ability to play well in the most inclement conditions, promoting talk of "Fritz-Walter-Wetter" or "Fritz Walter weather".

PRESSURE ON JULIAN

World champions Germany won their first FIFA Confederations Cup in Russia in 2017, despite coach Joachim Low resting many of his senior stars, including Thomas Muller, Mesut Ozil and Toni Kroos. Lars Stindl scored the only goal of the final, against Chile, while goalkeeper Marc-Andre ter Stegen was named man of the match. The Golden Ball for the tournament's best player went to 23-year-old captain **Julian Draxler** – Germany's youngest skipper at a tournament since Max Breunig at the 1912 Summer Olympics – and the Golden Boot went to three-goal team-mate Timo Werner. Germany also had the youngest average age for any FIFA Confederations Cup-winning squad: 24 years and four months.

SEPP'S SURPRISE

Sepp Herberger (1897–1977) was one of the most influential figures in Germany's football history. He was their longest-serving coach (28 years at the helm) and his legendary status was assured after West Germany surprised odds-on favourites Hungary to win the 1954 FIFA World Cup final – a result credited with dragging the country out of a post-war slump. Herberger took charge in 1936 and led the team into the 1938 FIFA World Cup finals. During the war years he used his influence to try to keep his best players away from the heavy fighting. When organized football resumed in 1949, the federation decided to advertise for a national coach, but Herberger persuaded DFB chief Peco Bauwens to give him back his old job. He had a clause in his contract guaranteeing him a totally free hand in organization and selection policy. Among Herberger's favourite sayings was: "The ball is round and the match lasts 90 minutes. Everything else is just theory."

ITALY

Only Brazil (with five victories) can claim to have won the FIFA World Cup more times than Italy. The *Azzurri* became the first nation to retain the trophy (winning in 1934 and 1938), were surprise champions in Spain in 1982 and collected football's most coveted trophy for a fourth time in 2006. Add the 1968 UEFA European Championship to the mix and few nations can boast a better record. The success story does not end there. Italian clubs have won the European Cup or UEFA Champions League on 12 occasions and the country's domestic league, Serie A, is considered among the strongest in the game. Even so Italy, despite being one of the world game's greatest powers, failed surprisingly to qualify for the finals of the 2018 FIFA World Cup.

GLOVE CONQUERS ALL

Walter Zenga went 517 minutes without conceding a goal at the 1990 FIFA World Cup, an all-time tournament record only brought to an end by Argentina's Claudio Caniggia in the semi-finals.

ROTTEN RETURN

Italy were knocked out of the FIFA World Cup in the first round in both 2010 and 2014 – the first time they had done so in consecutive tournaments since 1962 and 1966. At least the modern players did not suffer the fate of those arriving home from England in 1966: they were pelted with rotten fruit after a dismal showing most notable for a 1-0 defeat to minnows North Korea.

OFF THE SPOT

Only England have lost as many FIFA World Cup penalty shoot-outs as Italy – three apiece. **Roberto Baggio**, nicknamed "The Divine Ponytail", was involved in all three of Italy's spot-kick defeats, in 1990, 1994 and 1998. Left-back Antonio Cabrini is the only man to have missed a penalty during normal time in a FIFA World Cup final – the score was 0-0 at the time but, fortunately for him, Italy still beat West Germany 3-1 in 1982.

SO NEAR, SO ZAZA

Italy were one of only four teams to qualify unbeaten for the 2016 UEFA European Championship – and while Austria and Romania went out in the first round and England the second, Antonio Conte's side reached the quarter-finals before losing to Germany on penalties. Simone Zaza, brought on as a substitute just in time for the shoot-out, apologized afterwards for his missed spot-kick that followed a bizarrely intricate run-up. Italy's opening game against Belgium saw them field a starting-eleven with an average age of 31 years and 169 days – the oldest side in UEFA European Championship history.

IN SAFE KEEPING

During World War Two, the Jules Rimet Trophy, the FIFA World Cup – won by Italy in 1938 – was hidden in a shoebox under the bed of football official Ottorino Barassi. He preferred to keep it there, rather than at its previous home – a bank in Rome. The trophy was handed back to FIFA, safe and untouched, only when the FIFA World Cup resumed in 1950.

YOUNG ONE DON

Dino Zoff and Gianluigi Buffon were acclaimed not only for their goalkeeping skills and leadership for Italy, but also their longevity. In contrast, **Gianluigi Donnarumma**, aged 17 years 189 days, set a record as the country's youngest international goalkeeper when he replaced Buffon against France at half-time on 1 September 2016. He had previously become the second-youngest keeper to start a game in Serie A, when playing for AC Milan aged 16 years and 242 days on 25 October 2015 – exactly 73 years since Giuseppe Sacchi made his debut for the same club, just 13 days younger. Donnarumma was already Italy's youngest U21 player – 17 years and 28 days – having played in a 4-1 defeat of the Republic of Ireland in March. Italy's youngest international remains AC Milan defender Renzo De Vecchi, aged 16 years 112 days when he lined up against Hungary in May 1910.

BOSSI DE ROSSI

Central midfielder Daniele de Rossi was roundly condemned when he was sent off for elbowing Brian McBride of the USA in a 2006 FIFA World Cup group match. His suspension finished in time for him to be a substitute in the final, which Italy won against France. However, in March 2006, De Rossi had won widespread praise for his honesty. During a Serie A match his club AS Roma were awarded a goal against Messina when he diverted the ball into the net with his hand and he persuaded the referee to disallow the goal (Roma still won 2-1). De Rossi's international honours also include an Olympic bronze medal from 2004 and, in November 2014 he became only the sixth Italian to win 100 caps, in a 1-1 draw against Croatia in a UEFA European Championship 2016 qualifier.

TOP DRAW

No team have drawn more FIFA World Cup matches than Italy, who took their tally to 21 with 1-1 draws against both Paraguay and New Zealand in Group F at the 2010 competition in South Africa. Their first draw had also been 1-1, against Spain in a 1934 quarter-final tie. Italy's **Giuseppe Meazza** scored the only goal of a replay the following day, and Italy went on to lift the trophy for the first time that year.

TOURNAMENT SPECIALISTS

FIFA WORLD CUP: 18 appearances – winners 1934, 1938, 1982, 2006
UEFA EUROPEAN CHAMPIONSHIP: 9 appearances – winners 1968
FIRST INTERNATIONAL: Italy 6 France 2 (Milan, 15 May 1910)
BIGGEST WIN: Italy 9 USA 0 (Brentford, London, 17 August 1948 – Olympic Games)
BIGGEST DEFEAT: Hungary 7 Italy 1 (Budapest, 6 April 1924)

FLYING HIGH

Vittorio Pozzo is the only man to have won the FIFA World Cup twice as manager – both times with Italy, in 1934 and 1938 (only two players, Giuseppe Meazza and Giovanni Ferrari, were selected in both finals). Pozzo also led Italy to the 1936 Olympics title. Born in Turin on 2 March 1886, Pozzo learned to love football as a student in England, watching Manchester United. He returned home reluctantly when his family bought him a return ticket for his sister's wedding and then refused to let him leave Italy again. Pozzo fired up his Italian team ahead of their 1938 semi-final against Brazil by revealing their opponents had already booked their plane to Paris for the final – Italy won 2-1.

VENTURA'S MISADVENTURE

The 2018 FIFA World Cup in Russia was the first since 1958 not to feature Italy, after they lost a qualifying play-off 1-0 on aggregate to Sweden. The *Azzurri* had finished second, five points behind group-winners Spain, to go into the qualification playoff, but lost the first leg 1-0 in Sweden before only managing a goalless draw in the return fixture at Milan's San Siro stadium. Players and supporters were left visibly distraught at this unexpected failure, which cost both manager Gian Piero Ventura and Italian football association president Carlo Tavecchio their jobs. Four of Italy's star players also announced their international retirements following the November 2017 playoff: goalkeeper Gianluigi Buffon, defenders Giorgio Chiellini and **Andrea Barzagli** and midfielder Daniele De Rossi. However, caretaker manager Luigi Di Biagio selected both Buffon and Chiellini for friendlies in March 2018.

ITALY'S NATIONAL COACHES

Vittorio Pozzo	1912, 1924
Augusto Rangone	1925–28
Carlo Carcano	1928–29
Vittorio Pozzo	1929–48
Ferruccio Novo	1949–50
Carlino Beretta	1952–53
Giuseppe Viani	1960
Giovanni Ferrari	1960–61
Giovanni Ferrari/Paolo Mazza	1962
Edmondo Fabbri	1962–66
Helenio Herrera/Ferruccio Valcareggi	1966–67
Ferruccio Valcareggi	1967–74
Fulvio Bernardini	1974–75
Enzo Bearzot	1975–86
Azeglio Vicini	1986–91
Arrigo Sacchi	1991–96
Cesare Maldini	1997–98
Dino Zoff	1998–2000
Giovanni Trapattoni	2000–04
Marcello Lippi	2004–06
Roberto Donadoni	2006–08
Marcello Lippi	2008–10
Cesare Prandelli	2010–14
Antonio Conte	2014–16
Gian Piero Ventura	2016–17
Luigi Di Biagio	2018
Roberto Mancini	2018–

COMEBACK KID

Paolo Rossi was the unlikely hero of Italy's 1982 FIFA World Cup triumph, winning the Golden Boot with six goals – including a memorable hat-trick against Brazil in the second round, and the first of Italy's three goals in their final win over West Germany. But he only just made it to the tournament at all, having completed a two-year ban for his alleged involvement in a betting scandal only six weeks before the start of the tournament.

SAN SIRO HEROES

Italy extended their 94-year unbeaten run in Milan to 44 games when they drew 0–0 with Sweden at the San Siro stadium in a FIFA World Cup play-off second leg in November 2017. Unfortunately, that meant they failed to reach the 2018 finals. Their last defeat in Milan had been by 2-1 to Hungary on 18 January 1925.

ONCE BITTEN, TWICE SHY

Italy went out of the 2014 FIFA World Cup in Brazil in the first round despite beating England in their opening game. They then suffered a pair of 1-0 defeats, first to surprise group winners Costa Rica – Italy's first FIFA World Cup defeat to a Central American nation – then to Uruguay, for whom Diego Godin netted a late goal. Italy were incensed Uruguay striker Luis Suarez had not been sent off for biting Giorgio Chiellini on the shoulder. The defender pulled down his shirt to show Mexican referee Marco Rodriguez the toothmarks left in his skin, but to no avail. In October 2014, Chiellini scored all three goals in Italy's 2-1 victory against Azerbaijan in a 2016 UEFA European Championship qualifier in Palermo. He opened the scoring just before half-time, found his own net with 14 minutes to go, but went on to head the *Azzurri*'s 82nd-minute winner.

TOP CAPS

1	Gianluigi Buffon	176
2	Fabio Cannavaro	136
3	Paolo Maldini	126
4	Daniele De Rossi	117
5	Andrea Pirlo	116
6	Dino Zoff	112
7	Gianluca Zambrotta	98
8	Giorgio Chiellini	96
9	Giacinto Facchetti	94
10	Alessandro Del Piero	91

TOP SCORERS

1	Luigi Riva	35
2	Giuseppe Meazza	33
3	Silvio Piola	30
4	Roberto Baggio	27
=	Alessandro Del Piero	27
6	Alessandro Altobelli	25
=	Adolfo Baloncieri	25
=	Filippo Inzaghi	25
9	Francesco Graziani	23
=	Christian Vieri	23

MISTER INTER, GIACINTO

No Internazionale footballer will ever wear the No.3 shirt after it was retired in tribute to the legendary full-back **Giacinto Facchetti**, following his death in 2006 at the age of 64. He spent his entire senior career at Inter, between 1960 and 1978, and later served as the club's technical director and president. In his playing days he helped pioneer the role of a full-back as a stampeding, attacking presence – though favoured his right foot despite advancing on the left. He captained Italy 70 times, during his 94-cap international career and lifted the UEFA European Championship trophy in 1968.

ZOFF THE SCALE

Goalkeeper **Dino Zoff** set an international record by going 1,142 minutes without conceding a goal between September 1972 and June 1974. Zoff was Italy's captain when they won the 1982 FIFA World Cup – emulating the feat of another Juventus goalkeeper, Gianpiero Combi, who had been the victorious skipper in 1934. Zoff coached Italy to the final of the 2000 UEFA European Championship, which they lost 2-1 to France thanks to an extra-time "golden goal" – then quit a few days later, unhappy following the criticism levelled at him by Italy's then prime minister, Silvio Berlusconi.

⊛ SHARE AND SHARE ALIKE

Manager Marcelo Lippi used all of outfield squad members when winning Italy's fourth FIFA World Cup in Germany in 2006 – and all six of his named strikers found the net once apiece, apart from Luca Toni who scored twice. He might have had a third, but his 61st-minute header against France in the final was disallowed for a marginal offside. The other forwards to score were Alessandro Del Piero, Francesco Totti, Alberto Gilardino, Vincenzo Iaquinta and Filippo Inzaghi. Toni retired from football at the end of the 2015–16 season at the age of 39, having a year earlier become the oldest man to finish as Serie A's top scorer.

⊛ MOURNING FOR ASTORI

Italian and world football united in tribute to international defender **Davide Astori** after his sudden death from a cardiac arrest at the age of only 31 in March 2018. The Fiorentina skipper had been capped 14 times by Italy between 2011 and 2017, despite being sent off on his debut against Ukraine, 15 minutes after coming on as a 17th-minute substitute. He helped Italy to finish third at the 2013 FIFA Confederations Cup, scoring the opening goal of the 3-2 play-off victory over Uruguay. Italy captain Gianluigi Buffon said, in an emotional statement after Astori's death: "You were the best expression of an older football world, one that has moved on but one that was based on altruism and elegance." Both Fiorentina and former club Cagliari retired his shirt number.

⊛ RIGHT START

Torino defender Emiliano Moretti became Italy's oldest debutant when he made his international bow in November 2014, a friendly against Albania, at the age of 33 years and 160 days. His debut may yet pall compared to that of striker Christian Vieri, who not only marked his first appearance with a goal, the second in his side's 3-0 win over Moldova in March 1997 – it was also the 1,000th goal Italy had scored in all internationals.

⊛ ROLLING RIVA

Italy's all-time top scorer is **Luigi "Gigi" Riva**, who scored 35 goals in 42 appearances for his country. One of his most important strikes was the opening goal in the 1968 UEFA European Championship final win over Yugoslavia. Despite his prolific form after having switched from left-winger to striker, he never played for one of Italy's traditional club giants. Instead, Riva – born in Leggiuno on 7 November 1944 – spent his entire league career with unfashionable Sardinian club Cagliari, and at one point turned down a move to the mighty Juventus. His goals (21 of them) fired the club to their one and only league championship in 1970. Riva suffered his fair share of bad luck with injuries, breaking his left leg while playing for Italy in 1966, then his right leg in 1970, again when he was away on international duty.

⊛ HAPPY CENTENARY

After captaining Italy to the 2006 FIFA World Cup title, **Fabio Cannavaro** was named FIFA World Player of the Year – at 33, the oldest winner of the prize, as well as the first defender. Cannavaro, born in Naples in 1973, played every minute of the 2006 tournament and the final triumph against France was the ideal way to celebrate his 100th international appearance.

WHEN THE GOING GETS BUFF

Italy goalkeeper **Gianluigi Buffon** has not only been one of the finest modern-day goalkeepers in the world but has also even surpassed some of the achievements of legendary Italian predecessor Dino Zoff. Buffon emulated 1982 world champion Dino Zoff by being part of Italy's 2006 FIFA World Cup-winning side – only conceding two goals during the tournament, one an own goal and the other a penalty. Italy's progress to the 2012 UEFA European Championship final allowed him to play his 25th game at a finals for Italy, one more than Zoff – and behind only defenders Paolo Maldini (36) and Fabio Cannavaro (26). Italy's dismal first-round exit at the 2010 FIFA World Cup could be blamed at least more than a little on Buffon's back injury in the first half of their first match that ruled him out of the rest of the tournament. Unlike fellow veterans Cannavaro and Gennaro Gattuso, who retired from internationals after the finals, Buffon insisted he would go on and was rewarded with the captaincy by incoming coach Cesare Prandelli. Buffon became only the third footballer selected for five different FIFA World Cups when he made two appearances in Brazil in 2014, only missing the opening match against England due to a late ankle injury. Buffon equalled the European record of 167 international appearances – jointly held by Spain's goalkeeper Iker Casillas and Latvian midfielder Vitalijs Astafjevs – when keeping a clean sheet in a goalless draw against Germany in Milan on 15 November 2016, then broke the record in March 2017 with another clean sheet, against Albania, a match which marked his 1,000th career appearance.

CLEAN SWEEP

Italian clubs won all three UEFA trophies in the 1989–90 season, a unique treble. AC Milan took the European Cup (beating Benfica 1-0 in the final), Juventus the UEFA Cup (beating Fiorentina 3-1) and Sampdoria the Cup-Winners' Cup (beating Anderlecht 2-0 in the final).

KEEPING IT IN THE FAMILY

Cesare and **Paolo Maldini** are the only father and son to have hoisted the European Cup as winning captains – both with AC Milan and both for the first time in England. Cesare lifted the trophy after his team beat Benfica at Wembley, London, in 1963. Paolo repeated the feat 40 years later, when Milan defeated Juventus at Old Trafford, Manchester. Cesare was Italy coach and Paolo Italy captain at the 1998 FIFA World Cup, and they both featured at the 2002 tournament – though by now Cesare was in charge of Paraguay. A third generation Maldini, Christian, born in 1996, tried to emulate his father and grandfather, but he left Milan in 2016 without making a first-team appearance. He would have been the only player allowed to wear the No.3 shirt made famous by his father. Although he retired as Italy's second most-capped player, Paolo never managed to win an international tournament – he played for Italy sides that finished third and runners-up at the FIFA World Cup and runners-up in the UEFA European Championship. Cesare died on 3 April 2016, aged 84.

TAKING CARE OF BUSINESS

Italy's caretaker manager for two friendly matches in March 2018 was former international defensive midfielder **Luigi Di Biagio**, who had been put in charge of the country's U-20s in 2011 and their U-21s two years later. The senior side lost 2-0 at home to Argentina under his command, before drawing 1-1 away to England. Di Biagio held the distinction of scoring Italy's 100th FIFA World Cup goal, in a 3-0 first-round win over Cameroon in June 1998 – but missed the decisive spot-kick when losing to hosts France in the quarter-finals. He did make some amends, scoring in a UEFA Euro 2000 penalty shoot-out victory over the Netherlands. In May 2018 Roberto Mancini succeeded Di Biagio as permanent coach.

ITALY'S GREATEST PLAYERS

(as chosen by the Italian football association)

1 Giuseppe Meazza
2 Luigi Riva
3 Roberto Baggio
4 Paolo Maldini
5 Giacinto Facchetti
6 Sandro Mazzola
7 Giuseppe Bergomi
8 Valentino Mazzola

PEERLESS PIRLO

Deep-lying playmaker **Andrea Pirlo** – Italy's fifth  most-capped player with 116 – is one of the finest passers of a football in the modern era. He was one of the stand-out performers when Italy won the 2006 FIFA World Cup and the only player to win three man-of-the-match prizes at the 2012 UEFA European Championship. Perhaps his finest moment of Euro 2012 was the "Panenka" penalty he chipped down the centre of the goal in Italy's quarter-final shoot-out victory over England. Pirlo came to the tournament having gone through the Italian league season unbeaten, helping Juventus lift the Serie A title after joining them in 2011 from AC Milan on a free transfer.

MEDAL COLLECTORS

Giovanni Ferrari not only won both the 1934 and 1938 FIFA World Cup with Italy, he also shares the record for the most Serie A titles. He won it eight times, five with Juventus, two with Internazionale and one with Bologna. Virginio Rosetti won twice with Pro Vercelli and six with Juventus, while Giuseppe Furino and Gianluigi Buffon have eight Serie A titles with Juventus. In fact, Buffon has 11 titles, but the ones in 2004–05 and 2005–06 were rescinded in light of the Calciopoli scandal.

AZZURRI SEEING RED

Three men have been sent off twice for Italy, and three others have been dismissed on their debut. Pietro Rava marked his international bow by being sent off 53 minutes in, against the USA in August 1936 at the Berlin Olympics. Gianfranco Leoncini of Juventus, against Argentina in June 1966, and Cagliari's Davide Astori against Ukraine in March 2011 were also sent for early baths in their first appearances for Italy. The trio to have unhappily suffered two red cards apiece are Giancarlo Antognoni, Franco Causio and **Daniele De Rossi.**

ITALIAN LEAGUE TITLES

Club	Titles	Club	Titles
Juventus	34	Lazio	2
Internazionale	18	Napoli	2
AC Milan	18	Cagliari	1
Genoa	9	Casale	1
Bologna	7	Hellas Verona	1
Pro Vercelli	7	Novese	1
Torino	7	Sampdoria	1
Roma	3	Spezia	1
Fiorentina	2		

TRAGIC TORINO

Torino were Italy's most successful club side when their first-team squad was wiped out in an air crash at Superga, above Turin, on 4 May 1949. The club has only won the Serie A title once since then, in the 1976–77 season. Among the victims was star forward Valentino Mazzola, who had gone along on the trip despite being ill. His son **Sandro Mazzola**, only six at the time of the disaster, went on to star in the Italy teams that won the 1968 UEFA European Championship and finished as FIFA World Cup runners-up two years later.

BEEFING UP

The stadium shared by AC Milan and Internazionale is popularly known as the San Siro, after the district in which it is located. Its official title, however, is Stadio Giuseppe Meazza, named after the star inside-forward on the pitch and dance enthusiast off it who played for both clubs as well as Italy's 1934 and 1938 FIFA World Cup-winning sides. Meazza, born in Milan on 23 August 1910, was first spotted by an Inter scout while playing keepy-uppy in the street with a ball made of rags – but he was so thin he had to be fattened up with plenty of steaks. His last goal for Italy was a penalty in the 1938 World Cup semi-final against Brazil – taken while trying to pull up his shorts, whose elastic had broken.

WELL IN, EMANUELE

Emanuele Giaccherini scored Italy's fastest goal, just 19 seconds into their June 2013 friendly against Haiti – one second quicker than Salvatore Bagni's strike against Mexico 29 years earlier. The Haiti game finished 2-2 and was played to raise funds for victims of that country's 2010 earthquake.

NETHERLANDS

The walled banks of orange-shirted Netherlands fans may have become a regular feature at the world's major football tournaments, but that has not always been the case. It wasn't until the 1970s, with Johan Cruyff and his team's spectacular brand of "Total Football", that the country possessed a side worthy of the modern legend. They won the UEFA European Championship in 1988 and have regularly challenged for the game's major honours, but failed to qualify for both the 2016 UEFA European Championship and 2018 FIFA World Cup.

NETHERLANDS MANAGERS
(Since 1980)

Jan Zwartkruis	1978–81
Rob Baan	1981
Kees Rijvers	1981–84
Rinus Michels	1984–85
Leo Beenhakker	1985–86
Rinus Michels	1986–88
Thijs Libregts	1988–90
Nol de Ruiter	1990
Leo Beenhakker	1990
Rinus Michels	1990–92
Dick Advocaat	1992–95
Guus Hiddink	1995–98
Frank Rijkaard	1998–2000
Louis van Gaal	2000–02
Dick Advocaat	2002–04
Marco van Basten	2004–08
Bert van Marwijk	2008–12
Louis van Gaal	2012–14
Guus Hiddink	2014–15
Danny Blind	2015–17
Dick Advocaat	2017
Ronald Koeman	2018–

CRUYFF THE MAGICIAN

The football world united in tribute to one of the all-time legends and finest players ever when **Johan Cruyff** died aged 68 on 24 March 2016. Former Barcelona striker Gary Lineker said: "Cruyff did more to make the beautiful game beautiful than anyone in history," and Diego Maradona acclaimed the Dutch playmaker, captain and coach with the message: "We will never forget you, mate." Dutch prime minister Mark Rutte said: "The whole world knew him and, through him, the world knew the Netherlands." Cruyff, who was born in Amsterdam on 25 April 1947, was not only a genius with the ball at his feet but also an inspirational football philosopher, who spread the concept of "Total Football" not only with Ajax Amsterdam and the Netherlands in the 1970s but also in Spain where he played and managed Barcelona and acted as a mentor to those who followed him there, such as Pep Guardiola and Xavi Hernandez. He also gave the world the much-imitated "Cruyff turn", after managing to push the ball with the inside of his foot behind his standing leg before swivelling and surging past bemused Swedish defender Jan Olsson.

MICHELS THE MASTER

Rinus Michels (1928–2005) was named FIFA's Coach of the Century in 1999 for his achievements with the Netherlands and Ajax. The former Ajax and Netherlands striker took over the manager's job at his old club in 1965 and began creating the side that would dominate European football in the early 1970s. Michels built the team around Johan Cruyff – as he later did with the national side – and introduced the concept known as "Total Football". He moved to Barcelona after Ajax's 1971 European Cup victory, but he was called back to mastermind the Netherlands' 1974 FIFA World Cup bid. Nicknamed "The General", he was known as a disciplinarian who could impose order on the many different factions within the Dutch dressing room. Michels used that skill to great effect after taking over the national team again for their 1988 UEFA European Championship campaign. In the finals, the Dutch beat England and the Republic of Ireland to reach the last four, then knocked out hosts West Germany before beating the Soviet Union 2-0 in the final. Michels took charge for a third spell as manager when the Netherlands reached the semi-finals of Euro 92. He retired straight after the tournament.

KLAASSEN OF THE AJAX CLASS

Midfielder Davy Klaassen's first international appearance, a 2-0 defeat to France in March 2014, meant he was the 100th player to make his Netherlands debut as an Ajax Amsterdam player, having been brought up in the club's famed youth academy. Although he had to wait 12 months for his second appearance, he did manage to score his first international goal in a 2-0 victory over Spain in March 2015.

SENIOR ADVOCAAT

Dick Advocaat holds two records as Dutch national team coach. When he was re-appointed for his third spell in May 2017, he became, at 69, the oldest man to be national coach – one year older than Guus Hiddick had been when he was fired in 2015. Advocaat also has the most wins as national coach, victories in November 2017 friendlies over Scotland and Romania taking him to 37, one more than Englishman Bob Glendenning, who was in charge between 1925 and his death in 1940. After the Romania victory, however, Advocaat stood down as national coach and former player Ronald Koeman was appointed to replace him.

GOALS GALORE

Only four players have scored five goals in a game for the Netherlands: Jan Vos, as Finland were crushed 9-0 in July 1912; Leen Vente, in a 9-3 defeat of Belgium in March 1934; John Bosman, in an 8-0 home trouncing of Cyprus in October 1987; and Marco van Basten, in an 8-0 win in Malta in December 1990. Bosman scored three separate hat-tricks for the Dutch, as did Mannes Francken, Beb Bakhuys and Faas Wilkes. Two of Wilkes' trebles were scored in 1946 – the third came a full 13 years later.

HERO HAPPEL

Ernst Happel is second only to Rinus Michels for his coaching achievements with Dutch teams. The former Austria defender made history by steering Feyenoord to the European Cup in 1970 – the first Dutch side to win the trophy. He was drafted in to coach the Netherlands at the 1978 FIFA World Cup finals after guiding Belgian side Brugge to the European Cup final. In Johan Cruyff's absence, Happel drew the best from Ruud Krol, Johan Neeskens and Arie Haan as the Netherlands reached the final before losing in extra-time to Argentina in Buenos Aires.

ALL CHANGE FOR THE ORANJE

Ten of the 11 men who started the 2010 FIFA World Cup final were in the Dutch squad for a disastrous UEFA European Championship in 2012. They lost all three first-round games and missed the knock-out stages of a major tournament for the first time since failing to qualify for Euro 2004. Things improved dramatically at the 2014 FIFA World Cup as the Netherlands finished third after losing the semi-final to Argentina in a penalty shoot-out. Only nine members of the 23-man Euro 2012 squad made it to Brazil 2014. The most memorable Dutch display in Brazil came in their opening match: avenging their 2010 FIFA World Cup final defeat by demolishing champions Spain 5-1 in Salvador. **Robin van Persie**'s fantastic diving header from the edge of the area that looped over goalkeeper Iker Casillas was the highlight. Van Persie thus became the first Dutchman to score at three separate FIFA World Cups. The 2014 FIFA World Cup was the first one which the Netherlands ended with a win: their 3-0 third-place play-off defeat of hosts Brazil. This set another record as the Netherlands became the first country to beat Brazil in FIFA World Cup finals three times.

VAN BASTEN'S TOURNAMENT

Marco van Basten was the hero of the Netherlands' 1988 UEFA European Championship success. He netted a hat-trick to see off England in the group games, scored a semi-final winner against West Germany, and then cracked a spectacular flying volley to clinch a 2-0 victory over the Soviet Union in the final. The Dutch forward also starred in Italy's Serie A with AC Milan, and was twice the league's top scorer before persistent ankle trouble ended his career prematurely. He was then Netherlands coach for their runs to the second round of the 2006 FIFA World Cup and quarter-finals of the UEFA European Championship two years later.

HANGING AROUND

Goalkeeper Sander Boschker waited a long time for his full introduction to international football, but he set two Dutch records when coming on as a second-half substitute against Ghana in a June 2010 friendly. At the age of 39 years and 256 days, he was not only the oldest Dutchman to win his first cap – but also the oldest Dutch international ever. He retired in 2014 and it proved to be his only cap.

FLYING FEAR DENIED BERGKAMP MORE CAPS

Dennis Bergkamp would have won many more than 79 caps, but for his fear of flying. Bergkamp refused to board aircraft after the Netherlands squad were involved in a bomb hoax incident during the 1994 FIFA World Cup in the United States. He missed every away game for the Netherlands and his clubs unless he could reach the venue by road, rail or boat. His intricately-skilful last-minute winner against Argentina in the quarter-finals of the 1998 FIFA World Cup is seen by many as one of the tournament's finest and most elegant goals.

DIFFERENT SIDES OF SNEIJDER

On 9 June 2017, the Netherlands beat Luxembourg 5-0 in a 2018 FIFA World Cup qualifier, and midfield playmaker **Wesley Sneijder** not only became his country's most-capped footballer but also marked his 131st international appearance with his 31st goal. Five nights earlier, in a 5-0 friendly triumph over Ivory Coast, Sneijder had matched goalkeeper Edwin van der Sar's 130 caps total. He enjoyed an almost perfect 2010 as he won the treble with Italy's Internazionale – a domestic league and cup double and the UEFA Champions League – but just missed out on adding the FIFA World Cup, as the Netherlands lost 1-0 to Spain in the final. Sneijder also almost won the tournament's Golden Boot; his five goals put him level with Diego Forlan, Thomas Muller and David Villa.

TOP CAPS

1	Wesley Sneijder	133
2	Edwin van der Sar	130
3	Frank de Boer	112
4	Rafael van der Vaart	109
5	Giovanni van Bronckhorst	106
6	Dirk Kuyt	104
7	Robin van Persie	102
8	Phillip Cocu	101
9	Arjen Robben	96
10	John Heitinga	87
=	Clarence Seedorf	87

NEESKENS'S EARLY GOAL

The Netherlands took a first-minute lead in the 1974 World Cup final without a West German player having touched the ball. The Dutch built a move of 14 passes from the kick-off and Johan Cruyff was tripped in the box by Uli Hoeness. **Johan Neeskens** converted the first penalty in a World Cup final history ... but they still went on to lose.

KRUL TO BE KIND

Louis van Gaal pulled a masterstoke when he replaced goalkeeper Jasper Cillessen with Tim Krul in the 119th minute of the Netherlands' quarter-final against Costa Rica in the 2014 FIFA World Cup. He reasoned that the Dutch stood a better chance of winning the resulting shoot-out with Krul between the sticks as he is two inches taller than Cillessen. Sure enough, Krul saved two penalties and the Dutch went through. Enforced substitutions during the semi-final against Argentina meant van Gaal could not repeat the trick and Cillessen was unable to emulate Krul's earlier heroics. Third-choice goalkeeper Michel Vorm replaced Cillessen during stoppage-time of the third-place play-off against Brazil, making the Netherlands the first country to field all 23 squad-members during a FIFA World Cup.

NETHERLANDS' DOUBLE LOSERS

Nine Netherlands players were on the losing side in both the 1974 (2-1 to West Germany) and 1978 (3-1 to Argentina) FIFA World Cup finals. Jan Jongbloed, Ruud Krol, Wim Jansen, Arie Haan, Johan Neeskens, Johnny Rep and Rob Rensenbrink started both games. Wim Suurbier started in 1974 and was a substitute in 1978. Rene van de Kerkhof was a sub in 1974 and started in 1978. Rep is their seven-goal leading FIFA World Cup finals scorer, with four goals in 1974 and three in 1978.

THE WINNING CAPTAIN

With his distinctive dreadlocks, Ruud Gullit cut a swathe through world football through the 1980s and '90s. Twice a European Cup winner with AC Milan and a former European Footballer of the Year, he will always be remembered fondly by the Dutch fans as being the first man in a Netherlands shirt to lift a major trophy – the 1988 UEFA European Championship.

TOP SCORERS

1	Robin van Persie	50
2	Klaas-Jan Huntelaar	42
3	Patrick Kluivert	40
4	Dennis Bergkamp	37
=	Arjen Robben	37
6	Ruud van Nistelrooy	35
=	Faas Wilkes	35
8	Johan Cruyff	33
=	Abe Lenstra	33
10	Wesley Sneijder	31

DE BOER BOYS SET RECORD

Twins **Frank** and **Ronald de Boer** hold the record for the most games played by brothers together for the Netherlands. Frank won 112 caps, while Ronald won 67. Ronald missed a crucial spot-kick as the Dutch lost to Brazil in the semi-finals of the 1998 FIFA World Cup, while Frank suffered a similar unfortunate fate at the same stage of the UEFA European Championship two years later. Frank took over as Ajax Amsterdam manager in December 2010, having earlier that year been assistant to Bert van Marwijk to help the Netherlands to the FIFA World Cup final.

TWO LOOK FAMILIAR

Twin brothers Arnold and Anton Horburger were called up to the Netherlands' 12-man squad for a game against Belgium in April 1910, but only Arnold was picked to play in an era when substitutes were not permitted. However, Arnold left the pitch with a knee injury after half an hour but returned, seemingly fully fit, for the second half. The Belgians were convinced that twin Anton had taken the field instead, suggestions both players laughingly dismissed. Arnold went on to make eight international appearances, but Anton never played for his country – officially, at least.

VIRGIL RECORD

Virgil van Dijk became the world's most expensive defender in January 2018 after joining Liverpool from Premier League rivals Southampton for a reported £75 million. Two months later, he was named as the Netherlands' new captain, replacing Arjen Robben who had retired from international football the previous October. Robben is one of only two Dutch men to score at three separate FIFA World Cups – he and striker Robin van Persie both found the net in 2006, 2010 and 2014. Van Dijk's first international goal came in his 18th international appearance – second as skipper – in a 3-0 friendly win over European champions Portugal in March 2018.

WORK OF VAART

Rafael van der Vaart became the fifth player to make 100 appearances for the Netherlands, following Edwin van der Sar, Frank de Boer, Giovanni van Bronckhorst and Philip Cocu. Yet for a while it looked as if van der Vaart might just miss out on the milestone: he ended the 2012 UEFA European Championship on 99 caps and coach Bert van Marwijk said he may be left out of future squads. But Van Marwijk's departure after Euro 2012 was a boost for van der Vaart, who made his 100th appearance in a 4-2 friendly loss to Belgium in August 2012. Van der Vaart had marked his 99th cap with a stunning long-range goal against Portugal in the Netherlands' final first-round game at Euro 2012, and hit a post, in the 2-1 defeat that ended Dutch interest earlier than expected. Sadly, a calf injury ruled him out of the 2014 FIFA World Cup three days before Louis van Gaal announced his 23-man squad.

ALL-TIME LEADING SCORERS

Patrick Kluivert made his Netherlands debut in 1994 and, in the following ten years, won 79 caps and scored a then national record 40 goals. That mark was beaten by Robin van Persie, who was Netherlands captain at the 2014 FIFA World Cup, while Kluivert watched on as Louis van Gaal's assistant coach. Kluivert's son Justin, a winger at Ajax Amsterdam, made his Dutch international debut as a 78th-minute substitute against Portugal in March 2018, aged 18 – the same age at which Patrick first appeared for his country. Patrick's father and Justin's grandfather Kenneth Kluivert played three times for Surinam in 1964 and 1965, before he and his wife Lidwina moved to the Netherlands in 1970.

DUTCH CLOGS

The Netherlands became the first team to be shown as many as nine cards during a single FIFA World Cup match when they received eight yellows, including a lenient one for Nigel de Jong's chest-high challenge on Xabi Alonso, and a red during the 2010 final against Spain. The Netherlands were also involved in the FIFA World Cup game with the most cards: their second-round defeat to Portugal four years earlier, when 20 cards were shown in total – 16 yellows and four reds.

BLIND LEADING THE BLIND

Dutch defender Danny Blind won 42 caps between 1986 and 1996, and appeared at the FIFA World Cups of 1990 and 1994. He was also involved at the 2014 final, this time as an assistant to coach Louis van Gaal. He thus saw his son Daley – like Danny, a defender playing club football for Ajax Amsterdam – not only feature as a regular starter but score his first international goal, in the third-place play-off victory over Brazil. Danny Blind was appointed Guus Hiddink's assistant for the 2016 UEFA European Championship qualifying competition, but was appointed to the top job in May 2015 after Hiddink was sacked. Sadly, Blind could not turn around Dutch fortunes to qualify for France 2016 and, after a series of disappointing results in the qualification tournament for the FIFA World Cup 2018, he, too, was relieved of his duties in May 2017.

SIXTH SENSE

Maarten Stekelenburg, Edwin van der Sar's successor as the Netherlands' first-choice goalkeeper, impressed many with his performances at the 2010 FIFA World Cup, conceding just six goals in seven games – two of them penalties. His rise is all the more startling because he is deaf in one ear. He also has the unenviable distinction of being the first Dutch international goalkeeper to be shown a red card. On 6 September 2008, in a 2-1 friendly defeat against Australia in Eindhoven, he was sent off for fouling Josh Kennedy.

KOEMAN PEOPLE

Brothers **Ronald** and **Erwin Koeman** were Netherlands team-mates– helping them to win the 1988 UEFA European Championship – and also teamed up in management, with elder brother Erwin as Ronald's assistant at English clubs Southampton and Everton between 2014 and 2017. But when Ronald was appointed the Netherlands' new head coach in February 2018, Erwin opted not to join him. Ronald was the first man to both play for and manage all of Dutch domestic football's "big three" of Ajax Amsterdam, PSV Eindhoven and Feyenoord. He won the UEFA European Cup twice, with PSV Eindhoven in 1988 and – scoring the winning goal with a ferocious long-range free-kick – for Barcelona four years later. Despite largely playing in defence, he scored 14 goals in his 78 games for the Netherlands. Erwin played 31 times for the Netherlands and their father Martin won one cap for his country in 1964. Ronald Koeman's first game in charge of the Netherlands came two days after his 55th birthday, a 1-0 home defeat to England, as he began the challenge of improving prospects and morale after the Dutch – FIFA World Cup finalists in 2010 and finishing third four years later – failed to qualify for either the 2016 UEFA European Championship or the 2018 FIFA World Cup.

MATT START

At 17 years and 225 days, centre-back **Matthijs van Ligt** became the Netherlands' youngest player since Mauk Weber in 1931 (17 years and 92 days) when making his international bow against Bulgaria in March 2017. The youngest ever Dutch player was Jan van Breda Kolff, who scored on his debut against Belgium on 2 April 1911, aged 17 years and 74 days. It was no fairytale debut for van Ligt as he was blamed for Bulgaria's two first-half goals and replaced at half-time – albeit to widespread sympathy. Sixty days later, van Ligt came the youngest player to feature in a UEFA final, but his Ajax side lost to Manchester United in the Europa League final in Stockholm. Another Dutch defender, left-back Jetro Willems is the youngest player in UEFA European Championship finals history. In the Netherlands' Euro 2012 opener against Denmark on 9 June, Willems, aged 18 years and 71 days, was 44 days younger than Belgium's Enzo Scifo had been 1984.

ABE AND WILLING

Abe Lenstra was, until 2010, the oldest Dutchman to play in an international. He remains the nation's oldest goalscorer, aged 38 years and 144 days – when he netted in his final game, a 2-2 draw with Belgium, on 19 April 1959. The country's second oldest goalscorer, and his regular strike partner, Faas Wilkes, found the net for the last time exactly two years later – striking in a 2-1 defeat against Mexico, aged 37 years and 199 days. Lenstra scored 33 goals in 47 internationals while Wilkes – who endured a six-year hiatus from the national side when playing his club football abroad for Internazionale, Torino and Valencia – managed 35 in 38. Lenstra is also thought to be the first Dutch sports star to record and release a single, "Geen, maar daden" ("No words but deeds"), in 1958.

MEMPHIS SWELL

Substitute Memphis Depay became the youngest FIFA World Cup goalscorer in Dutch history – aged 20 years and 125 days – by netting in the 3-2 Group B victory over Australia at Porto Alegre in 2014. He also scored against Chile five days later, again as a substitute. Depay was one of three nominees for the Best Young Player award, but lost out to France's Paul Pogba.

PENALTY PLAGUE

Missed penalties have become a Dutch nightmare, causing their downfall in several tournaments. The jinx started in the 1992 UEFA European Championship semi-final, when Denmark's Peter Schmeichel won the shoot-out by saving from Marco van Basten. The Netherlands lost a Euro 96 quarter-final shoot-out to France and, two years later, went down on penalties to Brazil in a FIFA World Cup semi-final. And as co-hosts of Euro 2000, the Dutch missed two penalties in normal time in the semi-final against Italy and two more in the shoot-out. There was shoot-out joy at the 2014 FIFA World Cup when Costa Rica were beaten, but it turned to misery in the semi-final when they lost to Argentina on penalties.

NUMBER ONE EDWIN

Goalkeeper **Edwin van der Sar** (born in Voorhout on 29 October 1970) is the Netherlands' second most-capped player, having made 130 appearances for the national side. He joined Ajax in 1990 and helped them win the European Cup five years later. He made his Netherlands debut on 7 June 1995, against Belarus, and was their first-choice keeper for 13 years. He quit international football after the Netherlands' elimination at Euro 2008, but new coach Bert van Marwijk persuaded him to return briefly after injuries to his successors, Maarten Stekelenburg and Henk Timmer. Van der Sar has also won the UEFA Champions League with Manchester United, as well as spending spells with Juventus and Fulham.

HIGH-SCORING "LOW COUNTRIES DERBY"

The Netherlands' first official international was against Belgium on 30 April 1905, a 4-1 extra-time win in Antwerp with Eddy de Neve scoring all four Dutch goals, and they have since met another 125 times – more than three times more than any other opponent, which is Germany or West Germany with 40. Only Argentina and Uruguay (198) and Austria and Hungary (137) have met more often. The Netherlands' overall record against Belgium is 55 wins, 30 draws and 41 losses. One of the bitterest clashes was a goalless 1974 FIFA World Cup qualifier, which left the Netherlands top of the group but only after Belgium had a last-minute "goal" controversially disallowed. Memorable scorelines include Dutch wins 9-3 in March 1934, 8-0 in March 1936 and 9-1 in November 1959, defeats 7-1 in March 1940 and 7-6 in November 1951, and a 5-5 draw in September 1999. The most recent meeting was 1-1 draw in a November 2016 friendly.

SPAIN

Spanish clubs have won a record 18 European Cup/UEFA Champions Leagues between them and the country has produced some of world football's finest players. For years, however, the national team underachieved, winning only the 1964 UEFA European Championship. Things changed in 2008, when Spain won the UEFA European Championship and rose to a first-ever top position in the Coca-Cola/FIFA World Rankings. Two years later, it got even better as Spain added the FIFA World Cup, followed by a successful defence of the UEFA European Championship in 2012. But a disappointing first-round exit at the 2014 FIFA World Cup saw the run end and the 2018 tournament proved unexpectedly chaotic and underwhelming.

ANDRES THE GIANT

Andres Iniesta left Barcelona in 2018, having won nine La Liga titles, six Copa Del Rey trophies and four UEFA Champions League titles in 17 years at the club. He then bade farewell to international football after the 2018 FIFA World Cup, aged 34, having played 131 times for Spain and scored 13 goals – the most important of which won the 2010 FIFA World Cup. Uniquely, Iniesta has been named man of the match in the UEFA Champions League final (in 2015), UEFA European Championship final (2012) and FIFA World Cup final (2010).

DOUBLING UP

Spain's 2010 FIFA World Cup triumph made them the first country since West Germany in 1974 to lift the trophy as the reigning European champions. When France combined the two titles, they did it the other way around, by winning the 1998 FIFA World Cup and then the UEFA European Championship two years later. Yet no country had won three major tournaments in a row until Spain won Euro 2012, trouncing Italy 4-0 in the final. This also made Spain the first team to make a successful defence of their UEFA European Championship title. That scoreline was also the largest victory in a FIFA World Cup or UEFA European Championship final. The clean sheet in the final also stretched their run without conceding a goal in knockout games at major tournaments to 990 minutes.

HARD TO BEAT

Spain share with Brazil the record for longest international unbeaten run – the Brazilians went 35 games without a defeat between 1993 and 1996, a tally matched by the Spanish from 2007 until losing 2-0 to the United States in a 2009 FIFA Confederations Cup semi-final. That vintage Spain side also became the only country to secure 30 points out of 30 points in a FIFA World Cup qualification campaign, and they went on to to lift the trophy in South Africa in 2010.

THREE AND EASY

David Villa and Fernando Torres share Spain's record for most hat-tricks, with three. They even managed one apiece in the same match, the 10-0 crushing of Tahiti at the 2013 FIFA Confederations Cup. It was Spain's third-largest victory, behind only a 13-0 win over Bulgaria in 1933 and a 12-1 rout of Malta in 1983. Torres set another record at the 2009 FIFA Confederations Cup: the fastest ever hat-trick for Spain, all coming in the first 17 minutes of a 5-0 victory over New Zealand.

GROUNDS FOR APPEAL

No single country has provided more venues when hosting a FIFA World Cup finals than the 17 stadiums – in 14 cities – used by Spain in 1982. The 2002 tournament was played at 20 different venues but ten were in Japan and ten in South Korea. The 1982 competition was the first FIFA World Cup to be expanded from 16 to 24 teams. The final was played in Madrid's Estadio Santiago Bernabeu.

IAGO TURNS HERO ... THEN VILLAIN

Iago Aspas's spell in England, with Liverpool between 2013 and 2015 was something of a personal tragedy as he made only 14 – goalless – Premier League appearances. His return to England, for his Spain debut in a friendly on 15 November 2016 was much more successful. A substitute, he scored with his first shot at goal in the 90th minute and Isco then earned a last-gasp 2-2 draw. In Spain's 2018 FIFA World Cup second round penalty shoot-out loss to hosts Russia, however, Iago was again a villain as he (and Koke) failed from the spot.

MAJOR TOURNAMENTS

FIFA WORLD CUP:
15 appearances – winners 2010

UEFA EUROPEAN CHAMPIONSHIP:
10 appearances – winners 1964, 2008, 2012

FIRST INTERNATIONAL:
Spain 1 Denmark 0 (Brussels, Belgium, 28 August 1920)

BIGGEST WIN:
Spain 13 Bulgaria 0 (Madrid, 21 May 1933)

BIGGEST DEFEAT:
Italy 7 Spain 1 (Amsterdam, Netherlands, 4 June 1928); England 7 Spain 1 (London, England, 9 December 1931)

RED ALERT

Spain refused to play in the first UEFA European Championship in 1960, in protest at having to travel to the Soviet Union, a Communist country. But they changed their minds four years later, not only hosting the tournament but also winning it – by beating the visiting Soviets 2-1 in the final. Spain were captained by Fernando Olivella and managed by Jose Villalonga, who had been the first coach to win the European Cup, with Real Madrid in 1956.

RIGHT SAID FRED

When Spain came back from 2-0 and then 3-2 down to win 4-3 in Madrid in May 1929, they became the first non-British team to beat England. Spain's victory, in the Estadio Metropolitano, came with the help of their English coach Fred Pentland, who had moved to Spain in 1920. He had most success with Athletic Bilbao, leading them to league and cup doubles in 1930 and 1931 – and inflicting Barcelona's worst-ever defeat, a 12-1 rout in 1931.

NO DEFENCE

Spain went into the 2014 FIFA World Cup in Brazil aiming not only to successfully retain their crown but also to clinch a historic fourth successive international title, having won the UEFA European Championship in 2008 and 2012. Yet their defence was a disaster – despite taking the lead against the Netherlands in their opening game through a Xabi Alonso penalty, they lost the match 5-1: the heaviest FIFA World Cup finals defeat any reigning champion have suffered. A 2-0 defeat to Chile made them the first defending champions to be eliminated with a game remaining, though they gained a token consolation with a 3-0 defeat of Australia. The competition brought to an end the otherwise-glorious international careers of players such as Xavi Hernandez and David Villa.

WISE HEAD, OLD SHOULDERS

In 2008, a month short of his 70th birthday, Spain's **Luis Aragones** – full name Luis Aragones Suarez – became the oldest coach to win the UEFA European Championship. A former centre-forward and known only as "Luis" during his playing days, he won 11 caps for Spain. As coach, the "Wise Man of Hortaleza" won 38 matches between 2004 and 2008 – a national record since beaten by his successor Vicente Del Bosque. Aragones died from leukaemia on 1 February 2014, aged 75. Tributes were paid across football, but especially at his former club Atletico Madrid who, that same weekend, went top of La Liga for the first time since 1995–96 – when Aragones was coach. Atletico later won their first title since 1996. The players also wore his name embroidered in gold inside the collars of their shirts during the 2014 UEFA Champions League final.

TORRES! TORRES!

As a child, **Fernando Torres** wanted to be a goalkeeper, but made the wise decision to become a striker instead. He has a penchant for scoring the only goal in the final of a tournament, doing so in the 2008 UEFA European Championship, for Spain against Germany in Vienna, having done the same in the Under-16 UEFA European Championship in 2001 and for the Under-19s the following year. Torres became the most expensive Spanish footballer ever when Chelsea paid €58.5million to sign him from fellow English club Liverpool in January 2011. In 2012, Torres became the first player to score in the final of two different UEFA European Championships, when he came on as a substitute and found the net against Italy. Torres's goal in Spain's 3-0 victory over Australia in June 2014 was his first at a FIFA World Cup finals since Germany 2006. He thus became the ninth Spanish player to have scored four FIFA World Cup goals.

ADURIZ IS OLDEST

Aritz Aduriz became Spain's oldest goalscorer when finding the net in a 4-0 win over Macedonia on 13 November 2016 in a FIFA World Cup 2018 qualifier. He was aged 35 years and 275 days old – 50 days older than the previous record-holder Jose Maria Pena, who scored the only goal in 30 November 1930 friendly against Portugal. Athletic Bilbao striker Aduriz's strike against Macedonia came nine days after he scored all five of his club's goals in a 5-3 UEFA Europa League victory over Belgian side Genk. It was the first five-timer in the rebranded UEFA Europa League and the first since Italy's Fabrizio Ravanelli went nap for Juventus against CSKA Sofia in the UEFA Cup in 1994.

TOP SCORERS

1	David Villa	59
2	Raul Gonzalez	44
3	Fernando Torres	38
4	David Silva	35
5	Fernando Hierro	29
6	Fernando Morientes	27
7	Emilio Butragueno	26
8	Alfredo Di Stefano	23
9	Julio Salinas	22
10	Michel	21

HAPPY HERNANDEZ

When Spain's second most capped outfield player, with 133, retired from international football after the 2014 FIFA World Cup – and La Liga a year later – he was recognized as his country's most-decorated player. Curiously, both the first and final appearances of **Xavi Hernandez**'s international career were defeats to Netherlands sides coached by Louis van Gaal, 2-1 in 2000 and 5-1 in 2014. Triumph was far more familiar to the midfield playmaker, a mainstay of Spain's 2010 FIFA World Cup-winning side as well as the teams lifting the UEFA European Championship trophy in 2008 and 2012. The last match of his 24-year spell with Barcelona was, fittingly, their victory in the 2015 UEFA Champions League final, when he received the trophy from UEFA president Michel Platini, having come on as a late substitute for Andres Iniesta.

BEST CAS SCENARIO

Spain goalkeeper Iker Casillas has long been known to devotees back home as "Saint Iker" – an anointment richly supported by his haul of trophies and medals, both for team and individual. He is one of only three men to lift the FIFA World Cup, the UEFA European Championship and the UEFA Champions League trophies as captain, emulating Germany's Franz Beckenbauer and France's Didier Deschamps. As well as winning the 2008 and 2012 UEFA European Championships and 2010 FIFA World Cup, he remains Spain's most capped player and was Europe's joint most-capped. He claimed the Spanish record in a rare defeat, 1-0 to England in November 2011, before matching Latvia's Vitalijs Astafjevs and winning his 167th cap in a 6-1 friendly victory over South Korea in June 2016. Sadly, and to his evident disappointment, he was left on the bench as an unused substitute throughout the 2016 UEFA European Championship.

TOP CAPS

1	Iker Casillas	167
2	Sergio Ramos	156
3	Xavi	133
4	Andres Iniesta	131
5	Andoni Zubizarreta	126
6	David Silva	125
7	Xabi Alonso	114
8	Cesc Fabregas	110
=	Fernando Torres	110
10	Sergio Busquets	107

⚽ VILLA FILLS HIS BOOTS

David Villa became Spain's all-time top scorer in FIFA World Cups with his first-round goal against Chile in 2010, his sixth overall across the 2006 and 2010 tournaments. Villa also became the first Spaniard to miss a penalty in a FIFA World Cup match, when he wasted the chance of a hat-trick against Honduras, also in 2010, by putting his spot-kick wide. Spain had scored their previous 14 FIFA World Cup penalties, not counting shoot-outs. Villa became Spain's all-time leading scorer with a brace against the Czech Republic in March 2011, but a broken leg ruled him out of the 2012 UEFA European Championship, thus missing out on adding to his Euro 2008 and 2010 FIFA World Cup winners' medals. Villa retired from international football as Spain departed the 2014 FIFA World Cup, signing off with a neat backheel goal against Australia – his 59th international strike in 97 appearances and the first backheeled goal at a FIFA World Cup since Austria's Bruno Pezzey against Northern Ireland in 1982.

SERGING SERGIO

Sergio Ramos became the youngest-ever European player to reach 100 international caps, in March 2013, at the age of 26 years and 358 days – and marked the occasion by scoring Spain's goal in a 1-1 draw with Finland. Germany's Lukas Podolski, had been 21 days older when he won his 100th cap. South Korea's Cha Bum-Kun, who was 24 years and 139 days old when he achieved the landmark, holds the global record. Ramos, who can play both at right-back or in central defence, played in Spain's team that won the 2008 and 2012 UEFA European Championships, as well as the 2010 FIFA World Cup. He held those trophies in safer hands than he had done when he raised the Spanish Copa del Rey, won by his club Real Madrid, during an open-top bus tour in April 2011: on that occasion, he dropped the cup from the upper deck and saw it crushed beneath the bus's wheels. He passed Xavi Hernandez to become Spain's second most capped player during the 2016 UEFA European Championship.

⚽ VICTORY MARCH

Centre-back Carlos Marchena became the first footballer to go 50 internationals in a row unbeaten, when he played in Spain's 3-2 victory over Saudi Arabia in May 2009 – one more than Brazil's 1950s and 1960s winger Garrincha. Marchena was a member of Spain's successful 2010 FIFA World Cup squad, ending the tournament on 54 consecutive internationals without defeat. Marchena's 57-game unbeaten run came to an end when Argentina beat Spain 4-1 in September 2010.

⚽ FIT FOR PURPOSE

Luis Suarez played through injury for Spain in the 1964 UEFA European Championship final – luckily for his team-mates, since he set up both goals in a 2-1 triumph. He was named European Footballer of the Year in 1960 – the only Spanish-born player to have taken the prize.

⚽ ISCO INFERNO

Real Madrid attacker **Isco** scored Spain's 37th hat-trick – the first for five years – in a 6-1 friendly victory over Argentina on 27 March 2018. It equalled the South American team's heaviest ever defeat. Isco had helped Spain win the UEFA U21 European Championship in Israel in 2013, his three goals earning him the Bronze Boot. After joining Real Madrid in 2013, he has helped them win four UEFA Champions League titles in five years. Isco was among Spain's most impressive performers at the 2018 FIFA World Cup - but admitted losing to Russia on penalties was "the saddest day of my career".

TREASURE CHEST

The Spanish first division goalkeeper who concedes the fewest goals per game each season is awarded the Zamora Trophy. This is named after legendary keeper **Ricardo Zamora**, who played 46 times for Spain between 1920 and 1936 – including the legendary 4-3 win over England in Madrid in 1929. Zamora was the first Spanish star to play for both Barcelona and Real Madrid. Later he was league title-winning coach of ... Atletico Madrid.

LOPPING OFF LOPETEGUI

Spain's hopes of reclaiming their FIFA World Cup crown, having gone out in the 2014 group stage, were thrown into turmoil on 14 June 2018. Julen Lopetegui, appointed manager in the summer of 2016, was sacked one day before the opening game of the 2018 tournament in Russia. The decision came 24 hours after Lopetegui had announced he would be taking over from Zinedine Zidane at Real Madrid after the tournament. Spanish federation president Luis Rubiales claimed he was only given minutes' notice of Lopetegui's announcement and removed him from the post, putting Spain's sporting director **Fernando Hierro** in charge instead. Former Real Madrid centre-back Hierro – whose ten penalty goals for Spain remain a national record – oversaw progress from the first round, with a narrow victory over Iran and draws with Portugal and Morocco, but his side were surprisingly knocked out in the second round by hosts Russia on penalties.

Hierro stepped down from both his roles after elimination and former Real Madrid, Barcelona and Spain forward Luis Enrique – who had coached Barcelona to a treble of Spanish league and cup and UEFA Champions League in 2015 – was appointed as the nation's new permanent manager.

SPANISH LEAGUE CHAMPIONSHIPS

Real Madrid	33
Barcelona	25
Atletico Madrid	10
Athletic Bilbao	8
Valencia	6
Real Sociedad	2
Deportivo de la Coruna	1
Sevilla	1
Betis	1

THE RAUL THING

Raul Gonzalez Blanco – known as Raul – remains a Spain and Real Madrid icon, despite his record goal tallies being passed, respectively, by David Villa and Cristiano Ronaldo. He was an Atletico Madrid youth-teamer before signing for city rivals Real, where he scored 228 goals in 550 games and captained them from 2003 to 2010. But despite playing at five tournaments between the 1998 and 2006 FIFA World Cups, he was left out of Spain's UEFA Euro 2008 squad – and they won the trophy. After leaving Real, Raul enjoyed further success at Schalke in Germany, Al Sadd in Qatar and New York Cosmos in the United States.

SUPER PED

Spanish winger Pedro is the only player to have scored in six separate official club tournaments in one calendar year, managing to hit the net for Barcelona in Spain's Primera Liga, Copa del Rey and Super Cup in 2009, as well as the UEFA Champions League, UEFA European Super Cup and FIFA Club World Cup. He was also in the starting line-up for the 2010 FIFA World Cup final – less than two years after being a member of the Barcelona reserve team in Spain's third division and needing new club manager Pep Guardiola's intervention to prevent him being sent home to Tenerife.

PERFECT PICHICHI

The annual award for top scorer in La Liga is called the "Pichichi" – the nickname of Rafael Moreno, a striker for Athletic Bilbao between 1911 and 1921. He scored 200 goals in 170 games for the club, and once in five matches for Spain. Pichichi, who often took the field wearing a large white cap, died suddenly in 1922 aged just 29.

WAITING FOR BUS

Barcelona midfielder **Sergio Busquets** won the FIFA World Cup, UEFA European Championship and two UEFA Champions Leagues before turning 24 in July 2012, but he only broke his scoring duck for Spain in September 2014 – his 68th cap – in a 5-1 win over Macedonia. Since then, he has claimed a third UEFA Champions League, and second international goal. His father, Carles Busquets, was a Barcelona goalkeeper in the 1990s, part of Johan Cruyff's 1992 UEFA European Cup-winning squad, though he was mainly understudy to Andoni Zubizarreta.

FIFA FIRST

Real Madrid were the only Spanish club formally represented at FIFA's first meeting in Paris in 1904 – though the club was then known simply as Madrid FC. Spanish clubs, such as Real Madrid and Real Betis, dropped the word "Real" – meaning "Royal" – from their names during the Second Spanish Republic, between 1931 and 1939.

SILVA SERVICE

Spain entered the 2018 FIFA World Cup finals with an unbeaten qualifying run of 63 matches, the last defeat having been to Denmark in 1993. **David Silva** scored in his fourth consecutive international in a June 2017 qualifying victory over Macedonia and he was also on target in the 8-0 rout of Liechtenstein in September 2017. Other important Silva goals include the last in a 3-0 defeat of Russia in the 2008 UEFA European Championship semi-final, and the opener as Spain defeated Italy 4-0 in the Euro 2012 final to retain their crown. Silva ended the 2018 FIFA World Cup with 35 goals in 125 appearances for his country.

SPAIN'S PLAYERS IN EURO 2008/FIFA WORLD CUP 2010/ EURO 2012 SQUADS

Iker Casillas*
Sergio Ramos*
Andres Iniesta*
Xabi Alonso*
Xavi Hernandez*
Cesc Fabregas*
Fernando Torres*
David Silva
Alvaro Arbeloa
Raul Albiol
Pepe Reina

* = appeared in all three finals.

TOP BOSS DEL BOSQUE

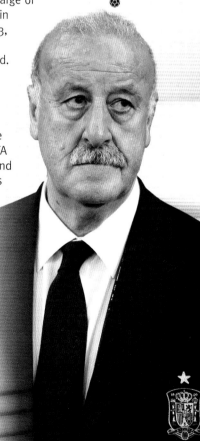

Vicente Del Bosque was an unused substitute during Ladislao Kubala's 68th and final match in charge of Spain in 1980. He was on Spain's bench again when *La Roja* played Denmark in March 2013, but this time as manager, and for the 69th time, enabling him to surpass Kubala's record. Del Bosque won the 2010 FIFA World Cup and the 2012 UEFA European Championship as Spain manager, adding to the two UEFA Champions League titles he claimed as Real Madrid boss. He and Italy's Marcelo Lippi are the only men to have won both the UEFA Champions League or European Cup and the FIFA World Cup – but Del Bosque's Euro 2012 triumph gave him an unprecedented hat-trick. Another unmatched feat was his 13 victories in his first 13 matches as Spain manager after he succeeded Luis Aragones in 2008. His 100th game in charge of Spain was a 2016 UEFA European Championship qualifier – a 1-0 win in Belarus in June 2015. Del Bosque stepped down as manager after Spain's second-round exit from the 2016 UEFA European Championship but was promised an ongoing role within the Spanish football association.

BELGIUM

Belgium embarked on a golden period in the Eighties after eight decades spent on the fringes of international competition: first a runners-up finish at the 1980 UEFA European Championship, then a run to the 1986 FIFA World Cup semi-finals. A new crop of elite European stars did, however, help Belgium to reach the 2014 FIFA World Cup quarter-finals – after which they rose to an all-time high No.1 in the FIFA World Rankings in November 2015 – and the "Red Devils" surpassed any previous achievements by finishing third at the 2018 FIFA World Cup.

TOP SCORERS

1	Romelu Lukaku	40
2	Paul Van Himst	30
=	Bernard Voorhoof	30
4	Marc Wilmots	28
5	Joseph Mermans	27
6	Robert De Veen	26
=	Raymond Braine	26
8	Eden Hazard	25
9	Wesley Sonck	24
10	Marc Degryse	23
=	Jan Ceulemans	23

OLD–TIMER TIMMY

Belgium's fourth most-capped player, Timmy Simons, became his country's oldest international when facing Estonia in November 2016 in a 2018 FIFA World Cup qualifier, aged 39 years and 338 days. He was barely troubled as Belgium ran out 8-1 winners.

HE'S OUR GUY

Unquestionably Belgium's greatest manager – as well as their longest-serving – was **Guy Thys**. He led them to the final of the 1980 UEFA European Championship and – with a team featuring the likes of Enzo Scifo and Nico Claesen – the semi-finals of the FIFA World Cup six years later. He spent 13 years in the job from 1976 to 1989, then returned for a second spell just eight months after quitting. He stepped down again after managing Belgium at the 1990 FIFA World Cup. During his playing days in the 1940s and 1950s, he was a striker and won two caps for Belgium. He died at the age of 80 in August 2003.

HAZ A GO HERO

Belgium, under Spanish manager Roberto Martinez, enjoyed their most successful FIFA World Cup in Russia in 2018, finishing third. They were the tournament's top scorers with 16 goals and won widespread admiration for such performers as centre-backs Jan Vertonghen and Toby Alderweireld, playmaker Kevin De Bruyne and attacking right-back Thomas Meunier. There were also individual prizes for goalkeeper Thibaut Courtois, who took the tournament's Golden Gloves award for best goalkeeper, and captain **Eden Hazard** who won the Silver Ball as second best player, behind Croatia's Luka Modric. Hazard scored Belgium's second goal as they beat England 2-0 in the third-place play-off – Meunier scored the first. Hazard is the son of not just one former footballer but two – his mother Carine only retired from the women's game when pregnant with Eden. He was born in La Louviere, the same birthplace as former star Enzo Scifo – once the youngest player at a UEFA European Championship, aged 18 years and 115 days when Belgium beat Yugoslavia in their opening game at the 1984 tournament. Scifo scored twice as Belgium finished fourth at the 1986 FIFA World Cup, their best result until 2018.

MOTHER'S BOY

Belgium's most-capped footballer, defender **Jan Vertonghen** made his 100th appearance
on 2 June 2018 against Portugal – 11 years to the day after his first cap, against
the same country. His mother Ria Matthews handed over a commemorative cap to
celebrate the 100-match landmark. Vertonghen, who scored in both the 2014 and
2018 finals, helped Belgium to a best-ever FIFA World Cup finish of third place in
2018. The man now second on Belgium's top caps list, Jan Ceulemans, also had
maternal influence as his mother recommended he did not move from Club
Brugge to AC Milan. Ceulemans also scored three goals in appearances at the
1982, 1986 and 1990 FIFA World Cups – and captained the team to fourth place in
1986. The longest-lasting Belgian international career belongs to Hector Goetinck,
who won 17 caps between 1906 and 1923.

COMEBACK KINGS

Belgium's 3-2 victory over Japan in Rostov at the 2018 FIFA World Cup was
the first time since 1970 that a team came back from two goals down
to win a knock-out game – and West Germany had needed extra-time to
beat England 3–2 in a quarter-final tie. Jan Vertonghen scored Belgium's
first goal after 69 minutes, followed by Marouane Fellaini's equalizer five
minutes later. Fellow substitute Nacer Chadli got the winner four minutes
into stoppage-time. Belgium's 10 different goalscorers in Russia equalled
the FIFA World Cup record held by France (1982) and Italy (2006).

TRIUMPHS AND TRAGEDY

The largest football venue in Belgium is the 50,000-capacity King
Baudouin Stadium in Brussels, which opened under its first name, the
Jubilee Stadium, on 23 August 1930 and was renamed Heysel in 1946. It
was the scene of tragedy in 1985 when a wall collapsed and 39 fans died
in disturbances while attending the European Cup final between Liverpool
and Juventus. The stadium was rebuilt and given its current name in 1995.
When Belgium and the Netherlands co-hosted the 2000 UEFA European
Championship, it staged the opening ceremony and first match, Belgium's
2-1 victory over Sweden. Now used for Belgium's home internationals, the
King Baudouin Stadium was chosen to stage four games, as one of 13
host cities, at the 2020 UEFA European Championship.

TOP CAPS

1	Jan Vertonghen	108
2	Jan Ceulemans	96
=	Axel Witsel	96
4	Timmy Simons	94
5	Eden Hazard	92
6	Marouane Fellaini	87
7	Eric Gerets	86
=	Franky Van Der Elst	86
9	Daniel Van Buyten	85
10	Enzo Scifo	84

DIVOCK'S DIVIDEND

Divock Origi was a late choice for Belgium's
2014 FIFA World Cup squad, picked by
manager Marc Wilmots to replace the injured
Christian Benteke. He justified that faith with
the only goal of Belgium's second game,
in the 88th minute, against Russia, half an
hour after coming on as a substitute. Aged
19 years and 65 days, he became Belgium's
youngest FIFA World Cup goalscorer. Divock's
father, Mike Origi, was an international for
his native Kenya, but spent most of his
career in Belgium, where Divock was born
and raised. Belgium's oldest FIFA World Cup
scorer remains centre-back Leo Clijsters,
aged 33 years and 250 days. He headed the
opener in a 3-1 win over Uruguay at Italia 90.

THE FOUR–MOST

Belgium enjoyed their largest winning margin
at a major tournament when they beat
Hungary 4-0 in the second round at the
2016 UEFA European Championship.
Until then, their most emphatic
victories had been 3-0 victories over
the Republic of Ireland in the previous
round and against El Salvador at the
1970 FIFA World Cup. Striker **Romelu
Lukaku**'s two goals in the Ireland game
made him the first Belgian player to
score a brace at a tournament since his
international manager Marc Wilmots did
similarly against Mexico at the 1998 FIFA World
Cup. Lukaku added two more braces in Belgium's
first two 2018 FIFA World Cup games, a 3-0 victory
over Panama and a 5-2 win over Tunisia in Group
G. Eden Hazard also scored twice against Tunisia.

BULGARIA

The glory days of the "golden generation" apart – when Bulgaria finished fourth at the 1994 FIFA World Cup in the United States, sensationally beating defending champions Germany 2-1 in the quarter-finals – a consistent pattern emerges with Bulgarian football. Regular qualifiers for the game's major competitions, and the birthplace of some of the sport's biggest names (such as Hristo Stoichkov and Dimitar Berbatov), the country has too often failed to deliver on the big occasions and make its mark on world football.

TOP SCORERS

1	Dimitar Berbatov	48
=	Hristo Bonev	48
3	Hristo Stoichkov	37
4	Emil Kostadinov	27
5	Liubomir Angelov	26
6	Peter Jekov	25
=	Ivan Kolev	25
8	Atanas Mihailov	23
=	Nasko Sirakov	23
10	Dimitar Milanov	20

A NATION MOURNS

Bulgaria lost two of its most popular footballing talents when a June 1971 car crash claimed the lives of strikers Georgi Asparukhov (28) and Nikola Kotkov (32). Asparukhov scored 19 goals in 50 internationals, including Bulgaria's only goal of the 1966 FIFA World Cup finals in a 3-1 defeat to Hungary.

MOB RULES

Much-travelled Bulgaria centre-forward **Dimitar Berbatov** claims to have learned English by watching the *Godfather* movies. Berbatov joined Manchester United from Tottenham in 2008 for a club and Bulgarian record fee of £30.75m. Before joining Spurs, he had been a member of the Bayer Leverkusen side who narrowly missed out on a treble in 2002. They lost in the final of both the UEFA Champions League and the German cup and finished runners-up in the German Bundesliga. Berbatov surprised and disappointed fans back home when he announced his international retirement aged just 29, in May 2010, having scored a national-record 48 goals in his 78 appearances for Bulgaria. He briefly considered a return to the national team in 2012, but ultimately opted against the idea, saying that he wanted to "give chances to younger players". After joining Fulham in the summer of that year, he raised eyebrows during one match by revealing a T-shirt with the slogan: "Keep calm and pass me the ball."

MAYOR WITH NO HAIR

Balding Yordan Letchkov headed the winning goal against holders and defending champions Germany in the 1994 FIFA World Cup quarter-final in the United States. At the time, he played for German club Hamburg. He later became mayor of Sliven, the Bulgarian town where he was born in July 1967.

POP OF HORRORS

Bulgaria captain Ivelin Popov has experienced a chequered career with the national side – including several scandals and banishments. He scored twice from the penalty spot in February 2011 in a 2-2 friendly draw with Estonia that was later officially expunged from the records by FIFA amid allegations of match-fixing involving the officials. He had previously been banned from the country's youth ranks in 2008 for allegedly throwing a bottle at a bus driver and then from the senior side in September 2010 for reportedly breaking a curfew to go out drinking with team-mates for striker Valeri Bojinov's birthday. He was barred from the national side again in 2014, but returned to favour in 2015 when recalled by new coach Ivaylo Petev, whose 2016 successor Petar Hubchev then restored Popov to the captaincy. Bulgaria missed out on the 2018 FIFA World Cup, however, despite Popov's two goals – finishing fourth in UEFA's Group A behind eventual champions France, play-off qualifiers Sweden and the Netherlands.

STAN THE BURGER VAN MAN

Stiliyan Petrov – nicknamed "Stan" by fans of his English club Aston Villa – was applauded onto the field when he became Bulgaria's first outfield player to reach 100 caps, against Switzerland in March 2011. The midfielder and Bulgaria captain has been playing in Britain since 1999, when he joined Scottish giants Celtic as a 20-year-old – but had to fight hard against a bout of homesickness. He later revealed that his English only improved when he started work behind the counter of a Scottish friend's burger van. Petrov said: "Some of the customers used to stare, thinking: 'That looks like Stiliyan Petrov, but it can't be.' But soon I started to understand things better." Tributes from across football and around the world poured in for Petrov when, in March 2012, he revealed he had been diagnosed with acute leukaemia. After 19 minutes of every home game for the rest of the season Villa fans stood and applauded for 60 seconds – 19 being his squad number.

TOP CAPS

1	Stiliyan Petrov	106
2	Borislav Mikhailov	102
3	Hristo Bonev	96
4	Krasimir Balakov	92
5	Dimitar Penev	90
=	Martin Petrov	90
7	Radostin Kishishev	83
=	Hristo Stoichkov	83
9	Nasko Sirakov	81
10	Zlatko Yankov	80

STOY STORY

Goalkeeper Vladislav Stoyanov has denied Cristiano Ronaldo from the penalty spot not once, but twice. The first was at club level in October 2014, when Real Madrid beat Ludogorets Razgrad 2-1 in the UEFA Champions League; the second was in a March 2016 international friendly when Bulgaria beat Portugal 1-0 – Ronaldo's fourth failure from 12 yards that season. It was Bulgaria's first victory over Portugal since December 1981, and was clinched by a debut goal by Brazilian-born attacking midfielder Marcelinho, a 31-year-old who had come to Bulgaria five years earlier.

MORE FROM '94

Former centre-back Petar Hubchev was appointed Bulgaria coach in September 2016, making him the second of his country's 1994 FIFA World Cup semi-finalists – after Hristo Stoichkov, 2004–07 – to manage the national side. Lubo Penev – in charge 2011–14 – is the nephew of the 1994 squad coach, Dimitar Penev, but missed that tournament as he was battling testicular cancer. He recovered to play at both Euro 1996 France 1998. Lothar Matthaus, in Germany's team which lost to them in 1994, was Bulgaria's coach 2010–11.

ALL–ROUNDER ALEKSANDAR

Defender Aleksandar Shalamanov played for Bulgaria at the 1966 FIFA World Cup, six years after representing his country as an alpine skier at the Winter Olympics at Lake Placid. He also went to the 1964 Tokyo Summer Olympics as an unused member of the volleyball squad. Shalamanov was voted Bulgaria's best sportsman in both 1967 and 1973.

HRISTO'S HISTORY

Hristo Stoichkov, born in Plovdiv, Bulgaria, on 8 February 1968, shared the 1994 FIFA World Cup Golden Boot, awarded to the tournament's top scorer, with Russia's Oleg Salenko. Both scored six times, though Stoichkov became the sole winner of that year's European Footballer of the Year award. Earlier the same year, he had combined up-front with Brazilian Romario to help Barcelona reach the final of the UEFA Champions League. He was banned for a year after a brawl earlier in his career, during the 1985 Bulgarian cup final between CSKA Sofia and Levski Sofia. Stoichkov won trophies with clubs in Bulgaria, Spain, Saudi Arabia and the United States before retiring as a player in 2003.

TEETHING TROUBLES

Martin Petrov suffered a terrible start to his international career when he was sent off for two yellow cards just eight minutes into his debut as a substitute in a Euro 2000 qualifier against England. He broke down in tears when leaving the field, but recovered from the experience to become one of his country's most-capped players and enjoyed spells with top clubs such as Atletico Madrid in Spain and Manchester City in England. His 90 caps and 20 goals included Bulgaria's only strike at the 2004 UEFA European Championship, against Italy.

CROATIA

Croatia's distinctive red-and-white chequered jersey has become one of the most recognized in world football – and their flamboyant attackers some of the most admired across the globe. Formerly part of Yugoslavia, they reached the quarter-finals in their very first senior competition (UEFA Euro 96) then finished third at the 1998 FIFA World Cup – and have remained regular qualifiers for both tournaments since, hitting a new peak in 2018 when reaching their first FIFA World Cup final.

TOP SCORERS

1	Davor Suker	45
2	Mario Mandzukic	33
3	Eduardo da Silva	29
4	Darijo Srna	22
5	Ivan Perisic	21
6	Ivica Olic	20
7	Niko Kranjcar	16
8	Nikola Kalinic	15
=	Ivan Rakitic	15
=	Goran Vlaovic	15

RAK ATTACKS

Only two footballers have won Croatia's Sportsman of the Year prize since Davor Suker in 1998: Mario Mandzukic in 2013 and **Ivan Rakitic** two years later – and Rakitic made history of his own at the 2018 FIFA World Cup. The Barcelona midfielder became the first man to convert the decisive penalty in two different shoot-outs at the same FIFA World Cup: against Denmark and Russia. Rakitic was born in Switzerland and played four times for that country's U17s, U19s and U21s before opting for Croatia, land of both his parents. He was named Croatian Footballer of the Year in 2015, the only time since 2013 it has not gone to six-time winner Luka Modric.

LUKA LOOPY

Croatia made history by reaching their first FIFA World Cup final in 2018 – and star of the show was captain and main playmaker **Luka Modric**, who won the Golden Ball prize as the tournament's best player despite their 4-2 final defeat to France. Modric began his career with Dinamo Zagreb before moving to Tottenham Hotspur in England and then winning four UEFA Champions League titles with Spain's Real Madrid. He made his international debut in March 2006 in a friendly against Argentina, scored at both the 2008 and 2016 UEFA European Championships and both scored and missed penalties at the 2018 FIFA World Cup. In Russia, Croatia became the first country since Argentina in 1990 to win two penalty shoot-outs at the same FIFA World Cup – beating Denmark in the second round and hosts Russia in the quarter-finals. Perhaps their best performance, however, was the 3-0 trouncing of Argentina in their second group match, with goals from Ante Rebic, Modric and Ivan Rakitic.

UNLUCKY MAND

Striker **Mario Mandzukic** was Croatia's hero in their 2018 FIFA World Cup semi-final – only to unwittingly turn villain four days later in the final. His goal, 19 minutes into extra-time, beat England 2-1 and sent Croatia to their first ever FIFA World Cup final. In the final, however, he headed an Antoine Griezmann free-kick into his own net after 18 minutes to give France the lead. Mandzukic did pull a goal back to make the score 4-2 to France with 21 minutes left. He thus became the first man to score for both sides in a FIFA World Cup final – only Dutch defender Ernie Brandts, against Italy in 1978 – had done it any FIFA World Cup finals match. Ivan Perisic, who equalized against England and France, also suffered misery at the other end because he conceded the handball penalty, which Antoine Griezmann converted, to restore France's lead in the final.

OLE, OLIC

Croatia's second game at the 2014 FIFA World Cup, a 4-0 trouncing of Cameroon, was doubly notable. It was the first time they had scored as many as four goals in a single FIFA World Cup finals match. It also saw striker Ivica Olic become the first player to score for Croatia at two separate FIFA World Cups, having previously found the net in 2002. His lengthy break between finals goals is matched only by Denmark's Michael Laudrup, who scored at the 1986 tournament and then had to wait until the 1998 finals to do so again. The other scorers against Cameroon in 2014, Mario Mandzukic and Ivan Perisic, then emulated Olic by scoring in the 2018 tournament – and both did so in the final defeat against France.

DEER DARIJO

Darijo Srna is Croatia's fourth top scorer of all time, despite playing many games as a right-back or wing-back. He has a tattoo on his calf in the shape of a deer, the Croatian word for which is "srna". He also has a tattoo on his chest – the name of his brother Igor, who has Down's syndrome and to whom he dedicates each goal he scores. Now Croatia's most capped player, Srna was one of three players to reach 100 appearances for their country against South Korea in February 2013. The other two were goalkeeper Stipe Pletikosa and defender Josip Simunic.

THE KIDNEYS ARE ALL RIGHT

Striker Ivan Klasnic returned to international duty with Croatia despite suffering kidney failure in early 2007. A first attempt at a transplant failed when his body rejected a kidney donated by his mother, but follow-up surgery – using a kidney from his father – proved successful. He recovered enough to play for Croatia again in March 2008 and represented his country in that summer's UEFA European Championship, scoring twice – including a winning goal against Poland.

DALIC'LL DO

Slaven Bilic and Igor Stimac were formidable central defensive partners as Croatia finished third at the 1998 FIFA World Cup and both went on to manage their country – but it was an uncapped player, Zlatko Dalic, who went one better by leading Croatia to the 2018 FIFA World Cup final. Bilic took Croatia to the 2008 and 2012 UEFA European Championships during his six-year spell in charge, but his successor Stimac only lasted 15 matches before being replaced by another former international Niko Kovac. Appointed in place of Ante Cacic in October 2017, Dalic's Croatia qualified for the 2018 finals with a 4-1 aggregate play-off victory over Greece. He stamped his authority on the side in Russia, sending home Nikola Kalinic after the striker allegedly refused to come on as a substitute in their opening game against Nigeria.

TOP CAPS

1	Darijo Srna	134
2	Stipe Pletikosa	114
3	Luka Modric	113
4	Josip Simunic	105
5	Ivica Olic	104
6	Vedran Corluka	103
7	Dario Simic	100
8	Ivan Rakitic	99
9	Mario Mandzukic	89
10	Robert Kovac	84

DOUBLE IDENTITY

Robert Jarni and Robert Prosinecki both have the rare distinction of playing for two different countries at different FIFA World Cup tournaments. They both represented Yugoslavia in Italy in 1990, then newly independent Croatia eight years later in France. Full-back Jarni actually played for both Yugoslavia and Croatia in 1990, then only Yugoslavia in 1991, before switching back – and permanently – to Croat colours in 1992 after the country officially joined UEFA and FIFA. He retired with 81 caps for Croatia, seven for Yugoslavia.

SUPER SUKER

Striker **Davor Suker** won the Golden Boot for being top scorer at the FIFA World Cup in 1998, scoring six goals in seven games as Croatia finished third. His strikes included the opening goal in Croatia's 2-1 semi-final defeat to eventual champions France, and the winner in a 2-1 triumph over Holland in the third-place play-off. Suker, by far his country's leading scorer of all time, had hit three goals at the UEFA European Championship in 1996 – including an audacious long-distance lob over Denmark goalkeeper Peter Schmeichel. Suker was named president of the Croatian Football Federation in July 2012.

CZECH REPUBLIC

The most successful of the former Eastern Bloc countries, as Czechoslovakia they finished as runners-up in the 1934 and 1962 FIFA World Cups, and shocked West Germany in a penalty shoot-out to win the 1976 UEFA European Championship. Playing as the Czech Republic since 1994, they lost – on a golden goal – in the UEFA Euro 96 final, and in the semi-final eight years later. Recent times have been tougher. The Czechs were quarter-finalists at Euro 2012 but have failed to qualify for the FIFA World Cup finals in 2010, 2014 and 2018.

PLASIL'S PLACE

Midfielder **Jaroslav Plasil** went into the 2016 UEFA European Championship having just become only the fourth Czech player to reach a century of caps, reaching the landmark in a 2-1 friendly defeat to South Korea. He had been part of the side which reached the semi-finals of the 2004 UEFA European Championship, scored against Turkey at the tournament four years later and also played every minute of his side's progress to the second round at Euro 2012. He was also a mainstay in helping reach the 2016 UEFA European Championship, although the 14 goals the Czechs conceded in qualifying were more than any other side to make the finals.

CHIP WITH EVERYTHING

One of the most famous penalties ever taken was **Antonin Panenka**'s decisive spot-kick for Czechoslovakia against West Germany in the final of the 1976 UEFA European Championship, giving the Czechs victory in the shoot-out. Despite the tension, and the responsibility resting on him, Panenka cheekily chipped the ball into the middle of the goal – as goalkeeper Sepp Maier dived to the side. That style of spot-kick is now widely known as a "Panenka", and has been replicated by the likes of France's Zinedine Zidane, in the 2006 FIFA World Cup final.

CZECHS STEP IN

Despite losing the 1996 UEFA European Championship final, the Czech Republic replaced winners Germany in the 1997 FIFA Confederations Cup in Saudi Arabia. The Czechs, coached at both tournaments by Dusan Uhrin, finished third after beating Uruguay 1-0 in a third-place play-off. Midfielder Edvard Lasota scored the only goal, but their top scorer was Vladimir Smicer, with five – including a hat-trick in a 6-1 triumph over the United Arab Emirates.

CECH CAP

Goalkeeper **Petr Cech** has worn a protective cap while playing ever since suffering a fractured skull during an English Premier League match in October 2006. He later added a chin protector after requiring a facial operation following a training accident. He was born as a triplet, along with sister Sarka and brother Michal, who died of an infection at the age of two. Cech served notice of his talents when he was beaten by only one penalty in a shoot-out against France in the 2002 UEFA U-21 European Championship final, helping the Czechs to win the trophy. He claimed winners' medals as Chelsea won the 2012 UEFA Champions League (he was named man of the match) and 2013 UEFA Europa League. Now the Czech Republic's most capped player, he marked his 100th international appearance in March 2013 with a clean sheet in a 3-0 defeat of Armenia. He played in all three games at the 2016 UEFA European Championship, but he retired after the team went out in the first round.

PASSING THE PUC

The final of the 1934 FIFA World Cup was the first to go into extra-time, with Czechoslovakia ultimately losing 2-1 to hosts Italy despite taking a 76th-minute lead through Antonin Puc. Puc was Czechoslovakia/the Czech Republic's top international scorer with 34 goals when he retired in 1938 until he was passed, first by Jan Koller, 67 years later, and, latterly, by Milan Baros.

WALK–OUT

Belgium's 1920 victory in the Olympic Games was overshadowed when Czechoslovakia walked off the pitch after half an hour in protest following what they saw as biased refereeing. Czechoslovakia are the only team in the history of Olympic football to have been disqualified.

MOSTLY MOZART

The last Czech Republic player to score at a FIFA World Cup was **Tomas Rosicky**, a double in a 3-0 victory over the United States at the 2006 tournament. Despite an injury-plagued career, he became only the third Czech to reach a century of caps, in a 2-1 2016 European Championship qualifier defeat to Iceland in June 2015. The midfielder, nicknamed "The Little Mozart" for the way he orchestrates play, has performed with rock band Tri sestry after taking up the electric guitar during a spell on the sidelines. His father and his brother, both named Jiri, were professional but uncapped footballers. Rosicky retired from international football after the Czech Republic were eliminated from Euro 2016 in the first round, during which he became the oldest Czech player to appear in a UEFA Euro finals, aged 35. He had also been their youngest, aged 19, in 2000.

THE CANNON COLLECTS

Pavel Nedved's election as European Footballer of the Year in 2003 ended an impatient wait for fans in the Czech Republic who had seen a string of outstanding players overlooked since Josef Masopust had been honoured back in 1962. Masopust, a midfield general, had scored the opening goal in the FIFA World Cup final that year before Brazil hit back to win 3-1 in the Chilean capital of Santiago. Years later, Masopust was remembered by Pele and nominated as one of his 125 greatest living footballers. At club level, Masopust won eight Czechoslovak league titles with Dukla Prague, the army club. He was also the winner, in 1962, of the first Czech Golden Ball as domestic footballer of the year. It was another day and in another age. Masopust was presented with his award before the kick-off of a European Cup quarter-final with Benfica – with a minimum of fuss. Years later, Masopust said: "Eusebio just shook hands with me, I put the trophy in my sports bag and went home on the tram."

TOP SCORERS

Czech Republic only

1	Jan Koller	55
2	Milan Baros	41
3	Vladimir Smicer	27
4	Tomas Rosicky	23
5	Pavel Kuka	22*
6	Patrick Berger	18
=	Pavel Nedved	18
8	Vratislav Lokvenc	14
9	Tomas Necid	12
10	Marek Jankulovski	11

* +7 goals for Czechoslovakia

TOP CAPS

Czech Republic only

1	Petr Cech	124
2	Karel Poborsky	118
3	Tomas Rosicky	105
4	Jaroslav Plasil	104
5	Milan Baros	93
6	Jan Koller	91
=	Pavel Nedved	91
8	Vladimir Smicer	80*
9	Marek Jankulovski	78
=	Tomas Ujfalusi	78

(Smicer also won 1 cap for Czechoslovakia. Pavel Kuka (87 total caps) and Jiri Nemec (84) played both before and after separation.)

TEN OUT OF TEN

Giant striker **Jan Koller** is Czech football's all-time leading marksman with 55 goals in 91 appearances. Koller scored on his senior debut against Belgium and struck ten goals in ten successive internationals. He scored six goals in each of the 2000, 2004 and 2008 UEFA European Championship qualifying campaigns. He began his career with Sparta Prague, who converted him from goalkeeper to goalscorer. Then, in Belgium, he was top scorer with Lokeren, before scoring 42 goals in two league title-winning campaigns with Anderlecht. Later, with Borussia Dortmund in Germany, he once went in goal after Jens Lehmann had been sent off and kept a clean sheet – having scored in the first half.

DENMARK

Denmark have been playing international football since 1908, but it was not until the mid-1980s that they became competitive at the game's major tournaments. The country's crowning moment came in 1992 when, after being called up as a replacement just ten days before the start of the tournament, they walked away with the UEFA European Championship crown, shocking defending world champions West Germany 2-0 in the final. They may not have been able to repeat that success, but remain a significant player in the world game.

LEADERSHIP STYLE

Morten Olsen captained Denmark at the 1986 FIFA World Cup and later became the first Dane to reach a century of caps, retiring in 1989 with four goals from 102 appearances. He then switched to coaching, first at club level with Brondby, FC Koln and Ajax Amsterdam, before taking on the job as Danish national coach in 2000 and leading them to the 2002 and 2010 FIFA World Cups. Denmark's 2-1 defeat to England in a February 2011 friendly was his 116th international in charge – taking him past the previous record set between 1979 and 1990 by his former national team boss Sepp Piontek. Olsen's 15-year reign as Denmark coach ended in November 2015, after a 4-3 aggregate defeat to Sweden in the 2016 UEFA European Championship qualifying play-offs. His 163 games in charge of his country comprised 79 victories, 42 draws and 42 defeats – an overall 48.47 win rate.

TOP CAPS

1	Peter Schmeichel	129
2	Dennis Rommedahl	126
3	Jon Dahl Tomasson	112
4	Thomas Helveg	108
5	Michael Laudrup	104
6	Martin Jorgensen	102
=	Morten Olsen	102
8	Thomas Sorensen	101
9	Christian Poulsen	92
10	John Sivebaek	87

GOLDEN GLOVES

Peter Schmeichel , a European champion with Denmark in 1992, was rated as the world's best goalkeeper in the early 1990s. His son Kasper Schmeichel emulated his father by enjoying club success in England and becoming Denmark's first-choice keeper. Peter was a very animated fan in the stands at the 2018 FIFA World Cup as Kasper saved three spot-kicks when Denmark lost a second round match against Croatia, 3-2 on penalties. He saved from Luka Modric in extra-time, and twice more in the shoot-out.

PENALTY REDEMPTION

Midfielder Morten Wieghorst is the only player to be sent off twice while playing for Denmark – yet has also received a special award for fair play. His first international red card came just three minutes after entering the field as a substitute, against South Africa in the 1998 FIFA World Cup. He was again dismissed after coming on as a sub against Italy in the 2000 UEFA European Championship, though this time he managed a whole 28 minutes of action – and scored a goal in Denmark's 3-2 victory. But the other side of his character was shown during a Carlsberg Cup match against Iran in February 2003, when he deliberately missed a penalty. The spot-kick had been awarded after Iranian defender Jalal Kameli Mofrad had picked the ball up, thinking wrongly that a whistle from the crowd was actually the referee blowing for half-time. The International Olympic Committee later presented Wieghorst with a special fair play prize for deliberately striking his penalty wide – a gesture which looked all the more sporting since Denmark went on to lose the game 1-0.

DANISH DYNAMITE

Denmark's 6-1 defeat of Uruguay in the 1986 FIFA World Cup first-round group stage in Neza ranks among the country's finest performances. Sadly, their adventure was ended by Spain in the last 16, losing 5-1 after a horrendous back pass by Manchester United's Jesper Olsen allowed the Spanish to open the scoring. The Danes had already been hampered by the loss of playmaker Frank Arsesen – suspended after being sent off during their final group game, a win over eventual runners-up West Germany. The side – popularly known as "Danish Dynamite" – was captained by future national coach Morten Olsen and managed by Sepp Piontek, a German who became the Danish national team's first professional coach when appointed in 1979. Michael Laudrup, a star member of the classic mid-1980s side, described them as "Europe's answer to Brazil".

CHRISTIAN AID

A T-shirt produced as Denmark approached the 2018 FIFA World Cup summed up their tactics as passing the ball to Christian Eriksen and waiting for him to score. The playmaker's hat-trick had secured his side's place at the finals, in a 5-1 qualification play-off win away to the Republic of Ireland in November 2017 – 32 years after Denmark had beaten the same country 4-1, also in Dublin, to reach the 1986 FIFA World Cup. Tottenham Hotspur midfielder Eriksen top-scored for Denmark with 11 goals in the 2018 qualification campaign – having previously only hit nine goals for his country since making his international debut in March 2010 against Austria. Eriksen was the youngest player at the 2010 FIFA World Cup, aged 18 years and four months, and at the time was playing for Dutch club Ajax Amsterdam, where Danish favourites Soren Lerby, Frank Arnesen, Jesper Gronkjaer and the Laudrup brothers – Michael and Brian – had all thrived. Eriksen moved to England in the summer of 2013 and ended his first season at Spurs voted as both player of the year and young player of the year by the North London club's supporters. But despite his heroics getting Denmark to the 2018 FIFA World Cup – and his elegant goal in their 1-1 draw with Australia – he hit the post with a penalty in their shoot-out defeat to Croatia in the second round. Eriksen ruefully remarked: "I'll see that kick many times – it will not be easy to forget."

TOP SCORERS

1	Poul Nielsen	52
=	Jon Dahl Tomasson	52
3	Pauli Jorgensen	44
4	Ole Madsen	42
5	Preben Elkjaer Larsen	38
6	Michael Laudrup	37
7	Nicklas Bendtner	30
8	Henning Enoksen	29
9	Christian Eriksen	23
10	Michael Rohde	22
=	Ebbe Sand	22

QUICK DRAW

Ebbe Sand scored the fastest FIFA World Cup goal ever scored by a substitute, when he netted a mere 16 seconds after coming onto the pitch in Denmark's clash against Nigeria at the 1998 FIFA World Cup.

TOMASSON'S JOINT TOP

Jon Dahl Tomasson, Denmark's joint-top goalscorer with 52, became his national side's assistant manager in 2016, working with Norwegian-born head coach Age Hareide. His final goal for Denmark came in a 3-1 defeat to Japan in the first round of the 2010 FIFA World Cup – tucking away the rebound after his penalty was saved by Eiji Kawashima. Tomasson won 112 caps, while Poul "Tist" Nielsen's 52 strikes came in just 38 appearances between 1910 and 1925. Pauli Jorgensen was also prolific, scoring his 44 goals in just 47 games 1925–39.

THE UNEXPECTED IN 1992

Few Danish football fans will forget June 1992, their national team's finest hour, when they won the UEFA European Championship, despite not qualifying for the finals in Sweden. Ten days before the tournament opened UEFA asked the Danes – who had finished second to Yugoslavia in their qualifying group – to take Yugoslavia's place, following their exclusion in the wake of international sanctions over the Balkan War. Expectations were minimal, but then the inconceivable happened. Relying heavily on goalkeeper Peter Schmeichel, his defence, and the creative spark of Brian Laudrup, Denmark crafted one of the biggest shocks in modern football history by winning the tournament, culminating in a 2-0 victory over world champions Germany. This victory was all the more remarkable in that Brian's brother Michael, their finest player, quit during the qualifying competition after falling out with coach Richard Moller Nielsen. Michael revived his international career in 1993, but Denmark failed to qualify for the 1994 FIFA World Cup in the United States. Among those paying their respects at Moller Nielsen's funeral after his death aged 76 in February 2014 were Schmeichel, Brian Laudrup and Euro 92 team-mates Preben Elkjaer Larsen and John Jensen.

IF THE SHIRT FITS

Danish striker Yussuf Poulsen had an eventful 2018 FIFA World Cup. In Denmark's opening game, he conceded a first-half penalty which was missed by Peru's Carlos Cueva, then scored the game's only goal and was officially voted man of the match. But he was booked in Denmark's first two games so missed their third against France. He wore his favoured middle name "YURARY" on the back of his Denmark shirt, despite wearing "POULSEN" for his German club Leipzig, because the club had already printed shirts with that name on them.

BROTHERS IN ARMS

Brian (left) and Michael Laudrup are among the most successful footballing brothers of modern times. As well as making a combined 186 international appearances, they played across Europe at club level. Michael (104 caps, 37 goals) played in Italy with Lazio and Juventus and in Spain with Barcelona and Real Madrid. Brian (82 caps, 21 goals) starred in Germany with Bayer Uerdingen and Bayern Munich, Italy with Fiorentina and Milan, Scotland for Rangers and England for Chelsea.

GREECE

There is no argument about Greece's proudest footballing moment – their shock triumph at the 2004 UEFA European Championship, one of the game's greatest international upsets. Guided by German coach Otto Rehhagel, it was only the Greeks' second appearance at a UEFA Euro finals. Greece also made the last eight at Euro 2012 in Poland and Ukraine. In the FIFA World Cup, South Africa 2010 marked just their second qualification and they reached the second round of a FIFA World Cup for the first time in 2014.

TOP SCORERS

1	Nikos Anastopoulos	29
2	Angelos Charisteas	25
3	Theofanis Gekas	24
4	Dimitris Saravakos	22
5	Mimis Papaioannou	21
6	Nikos Machlas	18
7	Demis Nikolaidis	17
8	Konstantinos Mitroglou	16
=	Panagiotis Tsalouchidis	16
10	Giorgos Sideris	14

SIMPLY THEO BEST

Theodoros "Theo" Zagorakis – born near Kavala on 27 October 1971 – was captain of Greece when they won the UEFA European Championship in 2004 and the defensive midfielder was also given the prize for the tournament's best player. He is the second most-capped Greek footballer of all time, with 120 caps. But it was not until his 101st international appearance – 10 years and five months after his Greek debut – that he scored his first goal for his country, in a FIFA World Cup qualifier against Denmark in February 2005. He retired from international football after making a 15-minute cameo appearance against Spain in August 2007.

PARTY CRASHERS

Shock UEFA Euro 2004 winners Greece became the first team to beat both the holders and the hosts on the way to winning either a UEFA European Championship or FIFA World Cup. In fact, they beat hosts Portugal twice – in both the tournament's opening game and the final, with a quarter-final victory over defending champions France in between.

GORGEOUS GEORGE

Georgios Samaras won and converted the last-minute penalty that sent Greece through to the knock-out stages of a FIFA World Cup for the first time, clinching a dramatic 2-1 victory over Group C opponents Ivory Coast at the 2014 tournament in Brazil. The goal, following a foul by Giovanni Sio, was former Celtic striker Samaras's ninth goal for his country – his first coming on his debut against Belarus in February 2006. Samaras could actually have played international football for Australia, because his father, Ioannis, was born in Melbourne and moved to Greece aged 13. Ioannis won 16 caps for Greece between 1986 and 1990, but he is a long way behind his son, who made 81 appearances.

ALL WHITE NOW

The surprise triumph at UEFA Euro 2004 brought a major change to Greek international football – they switched the national team's kit from blue to white. The former colours had been used since the Hellenic Football Federation was formed in 1926, but the success of Otto Rehhagel's men in their second kit prompted the permanent change of colours.

TOP CAPS

1	Giorgos Karagounis	139
2	Theodoros Zagorakis	120
3	Kostas Katsouranis	116
4	Angelos Basinas	100
5	Stratos Apostolakis	96
=	Vasileios Torosidis	96
7	Antonios Nikopolidis	90
8	Angelos Charisteas	88
9	Dimitrios Salpingidis	82
10	Georgios Samaras	81

HIT AND MISS

Full-back **Vasileios Torosidis**, later Greece captain, scored the winner against Nigeria in 2010 to secure his country's first ever victory at a FIFA World Cup – having earlier in the game been kicked by Sani Kaita, for which the Nigeria midfielder was sent off. He was also in Greece's squad for the 2008 and 2012 UEFA European Championships and 2014 FIFA World Cup. There was no third Euro for Torosidis as Greece finished bottom of the qualification group for Euro 2016, despite being the group's top seed. Their disastrous campaign included home and away defeats to the Faroe Islands.

TOP KAP

Goalkeeper Stefanos Kapino became Greece's youngest international when he made his debut in November 2011 in a friendly against Romania, at the age of 17 years and 241 days – 80 days younger than previous record-holder, striker Thomas Mavros, had been when facing the Netherlands in February 1972. Greece's oldest player was another goalkeeper, Kostas Chalkias – 38 years and 13 days old – when playing his final international, against the Czech Republic in June 2012. He conceded twice in the first six minutes and was replaced by Michalis Sifakis midway through the first half.

DIMI MORE

Striker Dimitrios Salpingidis not only struck the only goal of Greece's 2010 FIFA World Cup qualifying play-off victory against Ukraine, sealing their place in South Africa, he also then became the first Greek ever to score at a FIFA World Cup, with a 44th-minute deflected strike in the 2-1 Group B triumph over Nigeria. Yet another notable achievement was added with his equalizer against Poland in the opening game of UEFA Euro 2012: this made him the first Greek ever to score at a FIFA World Cup and a UEFA European Championship.

KOSTAS, BRAVO

Konstantinos "Kostas" Mitroglou played a crucial role as Greece qualified for the 2014 FIFA World Cup, scoring three goals in a 4-2 aggregate victory over Romania in a play-off. He was also his country's top scorer in qualifiers for the 2018 tournament, with six, but Greece missed out on the finals losing on aggregate to Croatia in another play-off. Mitroglou was three-goal top scorer at the 2007 UEFA U-19 European Championship, when Greece lost to Spain in the final, the country's best tournament performance apart from winning UEFA Euro 2004. Mitroglou has played in Germany, Greece, England, Portugal and, since 2017, France.

GRIEF AND GLORY FOR GIORGOS

It was a bittersweet day for captain **Giorgos Karagounis** when he equalled the Greek record for international appearances, with his 120th cap against Russia in their final Group A game at the UEFA Euro 2012. The midfielder scored the only goal of the game, giving Greece a place in the quarter-finals at Russia's expense – but a second yellow card of the tournament ruled him out of the next match, in which the Greeks lost to Germany. Karagounis was one of three survivors from Greece's Euro 2004 success, along with fellow midfielder Kostas Katsouranis and goalkeeper Kostas Chalkias – though it was only in Poland that Chalkias made the first of his UEFA European Championship appearances, having been understudy in 2004 and 2008. Manager Fernando Santos also surprised many by leaving the winning goalscoring hero of Euro 2004, Angelos Charisteas, out of the squad. Chalkias was Euro 2012's oldest player, making his 32nd and final international appearance during the tournament.

KING OTTO

German coach Otto Rehhagel became the first foreigner to be voted "Greek of the Year" in 2004, after leading the country to glory at that year's UEFA European Championship. He was also offered honorary Greek citizenship. His nine years in charge, after being appointed in 2001, made him Greece's longest-serving international manager. The UEFA Euro 2004 triumph was the first time a country coached by a foreigner had triumphed at either the UEFA European Championship or FIFA World Cup. Rehhagel was aged 65 at UEFA Euro 2004, making him the oldest coach to win the UEFA European Championship – though that record was taken off him four years later, when 69-year-old Luis Aragones lifted the trophy with Spain.

HUNGARY

For a period in the early 1950s, Hungary possessed the most talented football team on the planet. They claimed Olympic gold at Helsinki in 1952, inflicted a crushing first-ever Wembley defeat on England the following year, and entered the 1954 FIFA World Cup, unbeaten in almost four years, as firm favourites to win the crown. They lost to West Germany in the final and Hungary's footballing fortunes on the world stage have never been the same again.

TOP SCORERS

1	Ferenc Puskas	84
2	Sandor Kocsis	75
3	Imre Schlosser	59
4	Lajos Tichy	51
5	Gyorgy Sarosi	42
6	Nandor Hidegkuti	39
7	Ferenc Bene	36
8	Tibor Nyilasi	32
=	Gyula Zsengeller	32
10	Florian Albert	31

DZSUDZSAK'S NO DUD

Hungary have achieved an encouraging turnaround in the last few years, reaching the second round of the 2016 UEFA European Championship, less than three years after the nadir of an 8-1 defeat by the Netherlands in a 2014 FIFA World Cup qualifier. That equalled their heaviest ever losses, 7-0 to England in 1908 and to Germany in 1941. Under German coach Bernd Storck, and captained by **Balazs Dzsudzsak**, they beat Norway in a qualifying play-off to reach their first major tournament since the 1986 FIFA World Cup, where they lost 4-0 to Belgium in the round-of-16. Hungary reached another low during qualifying for the 2018 FIFA World Cup, a 1-0 defeat to Andorra in June 2017 – ending Andorra's 66-match winless run. Storck offered free tickets to a future game to Hungary fans in attendance. Failure to qualify cost Storck his job – but another embarrassing defeat followed, a 2-1 loss to Luxembourg in a November 2017 friendly.

TOP GERA

While no one can compare with Ferenc Puskas, elegant left-footed playmaker **Zoltan Gera** has been one of Hungary's finest footballers of recent times. He might have won even more international caps but for a brief retirement following a dispute with then-coach Erwin Koeman in 2009, after Gera had arrived late for a team meeting. The first three of his 26 international goals all came in a 3-0 victory over San Marino in October 2002, while his 25th strike was a stunning volley in a 3-3 draw with Portugal in the UEFA Euro 2016 first round. Aged 37 years and 62 days, he became the second oldest UEFA European Championship finals goalscorer – behind only Austria's Ivica Vastic, who was 38 years and 257 days old when he netted at Euro 2008.

GOLDEN HEAD

Sandor Kocsis, top scorer in the 1954 FIFA World Cup finals with 11 goals, was so good in the air he was known as "The Man with the Golden Head". In 68 internationals he scored an incredible 75 goals, including a record seven hat-tricks. His tally included two decisive extra-time goals in the 1954 FIFA World Cup semi-final against Uruguay, when Hungary had appeared to be on the brink of defeat.

GALLOPING MAJOR

Ferenc Puskas was one of the greatest footballers of all time, scoring a remarkable 84 goals in 85 international matches for Hungary and 514 goals in 529 matches in the Hungarian and Spanish leagues. Possessing the most lethal left-foot shot in the history of football, he was known as the "Galloping Major" – by virtue of his playing for the army team Honved before joining Real Madrid and going on to play for Spain. During the 1950s he was top scorer and captain of the legendary "Mighty Magyars" (the nickname given to the Hungarian national team), as well as of the army club Honved.

EMPEROR ALBERT

The only Hungarian footballer to win the Ballon d'Or prize for footballer of the year was **Florian Albert** in 1967, when it was organized by the magazine *France Football* rather than FIFA. Albert – nicknamed "The Emperor" – finished joint top scorer at the 1962 FIFA World Cup with four goals and helped his country to third place at the 1960 Olympics and the 1964 UEFA European Championship. Hungary's 5-0 home friendly win against Liechtenstein in November 2011 was dedicated to his memory following his death the previous month at the age of 70. His son Florian Albert Jr won six caps for Hungary as a midfielder between 1993 and 1996.

HUNGARY FOR IT

Hungary's 6-3 win over England at Wembley in 1953 remains one of the most significant international results of all time. Hungary became the first team from outside the British Isles to beat England at home, a record that had stood since 1901. The Hungarians had been undefeated for three years and had won the Olympic tournament the year before, while England were the so-called "inventors" of football. The British press dubbed it "The Match of the Century". In the event, the match revolutionized the game in England, Hungary's unequivocal victory exposing the naivete of English football tactics. England captain Billy Wright later summed up the humiliation by saying: "We completely underestimated the advances that Hungary had made, and not only tactically. When we walked out at Wembley … I looked down and noticed that the Hungarians had on these strangelightweight boots, cut away like slippers under the ankle bone. I turned to big Stan Mortensen and said: 'We should be all right here, Stan, they haven't got the proper kit.'"

YEARS OF PLENTY

Hungary's dazzling line-up of the early 1950s was known as the "*Aranycsapat*" – or "Golden Team". They set a record for international matches unbeaten, going 31 consecutive games without defeat between May 1950 and their July 1954 FIFA World Cup final loss to West Germany – a run that included clinching Olympic gold at Helsinki in Finland in 1952. That 31-match tally has been overtaken since only by Brazil and Spain. Hungary in the 1950s also set a record for most consecutive games scoring at least one goal – 73 matches – while their average of 5.4 goals per game at the 1954 FIFA World Cup remains an all-time high for the tournament.

SEVEN UP FOR SAROSI

No Hungarian man has scored more goals in one international than **Gyorgy Sarosi**'s seven when Czechoslovakia were beaten 8-3 in September 1937. He captained Hungary to the 1938 FIFA World Cup final, scored the second goal in their 4-2 defeat to Italy and ended the tournament as third top scorer with five. Ferenc Puskas is Hungary's all-time leading scorer, with 84 goals, but second-placed Sandor Kocsis – 75 – had more international hat-tricks, six to Puskas's four. The last man to score a hat-trick for Hungary was Adam Szalai, in an 8-0 rout of San Marino in October 2010 – almost exactly eight years after the previous most recent, his captain Zoltan Gera's against the same opposition in a 3-0 win. Szalai scored Hungary's opening goal in their 2-0 triumph over Austria in their first match of the 2016 UEFA European Championship.

NERVES AND STEEL

Gabor Kiraly may now have won more caps, and earned more attention for his customary tracksuit bottoms – often compared to pyjama trousers – but Gyula Grosics is still recognised as Hungary's greatest goalkeeper. Unusual for a goalkeeper of his era, he was comfortable with the ball at his feet and was willing to rush out of his area. The on-field confidence was not always displayed off it, however – and he was thought to be a nervous character, a hypochondriac and a loner. He allegedly asked to be substituted before the end at Wembley in 1953. He suffered after Hungary's surprise loss to West Germany in the 1954 FIFA World Cup final, being blamed for the equalizer.

TOP CAPS

1	Gabor Kiraly	108
2	Jozsef Bozsik	101
3	Zoltan Gera	97
4	Balazs Dzsudzsak	96
5	Roland Juhasz	95
6	Laszlo Fazekas	92
7	Gyula Grosics	86
8	Ferenc Puskas	85
9	Imre Garaba	82
10	Sandor Matrai	81

NORTHERN IRELAND

Northern Ireland have played as a separate country since 1921 – before that there had been an all-Ireland side. They have qualified for the FIFA World Cup on three occasions: in 1958, 1982 and 1986, but it would be 30 years before they qualified for another major tournament, reaching the second round of the 2016 UEFA European Championship – their first appearance in the Euro finals.

GEORGE BEST

One of the greatest players never to grace a FIFA World Cup, **George Best** (capped 37 times by Northern Ireland) nevertheless won domestic and European honours with Manchester United – including both a European Champions Cup medal and the European Footballer of the Year award in 1968. He also played in the United States, Hong Kong and Australia before his "final" retirement in 1984.

GIANT JENNINGS

Pat Jennings's record 119 appearances for Northern Ireland also stood as an international record at one stage. The former Tottenham Hotspur and Arsenal goalkeeper made his international debut, aged just 18, against Wales on 15 April 1964, and played his final game in the 1986 FIFA World Cup, against Brazil, on his 41st birthday.

HOSTILE HOSTS

Northern Ireland topped their first-round group at the 1982 FIFA World Cup, thanks to a 1-0 win over hosts Spain at a passionate Mestalla Stadium in Valencia. Watford striker Gerry Armstrong scored the goal and the Irish held on despite defender Mal Donaghy being sent off. A 4-1 second-round loss to France denied Northern Ireland a semi-finals place. Armstrong moved to Spain, joining Mallorca the following year and, predictably, was regularly booed by rival fans.

OH DANNY BOY

Northern Ireland's captain at the 1958 FIFA World Cup was Tottenham Hotspur's cerebral **Danny Blanchflower** – the first twentieth-century captain of an English club to win both the league and FA Cup in the same season, in 1960–61. When asked the secret of his national team's success in 1958, he offered the explanation: "Our tactic is to equalize before the others have scored." More famously, he offered the philosophy: "The great fallacy is that the game is first and foremost about winning. It's nothing of the kind. The game is about glory. It's about doing things in style, with a flourish, about going out and beating the other lot, not waiting for them to die of boredom."

TOP SCORERS

#	Player	Goals
1	David Healy	36
2	Kyle Lafferty	20
3	Colin Clarke	13
=	Billy Gillespie	13
5	Gerry Armstrong	12
=	Joe Bambrick	12
=	Iain Dowie	12
=	Jimmy Quinn	12
9	Olphie Stanfield	11
10	Billy Bingham	10
=	Johnny Crossan	10
=	Steven Davis	10
=	Jimmy McIlroy	10
=	Peter McParland	10

THE BOY DAVIS

Midfielder **Steven Davis** became Northern Ireland's youngest post-war captain when he led out the side against Uruguay in May 2006, aged just 21 years, five months and 20 days. He remained captain for more than a decade and maybe his finest moment came in October 2015 when his two goals in a 3–1 defeat of Greece helped to secure Northern Ireland's place at the 2016 UEFA European Championship finals.

McAULEY'S MIXED FORTUNES

Northern Ireland qualified for the 2016 UEFA European Championship as group-winners, and went into the finals on their longest ever unbeaten run – 12 games. A 2-0 victory over Ukraine in France was their first finals win since beating hosts Spain at the 1982 FIFA World Cup and Gareth McAuley's opener their first major tournament goal since Colin Clarke, also against Spain, at the 1986 FIFA World Cup. However, McAuley scored at the "wrong" end to give Wales the only goal of a "Battle of Britain" second-round tie, the first Northern Ireland own goal since October 2011, against Italy – and he got that one too!

TOP CAPS

#	Player	Caps
1	Pat Jennings	119
2	Aaron Hughes	112
3	Steven Davis	101
4	David Healy	95
5	Mal Donaghy	91
6	Sammy McIlroy	88
=	Maik Taylor	88
8	Keith Gillespie	86
9	Chris Baird	79
=	Gareth McAuley	79

GIVING A GOOD ACCOUNT

Michael O'Neill, who won 31 caps for Northern Ireland as a winger, retired from football in 2004. After his playing days were over he began working as an accountant before being tempted back into the game as assistant manager of Scottish club Cowdenbeath. Following success as manager of Shamrock Rovers in Ireland, he was given the Northern Ireland job in 2011 and led them to the second round of the 2016 UEFA European Championship, their first major tournament for 30 years. O'Neill was offered the Scotland manager's job in January 2018, two months after Northern Ireland had lost their 2018 FIFA World Cup qualification play-off 1-0 on aggregate to Switzerland, but insisted he would stay loyal to his IFA post.

"PETER THE LATE"

Peter Watson is thought to have had the shortest Northern Ireland international career, spending two minutes on the pitch in a 5-0 UEFA European Championship qualifying win over Cyprus in April 1971. A Distillery club-mate of Watson that season was law student Martin O'Neill – who went on to win international 64 caps, including captaining his country at the 1982 FIFA World Cup.

YOUNG GUN

Norman Whiteside became the then-youngest player at a FIFA World Cup finals (beating Pele's record) when he represented Northern Ireland in Spain in 1982 aged 17 years and 41 days. He won 38 caps, scoring nine goals, before injury forced his retirement aged just 26.

HERO HEALY

Northern Ireland's record goalscorer **David Healy** got off to the ideal start, scoring a brace on his international debut against Luxembourg in February 2000. But perhaps his two greatest days for his country came when he scored the only goal against Sven-Goran Eriksson's England in September 2005 – Northern Ireland's first victory over England since 1972 – and then, 12 months later, scoring a hat-trick to beat eventual champions Spain 3-2 in a 2008 UEFA European Championship qualifier. He did endure a four-year, 24-game scoring drought between October 2008 and November 2012, before hitting his final international goal against Israel in March 2013 and retiring from international football later that year, aged 34.

NORWAY

Although they played their first international, against Sweden, in 1908 and qualified for the 1938 FIFA World Cup, it would take a further 56 years, and the introduction of a direct brand of football, before Norway reappeared at a major international tournament. Success in such competitions has been rare – they have never progressed beyond the second round – but Norway retains the distinction of being the only nation in history never to have lost to Brazil.

JUVE DONE IT ALL

Jorgen Juve netted his national record 33 international goals in 45 appearances between 1928 and 1937. He did not score as Norway claimed bronze at the Berlin 1936 Olympics, but was playing when Norway beat Germany 2-0 in the quarter-finals, prompting spectators Adolf Hitler and other Nazi leaders to storm out in fury. After retiring in 1938, he worked as a legal scholar, sports journalist and author of books about the Olympics and football.

GOALS FOR EITHER IVERSEN

Steffen Iversen scored the only goal of Norway's only win at a UEFA European Championship – against Spain at the 2000 tournament. Iversen's father Odd had previously been one of the country's leading strikers, scoring goals in unexpected victories away to France in a qualifier for the 1970 FIFA World Cup and against Sweden in a 1978 FIFA World Cup qualifier. Odd scored a total of 19 times in 45 games for Norway between 1967 and 1979. Steffen equalled his father's international scoring tally with a hat-trick against Malta in November 2007 – then scored his next two goals against Iceland the following September. His 79th and final international cap came in 2011, aged 34, and he had 21 goals to his name.

YOUR BOYS TOOK A HELL OF A BEATING

Bjorge Lillelien's famous commentary after Norway beat England 2-1 in a qualifier for the 1982 FIFA World Cup remains one of the iconic moments of European football. A commentator from 1957 until just before his death from cancer in 1987, he concentrated on winter sports and football. Roughly translated, it sounded as follows: "Lord Nelson, Lord Beaverbrook, Sir Winston Churchill, Sir Anthony Eden, Clement Attlee, Henry Cooper, Lady Diana, Maggie Thatcher, can you hear me? Your boys took a hell of a beating." Although the commentary was for Norwegian radio, it soon made its way to an English audience and has achieved cliché status. In 2002, Lillelien's words were designated the greatest piece of sports commentary ever by the *Observer* newspaper's sports supplement. Such is its place in British sporting culture, parodies of the commentary have been written to celebrate a vast array of domestic sporting victories.

TOP SCORERS

1	Jorgen Juve	33
2	Einar Gundersen	26
3	Harald Hennum	25
4	John Carew	24
5	Tore Andre Flo	23
=	Ole Gunnar Solskjaer	23
7	Gunnar Thoresen	22
8	Steffen Iversen	21
9	Jan Age Fjortoft	20
10	Odd Iversen	19
=	Oyvind Leonhardsen	19
=	Olav Nilsen	19

LONG-DISTANCE RIISE

Fierce-shooting, ex-Liverpool, AS Monaco and AS Roma left-back Jon Arne Riise marked the game in which he matched Thorbjorn Svenssen's Norwegian appearances record, against Greece in August 2012, by getting onto the scoresheet, albeit in a 3-2 losing cause. He was also on the losing side when claiming the record for himself, a 2-0 loss in Iceland the following month, before scoring his 16th international goal in his 106th match four days later as Norway beat Slovenia 2-1. Midfielder Bjorn Helge Riise, Jon Arne's younger brother, joined him at English club Fulham, and made 35 full international appearances.

BOOT CAMPER

Egil Olsen, one of Europe's most eccentric coaches, was signed up for a surprise second spell as national manager when Norway put their faith in the direct-football specialist trying to qualify for the 2010 FIFA World Cup – 15 years after he had led the unfancied Scandinavians to the 1994 finals. That had been Norway's first finals appearance since 1938 and they followed it up by beating Brazil in the first round in France in 1998, making a hero out of the man in Wellington boots who guided his country to No. 2 in FIFA's official rankings. Before answering his country's call for a second stint as manager, Olsen's last job had been as manager of Iraq, but he left after only three months in charge. Remarkably, in his first match back at the helm for Norway, he masterminded a 1-0 win away to Germany with his route-one tactics.

COUSINS IN ARMS

Norway's Moroccan-born striker Tarik Elyounoussi took only four minutes after coming on at half-time on his debut to score his first international goal, in a 2-2 draw with Uruguay in May 2008. His cousin Mohamed Elyounoussi had won his own first Norway cap in January 2014 against Poland. He scored a hat-trick in an 8-0 win away to San Marino in October 2017 in a World Cup qualifier. Unfortunately Norway had already been eliminated.

NEW GAARD

Attacking midfielder **Martin Odegaard** became Norway's youngest international when he made his debut against the United Arab Emirates in August 2014, at the age of 15 years and 253 days. Forty-seven days later, he became the youngest player to feature in a UEFA European Championship qualifier, breaking a 31-year-old record held by Iceland's Siggi Jonsson. In March 2015, in a 5-1 loss to Croatia, Odegaard, at 16 years and 101 days, became the youngest European player to start in a competitive international. He was 164 days younger than Liechtenstein goalkeeper Peter Jehle, who played in a Euro 98 qualifier. Odegaard's rapid rise continued when he joined Real Madrid from Stromsgodset in January 2015 and made his Real debut four months later.

TOP CAPS

1	John Arne Riise	110
2	Thorbjorn Svenssen	104
3	Henning Berg	100
4	Erik Thorstvedt	97
5	John Carew	91
=	Brede Hangeland	91
7	Oyvind Leonhardsen	86
8	Morten Gamst Pedersen	83
=	Kjetil Rekdal	83
10	Steffen Iversen	79

LONG STAY TRAVELLERS

Norway's best finish at an international tournament was the bronze medal they clinched at the 1936 Summer Olympics in Berlin, having lost to Italy in the semi-finals but beaten Poland 3-2 in a medal play-off thanks to an Arne Brustad hat-trick. That year's side has gone down in Norwegian football history as the "*Bronselaget*", or "Bronze Team". However, they had entered the tournament with low expectations and were forced to alter their travel plans ahead of the semi-final against Italy on 10 August – Norwegian football authorities had originally booked their trip home for the previous day, not expecting their team to get so far. Italy beat Norway 2-1 in extra-time not only in that summer's Olympic semi-final, but also in the first round of the FIFA World Cup two years later – going on to win both tournaments.

OLDEST FRODE

Frode Johnsen waited six years since his last international call-up before recalled in September 2013. A month later, he became the oldest man ever to play for Norway. The striker was 39 years and 212 days old when winning the last of his 35 caps in a 1-1 FIFA World Cup qualifer against Iceland on 15 October 2013. The next oldest men to play for Norway were Gunnar Thoresen (38 years and 342 days, against Finland in June 1959) and Ronny Johnsen (38 years and 73 days, against Argentina in August 2007).

ROCK STAR

He no longer holds Norway's record for international appearances but Thorbjorn Svenssen captained the country more than any other player – leading them out 93 times. The defender did not score a single goal in his 104 games for Norway between 1947 and 1962, but did become the first Norwegian to reach a century of caps and, at the time, only the second footballer ever, behind only England's Billy Wright. Svenssen – nicknamed "Klippen", or "The Rock" – made his last appearance in May 1962, aged 38 years and 24 days. He died, aged 86, in January 2011.

POLAND

The history of Polish football is littered with tremendous highs and depressing lows. Olympic gold-medal success in 1972, and third-place finishes in the 1974 and 1982 FIFA World Cup competitions were followed by failure to qualify for any tournament until 1992. Poland first qualified for the UEFA European Championship in 2008 and co-hosted the tournament with Ukraine in 2012, making first round exits both times. At Euro 2016, however, they were quarter-finalists.

TOP SCORERS

1	Robert Lewandowski	55
2	Wlodzimierz Lubanski	48
3	Grzegorz Lato	45
4	Kazimierz Deyna	41
5	Ernest Pohl	39
6	Andrzej Szarmach	32
7	Gerard Cieslik	27
8	Zbigniew Boniek	24
9	Ernest Wilimowski	21
10	Jakub Blaszczykowski	20
=	Dariusz Dziekanowski	20

STAYING ON LATER THAN LATO

Record-breaking Polish stalwart **Michal Zewlakow** bowed out of international football on familiar turf, even though his country were playing an away game. The versatile defender's 102nd and final appearance for his country was a goalless friendly in Greece in March 2011, at the Karaiskakis stadium in Piraeus where he used to play club football for Olympiacos. Zewlakow had overtaken Grzegorz Lato's appearances record for Poland in his previous match, an October 2010 friendly against Ecuador. He had already helped make footballing history for his homeland when he and brother Marcin, a striker, became the first twins to line up together for Poland, against France in February 2000. Marcin would end his international career with 25 appearances and five goals.

LUBANSKI BOOTS

Wlodzimierz Lubanski was passed by Robert Lewandowski as Poland's all-time leading goalscorer in 2017, but he remains their youngest. Aged just 16 years and 188 days, and on his debut, he scored Poland's third goal in a 9-0 victory over Norway in 1963. Lubanski also scored in his final international in September 1980, a 1-1 draw with Czechoslovakia. His 48 strikes in 75 games also included Poland's second in a crucial 2-0 victory over England in June 1973, helping seal qualification for the 1974 FIFA World Cup at England's expense. But he was injured later in the match and missed the finals. Lubanski appeared five times at the 1978 World Cup, including two starts, but without scoring as Poland went out in the second group stage.

LOVING LEWANDOWSKI

Prolific striker **Robert Lewandowski** set a European record for goals in a FIFA World Cup qualifying competition with 16 for the 2018 FIFA World Cup – a tally which included three hat-tricks. His second treble, in a 6-1 away win over Armenia in October 2017, saw him become Poland's all-time leading scorer. Although Lewandowski made his World Cup finals debut in Russia, he didn't score and Poland finished bottom of Group H. Lewandowski, however, remains a feared striker – despite being rejected by Legia Warsaw aged 16 and as a 20-year-old failing to impress future Poland coach Franciszek Smuda, who chided the man who recommended him: "You owe me petrol money." Lewandowski eventually broke through with Lech Poznan, helped Borussia Dortmund to two Bundesliga titles in Germany and won four more after joining Bayern Munich in 2014. He scored on his international debut, against San Marino in September 2008, and also struck the opening goal of the 2012 UEFA European Championship co-hosted by Poland with Ukraine, in a 1-1 draw with Greece.

TOP CAPS

1	Michal Zewlakow	102
2	Jakub Blaszczykowski	100
=	Grzegorz Lato	100
4	Robert Lewandowski	98
5	Kazimierz Deyna	97
6	Jacek Bak	96
=	Jacek Krzynowek	96
8	Wladyslaw Zmuda	91
9	Antoni Szymanowski	82
10	Zbigniew Boniek	80

LATO'S MISSION

Grzegorz Lato is not only Poland's joint-second most-capped player and third highest scorer, the only Polish winner of the Golden Boot with his seven goals at the 1974 FIFA World Cup, and a member of the gold medal-winning team at the 1972 Summer Olympics. He was also a leading figure in Poland's co-hosting with Ukraine of the 2012 UEFA European Championship, having become president of the country's football federation in 2008. He vowed: "I am determined to change the image of Polish football, to make it transparent and pure." He was succeeded as federation president in 2012 by Zbigniew Boniek.

SUPER ERNEST

Ernest Wilimowski wrote his name into FIFA World Cup history in 1938 when he scored four goals but still finished on the losing side. Poland went down 6-5 after extra-time to Brazil in a first-round tie in Strasbourg, France.

PUNCTUALITY PUNISHMENT

Kazimierz Gorski was the coach – capped once as a player – who led Poland to third place at the 1974 FIFA World Cup, having won gold at the Olympics in Munich, Germany, two years earlier. While winning a reputation for closeness with his players, Gorski could also be ruthless – key player Adam Musial was dropped from the team for a second-round game against Sweden at the 1974 tournament as punishment for turning up 20 minutes late to training. Poland still won the game, 1-0.

TRAGEDY AND TRIUMPH

Jakub Blaszczykowski scored the winner against Ukraine in Poland's final group game at the 2016 UEFA European Championship to clinch a place in the knock-out stages for the first time. He scored again in the second-round draw against Switzerland – Poland won on penalties – making him the first Pole to score in successive games at a major tournament since Zbigniew Boniek at the 1982 FIFA World Cup. But Blaszczykowski's missed penalty meant Poland lost a quarter-final shoot-out to Portugal. He had been one of his country's few players to come out of Euro 2012 with credit, despite going into the tournament in testing circumstances. He joined the rest of the squad only after attending the funeral of his father. As a ten-year-old, Blaszczykowski had witnessed his mother Anna being stabbed to death by his father, who served 15 years in prison. Blaszczykowski was encouraged to pursue football as a teenager by his uncle Jerzy Brzeczek, a former Poland captain and 1992 Olympic Games silver medalist. Blaszczykowski became the third Pole to reach 100 caps, doing so against Senegal in Poland's 2018 FIFA World Cup opener. Sadly he was injured in the first half of the 2-1 defeat in Moscow and missed the rest of the tournament.

FIVE ASIDE

Poland had five different goalscorers when they beat Peru 5-1 at the 1982 FIFA World Cup: Wlodzimierz Smolarek, Grzegorz Lato, Zbigniew Boniek, Andrzej Buncol and Wlodzimierz Ciolek. The feat was not repeated until Phillip Cocu, Marc Overmars, Dennis Bergkamp, Pierre van Hooijdonk and Ronald de Boer gave Holland a 5-0 victory over South Korea at the 1998 FIFA World Cup.

MILIK DELIVERY

Arkadiusz Milik was the hero as Poland finally won a game at a UEFA European Championship in 2016, after three draws and three defeats in their two previous tournaments, in 2008 and 2012. The Ajax Amsterdam striker Milik struck in an opening win against Northern Ireland, kicking off what proved to be a run to the quarter-finals when only a penalty shoot-out defeat to Portugal ended Polish hopes. In fact, Poland did not trail for a single minute throughout the tournament until that 5-3 loss on spot-kicks.

A ZBIG IF

Zbigniew Boniek, arguably Poland's greatest ever player, earned a place among football's legends for his role in the country's progress to third place at the 1982 FIFA World Cup. However, his absence from the tournament's semi-final will go down as one of the great "what ifs" of the competition. Robbed of their star forward through suspension, could Poland have upset both Italy and the odds and reached the final? Instead they lost the match 2-0.

PORTUGAL

Portugal almost won their first international competition for which they qualified. Inspired by Eusebio, they reached the semi-finals of the 1966 FIFA World Cup, but lost to eventual champions England. A standout performance in the 1984 UEFA European Championship apart, more than 30 years would pass before Portugal enjoyed such giddy heights again. Two "golden" generations of players have made Portugal a consistent force on the world football stage for more than 20 years, but the 2016 UEFA European Championship was their first senior silverware.

TOP CAPS

1	Cristiano Ronaldo	154
2	Luis Figo	127
3	Joao Moutinho	113
4	Nani	112
5	Fernando Couto	110
6	Pepe	99
7	Bruno Alves	96
8	Rui Costa	94
9	Ricardo Carvalho	89
10	Pauleta	88

TOP SCORERS

1	Cristiano Ronaldo	85
2	Pauleta	47
3	Eusebio	41
4	Luis Figo	32
5	Nuno Gomes	29
6	Helder Postiga	27
7	Rui Costa	26
8	Nani	24
9	Joao Pinto	23
10	Nene	22
=	Simao	22

HAPPY EDER AFTER

Substitute striker **Eder** was the unlikely hero when Portugal finally ended their long wait for an international trophy to triumph at the 2016 UEFA European Championship. The forward – who spent the 2015–16 season on loan at French club Lille – scored the only goal of the final in Paris, in the 109th minute, to defeat host nation France. It was the latest opening goal scored in any UEFA European Championship final. Portugal, coached by Fernando Santos, drew their three first-round games to qualify as one of the best third-place teams. They then defeated Croatia 1-0 after extra-time, with Ricardo Quaresma's 117th-minute winner the game's only shot on target, Poland on penalties after a 1-1 quarter-final draw, and Wales 2-0 in the semi-finals. The final victory was Portugal's first against France in 11 attempts, stretching back to 1975 – and meant former Greece manager Santos remained unbeaten in his first 14 competitive matches in charge of his homeland. This triumph came 12 years after Portugal lost, as hosts themselves, the 2004 UEFA European Championship final against Greece.

THE BLACK PANTHER

Born in Mozambique, **Eusebio** da Silva Ferreira was named Portugal's "Golden Player" to mark UEFA's 50th anniversary in 2004. Signed by Benfica in 1960 at the age of 18, he scored a hat-trick in his second game – against Santos in a friendly tournament in Paris – outshining their young star, Pele. He helped Benfica win a second European Cup in 1962, was named European Footballer of the Year in 1965 and led Portugal to third place in the 1966 FIFA World Cup, finishing as top scorer with nine goals. A phenomenal striker, he scored 320 goals in 313 Portuguese league matches, won the first European Golden Boot in 1968 (and earned a second in 1973). The world of football united in paying tribute to Eusebio after he died aged 71 in January 2014. Portugal declared three days of mourning, his statue at Benfica's Estadio da Luz home was transformed into a shrine, his coffin was carried around the pitch and the Benfica players wore his name on their backs during a 2-0 win over rivals Porto.

PRESIDENTIAL POWER

Cristiano Ronaldo dos Santos Aveiro was given his second name because his father was an admirer of United States President Ronald Reagan. A Benfica fan in his youth, he began his career with arch-rivals Sporting Lisbon before moving to Manchester United, Real Madrid – who paid a then-world record fee of $93.9m in 2009 – and Juventus, to where he moved in July 2018 for a fee of $117m. The five-time FIFA World Player of the Year is Real's and the UEFA Champions League's all-time leading goalscorer – he has lifted that trophy five times. Already Portugal's top scorer, he became his country's most-capped player at the 2016 UEFA European Championship – and ended the competition lifting the trophy, despite going off injured 25 minutes into the final against France. Although he missed a penalty in his record-breaking game, he scored three in subsequent games, making him the first man to score at four different Euros. At the 2018 FIFA World Cup in Russia, Ronaldo became the first Portuguese player – and fourth ever – to score at four different FIFA World Cups. His four goals in Russia included a hat-trick against Spain in a 3-3 draw and it took him to 85, surpassing Hungary's Ferenc Puskas's old European record for international goals. But he missed a penalty in a 1-1 draw in the final group match against Iran and failed to score in Portugal's 2-1 second round loss to Uruguay.

THE FAMOUS FIVE

Eusebio, Mario Coluna, Jose Augusto, Antonio Simoes, and Jose Torres were the "Fabulous Five" in Benfica's 1960s Dream Team, who made up the spine of the Portuguese national side at the 1966 FIFA World Cup. Coluna (the "Sacred Monster"), scored the vital third goal in the 1961 European Cup final and captained the national side in 1966. Jose Augusto, who scored two goals in the opening game against Hungary, went on to manage the national side and later the Portuguese women's team. Antonio Simoes (the "Giant Gnome" – just 1.58 metres/5ft 3in tall) made his debut for Portugal and Benfica in 1962, aged just 18. Jose Torres – the only one of the five not to win the European Cup (though he played in the defeats in both 1963 and 1968) – scored the winner against Russia in the 1966 third-place match, and went on to manage the national side to their next appearance at the FIFA World Cup finals in 1986.

SILVA LINING

Striker **Andre Silva** missed a 14th-minute penalty in Portugal's 2-1 third-place play-off victory against Mexico at the 2017 FIFA Confederations Cup. This followed three missed penalties in the semi-final as they lost a shoot-out against Chile. Yet Silva can claim several Portuguese football milestones, having scored four goals in a 6-1 victory over Hungary at the 2014 UEFA European U-19 Championship – Portugal would finish as runners-up – then marked his debut for the Under-21s with a hat-trick against Albania. After graduating to the senior side, Silva became the youngest Portuguese man to score a hat-trick in a 6-0 victory over the Faroe Islands in a 2018 FIFA World Cup qualifier in October 2016 at the age of 20 years 339 days. In a May 2018 FIFA World Cup warm-up friendly against Tunisia, Silva scored Portugal's 1,000th international goal in a 2-2 draw.

NICE ONE, SAN

Renato Sanches is Portugal's youngest player at an international tournament, he was 18 years and 301 days for their 2016 UEFA European Championship opener against Iceland. He was one of the stars of the tournament, and was voted UEFA Euro 2016's best young player. His superb long-range strike against Poland in the quarter-finals made him the youngest scorer at any UEFA European Championship knock-out round, aged 18 years and 316 days. Ten days later, he was the youngest man to play in a UEFA European Championship final.

REP. OF IRELAND

It took a combination of astute management and endless searching through ancestral records before the Republic of Ireland finally qualified for the finals of a major tournament, at the 20th time of asking. But ever since Jack Charlton took the team to UEFA Euro 88, Ireland have remained one of Europe's most dangerous opponents.

ROBBIE KEEN

Much travelled striker **Robbie Keane** broke the Republic of Ireland's scoring record in October 2004 and added to it right up to 31 August 2016, when he marked his 146th and final appearance with his 68th goal, this in a 4–0 friendly victory against Oman. His most famous goals were last-minute equalizers against Germany and Spain at the 2006 FIFA World Cup. He marked the final game at the old Lansdowne Road with a hat-trick against San Marino in November 2006 and, four years later, won his 100th cap in the inaugural game at its replacement, the Aviva Stadium. Ireland's 2-1 win over Macedonia in March 2011 was Keane's 41st match as captain – equalling Andy Townsend's record. Two goals against Macedonia in June 2011 took him to 51, making him the first player from the British Isles to score a half-century of international goals. Keane's third international hat-trick, in a 7-0 win over Gibraltar in October 2014, took him to 65 goals and, with 21, he passed Turkey's Hakan Sukur for the most in UEFA European Championship qualifiers. After the final whistle of the Oman game, Keane was given a guard of honour by team-mates.

CHAMPION CHARLTON

Jack Charlton became a hero after he took Ireland to their first major finals in 1988, defeating England 1-0 in their first game at the UEFA European Championship. Things got even better at their first FIFA World Cup finals two years later, where the unfancied Irish lost out only to hosts Italy in the quarter-finals.

KILBANE KEEPS ON AND ON

Only England's Billy Wright, with 70, has played more consecutive internationals than **Kevin Kilbane**, whose 109th Republic of Ireland cap against Macedonia in March 2011 was also his 65th in a row, covering 11 years and five months. The versatile left-sider – nicknamed "Zinedine Kilbane" by fans – was given a rest for Ireland's next game three days later, though, a friendly against Uruguay.

KEANE CARRY–ON

Few star players have walked out on their country with quite the dramatic impact as Republic of Ireland captain **Roy Keane** in 2002 at their FIFA World Cup training camp in Saipan, Japan. The fiercely intense Manchester United skipper quit before a competitive ball had been kicked, complaining about a perceived lack of professionalism in the Irish preparations – and his loss of faith in manager Mick McCarthy. Ireland reached the second round without him, losing on penalties to Spain, but his behaviour divided a nation. When McCarthy stepped down Keane and the Irish football federation brokered a truce, and he returned to international duty in April 2004 under new boss Brian Kerr. Few expected his second comeback, however, when he was appointed assistant to new manager Martin O'Neill in November 2013. O'Neill, who played 64 times for Northern Ireland between 1971 and 1984 succeeded Italian veteran Giovanni Trapattoni, who resigned after failing to qualify for the 2014 FIFA World Cup finals.

BRADY BUNCH

Irish eyes were smiling again at Italy's expense in their final first-round group game at the 2016 UEFA European Championship, when **Robbie Brady** headed a late winning goal. It gave Martin O'Neill's team a place in the second round, where they took the lead through a Brady penalty against France, but succumbed 2-1. The spot-kick, after 118 seconds, was the earliest in the UEFA European Championship finals. Brady was the first Republic of Ireland player to score in consecutive UEFA European Championship games; Robbie Keane achieved the feat in the 2002 FIFA World Cup.

MORE FOR MOORE

Paddy Moore was the first player ever to score four goals in a FIFA World Cup qualifier when Ireland came from behind to draw 4-4 with Belgium on 25 February 1934. Don Givens became the only Irishman to equal Moore's feat when he scored all four as Ireland beat Turkey 4-0 in October 1975.

HOORAY FOR RAY

Ray Houghton may have been born in Glasgow and spoke with a Scottish accent, but he scored two of Ireland's most famous goals. A header gave the Republic a shock 1-0 win over England at UEFA Euro 88 in West Germany and, six years later, his long-range strike was the only goal of the game against eventual finalists Italy, in the first round of the 1994 FIFA World Cup in the USA. It was exactly 18 years to the day from that 1994 shock that Ireland – then managed by an Italian, Giovanni Trapattoni – lost 2-0 to Italy in their third and final Group C match of the 2012 UEFA European Championship. Playing for Ireland that day was defender John O'Shea, who had previously been part of the Irish team that beat Italy 2-1 in the final of the 1998 UEFA European U-16s Championship final in Scotland. The Republic's only other continental title was the UEFA European U-19s Championship trophy they lifted by beating Germany, also in 1998.

IS WINNING JERSEY MISSING IN ACTION?

Irish fans' happy memories of their past FIFA World Cup adventures were reawakened in June 2017 when English rapper MIA appeared to be wearing one of goalkeeper **Packie Bonner**'s old shirts in a photoshoot. Bonner starred at the 1988 European Championship and the 1990 and 1994 FIFA World Cups, and suggested one of several red-and-yellow patterned jerseys he gave away for charity after USA 94 may have ended up with one of MIA's stylists. Bonner enhanced his national hero status by saving Daniel Timofte's penalty in the second-round shoot-out victory against Romania at Italia 90, before veteran centre-back David O'Leary's winning spot-kick clinched their place in the quarter-finals where they narrowly lost 1-0 to hosts Italy.

TOP CAPS

1	Robbie Keane	146
2	Shay Given	134
3	John O'Shea	118
4	Kevin Kilbane	110
5	Steve Staunton	102
6	Damien Duff	100
7	Aiden McGeady	93
8	Niall Quinn	91
9	Tony Cascarino	88
10	Glenn Whelan	84

CAPTAIN COLEMAN

Attacking full-back **Seamus Coleman** skippered the Republic of Ireland when they defeated Italy 1-0 at the 2016 UEFA European Championship, and in the second-round defeat to hosts France – Ireland's first tournament knock-out match since the 2002 FIFA World Cup. Coleman was given the armband full-time in September 2016, after Robbie Keane's international retirement, but his career suffered a setback with a broken leg in a FIFA World Cup qualifier against Wales in March 2017. He returned to the national team a year later, again as captain, in a 1-0 friendly defeat to Turkey. Goalkeeper Colin Doyle won his second cap in the same game – ten years and 304 days after his first, against Ecuador.

TOP SCORERS

1	Robbie Keane	68
2	Niall Quinn	21
3	Frank Stapleton	20
4	John Aldridge	19
=	Tony Cascarino	19
=	Don Givens	19
7	Shane Long	17
8	Noel Cantwell	14
=	Kevin Doyle	14
=	Jonathan Walters	14

ROMANIA

The history of Romanian football is littered with a series of bright moments – they were one of four countries (with Brazil, France and Belgium) to appear in the first three editions of the FIFA World Cup – followed by significant spells in the doldrums – since 1938 they have qualified for the finals of the tournament only four times in 14 attempts. The country's football highlight came in 1994 when, inspired by Gheorghe Hagi, they reached the quarter-finals of the FIFA World Cup.

TOP CAPS

1	Dorinel Munteanu	134
2	Gheorghe Hagi	124
3	Gheorghe Popescu	115
4	Razvan Rat	113
5	Ladislau Boloni	102
6	Dan Petrescu	95
7	Bogdan Stelea	91
8	Michael Klein	89
9	Bogdan Lobont	85
10	Marius Lacatus	83
=	Mircea Rednic	83

FAMOUS FOURSOME

Gheorghe Hagi, Florin Raducioiu, Ilie Dumitrescu and Gheorghe "Gica" Popescu helped Romania light up the FIFA World Cup in the USA in 1994. Raducioiu (four), Dumitrescu (three) and Hagi (two) scored nine of their country's ten goals that summer and also the trio converted their penalties in a quarter-final shoot-out against Sweden, only for misses by Dan Petrescu and Miodrag Belodedici to send the Romanians home. As well as being team-mates, Popescu and Hagi are also brothers-in-law – their wives, Luminiya Popescu and Marlilena Hagi, are sisters. In charge was former international forward Anghel Iordanescu, in the first of his three separate spells as Romania manager (his terms were from 1993 to 1998, 2002–04 and 2014–16).

STANCU VERY MUCH

Romania conceded just two goals throughout the qualifying competition for the 2016 UEFA European Championship (the fewest of any team) – but then let in that same number in the tournament's opening match, a 2-1 defeat to hosts France. They exited the tournament in the first round after a 1-1 draw with Switzerland and 1-0 defeat against Albania. The two Romania goals in the finals were from the penalty spot, both being scored by striker Bogdan Stancu.

RUDOLF BY ROYAL APPOINTMENT

Romania played in the inaugural FIFA World Cup, in Uruguay in 1930, where they beat Peru 3-1 before being eliminated 4-0 by the hosts. Coach Constantin Radulescu filled in as a linesman for some games not featuring his own side. It is reputed the squad was picked by King Carol II and its captain was Rudolf Wetzer, the only Romania player to score five goals in a game. It was in a pre-tournament 8-1 victory over Greece in May 1930.

YELLOW PERIL

Despite topping Group G ahead of England, Colombia and Tunisia at the 1998 FIFA World Cup, Romania's players of that tournament might perhaps be best remembered for their collective decision to dye their hair blond ahead of their final first-round game. The **newly bleached Romanians** struggled to a 1-1 draw against Tunisia, before being knocked out by Croatia in the second round, 1-0.

TOP SCORERS

1	Gheorghe Hagi	35
=	Adrian Mutu	35
3	Iuliu Bodola	31
4	Viorel Moldovan	25
=	Ciprian Marica	25
6	Ladislau Boloni	23
7	Rodion Camataru	21
=	Dudu Georgescu	21
=	Anghel Iordanescu	21
=	Florin Raducioiu	21

CENTURY MAN

Gheorghe Hagi, Romania's "Player of the [twentieth] Century", scored three goals and was named in the Team of the Tournament at the 1994 FIFA World Cup in the United States, at which Romania lost out on penalties to Sweden after a 2-2 draw in the quarter-finals. Hagi made his international debut in 1983, aged just 18, scored his first goal aged 19 (in a 3-2 defeat to Northern Ireland) and remains Romania's joint-top goalscorer with 35 goals in 125 games. Despite retiring from international football after the 1998 FIFA World Cup, Hagi couldn't resist answering his country's call to play in UEFA Euro 2000. Sadly, two yellow-card offences in six minutes in the quarter-final against Italy meant Hagi's final bow on the international stage saw him receive a red card – and leave the field to take an early bath. Farul Constanta, in Hagi's hometown, named their stadium after him in 2000 – but fans stopped referring to it as such after he took the manager's job at rivals Timisoara.

CEMETERY SENTRY

It was second time luckier for former international striker Victor Piturca when he coached Romania at the 2008 UEFA European Championship in Austria and Switzerland, even though they were eliminated in the first round. He had previously been manager when the country qualified for the 2000 UEFA European Championship, but was forced out of the job before the tournament started following arguments with big-name players such as Gheorghe Hagi. Piturca's cousin Florin Piturca was also a professional footballer but died aged only 27 in 1978. Florin's father and Victor's uncle Maximilian, a cobbler, not only built a mausoleum for Florin but also slept at night in the cemetery until his own death in 1994.

MANEA OF THE MOMENT

Right-back Cristian Manea became Romania's youngest international when making his debut against Albania in May 2014, aged 16 years, nine months and 22 days, having played only five senior matches for his club Viitorul Constanta. He broke the record set back in 1928 by Gratian Sepi, aged 17 years, three months and 15 days when facing Turkey.

DAUM AND OUT

German coach Christoph Daum became only the second foreigner to take charge of Romania's national side when succeeding Anghel Iordanescu in July 2016 – the first was Austrian Josef Uridil, who worked alongside Constantin Radulescu at the 1934 FIFA World. But Daum was sacked in September 2017 after failure to qualify for the 2018 FIFA World Cup and was succeeded by former **Cosmin Contra**, who won 73 caps for Romania between 1996 and 2010, and appeared at the 2000 and 2008 UEFA European Championships.

ENDURING DORINEL

Dorinel Munteanu has played for Romania more times than any other although at one point his former team-mate Gheorghe Hagi's 125-cap record looked safe. Versatile defensive midfielder Munteanu was stuck on 119 appearances throughout an 18-month absence from the international scene before being surprisingly recalled at the age of 37 by manager Victor Piturca in February 2005. He ended his Romania career two years later, having scored 16 times in 134 games. Yet many Romanians believe he was wrongly denied a goal when a shot against Bulgaria at the 1996 UEFA European Championship appeared to bounce over the line, only to not be given. The match ended 1-0 to Bulgaria and Romania were eliminated in the first round following three straight defeats.

ADRIAN'S AID

Romania lost only once when **Adrian Mutu** scored – a fact made all the better for them since, with 35 goals, he is (with Gheorghe Hagi) his country's all-time leading goalscorer. Mutu matched Hagi with a FIFA World Cup qualifying game equalizer against Hungary in March 2013, though this was his first international goal in 21 months – and, it turned out, his final one, too. Unfortunately for Romania, controversy has followed their finest player of the 21st century: he has twice been banned for failed drugs tests. The first came when a test carried out by his club Chelsea, in September 2004, showed traces of cocaine and brought about his dismissal. After a seven-month ban he rehabilitated his career in Italy, first with Juventus and then Fiorentina, before receiving a nine-month suspension after he tested positive for a banned anti-obesity drug in January 2010.

RUSSIA

Before the break-up of the Soviet Union (USSR) in 1992, the team was a world football powerhouse, winning the first UEFA European Championship in 1960, gold at the 1956 and 1988 Olympic Games and qualifying for the FIFA World Cup on seven occasions. Playing as Russia since August 1992, the good times have eluded them – apart from being UEFA Euro 2008 semi-finalists. They did, however, reach the 2014 FIFA World Cup under Italian coach Fabio Capello but bettered their first-round exit then by reaching the quarter-finals as hosts four years later.

KERZH LIFTS HIS CURSE

Only one man was in Russia's squads for the 2002 FIFA World Cup finals and the next time they qualified, in 2014: Aleksandr Kerzhakov. He made his international debut as a 19-year-old a teenager in March 2002, and he played just eight minutes of the finals three months later. With five goals, he was Russia's leading scorer in qualifying for the 2014 finals, and Kerzhakov scored his 26th international goal to earn a 1-1 draw in Russia's opener against South Korea in Cuiaba. This goal equalled Russia's all-time scoring record set by a team-mate in 2002, Vladimir Beschastnykh. Kerzhakov went on to claim the all-time scoring record for himself with a brace in Russia's 4-0 victory in a friendly against Azerbaijan in September 2014.

TOP SCORERS

(Russia only)

1	Aleksandr Kerzhakov	30
2	Vladimir Beschastnykh	26
3	Roman Pavlyuchenko	21
4	Andrei Arshavin	17
=	Valeri Karpin	17
6	Dmitri Sychev	15
7	Artem Dzyuba	14
8	Roman Shirokov	13
9	Aleksandr Kokorin	12
=	Igor Kolyvanov	12
=	Fyodor Smolov	12

HOME RANGERS

Long-serving captain and centre-back **Sergei Ignashevich** first  appeared for Russia against Sweden in August 2002, but only made his FIFA World Cup finals debut in 2014 – and won his 100th cap in the 1-1 Group H draw against Algeria which saw them eliminated. He retired from international football after the 2016 UEFA European Championship, but came back at the 2018 FIFA World Cup, replacing the injured Ruslan Kambolov. Ignashevich scored an own goal in their second round match against Spain but atoned with one of their successful penalties in a shoot-out victory. Many of his appearances for Russia were alongside one or both of the Berezutskiy twins, Vasili (101 caps) and Aleksei (58). Russia were the only country at the 2014 FIFA World Cup whose entire 23-man squad played their club football domestically – and it happened again when they hosted the 2017 FIFA Confederations Cup. After beating New Zealand 2-0 in their first game, Russia exited at the group stage after losing to Portugal (1-0) and Mexico (2-1).

YOUNG PROMISE

Igor Akinfeev became post-Soviet Russia's youngest international footballer when he made his debut in a friendly against Norway on 28 April 2004. The CSKA Moscow goalkeeper was just 18 years and 20 days old. Akinfeev, by then past a century of caps, won the nation's acclaim by saving two penalties in Russia's 2018 FIFA World Cup second-round shoot-out victory over Spain. The youngest Soviet-era debutant was Eduard Streltsov, who hit a hat-trick on his debut against Sweden in June 1956, at the age of 17 years and 340 days and then scored another treble in his second game, against India.

ARTEM'S TIME

Artem Dzyuba scored his first international goal for Russia on 8 September 2014, in a 4-0 victory over Liechtenstein – and he enjoyed a happy anniversary precisely a year later in a 7-0 thrashing of the same opponents, scoring four of his side's strikes. The win equalled the biggest in Russia's history, 7-0 against San Marino in June 1995. Dzyuba was Russia's top scorer, with eight, during qualification for the 2016 UEFA European Championship but failed to score in the finals as Russia finished bottom of their group. However, Dzyuba came good at the 2018 FIFA World Cup, scoring three goals including the equalizer against Spain in the second round.

TOP CAPS

(Russia only)

1	Sergei Ignashevich	127
2	Igor Akinfeev	111
3	Viktor Onopko	109
4	Vasili Berezutskiy	101
5	Aleksandr Kerzhakov	91
6	Yuri Zhirkov	87
7	Aleksandr Anyukov	77
8	Andrei Arshavin	75
9	Valeri Karpin	72
10	Vladimir Beschastnykh	71

HAPPY HOSTS

Expectations on the field for 2018 FIFA World Cup hosts Russia, at 70th the lowest team in the FIFA World Football Rankings, were not great. In the opening game of the finals, they beat Saudi Arabia 5-0 and then downed Egypt 3-1 to guarantee a second-round place. Once there, Russia beat Spain on penalties before losing, again in a shoot-out, to Croatia in the last eight. Manager Stanislav Chercheshov, a former Russia goalkeeper, spoke of the pride felt nationwide by their unexpected progress. Winger **Denis Cheryshev** who scored four goals overall, replaced Alan Dzagoev against Saudi Arabia and scored – making him the first ever substitute to score in a FIFA World Cup opening game. Cheryshev might have played for Spain as he was born when his father Dmitri was playing for Sporting Gijon.

SUPER STOPPER

FIFA declared **Lev Yashin** to be the finest goalkeeper of the 20th century – naturally, he made it into their Century XI team, too. In a career spanning 20 years, Yashin played 326 league games for Dynamo Moscow – the only club side he ever played for – and won 78 caps for the Soviet Union, conceding on average less than a goal a game (only 70 in total). With Dynamo, he won five Soviet championships and three Soviet cups, the last of which came in his final full season in 1970. He saved around 150 penalties in his long career, and kept four clean sheets in his 12 FIFA World Cup matches. Such was Yashin's worldwide reputation, Chilean international Eladio Rojas was so excited at scoring past the legendary Yashin in the 1962 FIFA World Cup that he gave the surprised keeper a big hug with the ball still sitting in the back of the net. Yashin was nicknamed the "Black Spider" for his distinctive black jersey and his uncanny ability to get a hand, arm, leg or foot in the way of shots and headers of all kinds. In 1963, Yashin became the first, and so far only, keeper to be named European Footballer of the Year, the same year in which he won his fifth Soviet championship and starred for the Rest of the World XI in the English FA's Centenary Match at Wembley.

CAPPING IT ALL

Viktor Onopko, despite being born in the Ukraine, played all his career for the CIS and Russian national football teams. The first of Onopko's 113 international caps (the first four for the CIS) came in a 2-2 draw against England in Moscow on 29 April 1992. He played in the 1994 and 1998 FIFA World Cups, as well as the UEFA European Championship in 1996. He was due to join the squad for the UEFA European Championship in 2004 but missed out through injury. Onopko's club career, spanning 19 years, took him to Shakhtar Donetsk, Spartak Moscow, Real Oviedo, Rayo Vallecano, Alania Vladikavkaz and FC Saturn. He was Russian footballer of the year in 1993 and 1994.

GOLDEN BOY

Igor Netto captained the USSR national side to their greatest successes: gold at the 1956 Olympics in Melbourne and victory in the first-ever UEFA European Championship in France in 1960. Born in Moscow in 1930, Netto was awarded the Order of Lenin in 1957 and became an ice hockey coach after retiring from football.

SCOTLAND

A country with a vibrant domestic league and a rich football tradition – it played host to the first-ever international football match, against England, in November 1872 – Scotland have never put in the performances on the international stage to match their lofty ambitions. There have been moments of triumph, such as the unexpected defeat of The Netherlands at the 1978 FIFA World Cup, but far too many moments of despair. Scotland have not qualified for the finals of a major tournament since 1998.

TOP SCORERS

1	Kenny Dalglish	30
=	Denis Law	30
3	Hughie Gallacher	23
4	Lawrie Reilly	22
5	Ally McCoist	19
6	Kenny Miller	18
7	Robert Hamilton	15
=	James McFadden	15
9	Maurice Johnston	14
10	Bob McColl	13
=	Andrew Wilson	13

UPPER TIERNEY

Celtic defender **Kieran Tierney** became Scotland's fifth-youngest captain when given the armband for a friendly against the Netherlands in November 2017, aged 20 years and 157 days. The youngest ever is John Lambie, who led the team aged 17 years and 92 days, against Ireland in March 1886; the youngest since 1900 is Darren Fletcher, aged 20 years and 115 days, against Estonia in May 2004. Tierney had been appointed by temporary national coach Malky Mackay, who had taken over from the departed Gordon Strachan following Scotland's third place finish – behind England and Slovakia – in their 2018 FIFA World Cup qualifying group. In February 2018, former defender Alex McLeish was given the full-time job, his second spell as national coach, having spent ten months in charge in 2007, ending when Scotland narrowly failed to make the 2008 UEFA European Championship finals.

THE LAWMAN

Denis Law is joint top scorer for Scotland with Kenny Dalglish, scoring 30 goals in only 55 games compared to the 102 it took Dalglish to do the same. Law twice scored four goals in a match for Scotland, the first against Northern Ireland on 7 November 1962 – helping the Scots to win the British Home Championships – and then against Norway in a friendly on 7 November 1963. Law clearly enjoyed playing against Norway, having grabbed a hat-trick in Bergen just five months earlier.

KING KENNY

Kenny Dalglish is Scotland's joint-top international goalscorer (with Denis Law) and remains the only player to have won more than a century of caps for the national side, with 102 in total – 11 more than the next highest cap-winner, goalkeeper Jim Leighton. Despite growing up a Rangers fan (he was born in Glasgow on 4 March 1951), Dalglish made his name spearheading Celtic's domestic dominance in the 1970s, winning four league titles, four Scottish Cups and one League Cup. He then went on to become a legend at Liverpool, winning a hat-trick of European Cups (1978, 1981 and 1984) and leading the side as player-manager to their first-ever league and cup double in 1986. He later joined Herbert Chapman and Brian Clough as one of the few managers to lead two different sides to the league title – guiding Blackburn Rovers to the summit of English football in 1994–95. For Scotland, Dalglish scored at both the 1978 and 1982 FIFA World Cup finals, netting the first goal in the famous 3-2 victory over eventual runners-up Holland in the 1978 group stages. He played his last international in 1986.

TRUST IN LEIGH

It was both lucky 13 and lightning striking twice when **Leigh Griffiths** finally got off the mark in international football for Scotland. In his 13th appearance for his country, the Celtic striker hit the back of the net for the first time with an 87th-minute free-kick against old enemies England in a June 2017 FIFA World Cup qualifier – and repeated the trick with another magnificent set-piece strike three minutes later. This put Scotland 2-1 ahead and they seemed set for a first home win against their neighbours since centre-back Richard Gough's sole goal in a 1985 Hampden Park clash. Scottish hearts were broken, however when England captain Harry Kane volleyed an injury-time equaliser. Griffiths's quick-fire double came at the end of a season in which he had spearheaded Celtic's treble of League, FA Cup and League Cup as the first side to go an entire campaign undefeated in all domestic competitions.

DIVIDED LOYALTIES

Scottish-born winger Jim Brown played and scored for the USA side which lost to Argentina in the first FIFA World Cup in 1930. He had moved to New Jersey three years earlier and qualified through his US citizen father. Two of his brothers also played professionally: younger brother John, a goalkeeper, was capped by Scotland, but Tom did not play at international level. Jim's son George appeared once for the USA, in 1957, while two of John's sons, Peter and Gordon, both played rugby for Scotland.

The first brothers to play for different countries, were John and Archie Goodall – members of Preston North End's 1888–89 league and FA Cup double-winning squad – and although their parents were both Scottish, London-born John played for England and Belfast-born Archie represented Ireland. Another pair of brothers with Scottish parents were Joe and Gerry Baker – though Joe chose to play for England in the 1960s and Gerry appeared for the USA.

TOP CAPS

1	Kenny Dalglish	102
2	Jim Leighton	91
3	Darren Fletcher	80
4	Alex McLeish	77
5	Paul McStay	76
6	Tom Boyd	72
7	Kenny Miller	69
=	David Weir	69
9	Christian Dailly	67
10	Willie Miller	65

HOW GEMMILL DANCED TO THE MUSIC OF SCOTLAND'S WORLD CUP TIME

Archie Gemmill scored Scotland's greatest goal on the world stage in the surprise 3-2 victory over the Netherlands at the 1978 FIFA World Cup. He jinked past three defenders before chipping the ball neatly over Dutch goalkeeper Jan Jongbloed. Amazingly, in 2008, this magical moment was turned into a dance in the English National Ballet's "The Beautiful Game".

FLETCH LIVES

Steven Fletcher ended Scotland's 46-year wait for a hat-trick and his own six-year international goal drought when scoring three in his country's 6-1 victory over Gibraltar at Hampden Park in March 2015. He secured another treble in the return match – a 6–0 win played at the Estadio Algarve in Faro, Portugal, seven months later. He was the first Scottish international to score a hat-trick since Colin Stein's four goals in a FIFA World Cup qualifier against Cyprus in 1969. Since then, in September 2016, in Scotland's opening game of the qualification tournament for the 2018 FIFA World Cup, Robert Snodgrass also scored a hat-trick in a 5-1 win over Malta. Fletcher had been Scotland's top scorer as they finished runners-up in the 2006 UEFA U-19 European Championship, but both he and Snodgrass missed the final, a 2-1 defeat to Spain, through suspension.

WEIR ON THE BALL

Rugged Rangers centre-back **David Weir** became Scotland's oldest international footballer when he faced Lithuania in a 2012 UEFA European Championship qualifier on 3 September 2010, aged 40 years and 111 days, for his 66th appearance. He was still representing his country three caps and 39 days later, against reigning world and European champions Spain. The age record was previously held by ex-Aberdeen and Manchester United goalkeeper Jim Leighton, who was 40 years and 78 days old when he played his final international in 1998.

UNOFFICIAL WORLD CHAMPIONS

One of the victories most cherished by Scotland fans is the 3-2 triumph over arch-rivals and reigning world champions England in April 1967 at Wembley – the first time Sir Alf Ramsey's team had lost since clinching the 1966 FIFA World Cup. Scotland's man of the match that day was ball-juggling left-half/midfielder Jim Baxter, while it was also the first game in charge for Scotland's first full-time manager, Bobby Brown. Less fondly recalled is Scotland's 9-3 trouncing by the same opposition at the same stadium in April 1961, which made unfortunate goalkeeper Frank Haffey the butt of a popular joke that did the rounds across the border in England: "What's the time? Nearly 10 past Haffey." The game was Haffey's second – and last – for Scotland.

SERBIA

The former Yugoslavia was one of the strongest football nations in eastern Europe. They reached the FIFA World Cup semi-finals in 1930 and 1962, they were also runners-up in the UEFA European Championships of 1960 and 1968. In addition, Yugoslavia's leading club, Red Star Belgrade, were only the second team from eastern Europe (after Romania's Steaua Bucharest in 1986) to win the European Cup, when they beat Marseille on penalties in the 1991 final.

TOP CAPS
([United] Yugoslavia and Serbia)

1	Branislav Ivanovic	105
2	Dejan Stankovic	103
3	Savo Milosevic	102
4	Dragan Dzajic	85
5	Dragan Stojkovic	84
=	Vladimir Stojkovic	84
7	Aleksandar Kolarov	79
8	Zoran Tosic	76
9	Predrag Mijatovic	73
10	Zlatko Vujovic	70

STJEP UP

Yugoslavia/Serbia's all-time top goalscorer remains **Stjepan Bobek**, with 38 in 63 appearances. He also holds the record for most goals in a Yugoslavia/ Serbia top-flight game – in June 1948 he got nine for Partizan Belgrade in a 10-1 rout of 14 Oktobar. Although Partizan won the title that season, his 24 goals were four fewer than Franjo Wolfl of second-placed Dinamo Zagreb. Wolfl scored six goals in 12 international appearances and the pair combined to help Yugoslavia win the silver medal at the London 1948 Olympic Games. Bobek also was in Yugoslavia's squad that again won silver at the 1952 Games.

HITMAN MIT

Fiery striker **Aleksandar Mitrovic** was named player of the tournament at the 2013 UEFA European U19 Championship when Serbia beat France 1-0 in the final and he set up Andrija Lukovic for the goal. Also involved was winger Andrija Zivkovic, who that same year became Serbia's youngest senior international at the age of 17 years 92 days against Japan. Zivkovic also helped Serbia win the 2015 FIFA U20 World Cup, scoring the goal of the tournament, a free-kick against Mexico. Mitrovic was Serbia's focal point at the 2018 FIFA World Cup, scoring six goals in qualifying and their goal in the 2-1 loss to Switzerland, his sixth of 2018 and 17th overall. Aleksandar Kolarov scored the only goal in Serbia's Group E opener against Costa Rica, but a 2-0 loss to Brazil saw them go home after the group stage.

MITIC'S PITCH

Serbia's national stadium, in the capital Belgrade, was long known as the Marakana – after the famous Maracana in Rio de Janeiro, Brazil – but was renamed in 2014 in honour of former Yugoslavia striker and manager Rajko Mitic. He scored 32 goals in 59 games for his country between 1946 and 1951 – helping win silver at the 1948 and 1952 Olympics – before becoming national coach between 1966 and 1970. Under his stewardship, Yugoslavia had another runners-up finish, this one at the 1968 UEFA European Championship.

TOP SCORERS
([United] Yugoslavia and Serbia)

1	Stjepan Bobek	38
2	Milan Galic	37
=	Savo Milosevic	37
4	Blagoje Marjanovic	36
5	Rajko Mitic	32
6	Dusan Bajevic	29
7	Todor Veselinovic	28
8	Borivoje Kostic	26
=	Predrag Mijatovic	26
10	Zlatko Vujovic	25

STAN'S THE MAN

Midfielder **Dejan Stankovic** is the only man to have represented three different countries at separate FIFA World Cups, playing for Yugoslavia in 2002, Serbia and Montenegro in 2006, and Serbia in 2010. His pragmatic comment on his achievement was: "I'm happy with the record, but I'd rather win. It's OK to have been in three World Cups, but I would have liked to have better results." Stankovic scored twice on his international debut for Yugoslavia in 1998. He has also twice scored memorable volleyed goals from virtually on the halfway line – once for Internazionale against Genoa in 2009–10, with a first-time shot from the opposing goalkeeper's clearance, and an almost identical finish against German club FC Schalke 04 in the UEFA Champions League the following season. Stankovic tied Savo Milosevic's Serbian appearances record with his final competitive international in October 2011, but went one better in October 2013, when playing the first ten minutes of a 2-0 friendly defeat of Japan at Novi Sad.

SAV A GO HERO

Savo Milosevic was the first Serbian player to reach a century of international appearances – and he can claim to have played for his country in four different guises, representing Yugoslavia before and after it broke up, Serbia & Montenegro and finally Serbia alone. Milosevic's 100th international appearance was memorable for the wrong reasons, coming in a 6-0 defeat to Argentina at the 2006 FIFA World Cup. He returned to the fold for a final, farewell match: a friendly against Bulgaria on 19 November 2008. Milosevic played only the first 34 minutes yet managed not only to score twice but also miss two penalties. He joked: "Maybe those 34 minutes sum up my career, in the best possible way, with good moments and bad times, when you are at the top and at the bottom. Believe me, I have never missed two penalties before – not even in training."

BRAN POWER

Versatile defender **Branislav Ivanovic**, who became Serbia's most-capped player with two appearances at the 2018 FIFA World Cup, has enjoyed scoring significant late goals against Portuguese opposition. His first goal for his country was an 88th-minute equalizer in a UEFA European Championship qualifier away to Portugal in September 2007. His stoppage-time header gave Chelsea victory over Benfica in the final of the 2013 UEFA Europa League, a year after suspension ruled him out of the club's UEFA Champions League triumph over Bayern Munich. He was named Serb Footballer of the Year in 2012 and 2013, the first player to win the award in consecutive years since Serbia became independent – although this was then emulated by his Chelsea team-mate Nemanja Matic in 2014 and 2015.

MILORAD'S MILESTONE

The first man to captain and then coach his country at the FIFA World Cup was Milorad Arsenijevic, who captained Yugoslavia to the semi-finals at the inaugural tournament in Uruguay in 1930 and then managed their squad in Brazil 20 years later.

GOING IT ALONE

After Serbia and Montenegro competed at the 2006 FIFA World Cup, the 2010 tournament was the first featuring Serbia alone following Montenegro's independence. Topping their qualifying group ahead of France, Radomir Antic's Serbian side failed to make it through to the knockout stages in South Africa, despite a single-goal victory over Group D rivals Germany. A Serbian working for an opposing team was partly to blame – Milovan Rajevac was coach of the Ghana side that beat Serbia 1-0 in their opening first-round match. A mainstay in the Serbian defence was dominating centre-back **Nemanja Vidic**, a 2008 UEFA Champions League-winner and hero at Manchester United – but he announced his retirement from international football in October 2011.

SLOVAKIA

Slovakia have finally begun claiming bragging rights over their neighbours, the Czech Republic. A Slovak team did play games during the Second World War but then had to wait until post-war Czechoslovakia divided into Slovakia and the Czech Republic in 1993 before their next match. They returned to competitive action in qualifiers for the 1996 UEFA European Championship, finishing a promising third in their group. Continuing gradual progress culminated in qualification for their first FIFA World Cup, in 2010, at which they upset defending champions Italy 3-2 and reached the second round.

VLAD ALL OVER

Three relatives named Vladimir Weiss – different generations of the same family – have represented their country in international football, with two of them featuring at the 2010 FIFA World Cup. The first Vladimir won a footballing silver medal with Czechoslovakia at the 1964 Olympics, before his son Vladimir played for the same country at the 1990 FIFA World Cup. This second Vladimir then led Slovakia to the 2010 tournament as coach, picking his Manchester City winger son – yet another Vladimir – for three of the team's four matches. The first Vladimir made three appearances for Czechoslovakia, including the 1964 Olympics final in which he scored an own goal as Hungary triumped 2-1. The second Vladimir won 19 caps for Czechoslavakia and 12 for Slovakia, and the third, then aged only 20, ended the 2010 FIFA World Cup with 12. However, by the summer of 2018, the youngest Weiss was the most-capped family member with 64. The coach described their 3-2 victory over holders Italy at the 2010 FIFA World Cup as the second happiest day of his life – only beaten by the day his son was born. He stepped down as boss after failing to qualify for the 2012 UEFA European Championship.

ADAM'S PEAK

Adam Nemec had to wait more than three and a half years between his Slovakia debut against Luxembourg in February 2011 and his first international goal, the only one of the game as his side beat Malta in September 2014. Since then, he has scored regularly and his double, also against Malta in October 2017, in a 3-0 win, took him to 12 goals, joint seventh in Slovakia's all-time scorer ranks. More importantly, it ensured Slovakia finished second place in Group F of the 2018 FIFA World Cup qualifying competition, above Scotland and below only England. However they missed out on the finals because they were the "worst runners-up". At least three of Nemec's goals in Euro 2016 qualifiers were crucial in helping Slovakia to only their second major tournament.

TOP SCORERS

1	Robert Vittek	23
2	Szilard Nemeth	22
3	Marek Hamsik	21
4	Miroslav Karhan	14
=	Marek Mintal	14
6	Stanislav Sestak	13
7	Peter Dubovsky	12
=	Adam Nemec	12
9	Robert Mak	10
10	Martin Jakubko	9
=	Tibor Jancula	9
=	Lubomir Reiter	9

MAREK OFF THE MARK

Slovakia's biggest win is 7-0, a result they have achieved three times – with wing-back Marek Cech the only man to play in all three games: against Liechtenstein in September 2004 and twice versus San Marino, in October 2007 and June 2009. He scored twice in the most recent match and in fact four of his five international goals since his 2004 debut came against San Marino – he also scored a brace in a 5-0 victory in November 2007.

TOP CAPS

1	Miroslav Karhan	107
2	Marek Hamsik	105
3	Martin Skrtel	97
4	Jan Durica	91
5	Peter Pekarik	82
=	Robert Vittek	82
7	Stanislav Sestak	66
8	Filip Holosko	65
9	Vladimir Weiss	64
10	Tomas Hubocan	61

CZECH EIGHT

Eight Slovakia players played in Czechoslovakia's triumphant 1976 UEFA European Championship final against West Germany, including captain Anton Ondrus and both their scorers in the 2-2 draw: Jan Svehlik and Karol Dobias. Three of the team's successful penalty-takers in their 5-3 shoot-out win were Slovak-born: Marian Masny, Ondrus and substitute Ladislav Jurkemik. The other Slovaks to feature were Jan Pivarnik, Jozef Capkovic and Jozef Moder. Defender Koloman Gogh was born in what is now the Czech Republic, but had Slovak family ties and played most of his club football for Slovan Bratislava in the Slovak capital.

COOL DUDA

Slovakia made it to the second round when reaching their first ever UEFA European Championship finals in 2016, only then going out 3-0 to reigning world champions Germany. **Ondrej Duda** became the first man to score for Slovakia at a UEFA European Championship, with an equalizer in their opening game against Wales just 52 seconds after coming on – the fastest Euros goal by a substitute since Spain's Juan Carlos Valeron needed just 36 seconds against Russia in 2004. Slovakia's qualification campaign for the 2016 tournament included a national record six straight victories, including a surprise 2-1 win against defending champions Spain in Zilina in October 2014.

ROBERT THE HERO

Slovakia's **Robert Vittek** became only the fourth player from a country making their FIFA World Cup debut to score as many as four goals in one tournament, at the 2010 event in South Africa. He hit one against New Zealand, two against defending champions Italy, and a late penalty in a second-round defeat to Holland. The previous three players to have done so were Portugal's Eusebio in 1966, Denmark's Preben Elkjaer Larsen in 1986 and Croatia's Davor Suker in 1998. Vittek's last-minute penalty against Holland made him Slovakia's all-time leading scorer with 23 goals, overtaking former Sparta Prague and Middlesbrough striker Szilard Nemeth. His 2010 FIFA World Cup form was all the more striking since he had failed to score at all in the qualifiers.

CUTTING EDGE HAMSIK

Playmaker Marek Hamsik was just 17 when he left Slovakia in 2004 – after only six games for Slovan Bratislava – and moved to Italy, joining Brescia, then Napoli. After helping Napoli to win the 2012 Coppa Italia, he fulfilled a promise to shave off his Mohawk hairstyle. Hamsik captained Slovakia at the 2010 FIFA World Cup, where he helped to eliminate Italy in the opening round. It was a less happy story for Hamsik and Slovakia when it came to qualifying for the 2014 FIFA World Cup. Slovakia finished a disappointing third behind Greece and group G winners Bosnia & Herzegovina. He scored twice in eight appearances, but missed the final two games. The Mohawk was back at the 2016 UEFA European Championship where Hamsik helped to inspire Slovakia to advance to the second round and he scored in a 2-1 group win over Russia. He became the second Slovakia player to reach 100 appearances in a 1-0 defeat to Scotland in September 2017 in a FIFA World Cup qualifier.

BROKEN-DOWN KARHAN

Slovakia's defensive midfielder **Miroslav Karhan** helped his country qualify for the 2010 FIFA World Cup, taking his appearances tally to a national-record 95. But an Achilles tendon injury meant the team captain was ruled out of the tournament itself. After returning to action later in 2010, Karhan became the first Slovakia player to pass 100 caps and he retired in 2011 with 107 to his name.

SWEDEN

Twelve appearances at the FIFA World Cup finals (with a best result of second, as tournament hosts, in 1958) and three Olympic medals (including gold in London in 1948), bear testament to Sweden's rich history on the world football stage. Recent success has been harder to find, however, with semi-final appearances at the 1992 UEFA European Championship (again as hosts) and the 1994 FIFA World Cup the country's best performances in recent years. Their last-eight loss to England in 2018 was a 24-year best.

GRE-NO-LI OLYMPIC AND ITALIAN GLORY

Having conquered the world by leading Sweden to gold in the 1948 Olympics in London, Gunnar Gren, Gunnar Nordahl and **Nils Liedholm** were snapped up by AC Milan. Their three-pronged "Gre-No-Li" forward line led the Italian giants to their 1951 scudetto win. Nordahl, who topped the Serie A scoring charts five times between 1950 and 1955, remains Milan's all-time top scorer with 221 goals in 268 games. Gren and Liedholm went on to appear for the Swedish national team in the 1958 FIFA World Cup – where they finished runners-up.

TOP CAPS

1	Anders Svensson	148
2	Thomas Ravelli	143
3	Andreas Isaksson	133
4	Kim Kallstrom	131
5	Olof Mellberg	117
6	Zlatan Ibrahimovic	116
=	Roland Nilsson	116
8	Bjorn Nordqvist	115
9	Niclas Alexandersson	109
10	Henrik Larsson	106

ONE MORE ENCORE, AGAIN!

One of the most famous and decorated Swedish footballers of modern times, **Henrik Larsson** (a star on the club scene with both Celtic and Barcelona) quit international football after the 2002 FIFA World Cup ... and again after the 2006 FIFA World Cup in Germany. He then made a further comeback in the 2010 FIFA World Cup qualifiers. With 37 goals in his 106 appearances, including five in his three FIFA World Cups, fans and officials clamoured for his return each time he tried to walk away. Sweden's failure to qualify for the tournament in 1998 meant a record-equalling 12 years elapsed between Larsson's first FIFA World Cup finals goal against Bulgaria in 1994 and his last, a dramatic late equalizer in a 2-2 group-stage draw with England in 2006. After finally retiring for good in 2009, he became manager of Swedish second-tier club Landskrona BoIS.

TOP-STOPPER RAVELLI

Thomas Ravelli kept goal for Sweden a record 143 times – conceding 143 goals. He saved two penalties in a shoot-out against Romania in the 1994 FIFA World Cup quarter-final to send Sweden into the last four, where they lost 1-0 to Brazil. Sweden went on to finish third, and were also the tournament's highest scorers with 15 goals in all – four more than eventual champions Brazil. Sweden's tally included five for Kennet Andersson, four for Martin Dahlin and three for Tomas Brolin.

IBRA–CADABRA

Few modern footballers can claim such consistent success – or boast such an unrepentant ego – as Swedish forward **Zlatan Ibrahimovic**. His proclamations have included "There's only one Zlatan", "I am like Muhammad Ali" and – in response to criticism from Norway's John Carew – "What Carew does with a football, I can do with an orange". He christened the newly built Friends Arena in Solna with all four goals as hosts Sweden beat England 4-2 in a November 2012 friendly – his final strike topping the lot, a 30-yard overhead kick which won the FIFA Ferenc Puskas goal of the year award. Despite also qualifying for Bosnia and Croatia through his family, Malmo-born Ibrahimovic made his Sweden debut in January 2001 and went to score a national record 62 goals in 116 appearances before retiring from international football after Sweden's first-round departure from the 2016 UEFA European Championship. His clubs have included Ajax Amsterdam, Juventus, both Milan giants, Barcelona, Paris Saint-Germain and Manchester United. In 2018 he moved to Major League Soccer in the United States with LA Galaxy.

SUPER GRANQVIST

Sweden saw off the Netherlands and Italy to qualify for the 2018 FIFA World Cup, where they lost 2-0 to England in the quarter-finals. Substitute Jakob Johansson scored his first international goal, four minutes after coming on, in the second leg of the qualifying play-off against Italy, the only score of the tie. Their top scorer at the 2018 finals was centre-back and captain **Andreas Granqvist** – the successor to Zlatan Ibrahimovic as both captain and Swedish player of the year. He netted two penalties in Russia, the only goal against South Korea and the second strike in their 3-0 victory over Mexico that secured top spot in Group F. In between Sweden's two wins, they had lost 2-1 to Germany, the defending champions' only victory.

ANDERS KEEPERS

Midfielder Anders Svensson celebrated equalling Thomas Ravelli's Sweden appearances record by scoring in both his 142nd and 143rd games for his country: a long-range strike as Norway were beaten 4-2 and then the winning goal against the Republic of Ireland in a qualifier for the 2014 FIFA World Cup. He then became his country's most-capped player in a 1-0 victory over Kazakhstan, but he didn't score. Svensson retired from international football in 2013, aged 37, after Sweden lost to Portugal in the qualifying play-off. He made 148 appearances, and scored 21 goals.

TOP SCORERS

1	Zlatan Ibrahimovic	62
2	Sven Rydell	49
3	Gunnar Nordahl	43
4	Henrik Larsson	37
5	Gunnar Gren	32
6	Kennet Andersson	31
7	Marcus Allback	30
8	Martin Dahlin	29
9	Tomas Brolin	27
=	Agne Simonsson	27

ALEXANDER THE GREAT YOUNG HOPE

Borussia Dortmund striker Alexander Isak became Sweden's youngest international scorer on 12 January 2017 when he netted the opener in a 6-0 friendly defeat of Slovakia in Abu Dhabi. Aged 17 years and 113 days old, he beat the record set in 1912 by Erik Dahlstrom – aged 18 years and one day – when scoring against Finland. Four days earlier Isak had become Sweden's youngest international since record-holder Gunnar Pleijel faced Finland in 1911 aged 17 years and 72 days. Isak is also the youngest scorer in Sweden's top division, having struck for AIK Solna against Ostersunds FK at the age of 16 years and 199 days. However, his lack of experience cost him a place in Sweden's 2018 World Cup squad.

MANAGER SWAP

The most successful manager Sweden ever had was Englishman **George Raynor**, who led them to Olympic gold in London in 1948 and steered Sweden to third place and the runners-up spot in the 1950 and 1958 FIFA World Cups respectively. Raynor got one over on the country of his birth when Sweden became only the second foreign side to win at Wembley, with a 3-2 victory over England in 1959. Working in the opposite direction, in 2001 Sven-Goran Eriksson left Serie A side Lazio to become England's first foreign coach. He led the side to three consecutive quarter-finals – in the FIFA World Cups of 2002 and 2006 and, in between, the 2004 UEFA European Championship. Eriksson, however, failed to lead England to a win over his home country, recording three draws (1-1 in a 2001 friendly; 1-1 in a 2002 FIFA World Cup group game; 2-2 in a 2006 FIFA World Cup group game) and one defeat (0-1 in a 2004 friendly).

MAGICAL MELL

Centre-back Olof Mellberg became the first Swedish man to play in four UEFA European Championship finals when he appeared at Euro 2012. The 34-year-old also became Sweden's oldest UEFA European Championship goalscorer, netting in a 3-2 defeat against England. Mellberg's six previous international goals had all come in qualifying matches for either the UEFA European Championship or the FIFA World Cup.

SWITZERLAND

Switzerland did not concede a goal at the 2006 FIFA World Cup, other than in a penalty shoot-out, but, uniquely, still went out of the tournament. It sums up the country's football history: despite reaching three FIFA World Cup quarter-finals – in 1934, 1938 and (as hosts) 1954 – and three second rounds – in 2006, 2014 and 2018, Switzerland are not an international football powerhouse. The home of both FIFA and UEFA, Switzerland co-hosted the 2008 UEFA European Championship, with Austria, but went out in the group stage.

CLEAN SHEET WIPE-OUT

Switzerland remain the only team to exit the FIFA World Cup without conceding a goal in regulation time, which they did in 2006. However, in the shoot-out defeat to Ukraine in the second round, following a goalless 120 minutes, they failed to score a single penalty and lost 3-0. Despite being beaten three times in the shoot-out, goalkeeper Pascal Zuberbuhler's performances in Germany earned him a Swiss record for consecutive clean sheets at an international tournament. Another Swiss keeper, **Yann Sommer**, was out of luck at the 2018 FIFA World Cup. Late in the group match against Costa Rica, Brian Ruiz's penalty hit the crossbar, then his head and bounced into the net to make it 2-2. Sommer is only the third goalkeeper to score a FIFA World Cup own goal, after Spain's Andoni Zubizarreta in 1998 and Noel Valladeres of Honduras in 2014.

WHO'S HUGI

Only two men have scored more than three goals in one game for Switzerland and **Josef Hugi** leads the way with a five-timer. His 23 goals in 34 games for his country included five on 12 October 1960 as France were beaten 6-2 in Basel. Hugl found the net six times at the 1954 FIFA World Cup including a hat-trick in a 7-5 quarter-final defeat to Austria, as he finished second top scorer at the tournament. His six FIFA World Cup finals goals remains a national record. In the 1924 Paris Olympic Games, Paul Sturzenegger netted four in a 9-0 win over Lithuania.

LLAMA FARMER FREI-ING HIGH

After being compared to a llama by an angry Swiss sports press for spitting at Steven Gerrard at UEFA Euro 2004, **Alexander Frei**, Switzerland's all-time top scorer, adopted a llama at Basel zoo as part of his apology to the nation. Citing abuse from his own fans during recent matches, Frei announced his retirement from international football in April, leaving as Switzerland's all-time leading goalscorer with 42 in 84 games. These included a goalless draw against minnows Malta, when both Frei and team-mate Gokhan Inler missed penalties. Frei was joined in international retirement by strike partner Marco Streller, who had scored 12 goals in 37 games.

CHAMPION CHAPPI

Stephane "Chappi" Chapuisat – the third man to make 100 appearances for Switzerland – was the first Swiss player to win a UEFA Champions League medal when he led the line for Borussia Dortmund in their 3-1 victory over Juventus in 1997. But his most significant contribution in the final was to make way for Lars Ricken, whose goal with his first touch put the game beyond Juventus. Stephane's father, Pierre-Albert Chapuisat, was also a successful Swiss international – earning 34 caps for the national side in the 1970s and 1980s – but he failed to reach the heights of Stephane, who would later add both the Club World Cup and the Swiss super league (while playing for Grasshoppers) to his winners' medal collection.

ADMIR ADDS MORE

Switzerland reached the knock-out stages of the UEFA European Championship for the first time in 2016, and their 1-0 Group A victory over Albania – thanks to a goal by centre-back Fabian Schar – was the first time they had ever won their Euro tournament opener. In their next match they managed a 1-1 draw against Romania, courtesy of a second-half equalizer by Admir Mehmedi. Mehmedi thus became the first Swiss player to score in both FIFA World Cup and UEFA European Championship finals, after his strike against Ecuador in Brazil two years earlier. Ten days later, Xerdan Shaqiri emulated Mehmedi, equalizing against Poland in the round of 16.

SHAQIRI LOYALTY TEST

Playmaker **Xerdan Shaqiri** scored one of the most spectacular goals of the 2016 UEFA European Championship, an overhead kick from outside the penalty area to give Switzerland a 1-1 draw in their second-round match with Poland – the Poles, however, prevailed on penalties. Two years earlier he had scored the 50th hat-trick in FIFA World Cup history during his side's 3-0 triumph over Honduras in Manaus. Kosovo-born Shaqiri indicated he would be prepared to switch international allegiance to his native land – which became a full UEFA and FIFA member in 2016 – if permitted. However he stuck with Switzerland and, at the 2018 World Cup, scored a late winner against Serbia. The Swiss were thus the first team at these finals to come from behind to win. Shaqiri was later cautioned by FIFA for a nationalistic celebration gesture.

TOP SCORERS

1	Alexander Frei	42
2	Max Abegglen	34
=	Kubilay Turkyilmaz	34
4	Andre Abegglen	29
=	Jacques Fatton	29
6	Adrian Knup	26
7	Josef Hugi	23
8	Charles Antenen	22
9	Lauro Amado	21
=	Stephane Chapuisat	21
=	Xerdan Shaqiri	21

TOP CAPS

1	Heinz Hermann	118
2	Alain Geiger	112
3	Stephane Chapuisat	103
=	Stephan Lichtsteiner	103
5	Johann Vogel	94
6	Gokhan Inler	89
7	Hakan Yakin	87
8	Alexander Frei	84
9	Valon Behrami	83
10	Patrick Muller	81

THE ORIGINAL BOLT

Karl Rappan did so much for Swiss football – including founding its first national football fan club – that it is often forgotten that he was Austrian. After a moderately successful career as a player and coach in Austria, Rappan achieved lasting fame as an innovative manager in Switzerland, leading the national side in the 1938 and 1954 FIFA World Cups, as well as securing league titles and cups as manager of Grasshopper Club, FC Servette and FC Zurich. He developed a flexible tactical system – which allowed players to switch positions depending on the situation and putting greater pressure on their opponents. This revolutionary new idea became known as the "Swiss bolt" and helped the unfancied hosts defeat Italy on the way to the quarter-finals of the 1954 FIFA World Cup, before losing out to Rappan's home country, Austria. An early advocate of a European league, Rappan eventually settled for the simpler knockout tournament, the Intertoto Cup, which he helped devise and launch in 1961. Rappan was, until Kobi Kuhn, Switzerland's longest-serving and statistically most successful manager, with 29 victories in 77 games in charge.

"MERCI KOBI"

Former Swiss international player and manager, **Jakob "Kobi" Kuhn**, was left close to tears as his players unfurled a "thank you" banner at the end of his final game as Swiss national manager – the 2-0 victory over Portugal in the final group game of UEFA Euro 2008. How times have changed for Kuhn: while now a much-loved elder statesmen of the Swiss game, when he was just 22 years old, he was sent home from the 1966 FIFA World Cup for missing a curfew. He was then banned from the national side for a year. The shoe was on the other foot when Kuhn had to send Alexander Frei home from UEFA Euro 2004 after the centre-forward spat at England's Steven Gerrard. Kuhn spent most of his playing career, where he was described as playing "with honey in his boots", with FC Zurich, winning six league titles and five Swiss Cups. He played 63 times for the national side, scoring five goals. He then worked his way up through the ranks of the Swiss national team, leading first the Under-18s, then the Under-21s and finally the senior national team. He retired, aged 64, with a record of 32 victories, 18 draws and 23 defeats in 73 matches as Swiss coach.

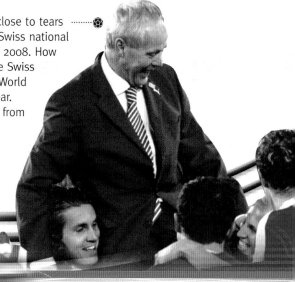

TURKEY

Galatasaray's penalty shoot-out success over Arsenal in the 2000 UEFA Cup final signalled a change in fortune for Turkish football. Prior to that night in Copenhagen, Turkey had qualified for the FIFA World Cup only twice (in 1950, when they withdrew, and 1954), and had consistently underachieved on the world stage. Since 2000, however, Turkish fans have had plenty to cheer about, including a third-place finish at the 2002 FIFA World Cup in Japan and South Korea, and a semi-final appearance at the 2008 UEFA European Championship.

SPOREL SPORTS

Zeki Riza Sporel scored Turkey's first goal in international football, against Romania on 26 October 1923. He actually hit a brace that day in a 2-2 draw, the first of 16 games for Turkey in which he hit 15 goals. Turkey's captain for their first international was his older brother Hasan Kamil Sporel.

SHOW ME MOR

Eighteen-year-old **Emre Mor** became Turkey's youngest player at a UEFA European Championship when he featured for them at the 2016 tournament in France, and the seventh youngest in the competition's history. But despite showing dazzling promise, Turkey were one of the two third-place finishers to miss out on a place in the knock-out stages. They lost 1-0 to Croatia and 3-0 Spain before beating the Czech Republic 2-0. Turkey have lost their opening match at every tournament finals they have reached.

QUICK OFF THE MARK

Hakan Sukur scored the fastest-ever FIFA World Cup finals goal – taking only 11 seconds to score Turkey's first goal in their third-place play-off match against South Korea at the 2002 FIFA World Cup. Turkey went on to win the game 3-2 to claim third place, their finest-ever performance in the competition. His total of 51 goals (in 112 games) is more than double his nearest competitor in the national team ranking. His first goal came in only his second appearance, as Turkey beat Denmark 2-1 on 8 April 1992. He went on to score four goals in a single game twice – in the 6-4 win over Wales on 20 August 1997 and in the 5-0 crushing of Moldova on 11 October 2006.

RUSTU TO THE RESCUE

With his distinctive ponytail and charcoal-black warpaint, Turkey's most-capped international **Rustu Recber** has always stood out. But perhaps never more so than as a star mainstay in Turkey's third-place performance at the 2002 FIFA World Cup. He was elected into the Team of the Tournament before being named FIFA's Goalkeeper of the Year. He had been relegated to the bench by the time Turkey opened their campaign at the 2008 UEFA European Championship but played in the quarter-final after first-choice goalkeeper Volkan Demirel was sent off in the final group-game and suspended – and Recber became the hero again, saving from Croatia's Mladen Petric in a penalty shoot-out to send Turkey into their first UEFA European Championship semi-final, a narrow defeat to Germany.

OLD GOLD

The last FIFA World Cup "golden goal" was scored by Turkey substitute Ilhan Mansiz, in the 94th minute of their 2002 quarter-final against Senegal – giving his side a 1-0 win on their way to finishing third overall. The "golden goal" rule was abandoned ahead of the 2006 FIFA World Cup, which went back to two guaranteed 15-minute periods of extra-time if a knockout fixture ended level after 90 minutes.

TWIN TURKS

Hamit Altintop (right) was born 10 minutes before identical twin brother **Halil** (left) – and he has been just about leading the way throughout their parallel professional footballing careers since their birth in the city of Gelsenkirchen, Germany, on 8 December 1982. Both began playing for German amateur side Wattenscheid, before defender-cum-midfielder Hamit signed for FC Schalke 04 in the summer of 2006 and striker Halil followed suit shortly afterwards. Hamit would stay just a season there, though, before being bought by Bayern Munich. Both helped Turkey reach the semi-finals of the 2008 UEFA European Championship – losing to adopted homeland Germany – though only Hamit was voted among UEFA's 23 best players of the tournament.

TAKE FAT

It seemed finally to be the end of an epic era when **Fatih Terim**'s third spell as national manager finished abruptly in July 2017, with the Turkish Football Federation announcing: "It would be healthier for both sides to part ways." This followed allegations of a fight involving Terim and a restaurant manager in a coastal town. But Terim remains Turkish football history's dominant force – befitting his nickname, "Emperor". After coaching Galatasaray to victory over Arsenal in the 2000 UEFA Cup final – the nation's first European trophy – he led Turkey on their surprise run to the 2008 UEFA European Championship semi-finals. They lost their first game to Portugal but came back from losing positions to beat Switzerland and the Czech Republic and even recovered from conceding a 119th-minute opening goal to Croatia in the quarter-finals. As their opponents celebrated, Terim urged his team to fight back and Semih Senturk's instant equaliser took the match to a penalty shoot-out, which the Turks won 3-1. Turkey led in the semi-final only to concede a last-minute winner to Germany. Terim returned to Galatasaray in 2009 but became national manager for the third time in 2013 – his first stint coming between 1993 and 1996. He was in charge, in total, for 136 matches, winning 70, drawing 34 and losing 32 – a win percentage of 51.48.

TOP SCORERS

1	Hakan Sukur	51
2	Burak Yilmaz	23
3	Tuncay Sanli	22
4	Lefter Kucukandonyadis	21
5	Nihat Kahveci	19
=	Metin Oktay	19
=	Cemil Turan	19
8	Arda Turan	17
9	Zeki Riza Sporel	15
10	Arif Erdem	11
=	Ertugrul Saglam	11
=	Cenk Tosun	11

TOP CAPS

1	Rustu Recber	120
2	Hakan Sukur	112
3	Bulent Korkmaz	102
4	Arda Turan	100
5	Emre Belozoglu	95
6	Tugay Kerimoglu	94
7	Alpay Ozalan	90
8	Hamit Altintop	82
9	Tuncay Sanli	80
10	Mehmet Topal	78

SO NEAR, SO SAH

Playmaker **Nuri Sahin** became both Turkey's youngest international and youngest goalscorer, on the same day. Sahin was 17 years and 32 days old when he made his debut against Germany in Istanbul on 8 October 2005, and his goal, one minute from time, gave Turkey a 2-1 win. Ironically, Sahin was actually born in Germany, to Turkish parents, and he has played most of his club career there, for Borussia Dortmund though he has also had spells with Feyenoord, Real Madrid and Liverpool.

WORK HARD, PLAY ARDA

Wing wizard Arda Turan – Turkey's captain at the 2016 UEFA European Championship – has survived cardiac arrhythmia, swine flu and a car crash to emerge as one of Turkish football's leading lights. His international achievements include key goals at the 2008 UEFA European Championship, the first a stoppage-time winner against Switzerland, then Turkey's late opener when overturning a two-goal deficit against the Czech Republic in a first-round qualification decider. After leaving Galatasaray, he has enjoyed great success in Spanish club football, winning European and domestic trophies with Atletico Madrid and Barcelona. His international career appeared to end rancourously in June 2017, when he was accused of attacking a journalist on a flight home from a 0-0 draw away to Macedonia. Turan said he would not play for his country again. But Turan changed his mind after coach Fatih Terim was succeeded by former Romania coach Mircea Lucescu and he made his 100th appearance for Turkey in a 3-0 defeat against FIFA 2018 World Cup qualifying group winners Iceland in October 2017.

UKRAINE

Ukraine has been a stronghold of football in eastern Europe for many years. A steady flow of talent from Ukrainian clubs with a rich European pedigree, such as Dynamo Kiev, provided the Soviet national team with many standout players in the years before independence. Since separating from the Soviet Union in 1991, Ukraine has become a football force in its own right, qualifying for the FIFA World Cup for the first time in 2006, reaching the quarter-finals.

YARMED AND DANGEROUS

Only Andriy Shevchenko has scored more goals for Ukraine than **Andriy Yarmolenko** – and no one has found the net more quickly after kick-off for the country than his opener just 14 seconds into their 3-2 friendly defeat against Uruguay in September 2011. Yarmolenko was crucial in helping Ukraine qualify for the 2016 UEFA European Championship, with six goals – including a hat-trick in a 6-0 victory over Luxembourg and strikes in both legs of their play-off victory over Slovenia. He was also Ukraine's leading scorer in their 2018 FIFA World Cup qualification bid, again with six goals, but the country failed to reach the tournament after finishing behind Iceland and Croatia in their group.

ROCKET MAN

Andriy Shevchenko beat team-mate **Anatoliy Tymoshchuk** to become the first Ukrainian footballer to reach a century of international appearances – but the defensive midfielder overtook Shevchenko and retired in 2016 and is the country's most-capped player with 144 appearances. He also had the rare honour of seeing his name in space, when Ukrainian cosmonaut Yuri Malenchenko launched into orbit wearing a Zenit St Petersburg shirt with "Tymoshchuk" on the back in 2007.

YURI-KA MOMENT

Denys Harmash and Dmytro Korkishko scored the goals against England that gave Ukraine their first major international footballing title, in the final of the 2009 UEFA Under-19 European Championship. The coach was Yuri Kalitvintsev, later assistant to Oleg Blokhin with the senior international side.

REB ALERT

Andriy Shevchenko's strike partner Ukraine and Dynamo Kiev 1994–99 was Ukraine's youngest international, Serhiy Rebrov. He was 18 years and 24 days old when making his debut against the USA in June 1992. Four years later Rebrov scored Ukraine's first ever FIFA World Cup goal, giving them a 1-0 win over Northern Ireland in an August 1996 qualifier for the 1998 tournament. He was part of the squad for Ukraine's first FIFA World Cup finals in 2006, scoring against Saudi Arabia to help his side towards the quarter-finals where they lost 3-0 to eventual champions Italy. After spells in England and Turkey, Rebrov returned to Kiev and, in 2014, went into management, steering Dynamo to two Ukrainian league titles.

SUPER SHEVA

In 2004, **Andriy Shevchenko** became the third Ukrainian to win the Ballon D'Or. The first to do so, in 1975, was his 2006 FIFA World Cup coach Oleg Blokhin (second was Igor Belanov in 1986), but he was the first to win the award since Ukraine's independence from the Soviet Union. Born on 29 September 1976, Shevchenko was a promising boxer as a youngster, before deciding to focus on football full-time. He has won trophies at every club he's played for, including five titles in a row with Dynamo Kiev, the Serie A and UEFA Champions League with AC Milan, and even two cups in his "disappointing" time at Chelsea. Shevchenko is Ukraine's second most-capped player and leading goalscorer, with 48 goals in 111 games. This includes two at the 2006 FIFA World Cup, where he captained his country in their first-ever major finals appearance, and a double to secure a 2-1 comeback win over Sweden in Ukraine's first match co-hosting the 2012 UEFA European Championship. Shevchenko was Ukraine's assistant coach at the 2016 UEFA European Championship and replaced Mykhailo Fomenko as manager after the tournament.

LEADING FROM THE FRONT

Oleg Blokhin, Ukraine's coach on their first appearance at a major tournament finals, made his name as a star striker with his hometown club Dynamo Kiev. Born on 5 November 1952, when Ukraine was part of the Soviet Union, Blokhin scored a record 211 goals in another record 432 appearances in the USSR national league. He also holds the goals and caps records for the USSR, with 42 in 112 games. He led Kiev to two victory in the European Cup-Winners' Cup in 1975 and 1986, scoring in both finals, and was named the 1975 European Footballer of the Year. Always an over-achiever, Blokhin managed Ukraine to the finals of the 2006 FIFA World Cup in Germany, where they lost out to eventual winners Italy 3-0 in the quarter-finals after knocking out Switzerland in the second round – also on penalties. Blokhin was renowned for his speed – when Olympic gold medallist Valeriy Borzov trained the Kiev squad in the 1970s, Blokhin recorded a 100 metres time of 11 seconds, just 0.46 seconds slower than Borzov's own 1972 medal-winning run. Blokhin quit as Ukraine manager in December 2007, but returned to the job in April 2011.

DEVASTATING DEVIC

Ukraine enjoyed their biggest win on 6 September 2013 thrashing San Marino 9-0 in a FIFA World Cup qualifier – then rubbed salt into the wounds by winning 8-0 away to the same opposition the following month, on 25 October 2013. There were eight different scorers in the first game, with the opening goal struck by striker **Marko Devic** – and he went on to hit a hat-trick in the rematch. Devic was actually born in Belgrade and brought up in Serbia but transferred to Ukrainian club Volyn Lutsk in 2005 and switched nationalities three years later.

TOP SCORERS

1	Andriy Shevchenko	48
2	Andriy Yarmolenko	35
3	Yevhen Konoplyanka	17
4	Serhiy Rebrov	15
5	Oleh Husyev	13
6	Serhiy Nazarenko	12
7	Yevhen Seleznyov	11
8	Andriy Husin	9
=	Andriy Vorobey	9
10	Tymerlan Huseynov	8
=	Artem Kravets	8
=	Artem Milevskyi	8
=	Ruslan Rotan	8
=	Andriy Voronin	8

GET ZIN IN

Ukraine performed disappointingly at the 2016 UEFA European Championship, failing to score and conceding five goals as they made a first-round exit. But hope for the future was provided by midfielder **Oleksandr Zinchenko**. He became Ukraine's youngest ever goalscorer two weeks before the tournament, in a 4-3 friendly win against Romania – then came on as a substitute in his country's tournament opener against Germany, aged 19 years and 179 days old, making him Ukraine's youngest player at an international finals. Also in the summer of 2016 Zinchenko left Russian club Ufa for England's Manchester City.

TOP CAPS

1	Anatoliy Tymoshchuk	144
2	Andriy Shevchenko	111
3	Ruslan Rotan	100
4	Oleh Husyev	98
5	Oleksandr Shovkovskyi	92
6	Andriy Pyatov	81
7	Andriy Yarmolenko	77
8	Serhiy Rebrov	75
9	Andriy Voronin	74
10	Yehven Konoplyanka	72

⚽ WALES

In a land where rugby union has long been the main national obsession, Wales struggled for many years to impose themselves on the world of international football despite producing many hugely talented players. But recent progress – including a semi-finals appearance at the 2016 UEFA European Championship – has inspired unprecedented excitement and optimism.

GOOD ON RAMSEY

Arsenal midfielder **Aaron Ramsey** became Wales's youngest captain when appointed to the role in March 2011 by new manager Gary Speed. Ramsey was 20 years 90 days old when he led the side out for the first time at Cardiff's Millennium Stadium in a 2012 UEFA European Championship qualifier that ended in a 2-0 win for England. The record had previously been held by centre-back Mike England, who was 22 years 135 days old when skipper against Northern Ireland in April 1964.

FAMILY MISFORTUNES

Full-back Chris Gunter's parents had a dilemma when Wales made the semi-finals of the 2016 UEFA European Championship – they were meant to be attending his brother Marc's wedding in Mexico the day Wales faced Portugal. They opted to watch Chris in action instead, sadly seeing Wales bow out 2-0 in Lille.

HEADLINING GIGGS

The most-decorated Welsh player of all-time took over as the country's national coach in 2018 – despite having no previous full-time managerial experience. **Ryan Giggs** scored 12 goals in 64 games for Wales between 1991 and 2007. However, he was criticised by some fans for failing to play in friendlies – he missed 18 in a row in one spell – and never represented Wales at a major tournament. On a domestic level, with his only senior club Manchester United, he won 13 English league titles, four FA Cups, three League Cups, two UEFA Champions Leagues and one FIFA Club World Cup – and appeared in more than 1,000 first-team matches before retiring, aged 40, in 2014. Following Wales's failure to qualify for the 2018 FIFA World Cup, manager Chris Coleman resigned and Giggs took over.

BRICKS TO BRILLIANCE

Goalkeeper **Neville Southall** made the first of his record 92 appearances for Wales in a 3-2 win over Northern Ireland on 27 May 1982. The former hod-carrier and bin man kept 34 clean sheets in 15 years playing for Wales and won the English Football Writers' Player of the Year in 1985 thanks to his performances alongside Welsh captain Kevin Ratcliffe at Everton. In his final match for Wales, on 20 August 1997, he was substituted halfway through a 6-4 defeat against Turkey in Istanbul.

RUSH FOR GOAL

Liverpool legend **Ian Rush** is Wales' second-top marksman, with 28 goals in 73 games. His first came in a 3-0 win over Northern Ireland on 27 May 1982; he scored his 28th and final goal in a 2-1 win over Estonia in Tallinn in 1994.

CAUGHT ON CAMERA

Pioneer movie-makers Sagar Mitchell and James Kenyon captured Wales v Ireland in March 1906, making it the first filmed international football match.

TOP CAPS

1	Neville Southall	92
2	Chris Gunter	88
3	Gary Speed	85
4	Ashley Williams	79
5	Craig Bellamy	78
6	Joe Ledley	77
7	Wayne Hennessey	76
8	Dean Saunders	75
9	Peter Nicholas	73
=	Ian Rush	73

TOP SCORERS

1	Gareth Bale	29
2	Ian Rush	28
3	Ivor Allchurch	23
=	Trevor Ford	23
5	Dean Saunders	22
6	Craig Bellamy	19
7	Robert Earnshaw	16
=	Mark Hughes	16
=	Cliff Jones	16
10	John Charles	15

BILLY IDOL

Winger Harry Wilson became Wales' youngest full international when replacing Hal Robson-Kanu in October 2013, in a 2014 FIFA World Cup qualifier. At 16 years and 207 days, he was 108 days younger than previous record-holder Gareth Bale. Wales' oldest international is Billy Meredith, whose 48th and final international came aged 45 years and 229 days in March 1920. Meredith's international career lasted a Welsh record 25 years.

ALL HAIL BALE

It was fitting – and predictable – that Wales' first goalscorer at the 2016 UEFA European Championship, their first finals since the 1958 FIFA World Cup, would be their undoubted "Galatico" **Gareth Bale**. The Real Madrid star – whose $100 million (£86 million) move from Tottenham Hotspur in August 2013 made him the world's most expensive footballer – opened the scoring with a free-kick in their 2-1 first-round win over Slovakia, and repeated the trick in their next game, against England. Before Bale, only France's Michel Platini in 1984 and Germany's Thomas Hassler in 1992, had scored twice from direct free-kicks at one UEFA European Championship. A month earlier Bale had won his second UEFA Champions League with Real Madrid, and there was another one in June 2017 – this time in the Millennium Stadium in Cardiff, the city of his birth. Once Wales's youngest international, Bale became the country's leading goalscorer with a hat-trick in a 6-0 defeat of China in March 2018.

HAT-TRICK HERO

Welsh striker Robert Earnshaw holds the remarkable record of scoring hat-tricks in all four divisions of English football, the FA Cup, the League Cup. He also grabbed a treble for Wales, against Scotland on 18 February 2004. In full internationals, Wales have registered 15 hat-tricks – each one by a different player. Gareth Bale ended a 14-year treble drought in March 2018.

SHOCK LOSS OF A MODEL PROFESSIONAL

Welsh and world football were united in shock and grief at the sudden death of Wales manager **Gary Speed** in November 2011. Former Leeds United, Everton, Newcastle United and Bolton Wanderers midfielder Speed, the country's most-capped outfield player, was found at his home in Cheshire, England. The 42-year-old had been manager for 11 months, overseeing a series of encouraging performances that saw a rise in the world rankings from 116th to 48th and a prize for FIFA's "Best Movers" of 2011. An official memorial game was played in Cardiff in February 2012 between Wales and Costa Rica – the country against whom he had made his international debut in May 1990.

RISE OF THE DRAGON

After reaching the quarter-finals of the 1958 FIFA World Cup, Wales had to wait another 58 years to play at another major tournament. They returned to the big time in style, reaching the semi-finals of the 2016 UEFA European Championship in France. Chris Coleman's men beat Slovakia 2-1 and Russia 3-0 in the first round, Northern Ireland 1-0 in a second-round clash and came from a goal down to defeat Belgium 3-1 in the quarter-finals. Their goals that day were all scored by English-born players: captain Ashley Williams, **Hal Robson-Kanu** and Sam Vokes. Robson-Kanu, who went into the tournament without a club after leaving English second-tier side Reading, was later acclaimed as one of the best goals of the tournament – his "Cruyff turn" solo effort against Belgium, rather than his winner against Slovakia. Coleman's side lost 2-0 to eventual champions Portugal in the semi-finals and were welcomed home with an open-top bus parade in the capital Cardiff. In qualifying for the finals, Wales reached a best-ever eighth in the FIFA World Rankings in October 2015.

OTHER TEAMS EUROPE

For the major European football powers, a qualifying campaign for one of the game's major international tournaments would not be the same without an awkward trip to one of the former Eastern Bloc countries or the chance of a goal-fest against the likes of San Marino or Luxembourg. For these countries' players, the thrill of representing their nation is more important than harbouring dreams of world domination.

UNDERDOGS HAVE THEIR DAY

Iceland became the smallest nation ever to qualify for a FIFA World Cup, with a 2-0 victory over Kosovo in October 2017 thanks to goals from star midfielder **Gylfi Sigurdsson** and Johann Berg Gudmundsson. Striker Alfred Finnbogason netted their first FIFA World Cup finals goal, in a 1-1 draw with two-time winners Argentina. Unlike in their first UEFA European Championship appearance two years earlier, Iceland missed out on the knock-out stages after going down 2-0 to Nigeria and 2-1 to Croatia. Manager and part-time dentist Heimir Hallgrimsson, resigned after the finals.

LIT'S A KNOCK-OUT

Perhaps it's not be too surprising that **Jari Litmanen** should have become a football star – both his parents played for the Lahti-based club Reipas while Litmanen's father Olavi also won five caps for the national team. But Jari's skills and achievements far outstripped them both – and, arguably, any other player the country has produced. It was fitting that Litmanen became the first Finnish player to get his hands on the UEFA European Cup – or Champions League trophy – when his Ajax Amsterdam side beat AC Milan in 1995. Despite a series of injuries, he remained dedicated to his country, captaining the side between 1996 and 2008, and was still playing and scoring for Finland in 2010 at the age of 39 – having notched up more international goals and games than any other Finn, scoring 32 times in 137 appearances.

SELVA SERVICE

San Marino, with a population of under 30,000, remain near the bottom of FIFA's world rankings but they finally had something to celebrate in November 2014, thanks to a goalless draw with Estonia – their first ever point in a UEFA European Championship qualifier – and ending a run of 61 successive defeats. They have avoided defeat only five times and have never recorded a competitive victory. In fact, San Marino's only win was a 1-0 friendly triumph over Liechtenstein in April 2004. Striker and captain Andy Selva, still playing after making his debut in 1998, is top scorer with eight goals and for a long time was San Marino's only multiple goalscorer until midfielder Manuel Marani scored his second, against Malta, in August 2012. Massimo Bonini, San Marino manager between 1996 and 1998, previously lifted the UEFA European Cup with Italian giants Juventus in 1985. Selva, aged 41, was an unused squad member for San Marino's 2-0 2018 FIFA World Cup qualifying defeat to Andorra in February 2017. His most recent international appearance, his 74th, had been as a substitute in a 4-1 2018 FIFA World Cup qualifying loss, to Norway, in October 2016.

MOSQUITO STINGS

Malta ended a 20-year wait for an away win in a competitive international when they shocked Armenia 1-0 in a 2014 FIFA World Cup qualifier in June 2013. Appropriately enough, the vital strike came from veteran forward **Michael Mifsud,** his country's captain and all-time leading scorer, who made his international debut in February 2000. He made his name in Germany with Kaiserslautern and in England with Coventry City. Nicknamed "Mosquito", the 1.65m-tall player's international exploits include five goals in the 7-1 trouncing of Liechtenstein in March 2008 – including a hat-trick within the first 21 minutes. Before Armenia, the last time Malta won a UEFA European Championship or FIFA World Cup away qualifier had been a 1-0 success in Estonia in May 1993.

GIVING IT UP

Lithuania and Estonia did not bother playing their final group game against each other in the 1934 FIFA World Cup qualifying competition. Sweden had already guaranteed themselves top spot, and the sole finals place available, by beating Lithuania 2-0 and Estonia 6-2.

BEYOND THE IRON CURTAIN

The break-up of the Soviet Union in 1990 led to 15 new footballing nations, though initially Russia played on at the 1992 UEFA European Championship as CIS, or the Commonwealth of Independent States – without the involvement of Estonia, Latvia and Lithuania. In the coming years, UEFA and FIFA approved the creation of separate teams for Russia, Armenia, Azerbaijan, Belarus, Estonia, Georgia, Kazakhstan, Kyrgyzstan, Latvia, Lithuania, Moldova, Tajikstan, Turkmenistan, Ukraine and Uzbekistan. Upheavals in the early 1990s would also fragment the former Yugoslavia into Croatia, Serbia, Bosnia-Herzegovina, Macedonia, Slovenia and Montenegro, while Czechoslovakia split into Slovakia and the Czech Republic.

YEAR FIRST AFFILIATED TO FIFA	
Albania	1932
Andorra	1996
Austria	1905
Belarus	1992
Bosnia-Herzegovina	1996
Cyprus	1948
Estonia	1923
Faroe Islands	1988
Finland	1908
Georgia	1992
Gibraltar	2016
Greece	1927
Iceland	1947
Israel	1929
Kazakhstan	1994
Kosovo	2016
Latvia	1922
Liechtenstein	1974
Lithuania	1923
Luxembourg	1910
Macedonia	1994
Malta	1959
Moldova	1994
Montenegro	2007
San Marino	1988
Slovenia	1992

REBORN BOURG

A long and painful wait finally ended for traditional whipping-boys Luxembourg when they beat Northern Ireland 3-2 in September 2013. It was the "Red Lions" first home win in a FIFA World Cup qualifier for 41 years, since overcoming Turkey 2-0 in October 1972. It was also five years to the day since their last FIFA World Cup qualifying victory, a 2-1 triumph in Switzerland in 2008. Luxembourg's goals came from Aurelien Joachim, Stefano Bensi and **Mathias Janisch**. The winning goal, with three minutes remaining, was the first of Janisch's international career.

HAPPY AND SADIKU

Armando Sadiku scored Albania's first goal at an international tournament, his late first-half effort beating Romania in their final group game at the 2016 UEFA European Championship. Coached by Italian Gianni De Biasi, they finished second in their qualifying group – ahead of Denmark, Serbia and Armenia – having beaten eventual UEFA Euro 2016 champions Portugal 1-0. Albania's captain and most-capped player Lorik Cana played a minor role in France – he saw yellow twice within 36 minutes of their opener against Switzerland and was sent off. Sadly, Albania were one of two third-place teams to miss the knockout stages.

TRAVELLING MEN

Israel looked like qualifying for the 1958 FIFA World Cup without kicking a ball, because scheduled opponents Turkey, Indonesia and Sudan refused to play them. But FIFA ordered them into a two-legged play-off against a European side – which Israel lost 4-0 on aggregate to Wales. Israel were unfortunate again in the 2006 FIFA World Cup qualifiers, ending the campaign unbeaten – yet failing even to make the play-offs, finishing third in their group behind France and Switzerland. Their star midfielder that campaign was Israel's most-capped player Yossi Benayoun, whose clubs included Liverpool, Chelsea and Arsenal, while their coach at the time was Avram Grant who would later take Chelsea to the 2008 UEFA Champions League final. Israel hosted, and won, the 1964 Asian Nations Cup, and qualified for the 1970 FIFA World Cup through a combined Asia/Oceania qualifying competition, but are now members of the European Federation.

KOS FOR CELEBRATION

Kosovo gained independence from Serbia in May 2008, but it took eight years for them to become UEFA's 55th member and, days later, receive FIFA affiliation. Their first international permitted by FIFA was a goalless draw with Haiti on 5 March 2014 and their first as a FIFA member, on 3 June 2016, saw a 2-0 victory over the Faroe Islands. Their first goal that day was scored by **Albert Bunjaku**, a former Swiss international striker, who was among several given official permission to switch allegiance to Kosovo. Bunjaku scored their first two goals between receiving FIFA approval and affiliation, in a 6-1 defeat to Turkey and a 3-1 loss to Senegal.

MORE SIND AGAINST

Austria's star player **Matthias Sindelar** refused to play for a new, merged national team when Germany annexed Austria in 1938. Sindelar, born in modern-day Czech Republic in February 1903, was the inspirational leader of Austria's so-called Wunderteam of the 1930s. He scored 27 goals in 43 games for Austria, who went 14 internationals unbeaten between April 1931 and December 1932, won the 1932 Central European International Cup and silver at the 1936 Olympics. During a special reunification match between the Austrian and German teams in Vienna in April 1938, Sindelar disobeyed orders and scored a spectacular solo goal. Austria went on to win 2-0 in a game which might have been expected to end in a diplomatic draw. Sindelar was mysteriously found dead from carbon monoxide poisoning in his Vienna apartment in January 1939.

THE GUD SON

Iceland striker **Eidur Gudjohnsen** made history on his international debut away to Estonia in April 1996. He was a substitute for his father, Arnor Gudjohnsen. Eidur was 17 at the time, his father 34 – though both were disappointed they did not get to play on the pitch at the same time. The Icelandic Football Association thought they would get a chance to do so in Iceland's next home game, but Eidur had an ankle injury and the opportunity never arose again. Eidur's goal for Iceland in a 3-0 win over Kazakhstan in March 2014 made him the fourth oldest scorer in UEFA European Championship qualifiers, behind only Jari Litmanen of Finland, the Republic of Ireland's John Aldridge and Krasimir Balakov from Bulgaria. At 37, Gudjohnsen came on twice as a substitute at the 2006 UEFA European Championship, Iceland's first major tournament.

THE GIB'S UP

The British Overseas Territory of Gibraltar became UEFA's 54th member state in time to take part in qualifiers for the 2016 UEFA European Championship, but they were deliberately kept apart from neighbours Spain in the draw. Their first official international ended goalless against Slovakia in November 2013. Gibraltar's competitive bow was a 7-0 defeat to Poland in September 2014, their first Euro 2016 qualifier. Kyle Casciaro was the hero with the only goal in their first victory, against Malta in June 2014, though near-namesake Lee Casciaro netted the first competitive goal, in a 6-1 defeat away to Scotland in March 2015. Kyle is a shipping agent, Lee a policeman and captain Roy Chipolina a customs officer.

GEORGIAN STYLE

Georgia became the lowest-ranked side ever to defeat Spain when they inflicted a shock 1-0 defeat in the reigning European champions' last friendly before competing in the 2016 UEFA European Championship finals. Georgia, for whom midfielder Tornike Okriashvili scored the only goal, stood 137th in the FIFA rankings – 131 places below their opponents. Missing that game was defender Zurab Khizanishvili, who, with 92 caps, is second in international appearances for Georgia, behind only 100-cap **Levan Kobiashvili**. The ex-Dinamo Tbilisi, Schalke and Hertha Berlin wing-back Kobiashvili, became president of the Georgian Football Federation in October 2015.

VETERAN VITALIJS

Estonia may have lost their June 2012 friendly against France 4-0 but they did make history that night, becoming the first country to play all 52 fellow UEFA nations. They also previously claimed the record for most-capped European footballer – holding midfielder Martin Reim scored 14 goals in 157 internationals between June 1992 and June 2009. He might have closed in on an unprecedented double century of caps but for missing 40 games between 2004 and 2007 following a dispute with Latvia's Dutch manager Jelle Goes. His European record was passed by Latvia midfielder Vitalijs Astafjevs, who played 167 internationals – including three at the 2004 UEFA European Championship – between his debut in 1992 and his final cap in November 2009 at the age of 38, in a friendly against Honduras. Spain goalkeeper Iker Casillas joined Istafjevs, but both were passed by Italy's No.1 Gianluigi Buffon.

HAIL CESAR

Slovenia were the only team to beat eventual champions Italy on their way to 2006 FIFA World Cup glory, winning an October 2004 qualifier, 1-0, thanks to a goal from Bostjan Cesar – the country's most capped player. His 100th appearance was against Scotland in October 2017, but it was marred by a late red card and he retired after one more game. Cesar starred in Slovenia's only FIFA World Cup appearance in South Africa in 2010. They beat Algeria 1-0, before drawing 2-2 with the United States and losing 1-0 to England.

MOST INTERNATIONAL APPEARANCES

Albania	Lorik Cana	93
Andorra	Ildefons Lima	112
Armenia	Sargis Hovsepyan	132
Austria	Andreas Herzog	103
Azerbaijan	Rashad Sadygov	111
Belarus	Alyaksandr Kulchy	102
Bosnia-Herz.	Emir Spahic	94
Cyprus	Ioannis Okkas	106
Estonia	Martin Reim	157
Faroe Islands	Frodi Benjaminsen	95
Finland	Jari Litmanen	137
Georgia	Levan Kobiashvili	100
Gibraltar	Liam Walker	29
Iceland	Runar Kristinsson	104
Israel	Yossi Benayoun	102
Kazakhstan	Samat Smakov	76
Kosovo	Samir Ujkani	19
Latvia	Vitalijs Astafjevs	167
Liechtenstein	Peter Jehle	132
Lithuania	Andrius Skerla	84
Luxembourg	Mario Mutsch / Jess Strasser	98
Macedonia	Goce Sedloski	100
Malta	Michael Mifsud	131
Moldova	Alexandru Epureanu	85
Montenegro	Elsad Zverotic	61
San Marino	Andy Selva	74
Slovenia	Bostjan Cesar	101

ED BOY

Edin Dzeko became Bosnia-Herzegovina's all-time leading scorer with a second-half hat-trick in an 8-1 2014 FIFA World Cup qualifier victory over Liechtenstein in September 2012. The goals not only took him past previous record-holder Elvir Bolic, but also ahead of Dzeko's international team-mate Zvejdan Misimovic whose brace earlier in the game had briefly put him in the lead. Midfielder Misimovic drew level again with Dzeko in the following game, scoring twice in a 4-1 win, before Dzeko's last-minute strike put him ahead again.

SUPER PAN

Macedonia celebrated 100 years of football in the country with a friendly against future world champions Spain in August 2009 – and striker **Goran Pandev** marked the occasion by becoming his country's all-time leading scorer. His first-half brace gave the hosts a 2-0 lead and although Spain came back to win 3-2, he replaced 16-goal Gorgi Hristov at the top of Macedonia's scoring charts. Pandev has played the majority of his club career in Italy, after signing for Internazionale from local team FK Belasica as an 18-year-old in 2001. Pandev helped Inter win a treble of the UEFA Champions League, Serie A and the Coppa Italia in 2009–10, before scoring in their 2010 FIFA Club World Cup victory.

LAT'S ENTERTAINMENT

The 1938 FIFA World Cup went ahead with 15 instead of 16 teams after qualifiers Austria found themselves annexed by Germany – to the frustration of Latvia, who had finished runners-up in the Austrians' qualification group. Latvia was subsumed by the Soviet Union between 1940 and 1991, but qualified for their first major finals by beating Turkey in a play-off to reach the 2004 UEFA European Championship. Their team at that tournament featured all-time leading scorer 29-goal Maris Verpakovskis, who retired from international football in 2014, and their most-capped player Vitalijs Astafjevs, 167 caps.

BASKET CASE

Captain Rashad Sadygov not only secured Azerbaijan's biggest win in their history when he scored the only goal against Turkey in a UEFA Euro 2012 qualifier in October 2010 – he was also delivering a blow against the country in which he was making his living. Having previously played for Turkish top-flight side Kayserispor, he had since moved on to rivals Eskisehirspor. Not every transfer has worked out well for Sadygov: he missed the transfer deadline when signing for Azeri side PFC Neftchi in 2006, so he decided to play basketball for a season to keep himself fit until allowed to resume football. Sadygov scored the final goal as Azerbaijan equalled their largest victory, beating San Marino 5-1 in a FIFA World Cup qualifier in Baku in September 2017.

MOST INTERNATIONAL GOALS

Albania	Erjon Bogdani	18
Andorra	Ildefonso Lima	11
Armenia	Henrikh Mkhitaryan	25
Austria	Toni Polster	44
Azerbaijan	Gurban Gurbanov	14
Belarus	Maksim Romaschenko	20
Bosnia-Herz.	Edin Dzeko	52
Cyprus	Michalis Konstantinou	32
Estonia	Andres Oper	38
Faroe Islands	Rogvi Jacobsen	10
Finland	Jari Litmanen	32
Georgia	Shota Arveladze	26
Gibraltar	Lee Casciaro / Jake Gosling / Liam Walker	2
Iceland	Eidur Gudjohnsen	26
Israel	Mordechai Spiegler	32
Kazakhstan	Ruslan Baltiev	13
Kosovo	Albert Bunjaku / Elba Rashani	3
Latvia	Maris Verpakovskis	29
Liechtenstein	Mario Frick	16
Lithuania	Tomas Danilevicius	19
Luxembourg	Leon Mart	16
Macedonia	Goran Pandev	31
Malta	Michael Mifsud	40
Moldova	Serghei Clescenco	11
Montenegro	Stevan Jovetic	24
San Marino	Andy Selva	8
Slovenia	Zlatko Zahovic	35

LIVING HAND TO FOOT

The part-time international footballers of the Faroe Islands have a motley collection of day jobs – and other sporting achievements. Bobble hat-wearing goalkeeper Jens Martin Knudsen, man of the match in their shock 1-0 win over Austria in 1989, made his living as a forklift truck driver – while also winning a national gymnastics title and playing handball. Team-mates who have also played both football and handball include Uni Arge and John Petersen. A latter-day Faroes hero emerged in former Newcastle United striker Joan Edmundsson, the only goalscorer in a shock win away to former European champions Greece in a Euro 2016 qualifier in November 2014. The Faroes – under Danish coach Lars Olsen – were ranked 187th in the world; Greece were 18th.

TU-WHIT TWO-NIL

Finland's adopted lucky mascot is an eagle owl called "Bubi" that occasionally swoops down on the Helsinki Olympic Stadium during international matches – making his debut during a 2-0 UEFA European Championship qualifier win over Belgium in June 2007 and holding up the game for several minutes as he flew about the pitch and perched on goalposts. The eagle owl was later voted the Finnish capital's "Resident of the Year".

BOHEMIAN RHAPSODY

Striker **Josef "Pepi" Bican** is, for many Austrian fans, the most prolific goalscorer of all time. Some authorities put his total tally in officially recognized matches at 805 goals, higher in the rankings than Romario, Pele and Gerd Muller. Bican played for Austrian clubs Rapid Vienna and Admira in the 1930s, but the bulk of his strikes came for Czech-based Slavia Prague between 1937 and 1948. He also scored 19 goals in 19 games for Austria from 1933 to 1936, before switching citizenship and hitting 21 in 14 matches for Czechoslovakia between 1938 and 1949. Although he reached the semi-finals of the 1934 FIFA World Cup with Austria, an administrative error meant he was not registered with his new country in time for the 1938 tournament. He also played one international match for a representative Bohemia and Moravia side in 1939, scoring a hat-trick.

ICELAND ICE ENGLAND IN NICE

Iceland not only competed at their first major tournament at the 2016 UEFA European Championship – with a population of 330,000 only 182,000 Tahiti (2013 FIFA Confederations Cup) has been a smaller nation at an international finals – but they also made a major impression both on and off the pitch. Their fans popularized a much-imitated "thunderclap"-style celebration in the stands, as their side not only got out of their group but reached the quarter-finals before losing 5-2 to hosts France. Swedish coach Lars Lagerback, one of two joint managers, was leading a team at a record fourth UEFA European Championship while his colleague – who took sole control after the tournament – was former player and part-time dentist **Heimir Hallgrimsson**. The pair picked an unchanged starting eleven for all five of their games at the tournament, making Iceland the first team to do so in the UEFA European Championship. Experienced centre-back Ragnar Sigurdsson and striker Kolbeinn Sigthorsson scored the goals to clinch the greatest result in Iceland's history: a 2-1 second-round victory over England in Nice. FC Basel midfielder Bikir Bjarnason scored Iceland's first tournament goal, in their opening match, a 1-1 draw with Portugal.

A SEQUEL TO HAMLET

Striker Hamlet Mkhitaryan played twice for post-Soviet state Armenia in 1994, though died two years later from a brain tumour at the age of just 33. His son Henrikh, seven when his father died, has gone on to become the country's all-time leading scorer – and one who often dedicates his achievements to his late parent. The younger Mkhitaryan became Armenia's joint top scorer, alongside Artur Petrosyan, with a goal against Denmark in June 2013. While Petrosyan's goals came in 69 games, Mkhitaryan's 11 were scored in 39 – and he pulled away on his own, with a 12th international strike, in a 2-2 draw with Italy in October 2012. **Henrikh Mkhitaryan** made his Armenia debut in 2007, and his international career overlapped with an unrelated player also named Hamlet Mkhitaryan – a midfielder who won 56 caps between 1994 and 2008. A hat-trick in a national record 7-1 win against Guatemala in May 2016 took Henrikh to 19 international goals and he had extended his total to 25 by the summer of 2018.

RECORD WINS

Albania	5-0	v Vietnam (Italy, February 2003);
	6-1	v Cyprus (H, August 2009)
Andorra	2-0	v Belarus (H, April 2000);
	2-0	v Albania (H, April 2002);
	2-0	v San Marino (A, February 2017)
Armenia	7-1	v Guatemala (USA, May 2016)
Austria	9-0	v Malta (H, April 1977)
Azerbaijan	4-0	v Liechtenstein (H, June 1999)
	5-1	v San Marino (H, September 2017)
Belarus	5-0	v Lithuania (H, June 1998);
	6-1	v Tajikstan (H, September 2014)
Bosnia-Herzegovina	7-0	v Estonia (H, September 2008);
	8-1	v Liechtenstein (A, September 2012)
Cyprus	5-0	v Andorra (H, November 2000);
	5-0	v Andorra (H, November 2014)
Estonia	6-0	v Lithuania (H, July 1928)
	6-0	v Gibraltar (A, October 2017)
Faroe Islands	3-0	v San Marino (H, May 1995)
	4-1	v Gibraltar (A, March 2014)
	3-0	v Liechtenstein (N, March 2018)
Finland	10-2	v Estonia (H, August 1922)
	8-0	v San Marino (H, November 2010)
Georgia	7-0	v Armenia (H, March 1997)
Gibraltar	1-0	v Malta (H, June 2014)
	1-0	v Latvia (H, March 2018)
Iceland	5-0	v Malta (H, July 2000)
Israel	9-0	v Chinese Taipei (A, March 1988)
Kazakhstan	7-0	v Pakistan (H, June 1997)
Kosovo	3-0	v Albania (N, May 2018)
Latvia	6-1	v Lithuania (H, May 1935);
	5-0	v Lithuania (Estonia, June 2012);
	5-0	v Gibraltar (A, March 2016)
Liechtenstein	4-0	v Luxembourg (A, October 2004)
Lithuania	7-0	v Estonia (H, May 1994)
Luxembourg	6-0	v Afghanistan (A, July 1948)
Macedonia	11-1	v Liechtenstein (A, November 1996)
Malta	7-1	v Liechtenstein (H, March 2008)
Moldova	5-0	v Pakistan (A, August 1992)
Montenegro	6-0	v San Marino (A, September 2012)
San Marino	1-0	v Liechtenstein (H, April 2004)
Slovenia	7-0	v Oman (A, February 1999)

RECORD DEFEATS

Albania	0-12	v Hungary (A, September 1950)
Andorra	1-8	v Czech Republic (A, June 2005);
	0-7	v Croatia (A, October 2006)
Armenia	0-7	v Chile (A, January 1997);
	0-7	v Georgia (A, March 1997)
Austria	1-11	v England (H, June 1908)
Azerbaijan	0-10	v France (A, September 1995)
Belarus	0-5	v Austria (A, June 2003)
Bosnia-Herzegovina	0-5	v Argentina (A, May 1998)
Cyprus	0-12	v West Germany (A, May 1969)
Estonia	2-10	v Finland (A, August 1922)
Faroe Islands	0-7	v Yugoslavia (A, May 1991);
	0-7	v Romania (A, May 1992);
	0-7	v Norway (H, August 1993);
	1-8	v Yugoslavia (H, October 1996)
Finland	0-13	v Germany (A, September 1940)
Georgia	0-5	v Romania (A, April 1996);
	1-6	v Denmark (A, September 2005)
Gibraltar	0-9	v Belgium (A, August 2017)
Iceland	2-14	v Denmark (A, August 1967)
Israel	1-7	v Germany (A, February 2002)
Kazakhstan	0-6	v Turkey (H, June 2006);
	0-6	v Russia (A, May 2008)
Kosovo	0-6	v Croatia (H, October 2016)
Latvia	0-12	v Sweden (A, May 1927)
Liechtenstein	1-11	v Macedonia (H, November 1996)
Lithuania	0-10	v Egypt (H, May 1924)
Luxembourg	0-9	v England (H, October 1960);
	0-9	v England (H, December 1982)
Macedonia	0-5	v Belgium (H, June 1995);
	0-5	v Slovakia (H, October 2001);
	0-5	v Hungary (A, November 2001);
	1-6	v Czech Republic (A, June 2005)
Malta	1-12	v Spain (A, December 1983)
Moldova	0-6	v Sweden (A, June 2001)
Montenegro	0-4	v Romania (A, May 2008);
	0-4	v Ukraine (H, June 2013)
San Marino	0-13	v Germany (H, September 2006)
Slovenia	0-5	v France (A, October 2002)

KULCHY COUP

Midfielder Alyaksandr Kulchy became the first player to win 100 caps for Belarus, skippering the side against Lithuania in a June 2012 friendly. He also ended ex-Arsenal and Barcelona playmaker Alexander Hleb's run of four successive Belarus footballer of the year awards by claiming the prize in 2009. Hleb, whose younger brother Vyacheslav has also played for Belarus, had previously won the accolade in 2002 and 2003 as well, only for Belarus's all-time top scorer Maksim Romashenko to take it in 2004.

HAPPY DAYS FOR ILDEFONSO

Andorra's long-serving captain **Ildefonso Lima** had double cause for celebration on 9 June 2017. Not only did he equal Oscar Sonejee's record of 106 international appearances, but also Andorra also beat Hungary 1-0 in a 2018 FIFA World Cup qualifier – only their second ever competitive victory and first in 66 matches. The winning goal came from his central defensive partner Marc Rebes, his first for Andorra in his ninth game. Lima made his debut, and scored, in Andorra's second international, a 4-1 defeat to Estonia, on 22 June 1997, and also played in their only other competitive win, 1-0, against Macedonia in a 2006 FIFA World Cup qualifier, when left-back Marc Bernaus nettted.

BY JOVE

Stevan Jovetic struck seven goals in seven games for Montenegro from September 2016 to June 2017, taking him past strike partner and captain **Mirko Vucinic** as the country's leading scorer with 23. His 2018 FIFA World Cup qualifying hat-trick helped to down Armenia 4-1 in June 2017. Vucinic's 17 goals included a winner against Switzerland in a Euro 2012 qualifier which he celebrated by removing his shorts and wearing them on his head – antics that earned him a yellow card.

XHAKA CLAN

Granit and Taulant Xhaka, both born in Swiss city Basel to Kosovo Albanian parents, became the first brothers to face each other on opposing sides at a UEFA European Championship on 11 June 2016 – midfielder Granit, 23, for Switzerland, 25-year-old defender Taulant for Albania. Granit and Switzerland won 1-0.

SARG'S 20-YEAR SERVICE

Armenia's first international was a goalless draw at home to Moldova on 14 October 1992. In their starting line-up that day was centre-back Sargis Hovsepyan, who went on to win a record 131 caps for the country before his international retirement in November 2012. He was then appointed the Armenian national team's football director.

SOUTH AMERICA

South America was very disappointed that none of its five teams achieved glory at the 2018 FIFA World Cup finals. Brazil and Uruguay went the furthest but "only" to the quarter-finals – repeating the failure in 2006. Nonetheless, many thousands of fans from South America flooded the 11 host cities in Russia, bringing happy and colourful displays of their passion and enthusiasm to the tournament. That love is also fuelling a three-way bid from Uruguay, Argentina and Paraguay to host the centenary World Cup in 2030.

Partying like its 1982 all over again, Peru's fans waited 36 years to see their team in FIFA World Cup action. Tens of thousands of supporters travelled to Russia to watch their heroes and they cheered despite losing to Denmark and France, but a win over Australia sent them into raptures.

ARGENTINA

Copa America champions on 14 occasions, FIFA Confederations Cup winners in 1992, Olympic gold medallists in 2004 and 2008 and, most treasured of all, FIFA World Cup winners in 1978 and 1986: few countries have won as many international titles as Argentina. The country has a long and rich football history (the first Argentine league was contested in 1891) and has produced some of the greatest footballers ever to have played the game.

LONGEST–SERVING MANAGERS

Guillermo Stabile	1939–60
Cesar Luis Menotti	1974–83
Carlos Bilardo	1983–90
Alfio Basile	1990–94
	2006–08
Marcelo Bielsa	1998–2004
Jose Maria Minella	1964–68
Daniel Passarella	1994–98
Manuel Seoane	1934–37
Juan Jose Pizzuti	1969–72
Alejandro Sabella	2011–14

FRINGE PLAYERS

Daniel Passarella was a demanding captain when he led his country to glory at the 1978 FIFA World Cup. He was the same as coach. After taking over the national side in 1994, he refused to pick anyone unless they had their hair cut short – and ordered striker Claudio Caniggia to get rid of his "girl's hair".

WORLD CUP WOES

The last trophy won by Argentina was the Copa America in 1993 and their drought continued at the 2018 FIFA World Cup. They qualified narrowly, needing a Lionel Messi hat-trick against Ecuador in the final round of the qualifying tournament to book their place for Russia, then in a March 2018 friendly against Spain, they suffered their equal-worst defeat – 6-1. In Russia, amid rumours of dressing room rebellion – denied by coach Jorge Sampaoli, who had coached Chile to victory (over Argentina) in the 2015 Copa America – they were held 1-1 by minnows Iceland, with Messi missing a penalty, and lost 3-0 to Croatia. A late winner by **Marcos Rojo**, gave them a 2-1 victory over Nigeria, to book a second round berth but, in the last 16, Argentina lost 4-3 to France having led 2-1, their first FIFA World Cup defeat in 90 minutes after scoring three goals.

MESSI ENDINGS

Argentina reached – and lost a final – for a third consecutive year when Chile won a penalty-shoot-out at the 2016 Copa America Centenario. This final – just as in 2015 when the then hosts Chile took the shoot-out 4-1 – in New Jersey's MetLife Stadium ended goalless after 120 minutes before Chile triumphed 4-2. Argentina had also fallen to Germany in the 2014 FIFA World Cup final. In fact, Argentina last won the Copa America in 1993 and the FIFA World Cup in 1986. Earlier in the 2016 tournament, Lionel Messi's goal in the semi-final win over the United States was his 55th for Argentina and he passed Gabriel Batistuta to top the country's all-time list. But Messi ended the final in despair, after failing in the shoot-out – missing high and wide – then shocked the sport by announcing his international football retirement, aged just 29. He had lost in three finals, in 2007, 2015 and 2016. He was persuaded to reverse his decision six weeks later and scored the only goal of the game in his return, against Uruguay in September 2016.

WORTH WAITING FOR

Argentina's national stadium, **"El Monumental"** in Buenos Aires, hosted its first game in 1938. But the original design was not completed until 20 years later – largely thanks to the £97,000 River Plate received for a transfer fee from Juventus for Omar Sivori. The stadium is a must-see stop on the itinerary of many global football tourists for the "Superclasico" derby between hosts River Plate and city rivals Boca Juniors.

NUMBERS GAME

Argentina's FIFA World Cup squads of 1978 and 1982 were given numbers based on alphabetical order rather than positions, which meant the No. 1 shirt was worn by midfielders Norberto Alonso in 1978 and Osvaldo Ardiles in 1982. The only member of the 1982 squad whose shirt number broke the alphabetical order was No. 10, Diego Maradona.

SECONDS OUT

Argentina have finished Copa America runners-up more times than any other nation, 14, three more than Brazil, most recently in 2015 and 2016. Both these losses came under coach Gerardo Martino, who played once for Argentina in 2001, and had previously led Paraguay to second place at the 2011 Copa America. Martino stepped down in July 2016 and was succeeded as Argentina manager by Edgardo Bauza, who lasted just eight months and eight games – three wins, two draws and three defeats – before being fired in April 2017.

A ROUND DOZEN

Argentina were responsible for the biggest win in Copa America history, when five goals by Jose Manuel Moreno helped them thrash Ecuador 12-0 in 1942. The much-travelled Moreno won domestic league titles in Argentina, Mexico, Chile and Colombia.

YELLOW GOODBYE

Some 20 years before France were forced to wear local Argentine club Atletico Kimberly's kit at the 1978 FIFA World Cup, Argentina themselves faced similar embarrassment for their first-round match against West Germany. The Argentines had neglected to bring along a second kit and a colour-clash with their opponents meant borrowing the yellow shirts of Swedish side IFK Malmo. Despite taking a third-minute lead, Argentina lost 3-1 and departed the tournament bottom of Group A.

THE KIDS ARE ALL RIGHT

Sergio Aguero struck in the final, and ended the tournament as six-goal top scorer, when Argentina won the FIFA World U-20 Championship for a record sixth time in 2007, in Canada, beating the Czech Republic 2-1. Two years later, Aguero married Giannina Maradona – the youngest daughter of Argentina legend Diego – and in February 2009 she gave birth to Diego's first grandchild, Benjamin. Sergio Aguero is widely known by his nickname of "Kun", after a cartoon character he was said to resemble as a child.

BEGINNER'S LUCK

Aged just 27 years and 267 days old, Juan Jose Tramutola became the FIFA World Cup's youngest-ever coach when Argentina opened their 1930 campaign by beating France 1-0. Argentina went on to reach the final, only to lose 4-2 to Uruguay. Top-scorer at the 1930 FIFA World Cup was Argentina's Guillermo Stabile, with eight goals in four games – the only internationals he played. He later won six Copa America titles as his country's longest-serving coach between 1939 and 1960.

GOLDEN GLOW FOR MASCHERANO

Argentina is one of only three countries, alongside France and Brazil, to have won the FIFA World Cup, FIFA Confederations Cup and Olympics Games gold medals. After winning Olympic silver in both 1928 and 1996, they claimed gold in 2004 with Roberto Ayala as captain and Carlos Tevez scoring the only goal against Paraguay in Athens. Four years later in Beijing, Argentina – with Ayala absent and Juan Roman Riquelme as skipper – they won gold again, also 1-0 in the gold medal game, this time over Nigeria, who had beaten them to gold in 1996. Angel Di Maria scored the only goal to beat Nigeria. Defensive midfielder **Javier Mascherano** was part of the 2004 and 2008 teams, making him the first man to win two Olympic football gold medals since 1928 and only the second Argentine sportsman after polo player Juan Nelson. Mascherano retired as Argentina's most-capped player – with 147 – hours after Argentina's dramatic 4-3 loss to France in the second round of the 2018 FIFA World Cup.

ARGENTINA'S RECORD

FIFA WORLD CUP	17 appearances
Matches (81)	W43, D15, L23, GF137, GA93
Winners (2)	1978, 1986
Runners-up (3)	1930, 1990, 2014
Quarter-finals/ Second Round (6)	1966, 1974, 1982, 1998, 2006, 2010
Round of 16 (2)	1994, 2018
First round/Group (4)	1938, 1958, 1962, 2002

COPA AMERICA	41 appearances
Winners (14)	1921, 1925, 1927, 1929, 1937, 1941, 1945, 1946, 1947, 1955, 1957, 1959, 1991, 1993

CONFEDERATIONS CUP	3 appearances
Winners (1)	1992
Runners-up (2)	1995, 2005

OLYMPIC GAMES	8 appearances
Gold medal (2)	2004, 2008
Silver medal (2)	1928, 1996

FIRST INTERNATIONAL	Uruguay 2, Argentina 3, Montevideo, 16 May 1901
BIGGEST WIN	Argentina 12 Ecuador 0, Montevideo (Uruguay), 22 January 1942
HEAVIEST DEFEAT	Czechoslovakia 6 Argentina 1, Helsingborg (Sweden), 15 June 1958 Argentina 0, Colombia 5, Buenos Aires, 5 September 1993 Bolivia 6 Argentina 1, La Paz, 1 April 2009 Spain 6 Argentina 1, Madrid, 27 March 2018

RIGHT ANGEL

Winger **Angel Di Maria** scored the only goal to give Argentina their first Olympic Games football gold medal, beating Nigeria at Beijing in 2008. The match was played in such heat that officials allowed both sides occasional water breaks. Di Maria is much travelled. He was playing in Portugal for Benfica in 2008, having joined Rosario Central in his homeland aged just four. Di Maria later played for Spain's Real Madrid – he was voted man of the match when they won the 2013 UEFA Champions League final against Atletico Madrid – before big-money moves to Manchester United in England and French club Paris Saint-Germain. He was a star performer on Argentina's run to the 2014 FIFA World Cup final – scoring a late winner in the second round against Switzerland and setting up Gonzalo Higuain's quarter-final decider against Belgium – until a muscle tear ruled him out of the semi-final and final. His second FIFA World Cup goal was a spectacular strike from outside the area to level the score at 1-1 in a second-round game against France in Kazan in 2018, but Argentina went down to a 4-3 defeat.

SPOT-KICK FLOP

If at first you don't succeed, try and try again – unfortunately Martin Palermo missed all three penalties he took during Argentina's 1999 Copa America clash with Colombia. The first hit the crossbar, the second flew over the bar and the third was saved. Colombia won the match 3-0.

WINNING TOUCH

Midfielder Marcelo Trobbiani played just two minutes of FIFA World Cup football – the last two minutes of the 1986 final, after replacing winning goalscorer Jorge Burruchaga. Trobbiani touched the ball once, a backheel. The former Boca star ended his international career with 15 caps and one goal to his name.

TOP SCORERS

1	Lionel Messi	65
2	Gabriel Batistuta	54
3	Sergio Aguero	39
4	Hernan Crespo	35
5	Diego Maradona	34
6	Gonzalo Higuain	32
7	Luis Artime	24
8	Leopoldo Luque	22
=	Daniel Passarella	22
10	Herminio Masantonio	21
=	Jose Sanfilippo	21

SECOND TIME LUCKY

Luisito Monti is the only man to play in the FIFA World Cup final for two different countries. The centre-half, born in Buenos Aires on 15 May 1901 but with Italian family origins, was highly influential in Argentina's run to the 1930 final. They lost the game 4-2 to Uruguay – after Monti allegedly received mysterious pre-match death threats. Following a transfer to Juventus the following year, he was allowed to play for Italy and was on the winning side when the *Azzurri* beat Czechoslovakia in the 1934 final. Another member of the 1934 team was Raimundo Orsi, who had also played for Argentina before switching countries in 1929.

DIVINE DIEGO

To many people **Diego Armando Maradona** is the greatest footballer the world has ever seen, better even than Pele. The Argentinian legend, born in Lanus on 30 October 1960, first became famous as a ball-juggling child during half-time intervals at Argentinos Juniors matches. He was distraught to be left out of Argentina's 1978 FIFA World Cup squad and was then sent off for retaliation at the 1982 tournament. Maradona, as triumphant Argentina captain in Mexico in 1986, scored the notorious "Hand of God" goal and then a spectacular individual strike within five minutes of each other in a quarter-final win over England. He again captained Argentina to the final in 1990, in Italy – the country where he inspired Napoli to Serie A and UEFA Cup success. He was thrown out of the 1994 FIFA World Cup finals in disgrace after failing a drugs test. Maradona captained Argentina 16 times in FIFA World Cup matches, a record, and was surprisingly appointed national coach in 2008, despite scant previous experience as a manager.

FITTER, JAVIER

Only Javier Mascherano has won more caps for Argentina than **Javier Zanetti**, who made 143 international appearances – despite being surprisingly left out of squads for both the 2006 and 2010 FIFA World Cups. Zanetti, who played at full-back or in midfield, also played more Serie A matches than any other non-Italian – and all for Internazionale of Milan, with whom he won the treble of Italian league, Italian Cup and UEFA Champions League in 2009–10. Despite those achievements, he and Inter team-mate Esteban Cambiasso failed to make Diego Maradona's squad for the 2010 FIFA World Cup – but Zanetti returned to the fold under Maradona's successor Sergio Batista and captained his country at the 2011 Copa America. Zanetti made his 600th appearance in Italy's Serie A in March 2013 and retired from club football, aged 40, in 2014.

THE ANGEL GABRIEL

Gabriel Batistuta, nicknamed "Batigol", is the only man to have scored hat-tricks in two separate FIFA World Cups. Argentina's former all-time leading goalscorer grabbed the first against Greece in 1994 and the second against Jamaica four years later. Hungary's Sandor Kocsis, France's Just Fontaine and Germany's Gerd Muller each scored two hat-tricks in the same FIFA World Cup. Batistuta, born in Reconquista on 1 February 1969, also set an Italian league record by scoring in 11 consecutive Serie A matches for his club Fiorentina at the start of the 1994–95 season.

SUPER MARIO

Mario Kempes, who scored twice in the 1978 FIFA World Cup final and won the Golden Boot, was the only member of Cesar Menotti's squad from a foreign club. Playing for Valencia, he had been the Spanish league's top scorer for the previous two seasons.

LEO BRAVO

Lionel Messi became only the second substitute to hit a Copa America hat-trick when he came off the bench to score three times in 19 minutes in Argentina's 5-0 victory over Panama in the opening round of the 2016 Copa America Centenario. Before then, only Paulo Valentim had done so, for Brazil in 1959 as they beat Uruguay 3-1, before ultimately finishing runners-up to Argentina. This was just the latest in a long line of feats achieved by Messi, who – rather less gloriously – had been sent off just two minutes into his national debut, against Hungary in August 2005 after coming on as a substitute. He went on to become his Argentina's all-time record goalscorer, youngest FIFA World Cup scorer (against Serbia and Montenegro in 2006, aged 19), their youngest captain (at 23 years old during the 2010 FIFA World Cup) and winner of the Golden Ball for best player at the 2014 FIFA World Cup, where his four Man of the Match awards were a record for one tournament.

TOP CAPS

1	Javier Mascherano	147
2	Javier Zanetti	143
3	Lionel Messi	128
4	Roberto Ayala	114
5	Diego Simeone	104
6	Angel Di María	97
=	Oscar Ruggeri	97
8	Sergio Romero	94
9	Diego Maradona	91
10	Sergio Aguero	89

HERO ROMERO

No man has kept goal for Argentina more than **Sergio Romero**. He won an Olympic Games gold medal in 2008 but had to wait until September 2009 for his senior international debut against Paraguay. Romero, who had won 94 caps by summer 2018, was ever-present for Argentina at both the 2010 and 2014 FIFA World Cups, helping them reach the 2014 final with two saves in a semi-final penalty shoot-out victory over the Netherlands. The 1-0 final defeat to Germany denied him the FIFA World Cup winner's medal earned by compatriot 'keepers Ubaldo Fillol (58 caps) in 1978 and Nery Pumpido (36) eight years later. Still the first-choice goalkeeper, Romero missed the 2018 FIFA World Cup after injuring his knee the day after the squad was announced.

BRAZIL

No country has captured the soul of the game to the same extent as Brazil. The country's distinctive yellow-shirted players have thrilled generations of football fans and produced some of the game's greatest moments. No FIFA World Cup tournament would be the same without Brazil – the nation that gave birth to Pele, Garrincha, Zico, Ronaldo and Kaka. The only nation to appear in every FIFA World Cup finals and competition winners a record five times, Brazil's widely-admired hosting of the 2014 tournament did not end with the sixth triumph they craved.

EARLY ARRIVAL ... AND DEPARTURE

Brazil became the first country outside host nation Russia to secure a place at the 2018 FIFA World Cup, after just 14 of South American federation CONMEBOL's scheduled 18 qualification rounds as they beat Paraguay 3-0 on 28 March 2017. They had been sixth of ten South American nations in the group when Tite took over as manager in summer 2016 but he led them to eight consecutive victories and comfortable qualification. Yet despite high hopes for the 2018 tournament – and surpassing Germany as the FIFA World Cup's all-time highest scorers, with 229 goals – they bowed out 2-1 to Belgium in the quarter-finals.

TAKING AIM WITH NEYMAR

Brazil's triumph in the 2013 FIFA Confederations Cup, a record third in a row, was consolation for "only" a silver medal at the London 2012 Olympic Games. **Neymar** scored three goals at London 2012, and later was voted South American Footballer of the Year for the second successive year and then, in 2013, was named player of the FIFA Confederations Cup. Those were his last matches as a Santos player before he joined Spanish giants Barcelona. He was Brazil's undoubted star at the 2014 FIFA World Cup, with four goals in four games before being injured in the quarter-final win against Colombia. Neymar missed the 2016 Copa America Centenario to play in the 2016 Rio Olympic Games. He scored in the final at the Maracana and took the winning penalty as Brazil finally won Olympic gold. In summer 2017, Neymar became the world's most expensive footballer – his fee was £198m – leaving Barcelona for France's Paris Saint-Germain. He scored twice at the 2018 FIFA World Cup, in victories over Costa Rica in the first round and Mexico in the second.

CLOSE ENCOUNTERS

Brazil have been involved in many memorable games. Their 3-2 defeat to Italy in 1982 is regarded as one of the classic games in FIFA World Cup finals history. Paolo Rossi scored all three of Italy's goals with Brazil coach Tele Santana much criticized for going all out in attack when only a 2-2 draw was needed. Brazil's 1982 squad, with players such as **Socrates**, **Zico** and Falcao, is considered one of the greatest teams never to win the tournament. In 1994, a 3-2 win over the Netherlands in the quarter-finals – their first competitive meeting in 20 years – was just as thrilling, with all the goals coming in the second half. Socrates – a qualified medical doctor, as well as elder brother to 1994 FIFA World Cup-winner Rai – was mourned across the globe when he died at the age of 57 in December 2011.

BRAZIL'S RECORD

FIFA WORLD CUP	21 appearances (every finals)
Matches (109)	W73, D18, L18, GF229, GA105
Winners (5)	1958, 1962, 1970, 1994, 2002
Runners-up (2)	1950, 1998
Third place (2)	1938, 1978
Fourth place (2)	1974, 2014
COPA AMERICA	35 appearances
Winners (8)	1919, 1922, 1949, 1989,
	1997, 1999, 2004, 2007
CONFEDERATIONS CUP	7 appearances
Winners (4)	1997, 2005, 2009, 2013
FIRST INTERNATIONAL	Argentina 3 Brazil 0
	(Buenos Aires, 20 September 1914)
BIGGEST WIN	Brazil 10 Bolivia 1 (Sao Paulo,
	10 April 1949)
HEAVIEST DEFEAT	Uruguay 6 Brazil 0 (Vina del
	Mar, Chile, 18 September 1920)
	Brazil 1 Germany 7
	(Belo Horizonte, 8 July 2014)

TOP OF THE FLOPS

Brazil's dreams of winning a sixth FIFA World Cup, but first on home soil, became a nightmare in 2014 – 64 years on from the trauma caused by Uruguay's surprise triumph at Rio de Janeiro's Maracana stadium. Luiz Felipe Scolari's 2014 vintage set a series of unenviable records as they crashed out, 7-1 to Germany, in the semi-final in Belo Horizonte. This was not only Brazil's heaviest FIFA World Cup defeat, but also the biggest any semi-finalist had ever suffered. It equalled the 6-0 trouncing by Uruguay at the 1920 Copa America as Brazil's worst defeat of all-time. Finally, it was Brazil's first home loss in a competitive international since Peru beat them 3-1 – also in Belo Horizonte – in a 1975 Copa America semi-final. A 3-0 setback against the Netherlands in the third-place play-off meant Brazil lost consecutive internationals at home for the first time since 1940, when Argentina, 3-0, and Uruguay 4-3, were victorious. The 14 goals Brazil conceded was their worst ever in a FIFA World Cup, three worse than in 1938, and they became the first FIFA World Cup hosts to concede the most goals in a tournament. Not only did Neymar miss the Germany game through injury, but centre-back and captain **Thiago Silva** was absent suspended.

LAND OF FOOTBALL

No country is more deeply identified with football success than Brazil, who have won the FIFA World Cup a record five times – in 1958, 1962, 1970, 1994 and 2002. They are also the only team never to have missed a FIFA World Cup finals and are favourites virtually every time the competition is staged. After winning the trophy for a third time in Mexico in 1970, Brazil kept the **Jules Rimet Trophy** permanently. Sadly, it was stolen from the federation's headquarters in 1983 and was never recovered. Brazilians often refer to their country as "o país do futebol" ("the country of football"). It is the favourite pastime of youngsters, while general elections are often held in the same year as the FIFA World Cup, with critics arguing that political parties try to take advantage of the nationalistic surge created by football and bring it into politics. Charles Miller, the son of a Scottish engineer, is credited with bringing football to Brazil in 1894. Yet the sport would only truly become Brazilian when blacks were able to play at the top level in 1933. At first, because of the game's European origin, it was the sport of Brazil's urban white elite. However, it quickly spread among the urban poor as Brazilians realized the only thing they needed to play was a ball, which could be substituted inexpensively with a bundle of socks, an orange, or even a cloth filled with paper.

CAPTAIN TO COACH

Brazil's 1994 FIFA World Cup-winning captain **Dunga** – real name Carlos Caetano Bledorn Verri – was appointed national coach in 2006, despite having no previous management experience, for the first of two separate spells in charge of his country. He led the team to 2007 Copa America and 2009 FIFA Confederations Cup successes before losing his job when Brazil departed the 2010 FIFA World Cup in the quarter-finals against the Netherlands. He returned four years later, but was sacked after Brazil failed to get past the first round for only the second time in Copa America history. Dunga had been on the bench both times – as an unused substitute in 1987 and as manager in 2016. Replacing him as national coach after the embarrassing 2016 exit was former Corinthians manager Adenor Leonardo Bacchi, better known as Tite.

EYE FOR GOAL

Centre-forward **Tostao** – full name Eduardo Goncalves de Andrade – was one of the stars of Brazil's legendary 1970 FIFA World Cup-winning team but almost did not make the tournament. He had suffered a detached retina when hit in the face by a football the previous year, prompting some doctors' warnings that he should be left out. Tostao eventually retired at the age of 26 in 1973, after another eye injury, and went to work as a doctor instead. His 1970 team-mate Pele also experienced failing eyesight.

TOP CAPS

1	Cafu	142
2	Roberto Carlos	125
3	Dani Alves	107
4	Lucio	105
5	Claudio Taffarel	101
6	Robinho	100
7	Djalma Santos	98
=	Ronaldo	98
9	Ronaldinho	97
10	Gilmar	94

TOP SCORERS

1	Pele	77
2	Ronaldo	62
3	Neymar	57
4	Romario	55
5	Zico	48
6	Bebeto	39
7	Rivaldo	35
8	Jairzinho	33
=	Ronaldinho	33
10	Ademir	32
=	Tostao	32

JOY OF THE PEOPLE

Garrincha, one of Brazil's greatest legends, was really Manuel Francisco dos Santos at birth but his nickname meant 'Little Bird' – inspired by his slender, bent legs. Despite the legacy of childhood illness, he was a star right-winger at Botafogo from 1953 to 1965. He and Pele were explosively decisive newcomers for Brazil at the 1958 FIFA World Cup finals. In 1962 Garrincha was voted player of the tournament four years later. He died in January 1983 at just 49. His epitaph was the title often bestowed on him in life: "The Joy of the People."

THE KING

Pele is considered by many as the greatest player of all time, a sporting icon *par excellence* and not only for his exploits on the pitch. When, for instance, he scored his 1,000th goal, Pele dedicated it to the poor children of Brazil. He began playing for Santos at the age of 15 and won his first FIFA World Cup two years later, scoring twice in the final. Despite numerous offers from European clubs, the economic conditions and Brazilian football regulations at the time allowed Santos to keep hold of their prized asset for almost two decades, until 1974. All-time leading scorer of the Brazilian national team, he is the only footballer to be a member of three FIFA World Cup-winning teams. Despite being in the Brazilian squad at the start of the 1962 tournament, an injury suffered in the second match meant he was not able to play on and, initially, he missed out on a winner's medal. However, FIFA announced in November 2007 that he would be awarded a medal retrospectively. After the disastrous 1966 tournament, when Brazil fell in the first round, Pele said he did not wish to play in the FIFA World Cup again. He was finally talked round and ended up, in 1970, playing a key role in what is widely considered as one of the greatest sides ever. Since his retirement in 1977, Pele has been a worldwide ambassador for football, as well undertaking various acting roles and commercial ventures.

PARTY ANIMAL

Brazil's captain when they played Argentina (twice), Costa Rica and Mexico in autumn 2011 was a man many had not even expected to be in the international side again – former two-time FIFA World Footballer of the Year, Ronaldinho. Having amazed the world with his fancy footwork and prolific goalscoring for Paris Saint-Germain in France, Barcelona in Spain and AC Milan in Italy, he returned to his homeland with Flamengo in 2011 – but was widely accused of being more interested in partying than playing. But a return to form won him a recall under Mano Menezes. That appearance against Mexico took him to 33 goals, level with 1970 FIFA World Cup winner Jairzinho, then his next match – his 94th for Brazil – equalled the caps tally of 1958 and 1962 FIFA World Cup champion goalkeeper Gilmar. Ronaldinho himself became a FIFA World Cup winner in 2002, aged 22, when his long-range goal against England gave Brazil victory in the quarter-finals – though he was sent off seven minutes later and had to sit out the semi-final, before returning for the final.

WHITHER RONALDO?

Only one person knows exactly what happened to **Ronaldo** in the hours before the 1998 FIFA World Cup final – the man himself. He sparked one of the biggest mysteries in FIFA World Cup history when his name was left off the teamsheet before the game, only for it to reappear just in time for kick-off. It was initially reported that Ronaldo had an ankle injury, and then a upset stomach. Finally team doctor Lidio Toledo revealed the striker had been rushed to hospital after suffering a convulsion in his sleep, but that he had been cleared to play after neurological and cardiac tests. The most dramatic account came from Ronaldo's roommate Roberto Carlos. "Ronaldo was scared about what lay ahead. The pressure had got to him and he couldn't stop crying," said the legendary full-back. "At about four o'clock, he became ill. That's when I called the team doctor and told him to get over to our room as fast as he could."

COUTINHO'S SHOOTING BOOTS

Brazil's first two goals at the 2018 FIFA World Cup were scored not by star striker and captain Neymar but by **Philippe Coutinho**, seen by many as Neymar's replacement at Barcelona after joining for £135m from Liverpool in January that year – six months after Neymar's had gone to Paris Saint-Germain. Coutinho's goals came in a 1-1 draw with Switzerland and 2-0 victory over Costa Rica, in the latter game opening the scoring as the game went into stoppage-time. Coutinho had previously scored a hat-trick for Brazil when they beat Haiti 7-1 at the 2016 Copa America Centenario, his country's 54th international treble. Paulinho scored the 55th, in a 4-1 away win against Uruguay in March 2017. Pele leads the way with seven hat-tricks, followed by Zico on five – but only one-time Flamengo and Barcelona centre-forward Evaristo de Macedo has scored five goals in one game for Brazil, against Colombia in March 1957.

INAUSPICIOUS START

Left-back/left-winger **Marcelo** achieved the dubious "honour" of being the first player to score the opening goal of a FIFA World Cup finals in his own net. He inadvertently gave Croatia the lead in the 2014 tournament's curtain-raiser in Sao Paulo, but Brazil did come back to win 3-1, thanks to a pair of goals from Neymar and one from Oscar. Marcelo, who a couple of weeks earlier had scored for his club, Real Madrid, as they won the UEFA Champions League final, also became the first Brazil player ever to score past his own goalkeeper in the FIFA World Cup finals. Four years later, in Russia, midfielder Fernandinho scored Brazil's second FIFA World Cup own goal in their 2-1 quarter-final defeat to Belgium.

BRAZIL'S YOUNGEST PLAYERS

1 Pele, 16 years and 257 days
   (v Argentina, 7 July 1958)
2 Ronaldo, 17 years and 182 days
   (v Argentina, 24 March 1994)
3 Adriano, 17 years and 272 days
   (v Australia, 17 November 1999)
4 Toninho, 17 years and 343 days
   (v Uruguay, 28 April 1976)
5 Carvalho Leite, 18 years and 26 days
   (v Bolivia, 22 July 1930)
6 Diego, 18 years and 60 days
   (v Mexico, 30 April 2003)
7 Marcelo, 18 years and 115 days
   (v Wales, 5 September 2006)
8 Philippe Coutinho, 18 years and 116 days (v Iran, 7 October 2010)
9 Doria, 18 years and 149 days
   (v Bolivia, 6 April 2013)
10 Neymar, 18 years and 186 days
   (v USA, 10 August 2010)

ROLLING RIVA

Brazilian legend Rivaldo played into his 40s – a decade after the highlight of his career, helping Brazil win the 2002 FIFA World Cup. He scored 34 goals in 74 matches for his country between 1993 and 2003, including three goals at the 1998 FIFA World Cup and five more in Japan and South Korea four years later. His 2002 FIFA World Cup was marred only by blatant play-acting that helped get Turkey's Hakan Unsal sent off and earned Rivaldo a fine. Rivaldo – full name Rivaldo Vitor Borba Ferreira – became one of the world's finest footballers despite suffering malnourishment in a poverty-stricken childhood. His individual achievements including FIFA World Footballer of the Year and European Footballer of the Year prizes in 1999 while playing in Spain for Barcelona. His later clubs included AC Milan in Italy, Olympiacos and AEK Athens in Greece, Bunyodkor in Uzbekistan and Kabuscorp in Angola before he returned home to Brazil where he played for Sao Caetano in 2013 and Mogi Mirim in 2014–15 before retiring aged 43 in August 2015.

WORLD-BEATING SAINTS

Right-back **Djalma Santos** is one of only two players to be voted into the official all-star team of a FIFA World Cup on three different occasions. He was honoured for his performances at the 1954, 1958 and 1962 finals – even though his only appearance in 1958 was in the final. West Germany's Franz Beckenbauer was the other, chosen in 1966, 1970 and 1974. On the opposite flank to Djalma Santos was the left-back Nilton Santos – no relation – who also played in 1954, 1958 and 1962 and had also been a member of Brazil's runners-up squad on home turf in 1950.

SILVA VALUE

Brazil qualified from the first round of a FIFA World Cup for the 13th time running at Russia in 2018. They clinched top place in Group E by winning their third game 2-0 against Serbia – with their second goal scored by veteran centre-back **Thiago Silva**, from a corner by Neymar. Silva's previous FIFA World Cup goal, in a quarter-final victory over Colombia in 2014, was also set up by a Neymar corner. Silva won Olympic Games bronze with Brazil at Beijing in 2008 and silver at London 2012. He was Brazil's captain when they won the 2013 FIFA Confederations Cup triumph on home soil.

YELLOW FEVER

The world-renowned yellow and blue kit now worn by Brazil was not adopted until 1954, as a replacement for their former all-white strip. The *Correio da Manha* newspaper organised a design competition which was won by 19-year-old Aldyr Garcia Schlee and the new colours were worn for the first time in March 1954 against Chile. Schlee was from Pelotas, close to Brazil's border with Uruguay and actually supported Uruguayan sides against Brazil.

THE OLD RIVALS: BRAZIL V ARGENTINA

Matches played: 104
Brazil wins: 40
Argentina wins: 38
Draws: 26
Brazil goals: 162
Argentina goals: 160
First match: Argentina 3 Brazil 0 (20 September 1914)
Latest match: Brazil 0 Argentina 1 (9 June 2017, Melbourne)
Biggest Brazil win: Brazil 6 Argentina 2 (20 December 1945)
Biggest Argentina win: Argentina 6 Brazil 1 (5 March 1940)

GRAND ACHIEVEMENT

Brazil played their 1,000th match on 14 November 2012, with Neymar's second-half equaliser securing a 1-1 draw against Colombia in New Jersey, United States. Brazil's first match is considered generally to have been a 2-0 victory over visiting English club Exeter City on 21 July 1914, at the Estadio das Laranjeiras in Rio – still used by Fluminense. Brazil won that day despite star striker **Arthur Friedenreich** losing two teeth in a collision. Brazil's first international against another country was a 3-0 defeat to Argentina on 20 September 1914.

BRAZIL'S 2014 WORLD CUP STADIA

1. Maracana, Rio de Janeiro (76,804)
2. Brasilia, Estadio Nacional Mane Garrincha (70,064)
3. Mineirao, Belo Horizonte (62,547, Atletico Mineiro and Cruzeiro)
4. Arena Corinthians, Sao Paulo (65,807)
5. Estadio Castelao, Fortaleza (64,846)
6. Estadio Beira-Rio, Porto Alegre (48,849)
7. Arena Fonte Neva, Salvador (48,747)
8. Arena Pernambuco, Recife (46,000)
9. Arena Pantanal, Cuiaba (42,968)
10. Arena da Amazonia, Manaus (42,374)
11. Arena das Dunas, Natal (42,086)
12. Arena da Baixaba, Curitiba (41,456)

BRAZIL HAVE HAD THEIR PHIL

The return of "Big Phil" **Luiz Felipe Scolari** as Brazil coach in November 2012 was meant to culminate, in 2014, with a repeat of his success spearheading the country to triumph at the 2002 FIFA World Cup. Yet although his second reign did bring glory at the 2013 FIFA Confederations Cup, the following year's FIFA World Cup on home turf will be remembered for the many unwanted records his team set and the embarrassment with which their efforts ended – most notably, the 7-1 defeat by Germany in their Belo Horizonte semi-final. Scolari was relieved of his role just days after a 3-0 defeat to the Netherlands in the third-place play-off. However, the tournament gave him a second fourth-place finish, achieving that mark as Portugal boss in 2006, and he became the first coach to be in charge in three different FIFA World Cup semi-finals.

ROM NUMBERS

Brazilian goal poacher supreme **Romario** is one of the few footballers to claim more than 1,000 career goals. He is also the last man to win both the FIFA World Cup and the Golden Ball award as the best player at the same tournament, something he achieved in 1994 when his five goals – including the semi-final winner against Sweden – helped Brazil to their fourth title. The former Barcelona and Fluminense forward moved into politics after retiring from playing to become elected as an MP, as did his 1994 FIFA World Cup strike partner Bebeto. The pair had not only teamed up as twin peaks of the Brazilian attack that summer, but also memorably celebrated a goal against the Netherlands in the quarter-finals with a much-imitated "cradling the baby" dance – it marked the birth of Bebeto's son Matheus, who would later become a professional footballer himself.

LETTING LUCIO

Elegant centre-back **Lucio** set a FIFA World Cup record during the 2006 tournament by playing for 386 minutes without conceding a foul – only ending in Brazil's 1-0 quarter-final defeat to France. While mostly noted for leadership and control at the back, he also had an eye for goal – heading the late winner that gave Brazil a 3-2 triumph over the USA in the 2009 FIFA Confederations Cup final. The following year he was part of Italian club Internazionale's treble success, clinching the Italian league and cup as well as the UEFA Champions League.

SUPER-POWERS' POWER CUT

There was a new addition to the annual international calendar in 2011: the Superclasico de los Americas, a two-legged event between Brazil and Argentina. Brazil were the first winners, thanks to a goalless draw followed by a 2-0 win. They dramatically retained the crown in 2012. Brazil won the first leg at home, 2-1, but the return game in Chaco was postponed after a power cut – possibly because Brazil's team bus hit an electricity trailer. The rearranged game ended 2-1 to Argentina, but Brazil won 4-3 on penalties, their goal being scored by Fred, while strike partner Neymar netted the winning spot-kick. For Brazil's coach Mano Menezes, however, his "reward" was the sack. There was no Superclasico in 2013 before a one-off match played in the Chinese capital Beijing in October 2014 ended 2-0 to Brazil, thanks to a brace by Diego Tardelli. After two matches in the 2018 FIFA World Cup qualifiers – Brazil won 3-0 at home and drew 1-1 away – they met in a friendly in Melbourne, Australia, in June 2017.

CHILE

Chile were one of four founding members of CONMEBOL, South America's football confederation, in 1916. They played in the first match at a South American football championship – losing the opener of the unofficial 1910 tournament 3-0 to Uruguay – and they played in the first official Copa America, in 1916. Their greatest glories were hosting and finishing third at the 1962 FIFA World Cup and winning their first two Copa America titles in 2015 and 2016. Yet, oddly, they missed out on the 2018 FIFA World Cup finals.

DEJA VU

You wait 99 years for a first Copa America triumph – and then a second comes around 12 months later. Just as they did in 2015, Chile beat Argentina on penalties in the final of the Copa America – the later version named the Copa America Centenario and held as a special one-off – in the USA – to mark the 100th anniversary of the inaugural tournament. In 2016, Chile were managed by Argentina-born former Spain international Juan Antonio Pizzi, who had succeeded Jorge Sampaoli five months earlier. After a goalless draw – just as in 2015 – Chile prevailed in a shoot-out, this time 4-2 rather than 4-1, in New Jersey's MetLife Stadium, the winning kick delivered by defensive midfielder Francisco Silva.

VIDAL ESCAPES TO VICTORY

Hosts Chile's 2015 Copa America campaign nearly careered off the road, literally. Star midfielder **Arturo Vidal** crashed his red Ferrari after over-enjoying a night out, having scored twice in a 3–3 draw with Mexico. Coach Jorge Sampaoli resisted public pressure to drop him for the deciding match of the group after Vidal promised to donate his tournament fee to charity and a 5-0 thrashing of Bolivia – he grabbed another double – sealed Chile's quarter-final place. Vidal was named Man of the Match in the final and was selected for the 2015 Copa America team of the tournament. He was again crucial in the 2016 Copa America Centenario, and was again named in the team of tournament.

ALL-GO IN SANTIAGO AT LAST

Having taken part in the first Copa America in 1916, Chile ended their 99-year wait to first lift the trophy by triumphing as hosts in summer 2015. They defeated Argentina 4-1 on penalties in the final following a goalless draw after extra-time in Santiago's Estadio Nacional. Forward Eduardo Vargas shared the Golden Boot prize with Peru's Paolo Guerrero after scoring four goals – two of them in Chile's 2-1 defeat of Peru in the semi-final – while captain **Claudio Bravo** was named best goalkeeper.

HAPPY SAMP

Chile had never reached the knock-out stages of consecutive FIFA World Cups until their 2014 vintage in Brazil emulated the achievement of the 2010 squad. And both times they had coaches from Argentina: Marcelo Bielsa was in charge in 2010 and **Jorge Sampaoli** four years later – and another compatriot, Claudio Borghi, served a spell in between. Sampaoli retired from playing aged 19, because of tibia and fibula injuries, and devoted himself to a coaching career that took in Peru and Ecuador before he took the Chilean hotseat in 2012.

CONFED UP

Chile made their FIFA Confederations Cup debut in 2017 and reached the final, after beating European champions Portugal 3-0 in a penalty shoot-out after a goalless draw in the semi-final. Goalkeeper and captain Claudio Bravo saved from Ricardo Quaresma, Joao Moutinho and Nani, while Arturo Vidal, **Charles Aranguiz** and Alexis Sanchez all found the net for Chile. Although world champions Germany won the final 1-0, Bravo collected the Golden Glove award as the tournament's best goalkeeper, and Sanchez claimed the Silver Ball as second best player, behind Germany's Julian Draxler. Chile and Germany also drew 1-1 in the first round, when Sanchez's goal put him alone at the top of his country's all-time scorers chart.

BRAVO, BEAUSEJOUR

Chile went precisely 48 years between victories at a FIFA World Cup, from a 1-0 third-place play-off success against Yugoslavia on 16 June 1962 to a first-round victory by the same scoreline over Honduras on 16 June 2010. That long-awaited winner in South Africa came from **Jean Beausejour**, who then hit Chile's third in their opening-game 3-1 triumph over Australia in Brazil four years later. It meant he became the first Chilean player ever to score at more than one FIFA World Cup. Goalkeeper and captain at both tournaments was Claudio Bravo, Chile's most-capped player.

ROCKET FOR ROJAS

Chile were banned from the 1994 FIFA World Cup after an infamous incident involving their goalkeeper Roberto Rojas in September 1989. Chile needed to win against Brazil to have any hope of reaching the 1990 FIFA World Cup but were 1-0 down when, in the 70th minute, a flare was thrown by Brazilian supporters in Rio's Maracana Stadium, and Rojas collapsed to the ground. His team-mates refused to play on and left the pitch, but video footage later revealed he was play-acting – the flare had fallen several feet away. Rojas, who played for Brazilian club Sao Paulo, ultimately confessed to injuring himself with a hidden razorblade. Brazil were awarded the game 2-0, Chile were prevented from taking part in qualifiers for the 1994 tournament, captain Fernando Astengo was suspended for three years and Rojas was banned from football for life – although it was lifted in 2001, and he spent seven months as Sao Paulo manager in 2003.

CHILE'S RECORD

FIFA WORLD CUP 9 appearances

Matches (33)	W11, D7, L15, GF40, GA49
Third place (1)	1962
Round of 16 (3)	1998, 2010, 2014
First round (5)	1930, 1950, 1966, 1974, 1982

COPA AMERICA 37 appearances

Winners (2)	2015, 2016

CONFEDERATIONS CUP 1 appearance

FIRST INTERNATIONAL Argentina 3 Chile 1
(Buenos Aires, 27 May 1910)

BIGGEST WINS
Chile 7 Venuezela 0
Santiago, 29 August 1979
Chile 7 Armenia 0
Vina del Mar, 4 January 1997
Chile 7 Mexico 0
Santa Clara (USA), 18 June 2016

HEAVIEST DEFEAT
Brazil 7 Chile 0
Rio de Janeiro, 17 September 1959

VARGAS LEADS RECORD CHASE

Eduardo Vargas scored four times as Chile matched their record win – and their biggest in a competitive match – by beating Mexico 7-0 in their June 2016 quarter-final at that summer's Copa America Centenario. Edson Puch added a brace and Alexis Sanchez struck the other. Chile had previously won by the same margin at home to Venezuela in August 1979 and Armenia in 1997. Their largest defeat was also 7-0, losing away to Brazil in September 1959.

BLAME IT ON BOLIVIA

Chile's failure to reach the 2018 FIFA World Cup was one of the major surprises of qualifying. The 2015 and 2016 Copa America winners came sixth in South America's ten-team FIFA World Cup qualifying table. Missing out on the finals cost manager Juan Antonio Pizzi his job. He was succeeded by Colombian-born Reinaldo Rueda – formerly coach of Colombia, Honduras and Ecuador. The last Chilean to manage his country was Juvenal Olmos, between 2003 and 2005. But the real blame for missing out on qualification lay at Bolivia's door. In early September 2016 they illegally fielded ex Paraguay international Nelson Cabrera in a 1-1 draw with Chile and a 2-0 win over Peru. FIFA awarded Chile and Peru 3-0 wins, giving the Chileans two more points but Peru an extra three. In the final round of matches, Chile lost 3-0 to Brazil and Peru drew 1-1 with Colombia. It made all the difference as both countries ended on 26 points, but Peru's goal difference was +1 and Chile's -1.

TOP SCORERS

1	Alexis Sanchez	39
2	Marcelo Salas	37
3	Eduardo Vargas	35
4	Ivan Zamorano	34
5	Carlos Caszely	29
6	Leonel Sanchez	24
=	Arturo Vidal	24
8	Jorge Aravena	22
9	Humberto Suazo	21
10	Juan Carlos Letelier	18

BRAVO, BRAVO

In March 2016 goalkeeper Claudio Bravo became the first Chilean international to reach a century of caps, in a 2-1 defeat to Argentina in the qualification campaign for the 2018 FIFA World Cup. But just three months later, against the same opponents, he lifted the Copa America trophy – a special new design, this one – for the second time. He was also named man of the match for the final, just as he had been 12 months earlier, and was awarded the Golden Glove prize for being the tournament's best goalkeeper – while there were also individual prizes for two of his team-mates: **Eduardo Vargas** claimed the Golden Boot as top scorer, with six goals, while Alexis Sanchez took the Golden Ball as the best player. Chile provided eight of the 11 players in the official team of the tournament: alongside Bravo, Vargas and Sanchez were defenders Mauricio Isla, Gary Medel and Jean Beausejour and midfielders Arturo Vidal and Charles Aranguiz.

TOP CAPS

1	Alexis Sanchez	121
2	Claudio Bravo	119
3	Gary Medel	111
4	Gonzalo Jara	110
5	Jean Beausejour	100
=	Mauricio Isla	100
=	Arturo Vidal	100
8	Leonel Sanchez	85
9	Eduardo Vargas	82
10	Jorge Valdivia	79

CENTRE-BACK'S HAT-TRICK

The first player to be named South American Footballer of the Year three times was not Pele, Garrincha or Diego Maradona but Chilean centre-back **Elias Figueroa**, who took the prize in three consecutive years from 1974 to 1976 while playing for Brazilian club Internacional. First awarded in 1971, the only other men to win the award three times are Brazil's Zico, in 1977, 1981 and 1982, and Carlos Tevez of Argentina, in 2003, 2004 and 2005. Two more Chileans have won the award: Marcelo Salas in 1997 and Matias Fernandez in 2006. In all, the 46 awards have gone to players from Brazil and Argentina 13 times each, followed by Chile, Uruguay and Paraguay, five apiece, Colombia, four, and Peru, one. Although Figueroa started and ended his playing career in Chile, he also played for clubs in Brazil, Uruguay and the US, while also representing his country for 16 years (winning 47 caps), from 1966 to 1982 – including FIFA World Cup appearances in 1966, 1974 and 1982.

SANCHEZ SETS MORE CHILE RECORDS

The winning spot-kick against Argentina to secure Chile's first Copa America in 2015 was struck by the well-travelled **Alexis Sanchez**, then of Arsenal in England, following spells in Italy with Udinese and in Spain with Barcelona. Sanchez holds the record as Chile's youngest international, having made his debut against New Zealand in April 2006 at the age of 17 years and four months. Since the 2017 FIFA Confederations Cup, Sanchez has extended his goals total to 39, two more than the previous record-holder Marcelo Salas. Then, in 2018, and now with Manchester United, the striker took over at the top of the appearances list with 121 caps.

SALAS DAYS

Chile's second leading scorer **Marcelo Salas** formed a much-feared striking partnership with Ivan Zamorano during the late 1990s and early 21st century. Salas scored four goals as Chile reached the second round of the 1998 FIFA World Cup in France despite not winning a game. The striker spent two years in international retirement, from 2005 to 2007, but returned for the first four games of qualification for the 2010 FIFA World Cup. His scored twice in Chile's 2-2 draw with Uruguay on 18 November 2007, but his international career ended for good three days later, following a 3-0 defeat to Paraguay.

LUCKY LEO

For many years **Leonel Sanchez** held the Chilean record for international appearances, scoring 23 goals in 84 games. But he was lucky to remain on the pitch for one of them. Sanchez escaped an early bath despite punching Italy's Humberto Maschio in the face during their so-called "Battle of Santiago" clash at the 1962 FIFA World Cup, when English referee Ken Aston could have sent off more than just the two players he did dismiss. Sanchez, a left-winger born in Santiago on 25 April 1936, finished the tournament as one of its six four-goal leading scorers – along with Brazilians Garrincha and Vava, Russian Valentin Ivanov, Yugoslav Drazan Jerkovic and Hungarian Florian Albert.

BIG MISS BY LITTLE FOX

Chile forward Carlos Vidal – nicknamed "Little Fox" – has the unfortunate distinction of being the first man to miss a penalty at a FIFA World Cup, seeing his spot-kick saved by France goalkeeper Alex Thepot after half an hour of their first-round Group A meeting on 19 July 1930. But his fellow striker Guillermo Subiabre headed the only goal of the game in the second half. Chile finished second in their group, the only one at the tournament to have four rather than three teams, but only Argentina went through to the semi-finals as group winners.

URUGUAY

Uruguay was the first country to win a FIFA World Cup, in 1930, and with a population of under four million, they remain the smallest to do so. They claimed the game's greatest prize for a second time in 1950, having already won Olympic gold in 1924 and 1928. Recent years were less productive, until a fourth-place finish at the 2010 FIFA World Cup and a record-breaking 15th Copa America triumph the following year.

PARTY-POOPERS

Uruguay is the only country to win the FIFA World Cup in anything other than a one-off, winner-takes-all final. The 1950 tournament had no knock-out games and the last four played in a round-robin final group. The last game was, effectively, the final – though Brazil needed only a draw to become champions. In front of an attendance estimated at anything up to 220,000 (FIFA's records now say 173,850), in Rio de Janeiro's Maracana stadium, hosts Brazil even took the lead through Friaca – but were stunned when goals by Juan Alberto Schiaffino and **Alcides Ghiggia** gave Uruguay the win they needed to clinch their second World Cup. Such was the frantic Brazilian disappointment, spilling on to the pitch, FIFA president Jules Rimet discreetly smuggled the trophy into the hands of Uruguay captain **Obdulio Varela** – and it was several hours before his team felt secure enough to emerge from their dressing-room and into the world outside.

DIFFERENT BALL GAME

Uruguay were the inaugural hosts – and the first winners – of the FIFA World Cup in 1930, having won football gold at the Olympics of 1924 in Paris and 1928 in Amsterdam. Among the players who won all three of those titles was forward Hector Scarone, now Uruguay's fourth top scorer with 31 goals in 52 internationals. Uruguay beat arch-rivals Argentina 4-2 in the 1930 final, a game in which two different footballs were used – Argentina's choice in the first half, in which they led 2-1, before Uruguay's was used for their second-half comeback. Uruguay declined the chance to defend their title in 1934, refusing to travel to host country Italy in pique at only four European nations visiting in 1930.

DUO'S TREBLES

Luis Suarez scored the only goal when Uruguay defeated Saudi Arabia in their second 2018 FIFA World Cup Group A match. It made him the first Uruguayan man to score at three different FIFA World Cups, having netted in both South Africa in 2010 and in Brazil four year later. Suarez's feat was emulated by strike partner Edinson Cavani in Uruguay's next match, a 3-0 win over hosts Russia. The pair had combined for 15 of Uruguay's 32 goals in qualifying for the 2018 finals. Not only did Uruguay win their first two games at a FIFA World Cup for the first time since 1954 but also they became the first country to win all three first-round group matches without conceding a goal since Argentina in 1998. Their winner in Uruguay's opener against Egypt came from defender **Jose Gimenez**, who four years earlier - aged 19 years and 149 days –became Uruguay's youngest player at a FIFA World Cup.

URUGUAY'S RECORD

FIFA WORLD CUP 13 appearances
Matches (56) W24, D12, L20, GF87, GA74
Champions (2) 1930, 1950
Fourth place (3) 1954, 1970, 2010
Quarter-finals (2) 1966, 2018
Round of 16 (3) 1986, 1990, 2014
First round (3) 1962, 1974, 2002

COPA AMERICA 43 appearances
Winners (15) 1916, 1917, 1920, 1923, 1924, 1926, 1935, 1942, 1956, 1959, 1967, 1983, 1987, 1995, 2011

CONFEDERATIONS CUP 2 appearances
Fourth place (2) 1997, 2013

OLYMPIC GAMES 3 appearances
Gold medal (2) 1924, 1928

FIRST INTERNATIONAL Uruguay 2, Argentina 3 (Montevideo, 16 May 1901)

BIGGEST WINS Uruguay 9 Bolivia 0 Lima (Peru), 9 November 1927

HEAVIEST DEFEAT Uruguay 0 Argentina 6 (Montevideo, 20 July 1902)

CLASS APART

No manager has overseen more international matches than the 191 – excluding the 2012 Olympic Games – of Uruguay's **Oscar Washington Tabarez**, a former schoolteacher known as "The Maestro". He led Uruguay to the second round of the 1990 FIFA World Cup and returned for a second spell in 2006, taking them back to the tournament in 2010 – and a fourth-place finish. When he took charge of his 168th Uruguay game in 2016, he passed West Germany's Sepp Herberger for the most matches coached for one team. His Uruguay teams set a national record of 18 matches unbeaten between 2011 and 2012 – and won the 2011 Copa America. Tabarez became the first man to take the same team to four FIFA World Cups in 2018 where, although battling Guillain-Barre syndrome, which required him to use a crutch in the dugout, Uruguay won four matches before losing 2-0 to France in the quarter-final.

PUNCHING ABOVE THEIR WEIGHT

Uruguay's population of 3.4 million and area of 176,000 sq km makes it the smallest nation to have lifted the FIFA World Cup trophy. The next smallest in terms of population is Argentina with 43m. Both are a long way off the 192 million residents and 8.5 million sq km of five-times winners Brazil.

HAPPY ANNIVERSARY

A so-called "Mundialito", or "Little World Cup", was staged in December 1980 and January 1981 to mark the 50th anniversary of the FIFA World Cup – and, as in 1930, Uruguay emerged triumphant. The tournament was meant to involve all six countries who had previously won the tournament, though 1966 champions England turned down the invitation and were replaced by 1978 runners-up Holland. Uruguay beat Brazil 2-1 in the final, a repeat of the scoreline from the two teams' final match of the 1950 FIFA World Cup. The Mundialito-winning Uruguay side was captained by goalkeeper Rodolfo Rodriguez and coached by Roque Maspoli, who had played in goal in that 1950 final.

BOYS IN BLUE

Uruguay's 3–2 home defeat to neighbours Argentina, in Montevideo on 16 May 1901, was the first official international match outside the UK. On 20 July 1902 Argentina inflicted Uruguay's heaviest loss 6-0 in Montevideo. The two countries have played each other a world record 193 times – with Uruguay winning 59, Argentina 89 and there have been 45 draws. Before an agreed kit-swap in 1910, Uruguay would often wear vertical light-blue and white stripes and Argentina would don pale-blue shirts. One of Uruguay's most momentous recent triumphs over their arch rivals came when they defeated hosts Argentina on penalties in the quarter-finals of the 2011 Copa America on the way to lifting the trophy. Defender **Martin Caceres** struck the winning spot-kick.

TOP SCORERS

1	Luis Suarez	53
2	Edinson Cavani	45
3	Diego Forlan	36
4	Hector Scarone	31
5	Angel Romano	28
6	Oscar Miguez	27
7	Sebastian Abreu	26
8	Pedro Petrone	24
9	Carlos Aguilera	22
=	Fernando Morena	22

CAV FAITH

It took just three minutes for **Edinson Cavani** to score his first international goal, after coming on as a substitute for his Uruguay debut against Colombia in February 2008. He not only helped Uruguay finish fourth at the 2010 FIFA World Cup and win a record 15th Copa America but the devout Christian won praise when playing for Italian club Napoli from the Archbishop of Naples Crescenzio Sepe, who declared: "God serves himself by having Cavani score goals." Yet his 2015 Copa America ended unhappily with a bizarre sending-off at the end of a quarter-final defeat to hosts Chile after retaliating when opponent Gonzala Jara prodded him in the bottom.

FORLAN HERO

Diego Forlan was Uruguay's star man at the 2010 FIFA World Cup, scoring five goals – including three from outside the penalty area, the first player to achieve that feat at a FIFA World Cup since Germany's Lothar Matthaus in 1990. He also hit the crossbar with a free-kick, the final touch of his country's 3-2 defeat to Germany in the 2010 third-place play-off. Uruguay's fourth-place finish in South Africa meant Diego fared better than his father Pablo, who had played in the Uruguay team that was knocked out in the first round of the 1974 FIFA World Cup.

MAX POWER

Right-back **Maxi Pereira** became only the second Uruguayan to reach 100 caps, in a 1-0 friendly victory over Morocco in March 2015. He made his international debut in 2005 and played in the 2010 and 2014 FIFA World Cups and Uruguay's 2011 Copa America triumph. His FIFA World Cup fortunes have been mixed. In 2010 he became the first Uruguayan to miss a FIFA World Cup penalty, in their winning quarter-final shoot-out against Ghana before scoring his first international goal in the 3-2 semi-final defeat against the Netherlands. Pereira opened the scoring in Uruguay's 5-0 play-off win over Jordan to reach the 2014 finals but became the first player of the tournament to be shown a red card, against Costa Rica. He became Uruguay's most-capped player when making his 113th international appearance at the 2016 Copa America Centenario, in a 1-0 defeat to Venezuela as they departed in the first round.

UNCLE'S INSPIRATION

The only uncle and nephew combination to have both picked up FIFA World Cup winners' medals as players are Uruguayan duo Jose Leandro Andrade, triumphant in 1930, and Víctor Rodríguez Andrade, who was on the winning side 20 years later. Víctor deliberately used the surname Andrade as well as Rodríguez, in honour of his uncle. Before winning fame as a footballer, José Leandro Andrade's jobs included carnival musician and street shoe-shiner.

BITE RETURN

Notoriety has cast many shadows over the career of **Luis Suarez** and the controversy he caused at the 2010 FIFA World Cup was mild compared to what followed in Brazil four years later. Uruguay's all-time leading scorer is one of the world's most talented strikers but is also a danger not only to others but to himself and team-mates. He earned infamy with a deliberate goal-line handball in the last minute of extra-time when Uruguay and Ghana were level in their 2010 FIFA World Cup quarter-final – then celebrated wildly when Asamoah Gyan missed – and Uruguay won the resulting shoot-out. Worse followed, however, at the 2014 FIFA World Cup, when he bit into the shoulder of Italian defender Giorgio Chiellini, earning himself a nine-match international ban and a four-month suspension from all football. Astonishingly, this was the third time Suarez had bitten someone on the football field – having previously done so while playing for both Ajax Amsterdam and Liverpool. His scoring instincts, are much more admirable – his 48 international goals include four during Uruguay's triumphant 2011 Copa America campaign. Suarez does inspire loyalty among supporters and team-mates, who even pegged his shirt up in the dressing-room before their 2014 second-round clash with Colombia despite his enforced departure from Brazil the previous day.

OSCAR AWARD

Oscar Miguez's double in the closing 15 minutes of Uruguay's penultimate game of the 1950 FIFA World Cup not only turned a 2-1 deficit into a 3-2 victory over Sweden, but also made meaningful their final group showdown against hosts Brazil. Uruguay's 2-1 victory gave resulted in their second world title. Miguez ended the tournament on five goals, having previously hit a hat-trick in an 8-0 trouncing of Bolivia. He found the net three more times four years later in Switzerland, and with eight goals, remains Uruguay's leading all-time scorer in the FIFA World Cup. That figure might have been greater, but Miguez was injured in 1954 and missed his team's 1954 semi-final and third-place play-off, losses, respectively, to Hungary and Austria.

LEAVE IT TO BEAVER

Goalkeeper **Fernando Muslera** has played more FIFA World Cup matches than any other Uruguayan, taking his tally to 16 with five appearances at the 2018 tournament in Russia. Muslera, nicknamed *Castorino* – "The Little Beaver" – during a spell with Italian club Lazio, saved two penalties as Uruguay defeated Ghana in a quarter-final penalty shoot-out at the 2010 FIFA World Cup and a match-deciding spot-kick from Argentina's Carlos Tevez in the 2011 Copa America. He celebrated his 100th cap with a clean sheet against the FIFA World Cup hosts in a 2018 Group A match – but made a rare error as Uruguay exited at the quarter-final stage. He allowed a long-range shot from France's Antoine Griezmann to skip through his hands to make it 2-0.

TOP CAPS

1	Maxi Pereira	125
2	Diego Godin	122
3	Diego Forlan	112
4	Cristian Rodriguez	109
5	Edinson Cavani	105
6	Luis Suarez	103
7	Fernando Muslera	102
8	Diego Lugano	95
9	Egidio Arevalo Rios	90
10	Diego Perez	89

OLE, FRANCESCOLI

Until Diego Forlan passed him in 2011, no outfield player had represented Uruguay more often than **Enzo Francescoli** (73 caps) – and few can have taken the field quite so gracefully as the playmaker whose club career included stints with River Plate in Argentina, Racing and Marseille in France and Cagliari and Torino in Italy. His international swansong for Uruguay brought Copa America glory in 1995, when he starred as both midfielder and emergency striker and also scored one of Uruguay's spot-kicks in their penalty shoot-out final victory over Brazil. Among Francescoli's high-profile fans was Zinedine Zidane, who later named his first-born son Enzo, in honour of the Uruguayan maestro.

OTHER TEAMS SOUTH AMERICA

GOING CARACAS FOR FOOTBALL

Baseball and boxing may have held more sway with Venezuelans in recent decades but football fever has been on the rise in the twenty-first century – given a big boost by the country staging its first Copa America in 2007. This not only saw extravagant investment in new stadia but also Venezuela's first Copa America victory since 1967 – and unprecedented progress into the knock-out stages. **Juan Arango,** a popular success in Spain with La Liga club RCD Mallorca, scored Venezuela's goal in a 4-1 quarter-final loss to Uruguay. However Venezuela have yet to qualify for the FIFA World Cup. Their best performance in the 2018 qualifying competition, when they finished bottom of the 10-team group, was a 1-0 win in Paraguay.

NATIONAL STADIUMS

Bolivia:
Estadio Hernando Siles,
La Paz (41,143 capacity)

Chile:
Estadio Monumental David Arellano
Santiago (48,665)

Colombia:
Estadio Metropolitano
Baranquilla (46,788)

Ecuador:
Estadio Olimpico Atahualpa,
Quito (35,742)

Paraguay:
Estadio Defensores del Chaco,
Asuncion (42,354)

Peru:
Estadio Nacional,
Lima (40,000)

Venezuela:
Estadio Polideportivo
de Pueblo Nuevo,
San Cristobal (38,755)

BOLIVIA LEAVE IT LATE

Bolivia have only ever won the Copa America once, but did so in dramatic and memorable style when playing host in 1963. They were the only team to finish the competition unbeaten in all six matches, topping the league table. But they almost threw away glory on the competition's final day, twice squandering two-goal leads against Brazil. Bolivia led 2-0 before being pegged back to 2-2, then saw a 4-2 advantage turn to 4-4, before Maximo Alcocer scored what proved to be Bolivia's winning goal with four minutes remaining.

ECUADOR'S EARTHQUAKE TRIBUTE

Ecuador reached the knock-out stages of the 2016 Copa America Centenario – the first time they had advanced from the opening round since 1987. They drew with Brazil (0-0) and Peru (2-2) and defeated Haiti 4-0. Head coach Gustavo Quinteros dedicated their progress to the more than 600 people killed by an earthquake in the country's Manabi region on 16 April 2016. Ecuador's opening goal against Haiti was scored by West Ham United striker **Enner Valencia,** who had netted three times at the 2014 FIFA World Cup, including a brace against Honduras in a 2-1 win – the first Ecuadorian to score more than once in a FIFA World Cup finals match.

TALKING HEAD

Colombia's record international remains frizz-haired midfielder **Carlos Valderrama** who played 111 times for the *Cafeteros,* scoring 11 goals, between 1985 and 1998. Valderrama stood out for both his hairstyle and his playmaking talent when he captained Colombia in a golden era for the national team. He was voted South American Footballer of the Year in 1987 and 1993 while appearing in the finals of the FIFA World Cup on three successive occasions in 1990, 1994 and 1998. Valderrama was a hugely popular figure at the 2018 finals in Russia when he undertook television pundit duties, still parading his famous hairstyle.

ABOVE-PAR PARAGUAY

Paraguay's two most-capped players, centre-back **Paulo da Silva** (148 appearances, first against Bolivia on 27 July 2000) and goalkeeper Justo Villar (120 caps, debut v Guatemala, 3 March 1999) were mainstays in their country's most successful FIFA World Cup performance: topping their group in 2010 and reaching the quarter-finals, only losing to eventual champions Spain. Both were still in the side in October 2016, helping Paraguay win a FIFA World Cup qualifier in Argentina for the first time – thanks to a Derlis Gonzalez strike. All three of Da Silva's international goals have come against Chile – twice on 21 November 2007 in Santiago and, almost nine years later, on 1 September 2016 in Asuncion.

BIGGEST WINS

Bolivia 7 Venezuela 0
(22 August 1993)
Bolivia 9 Haiti 2
(3 March 2000)
Bahrain 0 Colombia 6
(26 March 2015)
Ecuador 6 Peru 0
(22 June 1975)
Paraguay 7 Bolivia 0
(30 April 1949)
Hong Kong 0 Paraguay 7
(17 November 2010)
Peru 9 Ecuador 1
(11 August 1938)
Venezuela 7 Puerto Rico 0
(16 January 1959)

MINA MAKES HIS MARKS

Colombian centre-back Yerry Mina surprised even himself at the 2018 FIFA World Cup in Russia when he proved not only a tower of strength in defence but was his team's three-goal leading scorer. That equalled the record tally for a defender at the finals. Colombia lost their opening game to Japan, but Mina scored the first goal of their next game a 3-0 defeat of Poland. He then struck again with the lone goal which beat Senegal and sent Colombia into the second round. Mina headed the last-minute equaliser in a 1-1 draw with England before Colombia lost on penalties. Five months earlier he became the first Colombian to join Barcelona, costing them £10m from Brazil's Palmeiras.

HIGH LIFE

Bolivia and Ecuador play their home internationals at higher altitudes than any other teams on earth. Bolivia's showpiece Estadio Hernando Siles stadium, in the capital La Paz, is 3,637 metres (11,932ft) above sea level, while Ecuador's main Estadio Olimpico Atahualpa, in Quito, sits 2,800 metres (9,185ft) above sea level. Opposing teams have complained that the rarefied nature of the air makes it difficult to breathe, let alone play, but a FIFA ban on playing competitive internationals at least 2,500 metres (8,200ft) above sea level, first introduced in May 2007, was amended a month later – adjusting the limit to 3,000 metres (9,840ft) and allowing Estadio Hernando Siles to be used as a special case. The altitude ban was suspended entirely in May 2008. FIFA had changed its mind after protests by Bolivia, Ecuador and other affected nations Colombia and Peru. Other campaigners to overturn the law included Argentina legend Diego Maradona, but he may have regretted his decision when, in March 2009 Bolivia scored a 6-1 home win against Argentina in a FIFA World Cup qualifier. The Argentina coach was ... Maradona.

HERO GUERRERO

Veteran playmaker **Paolo Guerrero** had to battle all the way for the right to lead Peru at the 2018 World Cup, their first appearance in the finals for 36 years. Peru's captain was suspended for 12 months during the qualifiers for failing a dope test for what he claimed was coca tea after a tie against Argentina. The ban would have ruled him out of the finals, but it was lifted pending appeal, and Guerrero was allowed to play in the finals. He even scored in a 2-0 win over Australia, but Peru went out at the group stage. That goal was his record-extending 35th for Peru in 89 appearances over 14 years.

BIGGEST DEFEATS

Uruguay 9 Bolivia 0
(6 November 1927)
Brazil 10 Bolivia 1
(10 April 1949)
Brazil 9 Colombia 0
(24 March 1957, in Lima, Peru)
Argentina 12 Ecuador 0
(22 January 1942)
Argentina 8 Paraguay 0
(20 October 1926)
Brazil 7 Peru 0
(26 June 1997)
Argentina 11 Venezuela 0
(10 August 1975)

TIM'S TIME

Peru were coached at the 1982 FIFA World Cup by Tim, who had been waiting an unprecedented 44 years to return to the FIFA World Cup finals – after playing once as striker for his native Brazil in the 1938 tournament.

WINNING RON

Bolivia's most-capped player, centre-back **Ronald Raldes**, made his international debut in 2001 but had to wait 13 years to score for his country – finally finding the net in a 3-2 November 2014 victory over Venezuela. Just seven months later he notched his second, in another 3-2 win – this time against Ecuador at the 2015 Copa America, helping secure Bolivia's first Copa America victory since 1997. Their failure to qualify for the 2018 FIFA World Cup means 1994 remains their only finals – but the 2018 campaign did include back-to-back wins for the first time since 1998, including a surprise 2-0 victory over Argentina thanks to a brace from Marcelo Moreno – who had gone ten internationals without a goal beforehand. That took him third in his country's all-time scoring charts, with 15 goals, behind only Joaquin Botero (20, including a hat-trick in a 6-1 defeat of Argentina in April 2009, his final appearance) and Victor Ugarte (16).

NOT SO FAB

Colombia full-back Frank Fabra endured a bittersweet Copa America first at the 2016 Centenario tournament when he scored for both teams in one match – no other player had done this in the competition's 100-year history. He found the net at both ends as his side lost 3-2 to Costa Rica in the first round, although Colombia did recover to qualify for the next stage and ultimately reached the semi-finals.

COOL DUDAMEL

Venezuela suffered some bad defeats when missing out on the 1998 FIFA World Cup. They ended with no wins and 13 defeats in 16 games, scoring 13 and conceding 41 goals. The losses included 4-1 to Peru, 6-1 to Bolivia and 6-0 to Chile, for whom Ivan Zamorano scored five. But their goalkeeper Rafael Dudamel had a moment to savour against Argentina in October 1996, when he scored with a direct free-kick late in the game. Venezuela still lost 5-2. Dudamel became Venezuela coach in April 2016 and, two months later, led them to the second round of the Copa America Centenario.

FALCAO BITES BACK

Colombia captain **Radamel Falcao** made a remarkable recovery to play at the 2018 FIFA World Cup finals in Russia. Four years earlier it had been feared a knee injury might bring his goal-hungry career to a premature end. The striker – named after Brazil's 1980s midfielder Paulo Roberto Falcao – had earned the nickname *El Tigre* (The Tiger) in making his name initially with Argentinian club River Plate. In 2009 Portuguese club FC Porto bought Falcao for £2m, and it proved a bargain as he led them to a 2011 treble of league, cup and UEFA Europa League. He scored a then record 17 goals in the 2010-11 UEFA Europa League campaign and, following a move to Spain's Atletico Madrid, repeated the Europa League triumph 12 months later. He moved AS Monaco in 2013, but a serious knee injury in January 2014 meant he missed that summer's FIFA World Cup. Disappointing loans spells in England, at Manchester United and Chelsea followed, but Falcao's 2016 return to Monaco saw him regain his confidence and, in 2018, he fulfilled his ambition of leading Colombia into the FIFA World Cup finals.

CHRISTIAN TRIBUTE

Ecuador's footballers dedicated their 2014 FIFA World Cup campaign to former team-mate Christian "Chucho" Benitez, who died suddenly from a cardiac arrest in July 2013 at the age of only 27. Team-mate, and Ecuador's captain at the 2014 FIFA World Cup finals, Antonio Valencia had Benitez's number 11 tattooed on his arm in tribute and the number was officially "retired" by the Ecuador FA. FIFA World Cup rules, however, meant the number had to be worn, and it was given to striker Felipe Caicedo at the 2014 finals.

MOST INTERNATIONAL CAPS

Bolivia	Ronald Raldes	102
Colombia	Carlos Valderrama	111
Ecuador	Ivan Hurtado	168
Paraguay	Paulo Da Silva	148
Peru	Roberto Palacios	128
Venezuela	Juan Arango	129

RUID AWAKENING

Peru ended a 31-year wait to beat Brazil with a 1-0 win in the first round of the 2016 Copa America Centenario. It put Ricardo Gareca's side in the second round and eliminated Dunga's Brazilians. The goal was contentious, however, as Raul Ruidiaz seemed to knock the ball into the goal with his hand from Andy Polo's cross. Ruidiaz insisted he had used his thigh and denied comparisons to Diego Maradona's "Hand Of God" goal at the 1986 FIFA World Cup, claiming his strike was "thanks to God". Peru's previous win over Brazil – 2016 was only the fourth ever – had been in April 1985, when Julio Cesar Uribe got the only goal in a friendly in Brasilia. Their other Copa America defeats of Brazil were in 1953 and 1975.

CANIZA CAN DO

Centre-back and captain **Denis Caniza**, then aged 36, became the first Paraguayan to play at four different FIFA World Cups, with his one appearance against New Zealand during the 2010 tournament. The same event brought a milestone for team-mate Roque Santa Cruz – his goal in the first-round game against Brazil equalled Jose Saturnino Cardozo's all-time Paraguayan scoring record of 25. Fellow striker Salvador Cabanas missed out on the tournament after being shot in the head with a gun in a nightclub five months earlier. He did recover well enough to return to professional football in 2012.

MARKSMAN SPENCER

Ecuador's greatest player of all time is arguably prolific striker **Alberto Spencer,** even though he played much of his club football in Uruguay. Spencer holds the record for most goals in South America's Copa Libertadores club championship, scoring 54 times between 1960 and 1972 and lifting the trophy three times with Uruguay's Penarol. He also scored four goals in 11 games for Ecuador and once in four appearances for Uruguay. Spencer was nicknamed "Magic Head" and was even praised as a better header of the ball than Pele – the tribute coming from Pele himself.

MOST INTERNATIONAL GOALS

Bolivia	Joaquin Botero	20
Colombia	Radamel Falcao	30
Ecuador	Agustin Delgado	31
Paraguay	Roque Santa Cruz	32
Peru	Paulo Guerrero	35
Venezuela	Juan Arango	23

SAFE HANDS OSCAR

Keeping clean sheets for Colombia all the way through the 2001 Copa America was **Oscar Cordoba**, who went on to become his country's most-capped goalkeeper – with 73 appearances between 1993 and 2006.

HIGHS AND LOWS FOR LOLO

Teodoro "Lolo" Fernandez scored six goals in two games for Peru at the 1936 Summer Olympics, including five in a 7–3 defeat of Finland and another in a 4–2 victory over Austria. But Peru were outraged when the Austrians claimed that fans had been invading the pitch and were even more upset when officials ordered the match to be replayed. Peru withdrew from the tournament in protest, while Austria went on to claim silver. But Fernandez and his team-mates had a happier ending at the Copa America three years later, with Peru crowned champions and Fernandez finishing as top scorer with seven goals.

IVAN THE ADMIRABLE

Ecuador defender Ivan Hurtado is South America's most-capped footballer, playing 168 games after making his debut in 1992 – including five goals. He was one of Ecuador's most influential players at their first FIFA World Cup finals, in 2002, and captained them as they reached the second round of the competition four years later. Hurtado retired after an October 2014 friendly, a 5-1 away victory against El Salvador.

 AFRICA

The African confederation organized its inaugural Cup of Nations in 1957, only a year after it was founded. Egypt, with a record seven victories, were the first winners while most recent include Ivory Coast in Equatorial Guinea in 2015 and Cameroon in 2017 in Gabon. In the FIFA World Cup South Africa, in 2010, were Africa's first finals hosts but it is still waiting for a semi-finalist (Cameroon, Senegal and Ghana have all lost quarter-finals). In 2018 no African teams made it to the second round, all five falling in the group stage.

Nigeria's passionate fans created plenty of noise and colour at the 2018 FIFA World Cup and although their heroes could not advance beyond the group stage, there was a 2-0 victory over Iceland in Volgograd to celebrate.

NORTH AFRICA FIFA WORLD CUP RECORDS

FAWZI'S FIRST

Abdelrahman Fawzi became the first African footballer to score at a FIFA World Cup, when he pulled a goal back for Egypt against Hungary in the first round of the 1934 tournament – then scored an equalizer eight minutes later, to make it 2-2 at half-time. Egypt went on to lose the match 4-2, and would not return to the finals for another 56 years.

PLAY–OFF PIQUE

Morocco's qualification for the 1970 FIFA World Cup ended a 36-year African exile from the finals. No African countries played at the 1966 FIFA World Cup in Africa, with 16 possible candidate countries all boycotting the event because FIFA wanted the top African team to face a side from Asia or Oceania in a qualification play-off.

HAIL HALLICHE

Algeria became the first African nation to score four goals in one game at a FIFA World Cup finals when they defeated South Korea 4-2 at Porto Alegre in their Group H contest in the Brazil 2014 tournament. The Algerians went on to finish second in the group, behind winners Belgium, and thus qualified for the knock-out stages for the first time. In the second round they faced one of the tournament favourites, Germany, and Algeria only departed after losing a thrilling match 2-1 after extra time. One of Algeria's scorers in the victory over South Korea on 22 June – they had raced into a 3-0 half-time lead – was centre-back **Rafik Halliche** (he headed the second goal), who by the end of the 2014 tournament had made eight FIFA World Cup appearances – a new Algerian record.

AGELESS EL HADARY

Egypt goalkeeper **Essam El Hadary**, at 45 years and 161 days, became the oldest player in World Cup history when he played in a 2-1 defeat by Saudi Arabia in 2018. El Hadary beat the record set by Colombia's Faryd Mondragon in 2014 (43 years and 3 days). El Hadary marked the occasion by becoming the oldest keeper to save a penalty (from Fahad Al Muwallad) and the oldest to do so on his World Cup debut.

REDS IN A ROW

When Antar Yahia was sent off for a second bookable offence, three minutes into stoppage-time of Algeria's 1-0 defeat to the USA at the 2010 FIFA World Cup, it was not only the latest red card shown in any World Cup game not featuring extra-time. It also meant at least one player had been sent off on eight consecutive days of the 2010 tournament – a record run for any FIFA World Cup.

DJAB FAB

Barring penalty shoot-outs, no African has scored a later FIFA World Cup goal than Algerian midfielder **Abdelmoumene Djabou**. His consolation strike in a 2-1 second-round loss to Germany on 30 June 2014 was timed at 120 minutes and 50 seconds. This was the third meeting between the two teams. Algeria had followed a 2-0 friendly win in 1964 with a shock 2-1 success at the 1982 FIFA World Cup.

MOROCCAN ROLL

Morocco were the first North African country to reach the second round of a FIFA World Cup, though they were knocked out, 1-0, by eventual finalists West Germany. It was in Mexico in 1986 that Morocco were the first African team to top a FIFA World Cup group, finishing above England, Poland and Portugal. Crucial was their 3-1 victory over Portugal in their final group game, following goalless draws against the other two teams – including an England side who lost captain Bryan Robson to a dislocated shoulder and vice-captain Ray Wilkins to a red card. **Abderrazak Khairi** scored two of the goals against Portugal, while Lothar Matthaus's winning strike for Germany came with just three minutes remaining.

NORTH AFRICAN COUNTRIES' BEST FIFA WORLD CUP PERFORMANCES

ALGERIA: Second round 2014
EGYPT: First round 1934, 1990, 2018
MOROCCO: Second round 2006
TUNISIA: First round 1978, 1998, 2002,
             2006, 2018

NORTH AFRICAN COUNTRIES' FIFA WORLD CUP QUALIFICATIONS

MOROCCO: 5 (1970, 1986, 1994, 1998, 2018)
TUNISIA: 5 (1978, 1998, 2002, 2006, 2018)
ALGERIA: 4 (1982, 1986, 2010, 2014)
EGYPT: 3 (1934, 1990, 2018)

NORTH AFRICA: TOP FIFA WORLD CUP GOALSCORERS

Salah Assad	(Algeria)	2
Salaheddine Bassir	(Morocco)	2
Abdelmoumene Djabou	(Algeria)	2
Abdelrahman Fawzi	(Egypt)	2
Abdeljalil Hadda	(Morocco)	2
Abderrazak Khairi	(Morocco)	2
Wahbi Khazri	(Tunisia)	2
Mohamed Salah	(Egypt)	2
Islam Slimani	(Algeria)	2

NO WAITING GAME

Morocco's 2-1 defeat to Saudi Arabia in 1994 was one of the last two games to be played simultaneously at a FIFA World Cup, without falling on a final match-day of a group. Belgium were beating Holland 1-0 at the same time, with every team in Group F having still one game to play. At later tournaments, every match has been played separately until the climactic two fixtures of any group.

HOMEGROWN HERO

Of the six African countries at the 2010 FIFA World Cup, Algeria's was the only squad with an African coach – **Rabah Saadane**, in his fifth separate stint in charge since 1981. He previously led his country to the 1986 FIFA World Cup in Mexico, where they were also eliminated in the first round. Along with Honduras, the Algeria team of 2010 were one of only two countries failing to score a single goal. However, they did concede just twice in their three games: 1-0 defeats to Slovakia and the USA, and a surprise goalless draw with England – Algeria's first-ever FIFA World Cup clean sheet.

MOKHTAR RUNS AMOK

Egypt had to play only two matches to qualify for the 1934 FIFA World Cup, becoming the first African representatives at the tournament. Both games were against a Palestine side under the British mandate – and the Egyptians won both games handsomely, 7-1 in Cairo and 4-1 in Palestine. Captain and striker Mahmoud Mokhtar scored a hat-trick in the first leg, a brace in the second. Turkey were also meant to contest qualifiers against the two sides, but withdrew, leaving the path to the finals free for Egypt.

TUNISIA IN TUNE

Tunisia became the first African team to win a match at a FIFA World Cup finals when they beat Mexico 3-1 in Rosario, Argentina, in 1978 – thanks to goals from Ali Kaabi, Nejib Ghommidh and Mokhtar Dhouib. Tunisia share with Morocco the North African record of reaching five different World Cups, but they had to wait until 2018 to celebrate a second win. Second-half goals by Fakhreddine Ben Youssef and **Wahbi Khazri** gave Tunisia a 2-1 victory over Panama in their final group match in Saransk, Russia, but both teams were already unable to advance to the knock-out rounds.

NORTH AFRICA NATIONAL RECORDS

MAHREZ THE MARVEL

In spring 2016 Algeria's French-born winger **Riyad Mahrez** became the first African to be voted England's Footballer of the Year by his fellow professionals after helping minnows Leicester City to a surprise first Premier League title. When first approached by Leicester in January 2014, Mahrez thought it was Leicester Tigers rugby club showing interest, but he still signed for just £380,000. His slight build had raised doubts about his ability to thrive in England. The first Algerian to win a Premier League winners medal recalled growing up as a sports-mad "street footballer", saying: "I was always with a ball – that's why I was so skinny, I would miss dinner."

ABOUD AWAKENING

After the political upheaval in Libya in 2011, little was expected of the country's footballers at the 2012 Africa Cup of Nations. Yet they brought some joy to supporters with a surprise 2-1 victory over Senegal in their final first-round match – the first time Libya had ever won an Africa Cup of Nations match outside their own country. Their kit bore the new flag of the country's National Transitional Council. Among the star performers were Ihaab al Boussefi – scorer of both goals against Senegal – and goalkeeper and captain **Samir Aboud**, at 39 the oldest player at the tournament. Libya played their first competitive home game in the capital Tripoli since 2010 when they hosted the Democratic Republic of Congo in a 2014 FIFA World Cup qualifier in June 2013, the game ending in a 0-0 draw.

OFFICIAL INFLUENCE

The first African to referee a FIFA World Cup final was Morocco's Said Belqola, who controlled the 1998 climax in which hosts France beat Brazil 3-0. Perhaps his most notable moment was sending off France's Marcel Desailly in the 68th minute – brandishing only the third red card to be shown in a FIFA World Cup final. Belqola was 41 at the time. He died from cancer just under four years later.

STRIKING RIVALS

A homegrown hero regained top spot in Tunisia's scoring ranks after Gabes-born **Issam Jemaa** overtook Francileudo Santos to total 36 goals in 80 appearances between 2005 and 2014. Jemaa began his career with Esperance but since 2005 has played his club football in France for Lens, Caen, Auxerre and Brest and in the Gulf for Kuwait SC, Sl-Salliya (Qatar) and Dubai CSC. By contrast, Brazil-born Santos did not visit Tunisia until his late teens and only accepted citizenship at the age of 24 in 2004. Within weeks he was helping his new nation not only to host but win the 2004 Africa Cup of Nations, scoring four goals including the opener in the final against Morocco. Both Jemaa and Santos were hampered by injury ahead of the 2006 FIFA World Cup – Santos played only 11 minutes at the tournament, while while Jemaa missed out altogether. Jemaa's last two goals came in a 3–0 friendly win over Congo in August 2013 before he finally retired from national team duties the following year.

NORTH AFRICA: SELECTED TOP GOALSCORERS

ALGERIA:	Abdelhafid Tasfaout	34
EGYPT:	Hossam Hassan	67
LIBYA:	Fawzi Al-Issawi	40
MOROCCO:	Ahmed Faras	42
SUDAN:	Hatham Tambal	20
TUNISIA:	Issam Jemaa	36

CRISIS YEARS FOR FOOTBALL IN EGYPT

Football in Egypt has been in crisis since the political upheavals which saw the overthrow of Presidents Hosni Mubarak in 2011 and Mohamed Morsi and 2013. Politicized fans of leading clubs in Cairo, including record champions Al Ahly and rivals Zamalek, took a large role in street protests, and stadia were shut down for lengthy periods following violence in Port Said, when 74 fans were killed and 500 injured after an Egypt Premier League match between El Masry and Al Ahly. The national team is the Africa Cup of Nations most successful team – seven wins, but they have reached only three World Cups: in 1934, 1990 and 2018.

SALAH THE FOOTBALLING PHARAOH

Egypt winger **Mohamed Salah** established himself as one of the world's outstanding players on his way to the 2018 World Cup. Salah had made a youthful name for himself in being named African football's Most Promising Talent at the London 2012 Olympics. Then came a hat-trick against Zimbabwe in the 2014 World Cup qualifiers before his goals for both Egypt and Swiss club Basel earned an £11m transfer to Chelsea. Salah moved swiftly to Fiorentina and Roma before returning to the English Premier League in 2017 with Liverpool for a fee of £37m, then a club record. It proved a bargain as Salah broke the club's scoring record for a debut season and was the Premier League's top scorer with 32 goals and 44 in all competitions. He was voted footballer of the year by both the Football Writers Association and Professional Footballers Assocation, and might have achieved Champions League glory but for a shoulder injury early in Liverpool's defeat against Real Madrid in the final. The injury meant Salah missed Egypt's opening defeat by Uruguay at the 2018 World Cup, but he scored in both subsequent matches, against Russia and Saudi Arabia. Sadly, Egypt lost both matches so they, and Salah, headed home after the group stage.

DOUBLE CUP UPSET

Unlucky Morocco suffered a double defeat in Russia at the 2018 World Cup. The Moroccan FA had lodged a bid with FIFA for hosting rights to the 2026 finals. Despite an imaginative proposal, FIFA's Congress preferred a co-host bid from the United States, Canada and Mexico. The Atlas Lions had no better luck in the finals, going out at the group stage after losing to Iran and Portugal and drawing 2-2 with Spain, thanks to goals from **Khalid Boutaib** and Youssef En-Nesyri.

NORTH AFRICA: SELECTED TOP APPEARANCES

ALGERIA:	Lakhdar Belloumi	101
EGYPT:	Ahmed Hassan	184
LIBYA:	Tarik El Taib	77
MOROCCO:	Noureddine Naybet	115
SUDAN:	Muhannad El Tahir	69
TUNISIA:	Sadok Sassi	116

SORE LOSERS

Libya could claim the record for highest-scoring victory by an African side, having racked up a 21-0 lead over Oman during the Arab Nations Cup in April 1966. But the Oman players walked off with 10 minutes remaining, in protest at Libya being awarded a penalty, and played no further part in the competition.

SUDAN IMPACT

After two second-place and one third-place finishes, Sudan became the third and last of the Africa Cup of Nations founders to lift the trophy, when they beat Ghana in the 1970 final. Hosts Sudan left it late to reach the final, with two goals from El-Issed – the second 12 minutes into extra-time – seeing off Egypt. The same player scored the only goal of the final, after 12 minutes.

SO FARAS, SO GOOD

Ahmed Faras not only heads Morocco's all-time scoring charts, with 42 goals between 1965 and 1979, he was also the captain who lifted the country's only Africa Cup of Nations trophy in 1976 – and was named the tournament's best player after scoring three goals in six games. He had previously come on twice as a sub when Morocco made their FIFA World Cup finals debut in 1970, the first African representatives since 1934.

MAD FOR 'MADIBA'

Apart from the Dutch and Spanish sides competing in the 2010 FIFA World Cup final, one of the star attractions in Johannesburg's Soccer City stadium on 11 July 2010 was South Africa's legendary former president **Nelson Mandela**. The frail 91-year-old – known affectionately by his tribal name of "Madiba" – was driven on to the pitch before the game in a golf cart and given a rapturous reception by the crowd. It marked his one and only public appearance at the tournament. Mandela had hoped to attend the opening ceremony and game on 11 June, but was mourning the death of his 13-year-old great-granddaughter in a car crash the previous evening. He had been a high-profile presence at the FIFA vote in 2004 which awarded South Africa hosting rights for 2010.

GOING FOR A SONG

Two players have been sent off at two separate FIFA World Cups: Cameroon's Rigobert Song, against Brazil in 1994 and Chile four years later, and France's Zinedine Zidane – red-carded against Saudi Arabia in 1998 and against Italy in the 2006 final. Song's red card against Brazil made him the youngest player to be dismissed at a FIFA World Cup – he was just 17 years and 358 days old. Song, born in Nkanglikock on 1 July 1976, is Cameroon's most-capped player, with 137 appearances – including winning displays in the 2000 and 2002 finals of the Africa Cup of Nations. He has been joined in the national team by his nephew, Arsenal utility player Alexandre Song Billong.

MORE FOR ASAMOAH

Ghana's Asamoah Gyan has scored more FIFA World Cup goals than any other player representing an African nation. He took his overall tally to six with two strikes at the Brazil 2014 FIFA World Cup – putting him one ahead of Cameroon's Roger Milla. He also became the first African to score at three separate FIFA World Cups and his 11 matches took him level with Cameroon's Francois Omam-Biyik.

SUB–SAHARAN AFRICAN COUNTRIES' BEST FIFA WORLD CUP PERFORMANCES

ANGOLA:	First round 2006
CAMEROON:	Quarter-finals 1990
GHANA:	Quarter-finals 2010
IVORY COAST:	First round 2006, 2010, 2014
NIGERIA:	Second round 1994, 1998, 2014
SENEGAL:	Quarter-finals 2002
SOUTH AFRICA:	First round 1998, 2002, 2010
TOGO:	First round 2006
ZAIRE/CONGO DR:	First round 1974

JOLLY ROGER

Cameroon striker **Roger Milla**, famous for dancing around corner flags after each goal, became the FIFA World Cup's oldest scorer against Russia in 1994 – aged 42 years and 39 days. He came on as substitute during that tournament with his surname handwritten, rather than printed, on the back of his shirt. Milla, born in Yaounde on 20 May 1952, had retired from professional football for a year before Cameroon's president, Paul Biya, persuaded him to join the 1990 FIFA World Cup squad. His goals in that tournament helped him win the African Footballer of the Year award for an unprecedented second time – 14 years after he had first received the trophy. He finally ended his international career after the 1994 FIFA World Cup in the United States, finishing with 102 caps and 28 goals to his name.

SUB–SAHARAN AFRICAN COUNTRIES' FIFA WORLD CUP QUALIFICATIONS

CAMEROON:	7	(1982, 1990, 1994, 1998, 2002, 2010, 2014)
NIGERIA:	6	(1994, 1998, 2002, 2010, 2014, 2018)
SOUTH AFRICA:	3	(1998, 2002, 2010)
GHANA:	3	(2006, 2010, 2014)
IVORY COAST:	3	(2006, 2010, 2014)
ANGOLA:	1	(2006)
SENEGAL:	2	(2002, 2018)
TOGO:	1	(2006)
ZAIRE/CONGO DR:	1	(1974)

HISTORY LESSON

Senegal made unwanted World Cup history at the 2018 finals as the first country ever to be eliminated by yellow cards. The Lions of Teranga and Japan finished their group on four points but the tiebreaker came down to a new "fair play" regulation. They drew their match 2-2 and finished with the same points, goal difference and goals scored. But Senegal "lost" 6-5 on bookings so Japan went into the second round ... and Senegal went home.

RATOMIR GETS IT RIGHT

Ghana went through four different managers during qualifiers for the 2006 FIFA World Cup, with Serbian coach Ratomir Dujkovic finally clinching the country a place at the finals for the very first time. He led them through the whole of 2005 unbeaten, winning a FIFA prize for being the most-improved team of the year. Ghana were the only African country to make it through the first round of both the 2006 and 2010 FIFA World Cups, despite having the youngest average age of any squad each time. They were again coached by a Serb in 2010, this time Milovan Rajevac.

BROTHERS AT ARMS

The Boateng brothers made FIFA World Cup history in playing against each other at the 2010 finals in South Africa. Both were also selected for the 'replay' in 2014. In 2010 Jerome played left-back for Germany while elder half-brother **Kevin-Prince**, who had switched nationalities a month earlier, was in the Ghana midfield. In the group match in 2010 Jerome Boateng switched to right-back. Germany won 1-0 in South Africa while the return in Brazil ended up 2-2. Kevin-Prince was the only brother to play a full 90 minutes, in South Africa. He was substituted during the game in Brazil while Jerome was replaced during both games. In the total 180 minutes they were on the pitch together for 'only' 117 minutes.

SUB–SAHARAN AFRICAN COUNTRIES: TOP FIFA WORLD CUP GOALSCORERS

Asamoah Gyan (Ghana) 6
Roger Milla (Cameroon) 5
Ahmed Musa (Nigeria) 4
Papa Bouba Diop (Senegal) 3
Samuel Eto'o (Cameroon) 3
Daniel Amokachi (Nigeria) 2
Emmanuel Amunike (Nigeria) 2
Andre Ayew (Ghana) 2
Shaun Bartlett (South Africa) 2
Wilfried Bony (Ivory Coast) 2
Henri Camara (Senegal) 2
Aruna Dindane (Ivory Coast) 2
Didier Drogba (Ivory Coast) 2
Gervinho (Ivory Coast) 2
Patrick Mboma (Cameroon) 2
Benni McCarthy (South Africa) 2
Sulley Muntari (Ghana) 2
Francois Omam-Biyik (Cameroon) 2

CAPTAIN COOL

John Obi Mikel captained Nigeria in a crucial 2018 World Cup tie against Argentina, despite having just been told his father had been kidnapped back home. The midfielder arranged to pay a £21,000 ransom but told neither his coach Gernot Rohr nor any of his team-mates of his distress and the pressure on him because, "I couldn't let 180 million Nigerians down." Mikel's father was later released unharmed after a gunfight between kidnappers and police. Nigeria lost the game 2-1 and were eliminated.

THE FOURMOST

The only two African footballers to play at four FIFA World Cups – and the only three to be named in the squads for four – are all from Cameroon. Striker Samuel Eto'o became the latest in 2014, after playing in 1998, 2002 and 2010. He emulated defender Rigobert Song, who was in the Cameroon team in 1994, 1998, 2002 and 2010. Goalkeeper Jacques Songo'o was named in the country's squads for the four FIFA World Cups between 1990 and 2002, but he only actually played in the 1994 and 1998 versions.

SUB-SAHARAN AFRICA NATIONAL RECORDS

HOT DROG

Didier Drogba may have been raised in France but he was born in Ivory Coast and remains one of the African country's favourite sons for his actions both on and off the pitch. The Ivory Coast captain has a record 65 goals in 104 appearances for the Elephants. He has been credited with influence off the pitch, too, when he called for a ceasefire in the civil war-torn nation. He also pushed for an Africa Cup of Nations qualifier against Madagascar in June 2007 to be moved from the capital Abidjan to rebel army stronghold Bouake, in an effort to encourage reconciliation. Drogba, a two-time CAF African Footballer of the Year, captained the Ivory Coast team at the three FIFA World Cups they have reached, in 2006, 2010 and 2014, but he started only the third game in 2014.

SUB–SAHARAN AFRICA: SELECTED TOP GOALSCORERS

Country	Player	Goals
ANGOLA:	Akwa	38
BOTSWANA:	Jerome Ramatlhakwane	19
CAMEROON:	Samuel Eto'o	56
GHANA:	Asamoah Gyan	49
IVORY COAST:	Didier Drogba	65
NIGERIA:	Rashidi Yekini	37
SENEGAL:	Henri Camara	29
SOUTH AFRICA:	Benni McCarthy	32
TOGO:	Emmanuel Adabayor	30
ZAMBIA:	Godfrey Chitalu	79
ZIMBABWE:	Peter Ndlovu	38

FIFTEEN LOVE

Fifteen-year-old Samuel Kuffour became the youngest footballer to win an Olympic medal when Ghana took bronze at the 1992 Olympics in Barcelona – 27 days before his 16th birthday.

EAGLETS SOAR

The first African country to win an official FIFA tournament was Nigeria, when their "Golden Eaglets" beat Germany 2-0 in the final of the 1985 World Under-17 Championships.

FIRST ADE

Togo's all-time leading goalscorer – and 2008 African Footballer of the Year – **Emmanuel Adebayor** was captain during the country's only FIFA World Cup finals appearance, in Germany in 2006. They failed to win a game, but Adebayor's European club career has been more successful, with stints in France with Metz and Monaco, Spain with Real Madrid in England with Arsenal, Manchester City, Tottenham and Crystal Palace. His time with Spurs was disrupted by a family row in which he accused his mother of witchcraft against him.

KNOCKED OUT ON PENALTIES

Botswana goalkeeper and captain Modiri Marumo was sent off in the middle of a penalty shoot-out against Malawi in May 2003, after punching the opposing goalkeeper Philip Nyasulu in the face. Botswana defender Michael Mogaladi had to go in goal for the rest of the shoot-out, which Malawi won 4-1.

GODFREY THE GREAT

Zambians believes the world record for goals in a calendar year should belong to their own Godfrey Chitalu and not to Lionel Messi. In 2012, Messi scored 91 goals for Argentina and Barcelona, but the Zambia FA insists that Chitalu had scored 116 goals, apparently unnoticed abroad, in 1972. Chitalu was voted Zambia's player of the year five times and he scored a record 79 goals in 108 international appearances between 1968 and 1980. Later he managed the national team but he was among those killed in the tragic plane crash in 1993 as the team headed for a World Cup qualifying tie in Senegal.

SUPER FRED

In 2007, Frederic Kanoute became the first non-African-born player to be named African Footballer of the Year. The striker was born in Lyon, France, and played for France U-21s. But the son of a French mother and Malian father opted to play for Mali in 2004, scoring 23 goals in 37 appearances before retiring from international football after the 2010 Africa Cup of Nations. As well as going down in history as one of Mali's greatest-ever players, he is also a hero to fans of Spanish side CF Sevilla, for whom he scored 143 goals, winning two UEFA Cups along the way. Only three men have scored more goals for the club.

GABON ON SONG

Gabon's leading international goalscorer **Pierre-Emerick Aubameyang** ended Yaya Toure's four-year reign as CAF African Footballer of the Year in 2016. Toure had joined Cameroon's Samuel Eto'o as a four-time winner, but Aubameyang's 41 goals for club Borussia Dortmund and country relegated him to second. Born in Laval, France, Aubameyang launched his career in Italy with AC Milan, and was the first Bundesliga player to win the award. Later he joined Arsenal in 2018 for a club record £56m. Aubameyang, who played once for France under-21s, made his Gabon debut in 2009.

SUB–SAHARAN AFRICA: SELECTED TOP APPEARANCES

Country	Player	Appearances
ANGOLA:	Flavio Amado	91
BOTSWANA:	Mompati Thuma	84
CAMEROON:	Rigobert Song	137
GHANA:	Asamoah Gyan	106
IVORY COAST:	Didier Zokora	123
NIGERIA:	Vincent Enyeama / Joseph Yobo	101
SENEGAL:	Henri Camara	99
SOUTH AFRICA:	Aaron Mokoena	107
TOGO:	Mohamed Kader	85
ZAMBIA:	Kennedy Mweene	116
ZIMBABWE:	Peter Ndlovu	100

PRESIDENT GEORGE

George Weah made history in December 2017 when he became the first star African footballer to go on and become president of his country. In Liberia's first democratic handover in decades, Weah succeeded Ellen Johnson Sirleaf, Africa's first elected female president. Weah, raised in a slum in the capital Monrovia, is the only former FIFA World Player of the Year whose country has never qualified for the World Cup finals. He starred in attack for Monaco, Paris Saint-Germain, Milan, Chelsea and Manchester City and dipped into his own earnings to help pay his national team's travel costs and kit.

SHOOTING STAR

Zimbabwe's leading scorer **Peter Ndlovu** was the first African footballer to appear in the English Premier League when he made his Coventry City debut in August 1992. He ended his international career with 38 goals in 100 games for his country between 1991 and 2007 – before being appointed Zimbabwe's assistant manager in 2011. The man nicknamed "the Bulawayo Bullet" had spearheaded in 2004 the first Zimbabwe side to reach an Africa Cup of Nations finals, following that up with repeat qualification two years later. His international team-mates included brother Adam and flamboyant ex-Liverpool goalkeeper Bruce Grobbelaar. Adam Ndlovu tragically died in a car accident near Victoria Falls in Zimbabwe in December 2012. Peter was also in the car and although he suffered very serious head injuries and broken bones he managed to survive.

ASIA & OCEANIA

Asia will host the World Cup for the second time when the Gulf state of Qatar stages football's greatest showpiece in 2022. This will enhance the increasingly high status of the Asian game, allied to the remarkable investment in football emerging from China. Japan and South Korea co-hosted Asia's first World Cup in 2002 since when the region's football power Asia has been strengthened by the "transfer" of Australia out of the Oceania confederation.

Japan was a credit to world football on and off the pitch at the FIFA World Cup 2018 in Russia. The team exited after a narrow second-round loss to Belgium and the support team in the dressing room and fans in the stands cleaned up after themselves.

AUSTRALIA

Victims, perhaps, of an overcomplicated qualifying system that has limited the country's FIFA World Cup finals appearances, and hampered by its geographical isolation that, in the early years, saw other sports prosper in the country at football's expense, it has taken many years for Australia to establish itself on the world football map. However, driven by new generations of players, many based with top European clubs, Australia have become regular FIFA World Cup qualifiers and in 2015 hosted and lifted the AFC Asian Cup for the first time.

AUSTRALIA RECORDS

Honours: Oceania champions 1980, 1996, 2000, 2004; Asian champions 2015
First international: v New Zealand (lost 3-1), Auckland, 17 June 1922
Biggest win: 31-0 v American Samoa, Coffs Harbour, 11 April 2001
Biggest defeat: 7-0 v Croatia, Zagreb, 6 June 1998

NATIVE HERO

Harry Williams holds a proud place in Australian football history as the first Aboriginal player to represent the country in internationals. He made his debut in 1970 and was part of the first Australian squad to compete at a FIFA World Cup finals, in West Germany in 1974.

MOMENTOUS MORI

Damian Mori's then-Australian record tally of 29 goals, in just 45 internationals, included no fewer than five hat-tricks: trebles against Fiji and Tahiti, four-goal hauls against the Cook Islands and Tonga, and five in Australia's 13-0 trouncing of the Solomon Islands in a 1998 FIFA World Cup qualifier. His international career spanned from 1992 to 2002, but he never played in a FIFA World Cup finals as Australia didn't qualify. He did, though, claim a world record for scoring the fastest goal – after just 3.69 seconds for his club side Adelaide City against Sydney United in 1996.

NEILL APPEAL

 Tough-tackling Australia veteran **Lucas Neill** had to wait until his 91st international appearance before scoring his first goal for his country: the final strike in a 4-0 victory over Jordan in June 2013 that boosted their chances of reaching the 2014 FIFA World Cup. Qualification was clinched in the next game. Neill, however, was omitted from Australia's squad for Brazil and his international career ended after 96 apppearances for the Socceroos. Former Blackburn Rovers, West Ham United and Galatasaray defender Neill made his Australia debut in October 1996, becoming the country's third-youngest international. His scoring record, though, pales alongside that of fellow centre-back Robbie Cornthwaite, his goal against Romania in February 2013 was his third in his first six games for Australia.

TOP CAPS

1	Mark Schwarzer	109
2	Tim Cahill	107
3	Lucas Neill	96
4	Brett Emerton	95
5	Alex Tobin	87
6	Mark Bresciano	84
=	Paul Wade	84
8	Luke Wilkshire	80
9	Mile Jedinak	79
10	Tony Vidmar	76

CAHILL MAKES HISTORY

Tim Cahill's total of five FIFA World Cup goals is only three fewer than all other Australians put together. He scored Australia's first two World Cup goals, netting in the 84th and 89th minutes of a comeback 3-1 win over Japan in 2006. But he saved the most spectacular for last, a first-time volley in a 3-2 defeat to the Netherlands in 2014. Cahill also received his second yellow card of the competition later in that game and so missed Australia's final match. He scored twice in 2006, once in 2010 – but was also red-carded – and twice in 2014. Cahill led Australia's goalscorers with 11 in qualifying for the 2018 FIFA World Cup, but he saw only 37 minutes of action in Russia, coming on as a substitute against Peru in the final group game.

AUSTRALIA'S SHOOT-OUT RECORD

Australia are the only team to reach the FIFA World Cup finals via a penalty shoot-out – in the final qualifying play-off in November 2005. They had lost the first leg 1-0 to Uruguay in Montevideo. Mark Bresciano's goal levelled the aggregate score, which remained 1-1 after extra-time. Goalkeeper **Mark Schwarzer** made two crucial saves as Australia won the shoot-out 4-2, with John Aloisi scoring the winning spot-kick. Schwarzer passed Alex Tobin to become Australia's most-capped footballer with his 88th appearance, in January 2011, in the AFC Asian Cup final defeat to Japan. Tobin had been in defence when Schwarzer made his Australia debut against Canada in 1993.

1,000 MILE

Australia captain **Mile Jedinak** has scored his country's last three FIFA World Cup goals – all from the penalty spot. He found the net in their 3-2 defeat to the Netherlands in 2014, then four years later scored in a 2-1 defeat to France and a 1-1 draw with Denmark before Australia bowed out in the first round. Midfielder Jedinak had scored a hat-trick to secure Australia's place in Russia – including two penalties – when Honduras were beaten 3-1 in November 2017 play-off following a goalless first leg. In March 2015, Jedinak had scored Australia's 1,000th international goal, a stunning free-kick in a 2-2 friendly draw against world champions Germany. Bill Maunder had scored the first in a tour game against New Zealand in June 1922.

THREE-CARD TRICK

Graham Poll, in 2006, was not the first referee at a FIFA World Cup to show the same player three yellow cards. It happened in another game involving Australia, when their English-born midfielder Ray Richards was belatedly sent off against Chile at the 1974 FIFA World Cup. Reserve official Clive Thomas, from Wales, informed Iranian referee Jafar Namdar he had booked Richards three times without dismissing him. Richards played four unwarranted minutes before eventually receiving his marching orders.

BET ON BRETT

Brett Holman's goal against Ghana, in a 1-1 draw at the 2010 tournament, made him Australia's youngest marksman at a FIFA World Cup. He was 26 years 84 days old at the time, 105 days younger than Tim Cahill had been when striking against Japan in 2006. Holman added to his tally five days later, when Australia beat Serbia 2-1. Cahill himself was also on the scoresheet, though goal difference meant Australia failed to reach the second round.

TOP SCORERS

1	Tim Cahill	50
2	Damian Mori	29
3	Archie Thompson	28
4	John Aloisi	27
5	Attila Abonyi	25
=	John Kosmina	25
7	Brett Emerton	20
=	Mile Jedinak	20
=	David Zdrilic	20
10	Graham Arnold	19

BATTLER WILS

Tough-tackling defender **Peter Wilson** was born in England but, after emigrating to Australia in 1969, captained his adoptive country at their first FIFA World Cup in 1974. He became the first Australian to reach 50 caps, in 1976, before retiring from international football in 1979 with 65 appearances – a tally only overtaken in 1993, by Paul Wade. Another mainstay of the Australia side of that era was midfielder and later broadcaster Johnny Warren, after whom the annual award for the Australian A-League's best player is named.

JAPAN

The past two decades have seen great breakthroughs for Japanese football. Until the first professional league was introduced in 1993, clubs had been amateur and football was overshadowed in Japan's affections by other sports such as baseball, martial arts, table tennis and golf. Even more significantly, Japan co-hosted the 2002 FIFA World Cup – where the team reached the second round for the first time. And AFC Asian Cup wins in 1992, 2000, 2004 and 2011 were celebrated keenly as proof of surging standards.

POLITICAL FOOTBALL

Japan were surprise bronze medallists in the football tournament at the 1968 Olympic Games in Mexico City. Star striker Kunishige Kamamoto finished top scorer overall with seven goals. He remains Japan's all-time leading scorer, with 80 goals in 84 matches (Japan consider Olympic Games matches full internationals). Since retirement, he has combined coaching with being elected to Japan's parliament and serving as vice-president of the country's football association.

CLEAN BREAK

Japan's fans and players impressed many at the 2018 FIFA World Cup with their displays – and their manners. Japanese fans were filmed meticulously tidying up after themselves in the stands at full-time of their games, and the support staff took a similar approach to their dressing rooms. Japan reached the second round for the third time in Russia and almost enjoyed a first quarter-final appearance, despite having replaced their manager Valid Halilhodzic with former Japan international wmidfielder Akira Nishino just two months before the tournament. They led Belgium 2-0 in the second round, including a second goal of the tournament for Takashi Inui, but Belgium scored twice to equalize. Keisuke Honda then saw a long-range stoppage-time shot saved by Thibaut Courtois. Belgium counter-attacked from the resulting corner and Nacer Chadli scored to win the game. Despite their disappointment, Japan's team support staff tidied their dressing room and left a thank-you note, in Russian, for their Rostov-on-Don hosts.

TOP SCORERS

1	Kunishige Kamamoto	75
2	Kazuyoshi Miura	55
3	Shinji Okazaki	50
4	Hiromi Hara	37
=	Keisuke Honda	37
6	Shinji Kagawa	31
7	Takuya Takagi	27
8	Kazushi Kimura	26
9	Shunsuke Nakamura	24
10	Naohiro Takahara	23

HONDA INSPIRES

Skilful midfielder **Keisuke Honda** is Japan's highest scorer at FIFA World Cups – four goals – and the only Japanese player to find the net at three finals. It started at South Africa in 2010, when he scored in Japan's victories over Cameroon and Denmark, and continued with a goal in the defeat against Costa Rica in Brazil four years later. At Russia 2018, Honda came on after 72 minutes of the Group H game against Senegal and, six minutes later, scored the second equaliser in a 2-2 draw. Honda won two man-of-the-match awards at the 2010 FIFA World Cup and was named player of the tournament when Japan won the 2011 AFC Asian Cup. After Japan had exited the tournament in Russia, Honda – whose clubs include Nagoya Grampus in Japan, CSKA Moscow in Russia, AC Milan in Italy and Pachuca in Mexico – retired from international football, having scored 37 goals in 98 games.

TOP CAPS

1	Yasuhito Endo	152
2	Masami Ihara	122
3	Yoshikatsu Kawaguchi	116
=	Shinji Okazaki	116
5	Makoto Hasebe	114
6	Yuji Nakazawa	110
7	Yuto Nagatomo	109
8	Keisuke Honda	98
=	Shunsuke Nakamura	98
10	Shinji Kagawa	95

THE ENDO

Midfielder Yasuhito Endo scored the opening goal of Japan's defence of their AFC Asian Cup crown, as they began the 2015 tournament with a 4-0 win over debutants Palestine. However, after winning their three group matches, without conceding a goal, Japan lost next time out, a quarter-final against the United Arab Emirates, on penalties after a 1-1 draw. It was their worst showing at the AFC Asian Cup for 19 years. Endo had the consolation of becoming Japan's first international to reach 150 caps, but he left the international stage after the finals, having scored 15 times in 152 games.

OKAZAKI'S A-OK

Shinji Okazaki became only the fifth man to reach 100 appearances for Japan, in a match against Syria in March 2016. Two months later, the striker ended the season with an English Premier League winner's medal, having scored five goals in Leicester City's 5,000-1 triumph (and one in the FA Cup). He was on the scoresheet during Japan's 3-1 victory over Denmark in Bloemfontein at the 2010 FIFA World Cup, along with Keisuke Honda and Yasuhito Endo – the first time an Asian side had scored three goals in one FIFA World Cup match since Portugal had beaten North Korea 5-3 in the 1966 quarter-finals. His 50 goals for his country include hat-tricks in consecutive matches, against Hong Kong and Togo in October 2009.

KAZU CAN DO

Japan's second most prolific international goalscorer Kazuyoshi Miura is also the world's oldest active professional high-level footballer. On 12 March 2017, aged 50 years and 14 days, Miura scored for Yokohama FC against Thespakusatsu Gunma in J.League Division 2. His 55 goals in 89 international matches include 14 in qualifying for the 1998 FIFA World Cup, Japan's first. Miura moved to Brazil at the age of 15 and starred for Pele's old team Santos before returning home in 1990 with the launch of the country's J.League, then firing his nation to AFC Asian Cup glory two years later.

TA-DA, TADANARI

The goalscoring hero whose extra-time goal won a record fourth AFC Asian Cup for Japan in 2011 was a man who had not even played for his country before the tournament kicked off. Striker **Tadanari Lee** made his international debut in the first-round match against Jordan – and conjured perfect timing for his first Japan goal, with 11 minutes of extra-time left in the final against Australia. His midfield team-mate Keisuke Honda took the prize for the event's most valuable player, while forward Shinji Okazaki's first-round hat-trick against Saudi Arabia helped earn him a place in the team of the tournament.

JAPANESE GOAL GLUT

No team have scored more goals in one AFC Asian Cup tournament than Japan's 21 in six games on their way to winning the title for the second time, in Lebanon in 2000 – though the final against Saudi Arabia was settled with just a single goal, by Shigeyoshi Mochizuki. Nine different players scored for Japan during the tournament – including Akinori Nishizawa and Naohiro Takahara, who each managed five – while their team-mate Ryuzo Morioka scored once in his own net. Japan's most emphatic victory of the tournament came in the first round, 8-1 against Uzbekistan, with both Nishizawa and Takahara hitting hat-tricks.

SOUTH KOREA

"Be the Reds!" was the rallying cry of South Korea's fervent fans as they co-hosted the 2002 FIFA World Cup – and saw their energetic team become the first Asian side to reach the semi-finals, ultimately finishing fourth. South Korea also won the AFC Asian Cup the first two times it was staged (in 1956 and 1960). South Korea could well claim to be the continent's leading football nation, even if AFC Asian Cup triumphs have been thin on the ground since then. The country's professional K-League is making progress and South Korean teams have won the Asian club championship 10 times.

PARK LIFE

The tirelessly-energetic midfielder **Park Ji-Sung** can claim to be the most successful Asian footballer of all time. He became the first Asian player to lift the UEFA Champions League trophy when his club Manchester United beat Chelsea in 2008, despite missing the final. He also became the first Asian footballer to score at three successive FIFA World Cups – beginning on home turf in 2002, when his goal broke the deadlock in a first-round game against Portugal, putting South Korea through to the knock-out stages for the first time ever. Park shares the Korean record for most FIFA World Cup goals – three – with Ahn Jung-Hwan, who got all of his in Germany in 2006. Park became the eighth South Korean to reach a century of caps when he captained the side in their 2011 AFC Asian Cup semi-final defeat to Japan, before announcing his international retirement to allow a younger generation to emerge.

HERE COMES THE SON

South Korea have played more FIFA World Cup games than any other Asian country, taking their tally to 34 with three first-round games in 2018. Defeats against Sweden, 1-0, and Mexico, 2-1, meant they could not advance to the second round, but they went out on a high, beating defending champion Germany 2-0 and condemning them to bottom of the group. South Korea's latest hero, **Son Heung-Min**, scored the consolation against Mexico and the second against Germany, minutes after Kim Young-Gwon's injury-time opener. Son tapped the ball into an empty net after German goalkeeper Manuel Neuer was stranded at the other end of the pitch. That lifted Son to 23 goals in 70 internationals and put him level with Park Ji-Sung and Ahn Jung-Hwan on three FIFA World Cup goals for South Korea. He was picked for the 2014 FIFA World Cup despite his former international footballer father Son Woong-Chun believing he needed more time to develop as a player. Son became Asia's most expensive footballer when English club Tottenham Hotspur bought him for £22m from Germany's Bayer Leverkusen in 2015.

SPIDER CATCHER

Goalkeeper **Lee Woon-Jae** – nicknamed "Spider Hands" – made himself a national hero by making the crucial penalty save that took co-hosts South Korea into the semi-finals of the 2002 FIFA World Cup. He blocked Spain's fourth spot-kick, taken by winger Joaquin, in a quarter-final shoot-out. Lee, who also played in the 1994, 2006 and 2010 FIFA World Cups, provided more penalty saves at the 2007 AFC Asian Cup – stopping three spot-kicks in shoot-outs on South Korea's way to third place. Lee's form restricted his frequent back-up, Kim Byung-Ji, to just 62 international appearances. But Kim did at least set a new South Korean top-flight landmark of 200 clean sheets in June 2012, at the age of 42.

STIELIKE'S STEELY DEFENCE

On 1 September 2016, South Korea set a national record with their ninth consecutive FIFA World Cup qualifying victory, this time beating China 3-2 in Seoul. They also completed a FIFA World Cup qualifying run of 13 hours and 44 minutes without conceding a goal in qualifiers, dating back to a 2013 loss to Iran. Among South Korea's scorers against China was midfielder **Lee Chung-Yong**, who also struck twice at the 2010 FIFA World Cup in South Africa. Another national record fell on 1 June 2017, when former West Germany international Uli Stieleke became South Korea's first national coach to complete 1,000 days in charge. However this three-year reign ended 14 days later when he was sacked after three defeats in eight games. Former South Korea midfielder Shin Tae-Yong, capped 23 times, took over and was in charge at the 2018 FIFA World Cup.

TOP CAPS

1	Hong Myung-Bo	136
2	Cha Bum-Kun	134
3	Lee Woon-Jae	133
4	Lee Young-Pyo	127
5	Yoo Sang-Chul	120
6	Ki Sung-Yueng	104
=	Kim Tae-Young	104
=	Lee Dong-Gook	104
9	Hwang Seon-Hong	103
10	Park Ji-Sung	100

TOP SCORERS

1	Cha Bum-Kun	58
2	Hwang Sun-Hong	50
3	Lee Dong-Gook	33
4	Choi Soon-Ho	30
5	Huh Jung-Moo	29
=	Kim Do-Hun	29
7	Choi Yong-Soo	27
=	Lee Tae-Hoo	27
9	Park Chu-Young	25
10	Lee Young-Moo	24
=	Park Sung-Hwa	24

HONG SETS FIFA WORLD CUP RECORD

South Korea defender **Hong Myung-Bo** was the first Asian footballer to appear in four consecutive FIFA World Cup finals tournaments. He played all three games as South Korea lost to Belgium, Spain and Uruguay in 1990. He scored twice in three appearances in 1994 – his goal against Spain sparking a Korean fightback from 2-0 down to draw 2-2. In 1998 he started all three group games as South Korea were eliminated at the group stage. Four years later, on home soil, he captained South Korea to fourth place in the finals and was voted third-best player of the tournament. As coach of the U-23 squad, Hong led South Korea to Olympic bronze at the 2012 Summer Games – beating Japan 2-0 in the medal play-off. Those goals were scored by Arsenal's Park Chu-Young and Koo Ja-Cheol of WfL Wolfsburg. Hong became South Korea's national team coach in June 2013, and was in charge at the 2014 FIFA World Cup, where one group game pitted him against Belgium and their coach Marc Wilmots – the pair having played against each other at the 1998 finals.

CHA BOOM AND BUST

Even before South Korea made their FIFA World Cup breakthrough under Guus Hiddink, the country had a homegrown hero of world renown – thunderous striker **Cha Bum-Kun**, known for his fierce shots and suitable nickname "Cha Boom". He helped pave the way for more Asian players to make their name in Europe by signing for German club Eintracht Frankfurt in 1979 and later played for Bundesliga rivals Bayer Leverkusen. His achievements in Germany included two UEFA Cup triumphs – with Frankfurt in 1980 and with Leverkusen eight years later – while his performances helped make him a childhood idol for future German internationals such as Jurgen Klinsmann and Michael Ballack. His record 58 goals for the national team, in 134 appearances, included a seven-minute hat-trick against Malaysia in the 1977 Park's Cup tournament – levelling the score after South Korea had been trailing 4-1. "Cha Boom" later served as national coach, winning 22, losing 11 and drawing eight during his time in charge between January 1997 and June 1998 – but there was an unhappy ending when he was sacked two games into the 1998 FIFA World Cup, after South Korea's 5-0 defeat to the Netherlands.

OTHER ASIAN COUNTRIES

The lesser-known Asian footballing nations represent the true backwaters of world football. These may well be the countries in which true football obsession has yet to take hold, but competition between, and achievements by, these teams are no less vibrant. The regions are the home to many of the game's record-breakers – from the most goals in a single game to the most career appearances – and some of these records may never be broken.

IRAN TOP SCORERS

1	Ali Daei	109
2	Karim Bagheri	50
3	Javad Nekounam	39
4	Ali Karimi	38
5	Sardar Azmoun	23
6	Gholamhussein Mazloumi	19
=	Farshad Pious	19
8	Karim Ansarifard	18
=	Asghar Modir Rosta	18
10	Reza Ghoochannejhad	17

READY NEK

Javad Nekounam is second behind Ali Daei in matches as Iran's captain (56 to 80) but he replaced his former team-mate at the top of the appearances table. Nekounam captained Iran at the 2014 FIFA World Cup, surpassed Daei's record with his 150th cap against Chile in March 2015 and bowed out with his final game against Sweden five days later. He was promptly appointed as assistant to Iran's national coach Carlos Queiroz.

MASTER MANAGER

Iran won all 13 matches across their hat-trick of AFC Asian Cup triumphs in 1968, 1972 and 1976. Their 8-0 win over South Yemen in 1976 is a tournament record. Manager was Heshmat Mohajerani who later guided Iran to their FIFA World Cup finals debut in 1978.

SAUDIS LEAVE IT LATE

Saudi Arabia ended a run of 12 matches in the FIFA World Cup finals without a victory when they defeated Egypt 2-1 in their final group match in 2018. It was their first chance to celebrate a victory on the game's biggest stage since they defeated Belgium by 1-0 in June 1994. Egypt scored first, but the Saudis equalized with a penalty by midfielder Salman Al Faraj five minutes 50 seconds in first half stoppage time – the latest goal in the first half of a finals tie since 1966. Their winner was also late – winger **Salem Muhamed Al-Dawsari** striking five minutes into second half stoppage time.

AHMED'S CONSOLATION

UAE striker Ahmed Khalil had the honour of being the 16-goal joint leading scorer in the Asian qualifying competition for the 2018 FIFA World Cup in Russia. Unfortunately for him, the 2015 Asian Footballer of the Year was denied the opportunity to test his talents at the pinnacle of the international game because the Gulf state's failed to make the most of his goal-poaching instincts. In the UAE's initial qualifying group Khalil's haul included scored four goals in a 10-0 win over Malaysia and the team finished runners-up to Saudi Arabia. That sent them on to the final group stage, but they finished fourth in the group, behind Japan, Saudi Arabia and Australia – all of whom celebrated qualification for the finals in Russia.

IRAN TOP CAPS

1	Javad Nekounam	151
2	Ali Daei	149
3	Ali Karimi	127
4	Jalal Hosseini	116
5	Mehdi Mahdavikia	110
6	Andranik Teymourian	101
7	Ehsan Hajsafi	97
8	Karim Bagheri	87
9	Hossein Kaebi	84
10	Hamid Reza Estili	82

APPEARANCES IN THE FIFA WORLD CUP FINALS

Iran	5	(1978, 1998, 2006, 2014, 2018)
Saudi Arabia	5	(1994, 1998, 2002, 2006, 2018)
New Zealand	2	(1982*, 2010*)
North Korea	2	(1966, 2010)
China	1	(2002)
Indonesia**	1	(1938)
Iraq	1	(1986)
Israel	1	(1970)
Kuwait	1	(1982)
United Arab Emirates	1	(1990)

* Qualified for FIFA World Cup as Oceania Confederation member
** Played in the 1938 FIFA World Cup as Dutch East Indies

SHAKEN SHEIKH

Kuwait have qualified for the FIFA World Cup just once, in 1982 – though they made a memorable appearance when they almost walked off the field in protest at a decision. Kuwait's chief Olympic official, Sheikh Fahad Al-Ahmed, even stomped on to the pitch in Valladolid, Spain, when France's Alain Giresse scored a goal that would have given les Bleus a 4-1 lead. The Kuwaitis claimed they had heard a whistle and stopped playing and ultimately convinced referee Myroslav Stupar to disallow the strike. The game still finished 4-1 to France, though, and Kuwait were eliminated in the first round.

CHINA YET TO REALIZE POTENTIAL

China have qualified just once for the FIFA World Cup finals, in 2002, but they suffered in the finals, failing to score in defeats by Costa Rica (2-0), Brazil (4-0) and Turkey (3-0). That squad included record caps-holder Li Weifeng (112 appearances) and leading scorer Hao Haidong (37 goals). They were one of a record three teams (along with Japan and South Korea) to complete the first round of the 2015 AFC Asian Cup with three wins out of three and no goals conceded, the first time China had achieved maximum points in an opening stage. Under French coach Alain Perrin they lost 2-0 to eventual champions Australia in the quarter-finals. China's new domestic Super League has raised standards but too late to help China qualify for the 2018 FIFA World Cup finals.

OFFICIAL'S APPROVAL

Nawaf Shukralla made history in 2018 by becoming the first referee from Bahrain to be nominated to two successive FIFA World Cup finals tournaments. Shukralla had joined the international list in 2008 and worked his way up via the 2011 FIFA U-17 World Cup, the Asian Champions League, FIFA Club World Cup and then the 2014 senior World Cup. He refereed two matches in Brazil and two more four years later in Russia: Senegal's opening 2-1 win against Poland and Tunisia's closing 2-1 win over Panama.

PALESTINE THE PIONEERS

Palestine, then under British rule, were the first Asian team to enter the FIFA World Cup qualifiers. They lost 7-1 away to Egypt on 16 March 1934. They lost the return match at home on 6 April, 4-1. Four years later, they were eliminated by Greece, who won 3-1 in Tel Aviv and 1-0 at home. The former Palestine was split by partition in 1948. A "new" Palestine made their debut in the Asian Cup finals in 2015 in Australia, but lost all three first round games.

WORLD'S WORST

On the same day that Brazil and Germany contested the FIFA World Cup final on 30 June 2002, the two lowest-ranked FIFA countries were also taking each other on. Asian side Bhutan ran out 4-0 winners over CONCACAF's Montserrat, in a match staged in the Bhutan capital Thimphu. The winning side's captain, striker Wangay Dorji, scored a hat-trick.

IRAQ AND ROLL

One of the greatest – and most heart-warming – surprises of recent international football was Iraq's unexpected triumph at the 2007 AFC Asian Cup, barely a year after the end of the war that ravaged the country and forced them to play "home" games elsewhere. Despite disrupted preparations, they eliminated Vietnam and South Korea on the way to the 2007 final in which captain **Younis Mahmoud**'s goal proved decisive against Saudi Arabia. They were unable to retain their title four years later, losing to Australia in the quarter-finals. Mahmoud retired from international football in March 2014, ending his Iraq career with 50 goals in 124 matches – second in both categories – behind only Hussein Saeed, who scored 61 goals in 126 appearances between 1977 and 1990.

MOKH STAR

Mokhtar Dahari, who died aged just 37 in 1991, remains Malaysia's record scorer – with 45 official goals in 167 games between 1972 and 1985. In 1978 Dahari, known as "Super Mokh", scored with a solo run for the halfway line in a 1-1 draw with England B, a game played before a 45,000-strong crowd in Kuala Lumpur. Although not one of the 10 members of the AFC's Hall of Fame – they are compatriot Soh Chin Aun, Australia's Harry Kewell, China's Sun Wen, India's Baichung Bhutia, Iran's Homayoun Behzadi and Ali Daei, Japan's Homare Sawa and Yasuhiko Okudera, Saudi Arabia's Sami Al-Jaber and South Korea's Hong Myung-bo – he is a Malaysian national hero.

HAPPY DAEI

Iran striker **Ali Daei** became the first footballer to score a century of international goals, when his four in a 7-0 defeat of Laos on 17 November 2004 took him to 102. He ended his career having scored 109 times for Iran in 149 internationals between 1993 and 2006 – though none of his goals came during FIFA World Cup appearances in 1998 and 2006. He is also the all-time leading scorer in the AFC Asian Cup, with 14 goals, despite failing ever to win the tournament. His time as national coach was less auspicious – he lasted only a year from March 2008 to March 2009 before being fired, as Iran struggled in qualifiers for the 2010 FIFA World Cup.

ONE OF BARCA'S BEST

The first Asian footballer ever to play for a European club was also, for almost a century, the all-time leading scorer for Spanish giants Barcelona, before being finally overtaken by Lionel Messi in March 2014. Paulino Alcantara, from the Philippines, scored 369 goals in 357 matches for the Catalan club between 1912 and 1927. He made his debut aged just 15, and remains Barcelona's youngest-ever first-team player. Alcantara was born in the Philippines, but had a Spanish father, and appeared in internationals for Catalonia, Spain and the Philippines, for whom he featured in a record 15-2 trouncing of Japan in 1917. Alcantara became a doctor after retiring from football at the age of 31, though he did briefly manage Spain in 1951.

WORTH HIS KUWAIT IN GOLD

Bader Al-Mutawa is both Kuwait's most-capped player and leading goalscorer. He moved to 156 appearances and 51 goals for his country in September 2015, having made his debut 14 years earlier. He also finished runner-up as 2006 AFC Asian Footballer of the Year – having mistakenly been named third initially. Unfortunately for Al-Mutawa, his national team career was interrupted in 2015 when Kuwait was suspended from international football by FIFA, a decision which also cost Kuwait staging rights for the 2019 AFC Asian Cup – it was switched to the UAE.

DOUBLE TROUBLE

Juan Antonio Pizzi had an unpleasant surprise when he returned to Russia in 2018 for his second managerial visit in a year. In 2017, Pizzi, who was born in Argentina but later played centre-forward for Spain, was manager of Chile who reached the final of the 2017 FIFA Confederations Cup, losing 1-0 to Germany in St Petersburg. After Chile failed to reach the 2018 FIFA World Cup, Pizzi was hired by Saudi Arabia, becoming their third manager in as many months. But a lack of preparation saw them eliminated in the first round.

TIE LACK

The 2015 AFC Asian Cup set a remarkable international tournament record for consecutive matches without a draw. All 24 matches in the group stage and then the first two quarter-finals turned up positive results after 90 minutes. However Iraq (over Iran) and the United Arab Emirates (over Japan) needed penalty shootouts to reach the last four. Uniquely, the inaugural World Cup finals tournament in Uruguay in 1930 saw all 18 matches end in a decisive result.

AFC ASIAN CUP TOP SCORERS

1	Ali Daei (Iran)	14
2	Lee Dong-Gook (South Korea)	10
3	Naohiro Takahara (Japan)	9
4	Jassem Al-Houwaidi (Kuwait)	8
=	Younis Mahmoud (Iraq)	8
6	Behtash Fariba (Iran)	7
=	Hossein Kalani (Iran)	7
=	Choi Soon-Ho (South Korea)	7
=	Faisal Al-Dakhil (Kuwait)	7
10	Yasser Al-Qahtani (Saudi Arabia)	6
=	Tim Cahill (Australia)	6
=	Alexander Geynrikh (Uzbekistan)	6

PAK STRIKE MAKES HISTORY

North Korea's **Pak Doo Ik** earned legendary status
by scoring the goal that eliminated Italy from the
1966 FIFA World Cup finals. The shockwaves caused
by the victory were comparable to those caused by
the United States' 1-0 win over England in 1950. Pak
netted the only goal of the game in the 42nd minute
at Middlesbrough on 19 July. North Korea thus became
the first Asian team to reach the quarter-finals. Pak,
an army corporal, was promoted to sergeant after the
victory and later became a gymnastics coach.

AFC ASIAN CUP–WINNING COACHES

1956	**Lee Yoo-Hyung**	(South Korea)
1960	**Wi Hye-Deok**	(South Korea)
1964	**Gyula Mandl**	(Israel)
1968	**Mahmoud Bayati**	(Iran)
1972	**Mohammad Ranjbar**	(Iran)
1976	**Heshmat Mohajerani**	(Iran)
1980	**Carlos Alberto Parreira**	(Kuwait)
1984	**Khalil Al-Zayani**	(Saudi Arabia)
1988	**Carlos Alberto Parreira**	(Saudi Arabia)
1992	**Hans Ooft**	(Japan)
1996	**Nelo Vingada**	(Saudi Arabia)
2000	**Philippe Troussier**	(Japan)
2004	**Zico**	(Japan)
2007	**Jorvan Vieira**	(Iraq)
2011	**Alberto Zaccheroni**	(Japan)
2015	**Ange Postecoglou**	(Australia)

ASIAN FOOTBALLER OF THE YEAR

Year	Player	Country
1988	Ahmed Radhi	Iraq
1989	Kim Joo-Sung	South Korea
1990	Kim Joo-Sung	South Korea
1991	Kim Joo-Sung	South Korea
1992	not awarded	
1993	Kazuyoshi Miura	Japan
1994	Saeed Owarain	Saudi Arabia
1995	Masami Ihara	Japan
1996	Khodadad Azizi	Iran
1997	Hidetoshi Nakata	Japan
1998	Hidetoshi Nakata	Japan
1999	Ali Daei	Iran
2000	Nawaf Al Temyat	Saudi Arabia
2001	Fan Zhiyi	China
2002	Shinji Ono	Japan
2003	Mehdi Mahdavikia	Iran
2004	Ali Karimi	Iran
2005	Hamad Al-Montashari	Saudi Arabia
2006	Khalfan Ibrahim	Qatar
2007	Yasser Al-Qahtani	Saudi Arabia
2008	Server Djeparov	Uzbekistan
2009	Yasuhito Endo	Japan
2010	Sasa Ognenovski	Australia
2011	Server Djeparov	Uzbekistan
2012	Lee Keun-Ho	South Korea
2013	Zheng Zhi	China
2014	Nasser Al-Shamrani	Saudi Arabia
2015	Ahmed Khalil	UAE
2016	Omar Abdulrahman	UAE
2017	Omar Kharbin	Syria

AL-JABER TO THE FORE

Sami Al-Jaber (born on 11 December 1972 in Riyadh) became
only the second Asian player to appear in four FIFA World Cup
finals tournaments when he started against Tunisia in Munich
on 14 June 2006. He scored in a 2-2 draw, his third goal in nine
appearances at the finals. Al-Jaber played only one game in
1998 before he was rushed to hospital with a burst appendix,
which ruled him out of the competition. He became Saudi
Arabia's record scorer, with 44 goals in 163 matches.

A LONG JOURNEY FOR A BEATING

The first Asian country to play in a
FIFA World Cup finals was Indonesia,
who played in France in 1938
as the Dutch East Indies. The
tournament was a straight
knockout and, on 5 June in
Reims, Hungary beat them 6-0,
with goals from Gyorgy Sarosi,
Gyula Zsengeller (two each),
Vilmos Kohut and Geza Toldi.

BHUTAN DO THE BEATING

Bhutan enjoyed an unprecedented winning streak in March
2015. The world's then-lowest-ranked nation had won only
two official internationals in 34 years before they beat Sri
Lanka twice in a two-legged 2018 FIFA World Cup qualifier.
Tshering Dorji scored the only goal of the first leg and the nation's only
professional footballer – **Chencho Gyeltshan** – struck both in a 2-1 victory
a week later. The Himalayan nation reached the second round of the AFC
qualification for the first time, but lost all eight matches with a goal
difference of -52. The reign of their Japanese coach Norio Tsukitate's
ended in strange circumstances. He was fired at half-time when
Bhutan trailed the Maldives 3-0, but the match ended in a 4-3 loss.

FROM CAR WASH TO CLEAN SHEETS

Iran goalkeeper Alireza Beiranvand overcame a string of barriers before making his dream come true by playing at the 2018 FIFA World Cup in Russia. Beiranvand's father disapproved of his son's love of football, tearing his clothes and throwing away his gloves, so Alireza ran away to Tehran. He slept rough at first, and worked in a dressmaking factory, car wash and pizza shop before being spotted by a local club coach. His 12 clean sheets in World Cup qualifying played a key role in helping Iran reach the finals in Russia.

HONG KONG HISTORY–MAKER

Chan Yuen-Ting made history when Hong Kong club Eastern won the national title in May 2016 – the 27-year-old became the first woman in the world to win a top-flight league crown as coach of a men's team. Her side pipped 41-time champions South China to the prize.

CHINA'S 4X4

Four teams carry the name of China. The China national team receives the most attention, but Hong Kong (a former British colony) and Macau (a former Portuguese colony) both retain their autonomous status for football – as Hong Kong China and Macau China respectively. Meanwhile, the independent island state of Taiwan competes in the FIFA World Cup and other competitions as Chinese Taipei.

COACH WITH THE MOST

Only one coach has twice led a team to victory in the AFC Asian Cup and he did it with two different countries. Carlos Alberto Parreira first won the trophy with Kuwait in 1980 and repeated the feat in 1988, this time in charge of Saudi Arabia. He then managed his native Brazil to FIFA World Cup glory in the USA in 1994.

Iran dominate AFC Asian Cup records. The have the most victories (37), most draws (18) and most goals scored (119), and share with South Korea the top tally of 62 games played. South Korea have conceded the most goals (62), Singapore and Myanmar the fewest (four), while 2015 debutants Palestine must wait to add to their record low of one goal in their favour. The next AFC Asian Cup is due to be staged by the United Arab Emirates in 2019, their first time as hosts since finishing runners-up in 1996.

LOCAL COACHES MAKE THEIR MARK

No one has won the AFC Coach of the Year award more than once since it was introduced in 1994 – though Asians have claimed the prize every year except when it went to Japan's French boss Philipppe Troussier in 2000 and South Korea's Dutch manager Guus Hiddink two years later. The women's game was recognized with triumphs for China coach Ma Yuanan in 1996, North Korea's U-20 manager Choe Kwang-Sok ten years later and Japan's FIFA Women's World Cup-winning coach Norio Sasaki in 2011. The award 12 months later went to Kim Ho-Gon, in charge of South Korean club Ulsan Hyundai.

HIGHEST ... AND LOWEST

The highest attendance for an Asian team in a home FIFA World Cup qualifier was the 130,000 who watched Iran draw 1-1 with Australia in the Azadi Stadium, Tehran, on 22 November 1997. The game was the first leg of a final playoff for the last place in the 1998 finals. Iran advanced on away goals after drawing the second leg 2-2 in Melbourne. The lowest attendance was the "crowd" of 20 that turned out for Turkmenistan's 1-0 win over Taiwan, played in Amman, Jordan, on 7 May 2001.

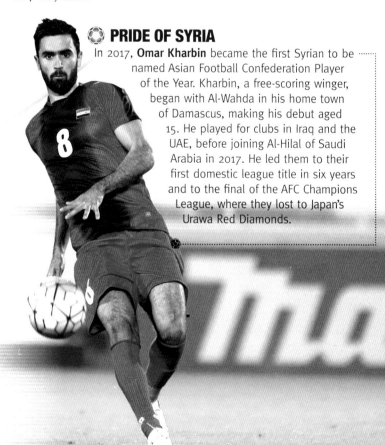

PRIDE OF SYRIA

In 2017, **Omar Kharbin** became the first Syrian to be named Asian Football Confederation Player of the Year. Kharbin, a free-scoring winger, began with Al-Wahda in his home town of Damascus, making his debut aged 15. He played for clubs in Iraq and the UAE, before joining Al-Hilal of Saudi Arabia in 2017. He led them to their first domestic league title in six years and to the final of the AFC Champions League, where they lost to Japan's Urawa Red Diamonds.

UAE KO ZAGALLO

Brazilian great Mario Zagallo, who won the FIFA World Cup as both player and manager, coached the United Arab Emirates when they qualified for their one and only FIFA World Cup finals in 1990. But despite his success in the Asian qualifiers, he was sacked on the eve of the FIFA World Cup itself. Zagallo was replaced by Polish coach Bernard Blaut, whose UAE team lost all three matches at Italia 90. Other big names to have managed the UAE over the years include Brazil's Carlos Alberto Parreira (another FIFA World Cup winner with Brazil), England's Don Revie and Roy Hodgson, Ukraine's Valery Lobanovsky and Portugal's Carlos Queiroz.

UZBEK RECORD-BREAKERS

Uzbekistan's Maksim Shatskikh retired from international football after winning his 61st cap, in a friendly against Oman in May 2014. He did not add to his national 34 goals that day. He equalled the top tally – 31 set by **Mirjalol Qosimov** – in a 7-3 defeat of Singapore in June 2008, and also holds the Uzbek single-game record with five goals against Taiwan in October 2007. Shatskikh has also enjoyed club success in Ukraine and, at Dynamo Kiev, he joined Qosimov as the only Uzbeks to score in a UEFA club competition. Qosimov was twice Uzbekistan's coach, 2008–10 and 2012–15, when the team were 2015 AFC Asian Cup quarter-finalists.

DOUBLE AGENT

Although North Korea's Kim Myong-Won usually plays as a striker, he was named as one of three goalkeepers in the country's 23-man squad for the 2010 FIFA World Cup. FIFA told North Korea he would only be able to play in goal, rather than outfield, though he failed to make it on to the pitch in any form during his country's three Group G matches.

THE ISRAEL ISSUE

Israel is, geographically, an Asian nation. It hosted – and won – the Asian Cup in 1964. But, over the years, many Asian confederation countries refused to play Israel on political grounds. When Israel reached the 1970 FIFA World Cup finals they came through a qualifying tournament involving two Asian nations – Japan and South Korea – and two from Oceania – Australia and New Zealand. In 1989, Israel topped the Oceania group, but lost a final play-off to Colombia for a place in the 1990 finals. They switched to the European zone qualifiers in 1992 and have been a full member of the European federation, UEFA, since 1994.

ASIAN CUP WINNERS

The Asian Cup is Asia's continental championship

Year	Winners
1956	South Korea
1960	South Korea
1964	Israel
1968	Iran
1972	Iran
1976	Iran
1980	Kuwait
1984	Saudi Arabia
1988	Saudi Arabia
1992	Japan
1996	Saudi Arabia
2000	Japan
2004	Japan
2007	Iraq
2011	Japan
2015	Australia

DEEP FREEZE THAWING

Mongolia went 38 years – 1960–98 – without playing a single international and, even in the years that followed, played few games due to below-freezing conditions in the country between October and June. They have been in more frequent action lately, and enjoyed their biggest ever win on 4 July 2016, 8-0 against North Mariana Islands – including a hat-trick by midfielder Monkh-Erdeniin Togoldor – in an East Asian Football Federation Cup first preliminary round match in Dededo, Guam.

OCEANIA

Football in Oceania can claim some of the most eye-catching football statistics – though not necessarily in a way many there would welcome, especially the long-suffering goalkeepers from minnow islands on the end of cricket-style scorelines. The departure to the Asian Football Confederation of Australia, seeking more testing competition, was a morale blow – but benefited New Zealand out on the pitch. The finals tournament of the 2010 FIFA World Cup was the first to feature both Australia and New Zealand.

PAIA FIRE IN VAIN

No team from Oceania other than Australia or New Zealand has ever qualified for the men's football tournament at the Summer Olympics – but Fiji came close to reaching the 2012 event, only losing 1-0 to New Zealand in the final of the qualifying competition. The top scorers were the Solomon Islands, but they didn't make it out of their opening group. They recorded a best first-round goal difference of +12 – thanks to a 16-1 destruction of American Samoa, including seven goals by Ian Paia. However, defeats by Fiji and Vanuatu left them third in the four-team section.

TOP SCORERS: NEW ZEALAND

1	Vaughan Coveney	28
2	Shane Smeltz	24
=	Chris Wood	24
4	Steve Sumner	22
5	Brian Turner	21
6	Jock Newall	17
7	Chris Killen	16
=	Keith Nelson	16
9	Grant Turner	15
10	Darren McLennan	12
=	Michael McGarry	12
=	Wynton Rufer	12

TOP CAPS: NEW ZEALAND

1	Ivan Vicelich	88
2	Simon Elliott	69
3	Vaughan Coveney	64
4	Ricki Herbert	61
5	Chris Jackson	60
6	Brian Turner	59
7	Duncan Cole	58
=	Shane Smeltz	58
=	Steve Sumner	58
10	Chris Zoricich	57

KAREMBEU A FIFA WORLD CUP WINNER

Christian Karembeu, born in New Caledonia, is the only FIFA World Cup winner to come from the Oceania region. He started for France in their 3-0 final victory over Brazil on 12 July 1998. The defensive midfielder had earlier begun against Denmark (group), Italy (quarter-finals) and Croatia (semi-finals). He played 53 times for France, scoring one goal, and was also a double European Champions League Cup winner with Real Madrid in 1998 in 2000.

THE WOOD LIFE

Chris Wood scored four goals at the 2016 OFC Nations Cup, only one behind the tournament's top scorer Raymond Gunemba of Papua New Guinea – as New Zealand lifted the trophy for a record fifth time. Wood had made his debut aged 17, against Tanzania, in June 2009 – the same year he became the fifth and youngest New Zealander to play in England's Premier League, for West Bromwich Albion. He scored his first international goal in October 2010 in a 1-1 draw with Honduras – though received an instant yellow card for his celebration, which involved revealing underpants bearing his nickname "Woodzee". On 14 November 2014, for a friendly against China, he became New Zealand's second-youngest captain, aged 22 years and 343 days. Wood, joint-second on the all-time scorers list, grabbed a hat-trick in a 6-1 win over the Solomon Islands in the first leg of their 2018 FIFA World Cup qualification tie in September 2017. A 2-2 second leg draw set up an intercontinental play-off against Peru. But the All Whites could only draw 0-0 in Wellington before falling and failing 2-0 in Lima.

RETURNING RICKI

Ricki Herbert is the only New Zealander to reach two FIFA World Cup finals. A left-back at the 1982 tournament in Spain, he then coached the country to their second World Cup appearance, in 2010. This second qualifcation came after a play-off defeat of Asian Football Confederation representatives Bahrain. Herbert resigned in November 2013, and briefly was in charge of The Maldives. The man currently in charge – he replaced Anthony Hudson who resigned after the All Whites failed to qualify for the 2018 FIFA World Cup finals – is Swiss coach Fritz Schmid. Herbert is one of only two New Zealand-born men to be national coach, along with Barrie Truman who was in charge between 1970 and 1976.

MAN OF THE PEOPLE MENAPI

Commins Menapi is the Solomon Islands' record scorer, with 34 in 37 games between 2000 and 2009 – including both his country's strikes in a 2-2 draw with favourites Australia at the 2004 OFC Oceania Nations Cup. He was mourned nationwide and in New Zealand – where he played much of his club football – after dying of illness at the age of just 40 in November 2017. Solomon Islands Football Federation chief executive Joseph Boso said: "Commins is very much an everyday figure in football in Solomon Islands – you cannot mention his name to people without them knowing his legacy and his calibre as a player. And also beyond his playing days he was still around trying to pass on his experience and his knowledge to the younger players."

TEHAU ABOUT THAT?

The Pacific Island underdogs of Tahiti finally broke the stranglehold Australia and New Zealand had over the OFC Nations Cup by winning the tournament when it was held for the ninth time in 2012, following four previous triumphs for Australia and four for New Zealand. Tahiti scored 20 goals in their five games at the event in the Solomon Islands – 15 of which came from the Tehau family: brothers Lorenzo (five), Alvin and Jonathan Tehau (four each) and their cousin Teaonui (two). Steevy Chong Hue scored the only goal of the final, against New Caledonia, to give the team managed by Eddy Etaeta not only the trophy but a place at the 2013 FIFA Confederations Cup in Brazil.

BAD LUCK OF THE DRAW

Despite featuring at only their second-ever FIFA World Cup – and their first since 1982 – New Zealand did not lose a game in South Africa in 2010. They drew all three first-round matches, against Slovakia, Italy and Paraguay. The three points were not enough to secure a top-two finish in Group F, but third-placed New Zealand did finish above defending world champions Italy. The only other three teams to have gone out despite going unbeaten in their three first-round group games were Scotland (1974), Cameroon (1982) and Belgium (1998).

WRONG BOX

A New Zealand player scored the opening goal of the 2017 FIFA Confederations Cup but, unfortunately for centre-back Michael Boxall, it was into his own net. The match, which ended 2-0 to hosts Russia, was watched in St Petersburg by FIFA president Gianni Infantino, Russian president Vladimir Putin and Brazilian football legend Pele.

FIJI TIPS

Fiji – with a population of just 900,000 – secured their first ever victory at a FIFA tournament with an unexpected 3-0 defeat of Honduras at the 2015 FIFA U-20 World Cup in New Zealand. Their victory, thanks to efforts from Iosefo Verevou, Saula Waqa and a Kevin Alvarez own goal, came days after an 8-1 trouncing by Germany. Although the hosts reached the round of 16, Fiji made the relatively short trip home after a 3-0 loss to Uzbekistan.

"WORLD'S WORST TEAM" TO SILVER SCREEN

Nicky Salapu was in goal when American Samoa set an unwanted international record, losing 31-0 to Australia in April 2001 – two days after Australia had crushed Tonga 22-0. Passport problems had denied American Samoa some of their best players for the Australia game and they had to field three 15-year-olds in a side with an average age of 18. Salapu was also playing when American Samoa finally won their first competitive international, 2-1 against Tonga in November 2011 thanks to goals by Ramin Ott and Shamin Luani. This was followed by a 1-1 draw with the Cook Islands, during a 2014 FIFA World Cup qualification campaign during which American Samoa were managed by Dutch coach Thomas Rongen and followed by film crews making a documentary movie, *Next Goal Wins*. It was released in 2014 to widespread critical acclaim – including for Jaiyah Saelua, the world's first transgender international footballer. He was born biologically male but is from the Fa'afafine people, a traditional American Samoan group with both masculine and feminine traits and often described as "third-gender".

CONCACAF

The passion of football in central and North America and the Caribbean will be illustrated when the United States, Canada and Mexico stage the first three-way hosting of the FIFA World Cup in 2026. Their "United 2026" bid was backed by the FIFA's congress in Russia in June 2018. Expanding the finals to 48 teams offers more slots to the region's nations. The 2018 finals saw Mexico reach the second round while Costa Rica and newcomers Panama fell in the group stage.

Costa Rica's 2018 FIFA World Cup adventure did not match the quarter-final achievements of the 2014 squad and their only goals and point in Russia came in their final group match, a 2-2 draw against Switzerland in Nizhny Novgorod.

MEXICO

Mexico may well be the powerhouse of the CONCACAF region and are regular qualifiers for the FIFA World Cup – they have missed out on the finals of the tournament just five times (in 1934, 1938, 1974, 1982 and 1990) – but they have always struggled to impose themselves on the international stage. Two FIFA World Cup quarter-final appearances (both times as tournament hosts, in 1970 and 1986) represent their best performances to date. A football-mad nation expects more.

TOP SCORERS

1	Javier Hernandez	50
2	Jared Borghetti	46
3	Cuauhtemoc Blanco	39
4	Carlos Hermosillo	35
=	Luis Hernandez	35
6	Enrique Borja	31
7	Luis Roberto Alves	30
8	Luis Flores	29
=	Luis Garcia	29
10	Benjamin Galindo	28

VICTOR HUGO

Javier Hernandez may have overtaken Jared Borghetti to hold the record as Mexico's all-time leading goalscorer, but perhaps the country's most inspirational striker remains **Hugo Sanchez,** famed for his acrobatic bicycle-kick finishes and somersaulting celebrations. Sanchez played for Mexico at the 1978, 1986 and 1994 FIFA World Cups and would surely have done so had they qualified in 1982 and 1990. During spells in Spain with Atletico Madrid and Real Madrid he finished as La Liga's top scorer five years out of six between 1985 and 1990. He was less successful as Mexico coach from 2006 to 2008, the best result being third in the 2007 Copa America.

MAKING HIS MARQUEZ

Commanding centre-back Rafael Marquez made history in 2014 as the first player to captain his country at four consecutive FIFA World Cups – and he extended that record four years later, when he emulated compatriot Antonio Carbajal and Germany's Lothar Matthaus in playing at five FIFA World Cups. Marquez is in elite Mexican company at the other end of the pitch, too, being one of only three players to have scored in more than one World Cup finals – Cuauhtemoc Blanco scored in two and Javier Hernandez in three. Marquez played twice in Russia in 2018 – taking his tournament tally to 19 appearances – and in their second round defeat to Brazil, he became the oldest outfielder to start a FIFA World Cup knock-out match since England's Stanley Matthews against Uruguay in 1954. At 39 years and 139 days old, Marquez was six days younger than Matthews.

PRECOCIOUS PEREZ

Mexico's youngest international remains midfielder Luis Ernesto "Lucho" Perez, who won the first of his 69 caps aged 17 years and 308 days old, against El Salvador on 17 November 1998. Less impressive was his red card in Mexico's third first-round match against Portugal at the 2006 FIFA World Cup. Hugo Sanchez was the nation's oldest player, 39 years and 251 days old for his final international, against Paraguay on 19 March 1998 – though this was a farewell game for Sanchez, coming four years after his previous appearance for Mexico, and he was replaced in the first minute by Luis Garcia.

TOP CAPS

1	Claudio Suarez	177
2	Andres Guardado	150
3	Rafael Marquez	147
4	Pavel Pardo	146
=	Gerardo Torrado	146
6	Jorge Campos	130
7	Carlos Salcido	124
8	Ramon Ramirez	121
9	Cuauhtemoc Blanco	120
10	Alberto Garcia-Aspe	109

SUAREZ IS NUMBER TWO ALL-TIME

Only Egypt's Ahmed Hassan (184) played more internationals than Mexico defender **Claudio Suarez**, who made 177 appearances between 1992 and 2006. Suarez – nicknamed "The Emperor" – played in all of Mexico's four games at the 1994 and the 1998 FIFA World Cups, but had to miss the 2002 finals after suffering a broken leg. He was a member of the squad for the 2006 tournament in Germany, but did not play and retired after the finals.

LITTLE PEA FROM A POD

Javier Hernandez's goal against Costa Rica on 24 March 2017 saw him join Jared Borghetti as Mexico's leading scorer – both men with 46 goals from 89 games. Further goals have followed – as has Hernandez's 100-cap milestone – and he reached 50 goals with a strike against South Korea in the 2018 FIFA World Cup. In June 2010, playing against South Africa in the opening match, he became the third generation of his family to play at a FIFA World Cup. Hernandez – nicknamed "Chicarito", or "Little Pea" – is the son of Javier Hernandez, who reached the quarter-finals with Mexico in 1986, and the grandson of Tomas Balcazar, a member of the 1954 squad. Another Mexican pair were the first grandfather-grandson duo to play at the finals: Luis Perez played in 1930 and grandson Mario Perez did so 40 years later.

SEVEN DOWN

Mexico's shock 7-0 trouncing by Chile in the quarter-finals of the 2016 Copa America Centenario was their heaviest defeat in an official competition – and brought to an end a 22-match unbeaten run, a Mexican international record. Their previous biggest tournament defeat had been a 6-0 loss to West Germany at the 1978 FIFA World Cup. What made this defeat against Chile even more painful was that it came in front of a 70,547 crowd of mainly Mexican supporters in the Levi's Stadium in Santa Clara, California.

MEXICO BEATS EARTHQUAKE

Mexico stepped in to host the 1986 FIFA World Cup finals after the original choice, Colombia, pulled out in November 1982. FIFA chose Mexico as the replacement venue because of its stadiums and infrastructure, still in place from the 1970 finals. The governing body turned down rival bids from Canada and the United States. Mexico had to work overtime to be ready for the finals, after the earthquake of 19 September 1985, which killed an estimated 10,000 people in central Mexico and destroyed many buildings in Mexico City.

ROSAS NETS HISTORIC PENALTY

Mexico's Manuel Rosas scored the first penalty ever awarded in the FIFA World Cup finals when he converted a 42nd-minute spot-kick in his country's match against Argentina in 1930. Rosas scored again in the 65th minute, but it was too little too late for the Mexicans: they crashed to a 6-3 defeat.

SECOND ROUNDS OUT

Only four countries – Argentina, Brazil, Germany and Italy – have more FIFA World Cup finals appearances than Mexico's 16. The central American nation, however, have yet to go beyond the quarter-finals, and those two last-eight visits, in 1970 and 1986, were only achieved when they hosted the tournament. Mexico's place at the 2018 finals in Russia owed plenty to winger **Hirving Lozano**, who top-scored with five goals in their qualifying campaign, including the only goal in a win over Panama in September 2017 that booked their place in Russia. He then got Mexico's challenge off to the ideal start with the only goal of their opening game, defeating defending champions Germany and winning himself the man of the match prize. But for the seventh consecutive FIFA World Cup, Mexico went out in the second round – going down 2-0 to Brazil in Samara. Another Mexican player set an unwanted record in Russia: Jesus Gallardo's yellow card after 15 seconds against Sweden in a group match was the fastest in FIFA World Cup history.

UNITED STATES

Some of football's biggest names – from Pele to David Beckham – have graced league football in the United States which remains one of only 17 nations to have hosted the FIFA World Cup. Domestic football is still working to step up popularity pressure behind American football, baseball and basketball despite impressive showings in the 2002, 2010 and 2014 World Cups. The shock of failing to reach the 2018 finals in Russia did not stop the US winning host rights, with Canada and Mexico, to the 2026 finals.

TOP CAPS

1	Cobi Jones	164
2	Landon Donovan	157
3	Clint Dempsey	141
4	Michael Bradley	140
5	Jeff Agoos	134
6	Marcelo Balboa	127
7	DaMarcus Beasley	126
8	Tim Howard	121
9	Claudio Reyna	112
10	Jozy Altidore	110
=	Carlos Bocanegra	110
=	Paul Caligiuri	110

ALTIDORE OPENS THE FLOODGATES

Jozy Altidore became the United States' youngest scorer of an international hat-trick in a 3-0 victory over Trinidad and Tobago on 1 April 2009, aged 19 years and 146 days. But he endured an 18-month barren spell between November 2011 and June 2013, when he scored the opener in a 4-3 win over Germany in a Washington DC friendly marking the 100th anniversary of the national team. Altidore then scored against Jamaica, Panama and Honduras to equal a national record of scoring four games in a row, joining William Lubb, Eric Wynalda, Eddie Johnson, Brian McBride and Landon Donovan. His scoring spree came in a 2012–13 season in which he also set a US record for goals in a European club league, with 31 for Dutch club AZ Alkmaar. Sadly his 2014 FIFA World Cup ended with a hamstring injury 23 minutes into the opening game against Ghana.

CALIGIURI'S SHOT MAKES HISTORY

The US's FIFA World Cup qualifying win in Trinidad, on 19 November 1989, is regarded as a turning point in the country's football history. The team included just one full-time professional, Paul Caligiuri, of (West) German second division club Meppen. He scored the only goal of the game with a looping shot after 31 minutes to take the US to their first finals for 40 years. Trinidad's goalkeeper, Michael Maurice, claimed to have been blinded by the sun, but the win raised the profile of the US team hugely, despite a first-round elimination in the 1990 FIFA World Cup.

LANDON HOPE AND GLORY

The US's joint all-time leading scorer **Landon Donovan** was the star of their 2010 FIFA World Cup campaign, scoring three goals in four matches, including a stoppage-time winner against Algeria to help his team top Group C. His four games at the tournament meant he featured in 13 FIFA World Cup matches for the USA, two ahead of Earnie Stewart, **Cobi Jones** and DaMarcus Beasley. His goal in the second-round loss to Ghana also made him the USA's all-time top scorer in the finals, with five – one more than 1930 hat-trick hero Bert Patenaude and Clint Dempsey, who scored twice in 2014. He was the first man to score more than one hat-trick for the US, with four goals against Cuba in July 2003 and trebles versus Ecuador in March 2007 and Scotland in May 2012. Jozy Altidore and Dempsey have now scored two hat-tricks, while nine others have one apiece.

BRUCE THE BOSS

No one has coached the USA men's team more often than Bruce Arena, who stepped down in October 2017, following the United States' shock failure to qualify for the 2018 FIFA World Cup. Arena – who won a third CONCACAF Gold Cup in 2017 and was coach for a total of 148 matches – returned for a second spell in November 2016, following Jurgen Klinsmann's dismissal after five years and 98 games. Former Germany striker Klinsmann had taken the USA to the 2014 FIFA World Cup second round – an extra-time loss to Belgium despite goalkeeper Tim Howard's tournament-record 16 saves – and fourth place at the 2016 Copa America Centenario, their equal best performance. The United States' fourth CONCACAF Gold Cup-winning coach when they triumphed in 2013, he joined Bora Milutinovic, Bob Bradley and Arena.

PAYING HIS DEUCE

The United States became the first CONCACAF nation to have two players each reaching a half-century of goals. **Clint Dempsey** equalled Landon Donovan's national record after scoring his 57th goal for his country in a 2-0 win over Costa Rica in July 2017. Dempsey – nicknamed "Deuce" – previously scored just 30 seconds into the USA's first game at the 2014 FIFA World Cup, against Ghana – the fifth fastest goal in the tournament's history. Also that summer, DaMarcus Beasley became the first American to play at four different FIFA World Cups.

ENGLAND STUNNED BY GAETJENS

The US's 1-0 win over England on 29 June 1950 ranks among the biggest surprises in FIFA World Cup history. England, along with hosts Brazil, were joint favourites to win the trophy. The US had lost their last seven matches, scoring just two goals. Joe Gaetjens scored the only goal, in the 37th minute, diving to head Walter Bahr's cross past goalkeeper Bert Williams. England dominated the game, but US keeper Frank Borghi made save after save. Defeats by Chile and Spain eliminated the US at the group stage, but their victory over England remains the greatest result in the country's football history.

MAGIC CHRISTIAN

Striker **Christian Pulisic** became the United States' youngest international goalscorer when he netted against Bolivia, aged 17 years and 253 days, in May 2016. The Philadelphia native moved to Germany as a 16-year-old in 2015 to sign for Borussia Dortmund. He was joined there a year later by his cousin Will, a goalkeeper who has played for the USA's U-17s. In March 2017 Christian Pulisic scored the USA's fastest second-half goal, taking just 12 seconds after the restart to find the net in a 6-0 victory over Honduras. In the same game Clint Dempsey scored a 22-minute hat-trick – his country's third fastest behind Brian McBride (12 minutes, v El Salvador, 2002) and Eddie Johnson (17 minutes, v Panama, 2004).

TOP SCORERS

1	Landon Donovan	57
=	Clint Dempsey	57
3	Jozy Altidore	41
4	Eric Wynalda	34
5	Brian McBride	30
6	Joe-Max Moore	24
7	Bruce Murray	21
8	Eddie Johnson	19
9	DaMarcus Beasley	17
=	Michael Bradley	17
=	Earnie Stewart	17

WEAH ON THE WAY

In March 2018, striker **Tim Weah** became the first man born in the 21st century to appear in a full international for the United States when an 86th-minute substitute in a 1-0 friendly victory over Paraguay. Weah – the son of former World Footballer of the Year and now Liberian president George Weah – was born in New York City on 22 February 2000, but moved to join French club Paris Saint-Germain in 2014. One of Weah's U-17 team-mates, Werder Bremen forward Josh Sargent, became in November 2017, became the first man to be selected for US squads at U-17, U-20 and senior level in the same calendar year, but was an unused substitute for the senior side.

KEEPING UP WITH JONES

His dreadlocked hair helped catch the attention, but Cobi Jones's raiding runs down the wing also made him one of the host country's most high-profile performers at the 1994 FIFA World Cup. Jones went on to become the US's most-capped player, with 164 international appearances between 1992 and 2004. When he finally retired from all forms of the game in 2007, his number 13 shirt was officially "retired" by the Los Angeles Galaxy – the first time a Major League Soccer club had honoured a player in such a way. Jones had been with the Galaxy since the MLS was launched in 1996 and later served the club as assistant coach and caretaker manager.

CONCACAF OTHER TEAMS

Mexico and the United States (with 25 FIFA World Cup finals appearances between them) are clearly the powerhouses of the CONCACAF region, which takes in North and Central America and the Caribbean. But Mexico only reached the 2014 finals via a play-off, after finishing behind automatic qualifiers USA, Honduras and Costa Rica. The surprising Costa Ricans were one of the stand-out performers in the finals, outdoing their Confederation rivals by reaching the quarter-finals.

DWAYNE'S REIGN

Canada's all-time leading goalscorer with 22, **Dwayne De Rosario** ended his footballing career in fitting style, playing in a January 2015 international friendly against Iceland – and he scored his team's goal in a 1-1 draw. De Rosario's 18-year playing career took in five different Major League Soccer clubs – including two stints with Toronto FC. When he played for DC United, he registered the fastest ever MLS hat-trick, in nine minutes. He was part of the Canada side which lifted their first CONCACAF Gold Cup in 2000, although team-mate Carlo Carazzin finished tournament top scorer with four goals. De Rosario could also claim to be a footballing rarity in being vegetarian and was even vegan for ten years until taking up fish in 2004.

KEYLOR IS KEY

Costa Rica made their FIFA World Cup finals debut in 1990 and goalkeeper Luis Gabelo Conejo shared the best goalkeeper award with Argentina's Sergio Goycochea as his displays helped his team reach the knock-out stages. "Los Ticos" did even better in 2014 and while goalscorers Joel Campbell and Bryan Ruiz impressed, again a goalkeeper was crucial: **Keylor Navas** was named man of the match four times in five games. Costa Rica went to the quarter-finals, where the Netherlands beat them, but only on penalties. They had topped the so-called "Group Of Death" by beating two former FIFA World Cup winners, Uruguay and Italy, and drawing with another, England. Navas conceded only two goals at the finals and his penalty shoot-out save from Theofanis Gekas helped his side defeat Greece in the second-round. Costa Rica became only the second CONCACAF side, after Mexico in 1986, to go out without losing a game in regulation-time.

ALL FOR EL SALVADOR

El Salvador can claim to be the first Central American country – other than Mexico or the United States – to have qualified for the FIFA World Cup twice, doing so in 1970 and 1982. Recent years have brought more struggles, however, although left-back Alfredo Pacheco became his country's pride and most-capped player with 86 appearances between 2002 and 2013. His life ended tragically, however, with a life ban for match-fixing in 2013 followed by his fatal shooting at a petrol station two years later at the age of 33.

PAN-TASTIC TORRES

Panama made their FIFA World Cup finals debut in 2018 in Russia, captained by mighty centre-back **Roman Torres,** whose goal three minutes from time sealed a 2-1 win over Costa Rica and secured their place at the expense of the USA, who lost by the same scoreline to Trinidad and Tobago that night. Panama's president Juan Carlos Valera declared a national holiday to celebrate and Torres had an image of the goal tattooed on his leg. Panama lost all three games in Russia – 3-0 to Tunisia, 6-1 to England and 2-1 to Tunisia – but their fans celebrated exuberantly in Nizhny Novgorod when substitute Felipe Baloy scored their first ever FIFA World Cup goal, against England. Weighing 99kg, Torres was the heaviest player at the 2018 FIFA World Cup, and he announced his international retirement after the tournament, having scored ten goals in 114 appearances.

CELSO LIKE HIS FATHER

Costa Rica playmaker Celso Borges was delighted, in 2014, to emulate his father by reaching the knock-out stages of the FIFA World Cup. He actually went one better as he scored the first penalty of Los Ticos' 5-3 shoot-out defeat of Greece in the second round. His Brazilian-born father, Alexandre Borges Guimares, played at the 1990 FIFA World Cup and set up the late winner scored by Hernan Medford against Sweden to take the FIFA World Cup finals debutants beyond the first round. The man affectionately known as "Guima" was Costa Rica's coach at both the 2002 and 2006 FIFA World Cup finals, but they failed to go beyond the group stage on either occasion.

REGGAE BOYZ STEP UP

In 1998, Jamaica became the first team from the English-speaking Caribbean to reach the FIFA World Cup finals. The "Reggae Boyz", as they were nicknamed, included several players based in England. They were eliminated at the group stage, despite beating Japan 2-1 in their final game thanks to two goals by Theodore Whitmore. They had earlier lost 3-1 to Croatia and 5-0 against Argentina.

CONCACAF TEAMS IN THE FIFA WORLD CUP FINALS

Appearances made by teams from the CONCACAF region at the FIFA World Cup finals

1	Mexico	16
2	United States	10
3	Costa Rica	5
4	Honduras	3
5	El Salvador	2
6	Canada	1
=	Cuba	1
=	Haiti	1
=	Jamaica	1
=	Panama	1
=	Trinidad & Tobago	1

BROTHERS IN ARMS

Honduras became the first team to field not one, not two, but three siblings at a FIFA World Cup, when they picked defender Johnny, midfielder Wilson and striker Jerry Palacios in the 2010 squad. Stoke City defensive midfielder **Wilson Palacios** was perhaps the most famous and acclaimed player in the first Honduras side to reach a FIFA World Cup in 28 years. Like the 1982 side, though, Reinaldo Rueda's men went three games without a win. An older brother, Milton Palacios, played 14 times as a defender for Honduras between 2003 and 2006. Both Jerry and Wilson made it into the 2014 FIFA World Cup squad, but it was not a happy time, especially for Wilson, who was sent off in the opener against France, and Honduras lost all three matches, but did at least score in the defeat against Ecuador. Honduras's captain in South Africa was their most-capped player, midfielder Amado Guevara, who retired after the tournament, having won 138 caps in a 16-year international career.

CUBA SHOW THE WAY

In 1938, Cuba became the first island state of the CONCACAF region to reach the FIFA World Cup quarter-finals. They drew 3-3 with Romania after extra-time in the first round, then won the replay 2-1 with goals by Hector Socorro and Carlos Oliveira after trailing at half-time. They were thrashed 8-0 by Sweden in the last eight. Haiti were the next Caribbean island to play in the finals, in 1974. They lost all three group games, 3-1 to Italy, 7-0 against Poland and 4-1 to Argentina.

SCALING THE HEIGHTS

In the school of both Guatemalan internationals and FIFA World Cup qualification goalscorers **Carlos Ruiz** – nicknamed "Pescado", or "Fish" – swims alone. He is the leading marksman in FIFA World Cup qualifying history, with 39 in 47 ties – three more than Iran's Ali Daei. He reached the tally with seven goals in two games in September 2016: both Guatemala's goals in a 2-2 draw with Trinidad and Tobago and then five in their 9-3 defeat of St Vincent and the Grenadines. He previously brought up a century of caps and half-century of goals on the same day in August 2012, in a 3-3 draw with Paraguay. Only one other Guatemalan, Juan Manuel Funes, has played in five separate FIFA World Cup qualification campaigns.

STERN OPPOSITION

Only 13 men have netted more than the 70 international goals – in 115 matches – scored by Trinidad and Tobago's **Stern John** between his debut in 1995 and his final game in 2011. He was Trinidad and Tobago's top scorer and second-highest appearance-maker, behind midfielder Angus Eve – who quit the international scene with 117 caps when omitted from the squad for the 2006 FIFA World Cup. John spent more than a decade playing his club football in England but, after a brief retirement, returned at the age of 37 in January 2014 to play for WASA FC in his homeland's top-flight.

LOVE HAITI

Italy goalkeeper Dino Zoff's international record of 1,142 minutes without conceding a goal was broken at the 1974 FIFA World Cup by Emmanuel Sanon, Haiti's all-time leader in caps (100) and goals (47). He also scored Haiti's other goal at those finals, against Argentina. Recent promise saw a 2-2 friendly draw with Italy in June 2013 and a place at the 2016 Copa America Centenario.

PART 2:
FIFA ALL-TIME RECORDS
WORLD CUP

France celebrated the 20th anniversary of their first FIFA World Cup triumph in the most joyous manner possible, by winning the trophy again in 2018. Victory, 4-2 over Croatia at the Luzhniki Stadium in Russia's capital Moscow, brought thunderous applause – even from the weather as a storm burst over the presentation ceremony. France's second success was achieved at the climax to the first FIFA World Cup staged in eastern Europe. *Les Bleus* have a long way to go still to catch Brazil who remain record five-times champions.

That on top of the world feeling engulfs France's players after their 4-2 victory over Croatia in the 2018 FIFA World Cup final at Moscow's Luzhniki Stadium confirmed they were world champions for the second time.

FIFA WORLD CUP 2018 RUSSIA REVIEW

France triumphed at the 2018 FIFA World Cup for the second time when *Les Bleus* climaxed a thrilling tournament in Russia by defeating surprise outsiders Croatia 4-2 in the final at Luzhniki stadium in Moscow. France had won football's top prize for the first time, on home soil in 1998, defeating Brazil 3-0 at the Stade de France. A link between the two was Didier Deschamps, who was captain in 1998 and coach in Russia. France's 4-3 victory over Argentina in the second round was arguably the best game of the finals. It also made history as the first 4-3 90-minute scoreline in the 88-year history of the World Cup finals.

EUROPE SUPREME

The 2018 FIFA World Cup in Russia was the first time in history that none of the "big five" – Argentina, Brazil, Germany, Italy or Spain – reached the final. Italy did not even qualify, Germany fell in the first round, Argentina and Spain in the second round and Brazil in the quarter-finals. This was only the fifth time that Europe had provided all four semi-finalists.

2018 FIFA WORLD CUP RUSSIA IN FIGURES

Matches:	64
Goals:	169
Goals per match ave:	2.64
Red cards:	4
Red cards per match ave:	0.06
Yellow cards:	219
Yellow cards per match ave:	3.42
Passes completed:	49,651
Passes completed per match ave:	775.80
Most goal attempts:	Neymar (Brazil) 27 (13 on target, 14 off/blocked)
Most distance run:	Ivan Perisic (Croatia) 72km
Most passes completed:	Sergio Ramos (Spain) 485
Most saves made:	Thibaut Courtois (Belgium) 27

PRESIDENT'S PRIDE

FIFA president **Gianni Infantino** hailed Russia 2018 as "the best FIFA World Cup ever" after the successful staging of the tournament in eastern Europe for the first time. The stadia saw 98 per cent capacity, the Fan Fests drew 7.7m visitors, Russia recorded more than 1m tourists and the tournament had attracted more than three billion television viewers and record numbers to FIFA's digital channels. The Russian organizers had called on more than 100,000 staff and volunteers for an event which President **Vladimir Putin** considered as having "broken down stereotypes about our country." One issue FIFA and Russia could not control was the weather. Putin and Infantino huddled under umbrellas as torrential rain streamed down on the presentation ceremony after the final.

WORLD CUP HISTORY

Year	Host	Final	Venue
1930	Uruguay	Uruguay 4, Argentina 2	Montevideo
1934	Italy	Italy 2, Czechoslovakia 1	Rome
1938	France	Italy 4, Hungary 2	Paris
1950	Brazil	Uruguay 2, Brazil 1	Rio de Janeiro
1954	Switzerland	West Germany 3, Hungary 2	Bern
1958	Sweden	Brazil 5, Sweden 2	Stockholm
1962	Chile	Brazil 3, Czechoslovakia 1	Santiago
1966	England	England 4, West Germany 2 aet	Wembley
1970	Mexico	Brazil 4, Italy 1	Mexico City
1974	West Germany	West Germany 2, Netherlands 1	Munich
1978	Argentina	Argentina 3, Netherlands 1 aet	Buenos Aires
1982	Spain	Italy 3, West Germany 1	Madrid
1986	Mexico	Argentina 3, West Germany 2	Mexico City
1990	Italy	West Germany 1, Argentina 0	Rome
1994	United States	Brazil 0, Italy 0 aet Brazil 3-2 pens	Pasadena
1998	France	France 3, Brazil 0	Saint-Denis
2002	Japan/South Korea	Brazil 2, Germany 0	Yokohama
2006	Germany	Italy 1, France 1, aet Italy 5-3 pens	Berlin
2010	South Africa	Spain 1, Netherlands 0 aet	Johannesburg
2014	Brazil	Germany 1, Argentina 0 aet	Rio de Janeiro
2018	Russia	France 4, Croatia 2	Moscow

FOURTH TIME LUCKY

England ended a 28-year World Cup jinx when they beat Colombia 4-3 on penalties after a 1-1 draw in the second round at Spartak stadium in Moscow. Previously the Three Lions had lost on penalties to West Germany in the 1990 semi-finals, to Argentina in the 1998 second round and to Portugal in the 2006 quarter-finals. Manager **Gareth Southgate** had suffered his own personal shoot-out nightmare with the decisive failure in England's defeat on penalties by Germany in the 1996 European Championship semi-final at Wembley.

KING KYLIAN

Kylian Mbappe was named as Best Young Player at the 2018 FIFA World Cup finals after his explosive performances for France. Mbappe, 19, had cost Paris Saint-Germain €180m from Monaco the previous year and he justified the fee in Russia. His winning goal against Peru made him the youngest French marksman at the World Cup. He scored two more against Argentina in the second round and thus became the first teenager to score twice in the knockout stages since Brazil's Pele in 1958. Mbappe scored again against Croatia in the final to become the tournament's joint second-top scorer.

BITE TO AVOID

Minnows Iceland caused more trouble for the giants at the 2018 FIFA World Cup as they had in the 2016 UEFA European Championship. In France in 2016, Iceland, newcomers on the big stage, defeated England in the second round. They followed up in Russia by holding Lionel Messi's Argentina 1-1 on their debut in the World Cup finals. But they kept their feet firmly on the ground. Part-time manager Heimar Hallgrimsson said: "I am still a dentist and I will never stop being a dentist."

PAIN FOR SPAIN

Spain had the worst possible start to a World Cup campaign when the federation sacked manager Julen Lopetegui three days before their opening match in Russia against neighbours Portugal. It had just emerged that the former national youth coach had agreed to take over from Zinedine Zidane at Real Madrid after the finals. Sporting director Fernando Hierro stepped in as emergency manager then quit himself after defeat on penalties by Russia in the second round.

VAR's PERFECT DEBUT

Russia's 2018 FIFA World Cup saw the revolutionary introduction of Video Assistant Referees (VARs). Their presence had a dramatic effect on decision-making with the number of penalties doubling compared with 2014. One of those VAR-assisted penalties was awarded to France by Argentinian referee **Nestor Pitana** in the final. Goal-line technology had been applied in 2014 and, in early 2018, the law-making International Board approved VAR for the World Cup. The VAR team consisted of a FIFA referee and three assistants focusing on game-changing situations from a central studio. Some 455 incidents were checked in the 64 matches, prompting 20 reviews by the match referees. The "correctness' of referees" decisions rose from 95 per cent to 99.3 per cent with the use of VAR.

FIFA WORLD CUP QUALIFIERS

BALLON D'ORIBE

Mexico booked the final spot at the 2014 FIFA World Cup by beating Oceania representatives New Zealand 9-3 on aggregate in a two-legged November 2013 play-off. Caretaker manager Miguel Herrera – Mexico's fourth boss of the year – earned the job on a permanent basis, masterminding 5-1 home and 4-2 away wins. His squad relied purely on domestic-based players, meaning there were no European-based stars such as Villarreal's Giovani dos Santos or Manchester United's Javier Hernandez. The goalscoring hero was **Oribe Peralta,** who scored five goals in the two games – including the first three in the victory at Wellington's Westpac Stadium.

TAKING AIM

The 2018 World Cup qualification tournament saw all 210 FIFA member nations enter – the 211th, Russia, qualified automatically as hosts – but both Zimbabwe and Indonesia were excluded before they had played a match. Four nations made their World Cup debuts: **Bhutan**, Gibraltar, Kosovo and South Sudan.

MORE COLLAPSE THAN CALYPSO FOR TEAM USA

In 2017, the United States failed to reach the World Cup finals for the first time since 1986. After a 4–0 defeat away to Costa Rica in the final group stage, World Cup old-hand Bruce Arena replaced coach Jurgen Klinsmann, but it was not enough to save them. Team USA would have made it to Russia with a win in their last match, away to **Trinidad & Tobago**, the group's bottom team. Instead they lost 2-1 and victories for Panama and Honduras dropped them from third to fifth in the group.

BIGGEST WINS IN WORLD CUP QUALIFIERS

1	**Australia**	31–0	American Samoa	11 April 2001
2	Australia	22–0	Tonga	9 April 2001
3	Maldives	0–17	Iran	2 June 1997
4	Australia	13–0	Solomon Islands	11 June 1997
=	New Zealand	13–0	Fiji	16 August 1981
=	Fiji	13–0	American Samoa	7 April 2001
7	Syria	12–0	Maldives	4 June 1997
=	Maldives	0–12	Syria	9 June 1997
=	West Germany	12–0	Cyprus	21 May 1969
10	Australia	11–0	Samoa	16 April 2001
=	Mexico	11–0	St Vincent & The Grenadines	6 December 1992

ORANJE AND AZZURRI OFF COLOUR

Among the notable European absentees from the party in Russia were Italy, winners in 2006, and the Netherlands, runners-up in 2010 and third in Brazil in 2014. The *Oranje* were eliminated after finishing third in Group A, behind Sweden on goal difference. Italy lost 1-0 on aggregate to Sweden in the playoffs. The Swedes won 1-0 at home then withstood everything the *Azzurri* could throw at them at the Stadio Giuseppe Meazza in Milan. Veteran goalkeeper and captain Gianluigi Buffon twice charged upfield at stoppage-time corners, but in vain. Italy – in 1934 the only hosts ever to go through the qualifying competition – were left to rue only their third-ever absence from the finals: they did not enter in 1930; and failed to qualify in 1958.

GERMANY IN A HURRY

Germany were the only European team to complete their 2018 qualifying programme with a 100 percent record, winning all 10 group stage matches. Coach Joachim Low's team scored 43 goals and conceded only four. Remarkably Germany's goals were shared among 22 players (including one own goal). Their top marksmen, Thomas Muller and Sandro Wagner, scored a modest five goals apiece.

ABSENT HEROES

Remarkably, the 2018 World Cup finals lacked the regional champions of South America, Africa, central and north America as well as Oceania. Chile, Copa America winners in 2015 and 2016, were bitterly disappointed to miss out, having also finished runners-up in the FIFA Confederation Cup in Russia in 2017. African title-holders Cameroon led a sad parade of absent continental former finalists who included Algeria, Ghana, Ivory Coast, South Africa and Togo. The United States, CONCACAF Gold Cup holders, fell in the last group stage while Oceania champions New Zealand were beaten by Peru in the intercontinental play-offs.

THE GROWTH OF THE QUALIFYING COMPETITION

This charts the number of countries entering qualifiers for the FIFA World Cup finals. Some withdrew before playing.

World Cup	Teams entering
Uruguay 1930	-
Italy 1934	32
France 1938	37
Brazil 1950	34
Switzerland 1954	45
Sweden 1958	55
Chile 1962	56
England 1966	74
Mexico 1970	75
West Germany 1974	99
Argentina 1978	107
Spain 1982	109
Mexico 1986	121
Italy 1990	116
USA 1994	147
France 1998	174
Japan/South Korea 2002	199
Germany 2006	198
South Africa 2010	205
Brazil 2014	203
Russia 2018	210

WELCOME NEWCOMERS

Panama and **Iceland** qualified for their first World Cup finals in Russia. The Icelanders followed up their historic quarter-finals run at UEFA Euro 2016 by becoming the smallest nation (population 335,000) to qualify for the FIFA World Cup finals. Panama left it late to make their own little bit of history. A goal two minutes from time by defender Roman Torres earned a 2-1 win over Costa Rica in their last game to clinch an all-important third place in the final CONCACAF group.

QUITO IN THE HISTORY BOOK

Quito (Chiquito do Carmo) of Timor-Leste made a little bit of history, scoring the first goal of the 2018 World Cup in a 4-1 defeat of Mongolia in Dili on 12 March 2015, in the Asian qualifiers. The tournament also doubled as preliminaries for the Asian Cup. Unfortunately, some months after the match, Timor-Leste had the victory annulled and awarded as a 3-0 win to Mongolia because they had used ineligible players.

PALMER BEATS THE WHISTLE

Carl Erik Palmer's second goal in Sweden's 3-1 win over the Republic of Ireland in November 1949 was one of the most bizarre in qualifying history. The Irish defenders stopped, having heard a whistle, while Palmer ran on and put the ball in the net. The goal stood, because the whistle had come from someone in the crowd, not the referee. The 19-year-old forward went on to complete a hat-trick.

LEWANDOWSKI TAKES POLE POSITION

Poland's **Robert Lewandowski** was the 16-goal joint-leading marksman in the qualifying campaign for the 2018 finals, level with Mohammad Al-Sahlawi from Saudi Arabia and Ahmed Khalil from the United Arab Emirates. The trio scored one more than Portugal captain Cristiano Ronaldo, FIFA's Best Player in both 2016 and 2017. Both Lewandowski and Ronaldo – now the all-time leading goalscorer in European qualification history with 30 – beat the 14-goal European record set by Yugoslavia's Predrag Mijatovic in the 1998 preliminaries.

THE FASTEST SUBSTITUTION

The quickest-ever substitution in the history of FIFA World Cup qualifiers came on 30 December 1980, when North Korea's Chon Byong Ju was substituted in the first minute of his country's home game against Japan.

BWALYA LEAVES IT LATE

Zambia's **Kalusha Bwalya** is the oldest player to have scored a match-winning goal in a FIFA World Cup qualifying match. The 41-year-old netted the only goal against Liberia on 4 September 2004 after coming on as a substitute. He had also scored in his first qualifier, 20 years previously, in Zambia's 3-0 win over Uganda.

KOSTADINOV STUNS FRANCE

On 17 November 1993, in the last game of the Group Six schedule, Bulgaria's Emil Kostadinov scored one of the most dramatic goals in qualifying history to deny France a place at the 1994 finals. France seemed to be cruising with the score at 1-1 in stoppage time, but Kostadinov earned Bulgaria a shock victory after David Ginola lost possession. The Bulgarians reached the semi-finals of the tournament in the United States, losing 2-1 to Italy.

THOMPSON SETS UNLIKELY MARK

Archie Thompson eased past Iran striker Karim Bagheri's record for the number of goals in a single qualifying match (seven) as Australia thrashed American Samoa 31-0 on 11 April 2001. He netted 13 goals. David Zdrilic also beat Bagheri's total with eight goals. Two days earlier, Australia had previously smashed Iran's scoring record after completing a 22-0 victory over Tonga.

THE FASTEST GOALS

Belgium striker **Christian Benteke** took just 8.1 seconds to give his side the lead against Gibraltar on 10 October 2016, making it the fastest goal in FIFA World Cup qualification history. His team went on to win 6-0, with Benteke completing a hat-trick. His opener was even quicker than **Davide Gualtieri**'s nine-second goal for San Marino against England on 17 November 1993.

SYRIA SO CLOSE TO GLORY

The seven-goal leadership of Saudi Arabia-based forward Omar Kharbin was responsible for Syria's remarkable feat of reaching the AFC qualifying group play-offs despite the warfare ravaging the region. Kharbin's achievement earned him the 2017 Asian Footballer of the Year award. In the play-off, against Australia, Syria drew 1-1 in their "alternative" home leg in Malaysia. then went all the way to extra time in Sydney before losing 2-1 and 3-2 on aggregate. The Socceroos went on to defeat Honduras and claim the AFC's fifth slot in the finals.

MESSI SHOWS THE WAY

Lionel Messi played an inspirational captain's role in leading Argentina to the 2018 World Cup finals. The Barcelona superstar was their seven-goal leading marksman after grabbing a decisive hat-trick against Ecuador in their concluding match – one they had to win. Thanks to *La Pulga* "The Flea", they did so 3–1 after the early scare of an opening goal by Ecuador.

RECORD HAT–TRICK

Abdel Hamid Bassiouny of Egypt scored the fastest-ever hat-trick in qualifying history in their 8-2 win over Namibia on 13 July 2001. He netted three times in just 177 seconds between the 39th and 42nd minutes.

YOUNGEST AND OLDEST

The youngest player to appear in the FIFA World Cup qualifiers is Souleymane Mamam of Togo, who was 13 years 310 days when he played against Zambia on 6 May 2001. The oldest was MacDonald Taylor, who was 46 years, 180 days when he played for the Virgin Islands against St Kitts Nevis on 18 February 2004.

HORST THE FIRST TO GIVE WAY

The first player to be substituted during a FIFA World Cup qualifier was West Germany's **Horst Eckel**, when he was replaced by Richard Gottinger in their 3-0 victory over the short-lived protectorate of Saarland in October 1953. Eckel would go on to play on the right side of midfield in the side that beat Hungary in the 1954 FIFA World Cup final, while Gottinger's delayed appearance against Saarland was his first and last for his country. By the time of the 1958 FIFA World Cup qualifiers, Saarland had been integrated within West Germany.

CARLOS ON TOP

Guatemala's Carlos Ruiz is the all-time top scorer in FIFA World Cup qualifiers, despite never reaching the finals. His nine goals in the 2018 qualifying campaign took him to 39, four ahead of Iran's Ali Daei. Ruiz scored eight goals in the 2002 qualifiers, ten in the preliminaries for 2006 and six each in the 2010 and 2014 campaigns. He went out on a high, leap-frogging Daei with a five-timer in his final international, a 9-3 2018 qualifying rout of St. Vincent and the Grenadines.

UNITED STATES LEAVE IT LATE

The latest of all qualifying play-offs took place in Rome on 24 May 1934, when the USA beat Mexico 4-2 to clinch the last slot in the FIFA World Cup finals. Three days later, the Americans were knocked out 7-1 by hosts Italy in the first round of the tournament.

ITALY FORCED TO QUALIFY

Italy are the only host country who have been required to qualify for their own tournament. The 1934 hosts beat Greece 4-0 to go through. FIFA decided that, for the 1938 finals, the holders and the hosts would qualify automatically. That decision was changed for the 2006 finals. Since then, only the hosts have been exempt from qualifying, though South Africa played in the second round of qualifying for 2010. This is because it doubled up as qualifiers for the 2010 Africa Cup of Nations.

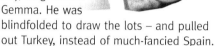

TURKEY THROUGH ON LUCK OF THE DRAW

Turkey were the first team to qualify for the FIFA World Cup finals after the drawing of lots. Their play-off against Spain, in Rome on 17 March 1954, ended 2-2. Qualification was decided by a 14-year-old Roman boy, Luigi Franco Gemma. He was blindfolded to draw the lots – and pulled out Turkey, instead of much-fancied Spain.

FIRST-TIME QUALIFIERS

1930:	Argentina, Belgium, Bolivia, Brazil, Chile, France, Mexico, Paraguay, Peru, Romania, USA, Uruguay, Yugoslavia
1934:	Austria, Czechoslovakia, Egypt, Germany, Hungary, Italy, Netherlands, Spain, Sweden, Switzerland
1938:	Cuba, Dutch East Indies, Norway, Poland
1950:	England
1954:	Scotland, South Korea, Turkey, West Germany
1958:	Northern Ireland, Soviet Union, Wales
1962:	Bulgaria, Colombia
1966:	North Korea, Portugal
1970:	El Salvador, Israel, Morocco
1974:	Australia, East Germany, Haiti, Zaire
1978:	Iran, Tunisia
1982:	Algeria, Cameroon, Honduras, Kuwait, New Zealand
1986:	Canada, Denmark, Iraq
1990:	Costa Rica, Republic of Ireland, United Arab Emirates
1994:	Greece, Nigeria, Russia, Saudi Arabia
1998:	Croatia, Jamaica, Japan, South Africa, Yugoslavia
2002:	China, Ecuador, Senegal, Slovenia
2006:	Angola, Czech Republic, Ghana, Ivory Coast, Serbia and Montenegro, Togo, Trinidad and Tobago, Ukraine
2010:	Serbia, Slovakia
2014:	Bosnia and Herzegovina
2018:	Iceland, Panama

THE "FOOTBALL WAR"

War broke out between El Salvador and Honduras after El Salvador beat Honduras 3-2 in a play-off on 26 June 1969 to qualify for the 1970 finals. Tension had been running high between the neighbours over a border dispute and there had been rioting at the match. On 14 July, the Salvador army invaded Honduras.

THE FIRST SHOOT-OUT

The first penalty shoot-out in qualifying history came on 9 January 1977 when Tunisia beat Morocco 4-2 on spot-kicks after a 1-1 draw in Tunis. The first game, in Casablanca, had also finished 1-1. Tunisia went on to qualify for the finals.

TITE TURNS BRAZIL AROUND

Brazil, winners of a record five World Cups and 2016 Olympic Games gold medallists, were the first nation to qualify to join Russia in the 2018 finals after winning the South American group with four matches to spare. New coach **Tite** instilled a new aura of confidence after disappointing results in the 2016 Copa America Centenario and initial World Cup qualifiers under former Cup-winning captain Dunga. **Gabriel Jesus** was their seven-goal top scorer, supported by Neymar and Paulinho with five apiece.

THIERRY'S TRICKERY

France qualified for the 2010 FIFA World Cup finals thanks to one of the most controversial international goals of recent history. The second leg of their play-off against the Republic of Ireland in November 2009 was 14 minutes into extra-time when striker **Thierry Henry** clearly controlled the ball with his hand, before crossing to William Gallas who gave his side a decisive 2-1 aggregate lead. After Swedish referee Martin Hansson allowed the goal to stand, the Football Association of Ireland first called for the game to be replayed, then asked to be allowed into the finals as a 33rd country – but both requests proved in vain.

ALL-TIME QUALIFICATIONS BY REGIONAL CONFEDERATION

1934–2018

1	Europe	245
2	South America	85
3	Africa	44
4	North/Central America & Caribbean	42
5	Asia	37
6	Oceania	4

GOING UNDERCOVER

The Kingdome in Seattle, United States, hosted the first FIFA World Cup qualifier to be played indoors, when the US beat Canada 2-0 in October 1976 – just a few months after the same venue had staged its first rock concert, by Paul McCartney's post-Beatles band Wings, and a religious rally featuring evangelist Billy Graham and country singer Johnny Cash. Canada gained revenge by beating the US 3-0 in a play-off, hosted in Haiti, to reach the next stage of the CONCACAF qualifying round. But only Mexico would go on to represent the Confederation at the 1978 FIFA World Cup in Argentina.

WORLD CUP QUALIFICATION COMPETITION RECORD

Team	P	W	D	L	GF	GA	Q*
Mexico	175	113	37	25	436	126	16
Costa Rica	172	85	43	44	295	176	5
United States	154	77	36	41	266	181	10
Uruguay	154	69	42	43	218	164	13
Paraguay	154	66	30	58	201	189	8
Colombia	152	57	46	49	180	159	6
Honduras	150	69	40	41	255	173	3
Bolivia	150	39	29	82	177	284	3
Peru	149	43	37	69	164	211	5
Chile	146	61	29	56	217	195	9

*Total number of FIFA World Cup tournaments qualified for

NOT SO FASO

Burkina Faso lost their final qualifying play-off in the Africa section on away goals to Algeria, following a 3-2 victory at home and a 1-0 defeat away. They then tried to have Algeria disqualified, claiming that crucial goalscorer **Madjid Bougherra** was ineligible. Burkina Faso officials, hoping to reach their first FIFA World Cup, claimed he should have been suspended following two yellow cards in previous matches but FIFA ruled he had been booked only the once.

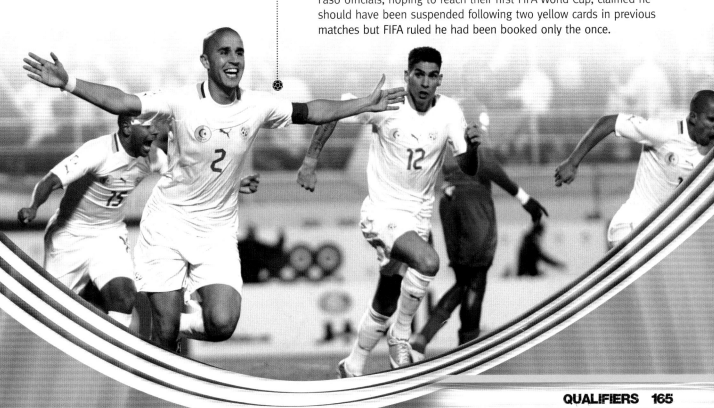

FIFA TEAM RECORDS
WORLD CUP

EXTRA SPECIAL GERMANS

Germany, in beating Argentina 1-0
in the Maracana stadium in 2014,
became the fifth team to win the
FIFA World Cup Final in extra time
after Italy (1934), England (1966),
Argentina (1978) and Spain (2010).
In both 2010 and 2014, the Final had
finished goalless after 90 minutes.
Andres Iniesta, for Spain in 2010, and
Mario Gozte, for Germany in Rio de
Janeiro, both struck their lone winning
goals in the second period of the
additional 30 minutes. Extra time
was not enough in 1994 and
2006, when Brazil and Italy,
respectively, won on
penalties.

CHAMPION
2014 FIFA World Cup

SHARING THE GOALS

France in 1982, winners Italy in 2006
and third-placed Belgium in 2018
supplied the most individual goalscorers
during a FIFA World Cup finals tournament –
ten. Germany's 17 goals were shared among
seven players on their way to ultimate success
in Brazil in 2014: Thomas Muller (five), Andre
Schurrle (three), Mats Hummels (two), Miroslav
Klose (two), Toni Kroos (two), Mario Gotze (two)
and Mesut Ozil (one). Belgium's top scorer in 2018
was Romelu Lukaku, joint second overall with four.

BRAZIL COLOUR UP

Brazil's yellow shirts are famous around the world. But they wore
white shirts at the first four FIFA World Cup finals. However, their
2-1 loss to Uruguay in the 1950 tournament's final match – when
a draw would have given Brazil the Cup – was such a shock they
switched to yellow. The Brazilian confederation insisted no further
colour change would follow the shock of the 7-1 semi-final defeat
by Germany and 3-0 third-place play-off loss to Holland in 2014.

COLOUR FAST JAPAN

Japan and Poland were the only teams in 2018
to play in their first-choice kit in all their first
round ties. Japan's blue shirts incorporated
the national flag and a crest to mark the 20th
anniversary of their first appearance in the finals.

ITALY KEEP IT TIGHT

Italy set the record for the longest
run without conceding a goal at the
FIFA World Cup finals. They went five
games without conceding at the 1990
finals, starting with their 1-0 group win
over Austria. Goalkeeper Walter Zenga
was not beaten until Claudio Caniggia
scored Argentina's equalizer in the
semi-final. And a watertight defence
did not bring Italy the glory it craved:
Argentina reached the final by winning
the penalty shoot-out 4-3.

TODAY EUROPE, TOMORROW THE WORLD

Spain's 2010 trophy-lifting coach **Vicente del Bosque** became only the second manager to have won both the FIFA World Cup and the UEFA Champions League or its previous incarnation, the European Champions' Cup. Marcello Lippi won the UEFA prize with Juventus in 1996, 10 years before his Italy team became world champions. Del Bosque won the UEFA Champions League twice with Real Madrid, in 2000 and 2002, though he was sacked in summer 2003 for "only" winning the Spanish league title the previous season.

CHAMPIONS CURSE

Germany, at the 2018 FIFA World Cup finals, became the third successive holders to be eliminated at the group stage. Italy went out in the first round in 2010 in South Africa and Spain followed their unfortunate example in Brazil four years later. In 2018, the Germans never recovered from an opening 1-0 defeat by Mexico. They beat Sweden 2-1, only with a stoppage-time goal from **Toni Kroos**, before losing 2-0 to South Korea and thus suffering the added embarrassment of finishing bottom of Group F.

MOST APPEARANCES IN THE FIFA WORLD CUP FINAL

1	Germany/West Germany	8
2	Brazil	7
3	Italy	6
4	Argentina	5
5	France	3
=	Netherlands	3
7	Czechoslovakia	2
=	Hungary	2
=	Uruguay	2
10	Croatia	1
=	England	1
=	Sweden	1

BRAZIL PROFIT FROM RIMET'S VISION

Jules Rimet, president of FIFA 1921–54, was the driving force behind the first FIFA World Cup, in 1930. The tournament, in Uruguay, was not high-profile, with only 13 nations taking part. The long sea journey kept most European teams away, and only Belgium, France, Romania and Yugoslavia made the trip. Rimet's dream has been realized and the FIFA World Cup has grown enormously in popularity. Brazil have been the competition's most successful team, winning five times. The only FIFA World Cup finals ever-presents, Brazil have more wins (70) than any other country, though Germany (66 wins) have played more matches: 106 to Brazil's 104. Germany and Italy are the most successful European nations with four World Cup wins apiece. The original finalists, Uruguay and Argentina, are both two-time champions, though Argentina have also lost two Finals. England (1966) and France (1998) both won once as hosts. Spain failed as hosts in 1982 but won in South Africa in 2010.

WHY THE BRITISH TEAMS STAYED OUT

England and Scotland may be the homelands of football but none of the home nations, including Wales and Northern Ireland, entered the World Cup until 1950 as they were not members of FIFA in the 1930s. England and Scotland both qualified for the 1950 finals but the Scots refused to go to Brazil because they finished only "second" in the British qualifying group.

ONE-TIME WONDERS

Indonesia, then known as the Dutch East Indies, made one appearance in the finals, in the days when the tournament was a strictly knockout affair. On 5 June 1938, they lost 6-0 to Hungary in the first round, and have never qualified for the tournament since.

MOST APPEARANCES IN FINALS TOURNAMENTS

1	Brazil	21
2	Germany/West Germany	19
3	Italy	18
4	Argentina	17
5	Mexico	16
6	England	15
=	France	15
=	Spain	15

FIFA WORLD CUP STOPS THE WORLD

The FIFA World Cup finals is the world's biggest single-sport event. Television was in its infancy when the first finals were held in 1930 but they are now one of the most popular of all TV events. The 2018 tournament in Russia was estimated to have attracted a cumulative three billion viewers worldwide, with one billion watching France defeat Croatia 4-2 in the final. FIFA's ever-expanding digital channels recorded 11 billion hits over the 32 days. In France, TF1's live coverage of *Les Bleus'* triumph in Moscow was watched by an average of 19.34m viewers with 22.21m watching the award ceremony alone. A further 1.01m followed the final on beIN Sports1, bringing the combined average audience to 20.35m, one of the highest in French history. More than 80 per cent of people watching TV at the time tuned into the final.

GOLDEN NARROWS

Before 2010, no country had won five consecutive FIFA World Cup matches by a one-goal margin – but **Arjen Robben** and the Netherlands became the first, thanks to their 3-2 semi-final victory over Uruguay. Before then, the record rested with Italy, who managed four single-goal wins in a row across the 1934 and 1938 FIFA World Cups. Spain's 1-0 defeat of the Dutch in the 2010 FIFA World Cup was also their fifth consecutive single-goal victory and fourth in the knockout stages.

BRAZIL'S GOALS GLOOM

The 14 goals conceded by Brazil in the 2014 FIFA World Cup finals are the most ever conceded by the host nation. The overall record was 16 goals shipped by South Korea in Switzerland in 1954. In those finals, West Germany let in 14 but still won the tournament for the first time. It included eight in a group match against beaten finalists Hungary.

EVER RED

England's victory in 1966 remains the only time the FIFA World Cup final has been won by a team wearing red. Spain, who usually wear red, changed into blue for their 2010 victory over the Netherlands to avoid a colour-clash. **Luka Modric** and his Croatia teammates did wear their unique red-and-white checks in the 2018 final but lost to France. Wearing red also proved unlucky for losing finalists Czechoslovakia in 1934 then Hungary in both 1938 and 1954.

THE FEWEST GOALS CONCEDED

FIFA World Cup winners France (1998), Italy (2006) and Spain (2010) hold the record for the fewest goals conceded on their way to victory. All three conceded just two. Spain also hold the record for fewest goals scored by FIFA World Cup winners. They netted just eight in 2010, below the 11 scored by Italy in 1938, England in 1966 or Brazil in 1994.

SPONSORS MAKE THE FINALS PAY

The Brazil 2014 FIFA World Cup was the most lucrative ever, with world football's governing body, FIFA, achieving a surplus of more than $2 billion. Two-thirds of FIFA World Cup revenues come from TV rights. This was the fifth finals played with 32 teams, the number going up from 24 for the France 1998 FIFA World Cup.

FEWEST GOALS CONCEDED IN ONE TOURNAMENT:
Switzerland: 0, 2006

MOST GOALS SCORED IN ONE TOURNAMENT
Hungary: 27, 1954

MOST WINS IN ONE TOURNAMENT
Brazil: 7, 2002

MOST GOALS SCORED IN ONE TOURNAMENT
Just Fontaine (France): 13, 1958

MOST CONSECUTIVE MATCHES SCORING A GOAL AT FIFA WORLD CUP FINALS

18	Brazil	1930–58
18	Germany	1934–58, 1986–98
17	Hungary	1934–62
16	Uruguay	1930–62
15	Brazil	1978–90
15	France	1978–86

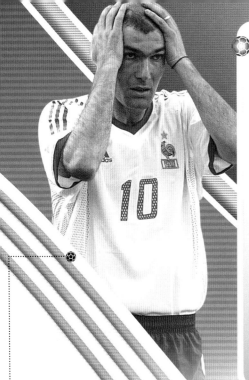

PERFORMANCES BY HOST NATION AT FIFA WORLD CUP FINALS

1930	Uruguay	Champions
1934	Italy	Champions
1938	France	Quarter-finals
1950	Brazil	Runners-up
1954	Switzerland	Quarter-finals
1958	Sweden	Runners-up
1962	Chile	Third place
1966	England	Champions
1970	Mexico	Quarter-finals
1974	West Germany	Champions
1978	Argentina	Champions
1982	Spain	Second round
1986	Mexico	Quarter-finals
1990	Italy	Third place
1994	United States	Second round
1998	France	Champions
2002	South Korea	Fourth place
	Japan	Second round
2006	Germany	Third place
2010	South Africa	First round
2014	Brazil	Fourth place
2018	Russia	Quarter-finals

SAFE EUROPEAN HOME

Germany's 1-0 victory over Argentina in the 2014 FIFA World Cup final meant they became the first European nation to win the FIFA World Cup in any of the eight tournaments staged in North, Central or South America, going back to 1930. Spain, winners of the 2010 FIFA World Cup in South Africa, were the first European victors to achieve it outside their home continent.

HOLDERS CRASH OUT

France produced the worst performance by a defending FIFA World Cup winner in Japan and South Korea in 2002: they lost their opening game 1-0 to Senegal, drew 0-0 against Uruguay and were eliminated after losing 1-0 to Denmark. They were the first defending champions to be knocked out without scoring a goal. In 2010 Italy emulated France by exiting at the first-round stage, and without winning a match – nor indeed ever taking the lead. At least Italy did achieve two draws – and scored four goals. They opened with a 1-1 draw against Paraguay, needed a penalty to force another 1-1 draw against minnows New Zealand, and they were on their way home after losing 3-2 to Slovakia.

SMALL IS BEAUTIFUL

Croatia, coached by **Zlatko Dalic**, became the second-smallest nation (population 4m) to appear in the FIFA World Cup final when they lost to France in Moscow in 2018. They were also the youngest, being only 27 years old. The only smaller finalist nation was Uruguay (population 3m) who had last reached the showdown back in 1950.

BRAZIL LEAD THE WAY

Brazil scored the most victories in finals tournaments when they won all their seven games in 2002. They began with a 2-1 group win over Turkey and ended with a 2-0 final triumph over Germany. They scored 18 goals in their unbeaten run and conceded on only four occasions.

HOME DISCOMFORT

South Africa became the first host nation to fail to reach the second round of a FIFA World Cup, when staging the 2010 tournament – though their first-round record of one win, one draw and one defeat was only inferior on goal difference to the opening three games played by hosts Spain, in 1982, and the USA, in 1994, both of whom reached the second round. Uruguay's 3–0 victory over South Africa in Pretoria on 16 June 2010 equalled the highest losing margin suffered by a FIFA World Cup host, following Brazil's 5–2 win over Sweden in the 1958 final and Italy's 4–1 trouncing of Mexico in their 1970 quarter-final.

FIFA GOALSCORING
WORLD CUP

HOST WITH THE MOST

Brazil have scored more goals (nine) in the opening matches of the FIFA World Cup than any other nation, though their status as double hosts in 1950 and 2014 certainly helped. Between 1974 and 2002 the holders, rather than the hosts, also had the honour of kicking off proceedings. Brazil beat Mexico easily by 4-0 in the 1950 opener in the Maracana stadium, with goals from Jair, Baltazar and Ademir (two). They defeated Scotland 2-1 in the Opening Match of France 1998 (Cesar Sampaio and Tom Boyd, own goal) and then Croatia, 3-1, in 2014, thanks to a double (one a penalty) from **Neymar** and a third from Oscar. A Brazilian also netted the very first goal of the 2014 finals, as left-back Marcelo gave Croatia the lead with an own goal. Italy's total of eight goals in the Opening Match was mainly thanks to a 7-1 beating of the United States in 1934 – they drew 1-1 with Bulgaria in 1986.

HIGHEST SCORES

The highest-scoring game in the FIFA World Cup finals was the quarter-final between Austria and Switzerland on 26 June 1954. Austria staged a remarkable comeback to win 7-5, with centre-forward **Theodor Wagner** scoring a hat-trick, after trailing 3-0 in the 19th minute. Three other games have produced 11 goals – Brazil's 6-5 win over Poland in the 1938 first round, Hungary's 8-3 win over West Germany in their 1954 group game and the Hungarians' 10-1 rout of El Salvador at the group stage in 1982.

LOW-SCORING SPAIN

Spain won the 2010 FIFA World Cup despite scoring just eight goals in seven games on their way to the title – fewer than any world champions in history, including 11-goal Italy in 1934, England in 1966 and Brazil in 1994. Vicente del Bosque's Spain were also the first team to win 1-0 in all four of their knockout matches. David Villa scored the decisive goal in two of those matches.

GENEROUS OPPONENTS

Chile were the first team to benefit from an opponent's own goal at the FIFA World Cup. Mexico's Manuel Rosas put the ball into his own net during the Chileans' 3-0 win at the inaugural 1930 finals in Uruguay. France, courtesy of two in both 2014 and 2018 are out on their own as recipients of the most own goals with six – Germany and Italy have four apiece. In 2014, Honduras goalkeeper Noel Valladares was struck by a shot rebounding off a post from Karim Benzema – denying him a hat-trick – and it was the first goal to be ratified by goal-line technology, in use in the finals in Brazil for the first time. In 2018 Mario Mandzukic of Croatia scored the first own goal in a FIFA World Cup final, while the other France own goal came from Australia's Aziz Behich in the groups.

PENALTY PROGRESS

The 2018 FIFA World Cup finals in Russia equalled the number of shoot-outs in the knock-out stage, with four matches decided from the penalty spot, matching the number in 1990, 2006 and 2014. **Croatia** became only the second team, after Argentina in 1990, to win consecutive shootouts, against Denmark and Russia. They were also the first team to be taken to extra-time in all three knock-out ties on their way to the final.

THE FASTEST GOAL

Turkey's **Hakan Sukur** holds the record for the quickest goal scored in the FIFA World Cup finals. He netted after 11 seconds against South Korea in the 2002 third-place play-off. Turkey went on to win 3-2. The previous record was held by Vaclav Masek of Czechoslovakia, who struck after 15 seconds against Mexico in 1962.

BIGGEST FIFA WORLD CUP FINALS WINS

Hungary 10, El Salvador 1 (15 June 1982)
Hungary 9, South Korea 0 (17 June 1954)
Yugoslavia 9, Zaire 0 (18 June 1974)
Sweden 8, Cuba 0 (12 June 1938)
Uruguay 8, Bolivia 0 (2 July 1950)
Germany 8, Saudi Arabia 0 (1 June 2002)

MOST GOALS IN ONE FIFA WORLD CUP

Goals	Country	Year
27	Hungary	1954
25	West Germany	1954
23	France	1958
22	Brazil	1950
19	Brazil	1970

MOST GOALS IN FIFA WORLD CUP FINALS (MINIMUM 100)

1	Brazil	229
2	Germany/W Germany	226
3	Argentina	137
4	Italy	128
5	France	120

FINAL FLURRY

France's 4-2 victory over Croatia in the 2018 World Cup Final was the highest 90-minute aggregate in the showdown since Brazil defeated hosts Sweden by 5-2 in 1958 in Stockholm. England and West Germany tallied six goals in the hosts' 4-2 victory in 1966, but the score was 2-2 after 90 minutes. The overall goals total at the 2018 tournament was 169, two short of the 171 from both 1998 and 2014, which is the record for the 32-team, 64-match finals.

YOUNGEST AND OLDEST

The youngest-ever scorer of a goal in FIFA World Cup finals history is **Pele.** He was 17 years and 239 days old when he notched Brazil's winner against Wales in the 1958 quarter-finals. Cameroon's **Roger Milla** – aged 42 years and 39 days – became the oldest scorer when he netted his country's only goal in a 6-1 defeat by Russia in 1994.

KING HARRY

Harry Kane became, in Russia in 2018, the second England striker to win the Golden Boot as leading scorer at the FIFA World Cup finals. The first was Gary Lineker who scored six goals when England reached the quarter-finals in Mexico in 1986. Kane first had been appointed England captain by manager Gareth Southgate during the 2017-18 season and was confirmed as skipper for the 2018 tournament in May. He rose to the challenge in Russia and led by example, scoring both goals in England's opening 2-1 win over Tunisia and then struck a hat-trick, including two penalties, in the 6-1 beating of Panama. It meant that in his seven games as captain, Kane had scored 11 goals. Kane scored a sixth goal, from yet another penalty, in the 1-1 second-round draw against Colombia. He also converted England's first kick in the shootout.

KLOSE ENCOUNTERS

Eight players have scored at FIFA World Cups 12 years apart. The most notable was Miroslav Klose. The Polish-born centre-forward opened with a hat-trick when Germany beat Saudi Arabia 8-0 in Japan in 2002 and scored a 16th goal in the 7-1 destruction of hosts Brazil in the 2014 semi-finals. That established Klose as the finals' all-time record marksman with one more goal than Brazil's Ronaldo. The other seven men to have scored in FIFA World Cups 12 years apart are: Pele (Brazil), Uwe Seeler (West Germany), Diego Maradona (Argentina), Michael Laudrup (Denmark), Henrik Larsson (Sweden), Sami Al-Jaber (S Arabia) and Cuauhtemoc Blanco (Mexico).

EUSEBIO THE STRIKE FORCE

Portugal's **Eusebio** was the striking star of the 1966 FIFA World Cup finals. Ironically, he would not be eligible to play for Portugal now. He was born in Mozambique, then a Portuguese colony, but now an independent country. He finished top scorer with nine goals, including two as Portugal eliminated champions Brazil and four as they beat North Korea 5-3 in the quarter-finals after trailing 3-0.

TUNISIAN TALLY

Tunisia's **Fakhreddine Ben Youssef** scored the 2,500th FIFA World Cup finals goal against Panama in 2018. His goal levelled the score at 1-1, before Tunisia won 2-1, their first victory at the finals since 1978. The first goal in the World Cup was scored by France's Lucien Laurent in 1930.

FIFA WORLD CUP FINALS TOP SCORERS

Maximum 16 teams in finals

Year	Venue	Top Scorer	Country	Goals
1930	Uruguay	Guillermo Stabile	Argentina	8
1934	Italy	Oldrich Nejedly	Czechoslovakia	5
1938	France	Leonidas	Brazil	7
1950	Brazil	Ademir	Brazil	9
1954	Switzerland	Sandor Kocsis	Hungary	11
1958	Sweden	Just Fontaine	France	13
1962	Chile	Garrincha	Brazil	4
		Vava	Brazil	
		Leonel Sanchez	Chile	
		Florian Albert	Hungary	
		Valentin Ivanov	Soviet Union	
		Drazen Jerkovic	Yugoslavia	
1966	England	Eusebio	Portugal	9
1970	Mexico	Gerd Muller	West Germany	10
1974	West Germany	Grzegorz Lato	Poland	7
1978	Argentina	Mario Kempes	Argentina	6

24 teams in finals

Year	Venue	Top Scorer	Country	Goals
1982	Spain	Paolo Rossi	Italy	6
1986	Mexico	Gary Lineker	England	6
1990	Italy	Salvatore Schillaci	Italy	6
1994	United States	Oleg Salenko	Russia	6
		Hristo Stoichkov	Bulgaria	6

32 teams in finals

Year	Venue	Top Scorer	Country	Goals
1998	France	Davor Suker	Croatia	6
2002	Korea/Japan	Ronaldo	Brazil	8
2006	Germany	Miroslav Klose	Germany	5
2010	South Africa	Thomas Muller*	Germany	5
		Diego Forlan	Uruguay	5
		Wesley Sneijder	Netherlands	5
		David Villa	Spain	5
2014	Brazil	James Rodriguez	Colombia	6
2018	Russia	Harry Kane	England	6

* = Won Golden Boot (had most assists)

KEMPES MAKES HIS MARK

Mario Kempes was Argentina's only foreign-based player in the hosts' squad at the 1978 finals. Twice top scorer in the Spanish league, Valencia's Kempes was crucial to Argentina's success. Coach Cesar Luis Menotti told him to shave off his moustache after he failed to score in the group games. Kempes then netted two against Peru, two more against Poland, and two decisive goals in the final against the Netherlands.

NO GUARANTEES FOR TOP SCORERS

Topping the FIFA World Cup finals scoring chart is a great honour for all strikers, but few have gained the ultimate prize and been leading scorer. Argentina's Guillermo Stabile started the luckless trend in 1930, topping the scoring charts but finishing up on the losing side in the final. The list of top scorers who have played in the winning side is small: Garrincha and Vava (joint top scorers in 1962), Mario Kempes (top scorer in 1978), Paolo Rossi (1982) and Ronaldo (2002). Gerd Muller, top scorer in 1970, gained his reward as West Germany's trophy winner four years later. Other top scorers, such as Sandor Kocsis, in 1954, Frenchman Just Fontaine in 1958 and both England strikers Gary Lineker in 1986 and Harry Kane in 2018 were disappointed in the final stages. Hungarian Kocsis was the only one of them to have reached the final, which the Magical Magyars lost 3-2 to West Germany, their first defeat in four years.

STABILE MAKES AN IMPACT

Guillermo Stabile, top scorer in the 1930 FIFA World Cup finals, had never played for Argentina before the tournament. He made his debut – as a 25-year-old – against Mexico because first-choice Roberto Cherro had suffered a panic attack. He netted a hat-trick then scored twice against both Chile and the United States as Argentina reached the final. He struck one of his side's goals in the 4-2 defeat by Uruguay in the final.

SUPER SUBS

Germany's winner in the 2014 FIFA World Cup Final was scored by **Mario Gotze** and created by a pass from Andre Schurrle. This was the first time both the assist and goal itself in a FIFA World Cup Final had come from two substitutes. It was also the first winning goal scored by a substitute.

HURST MAKES HISTORY

England's **Geoff Hurst** became the first and to date only player to score a hat-trick in a FIFA World Cup final when he netted three in the hosts' 4-2 victory over West Germany in 1966. Hurst headed England level after the Germans took an early lead, then scored the decisive third goal with a shot that bounced down off the crossbar and just over the line, according to the Soviet linesman. Hurst hit his third in the last minute. The British TV commentator Kenneth Wolstenholme described Hurst's strike famously with the words: "Some people are on the pitch ... They think it's all over ... It is now!"

⚽ JUST BRILLIANT

Just Fontaine of France scored 13 goals in the 1958 FIFA World Cup finals in Sweden, a record which has stood for 60 years. Fontaine – who was promoted into the team only because of an injury to Reims clubmate Rene Bliard – played in all six of France's matches, and scored at an average of 2.17 goals per game.

⚽ GRIEZ LUCK CHARM

France maintained, at the 2018 FIFA World Cup, their fine record of never losing in the 21 matches in which **Antoine Griezmann** has scored a goal. In Russia he opened the scoring for *Les Bleus* with a penalty in a 2-1 group stage win over Australia. The Atletico Madrid striker followed up with further goals against Argentina and Uruguay in the knockout stages and another penalty against Croatia in the final – his 24th in 61 appearances.

🏆 FIFA WORLD CUP FINALS ALL-TIME LEADING GOALSCORERS

	Name	Country	Tournaments	Goals
1	Miroslav Klose	Germany	2002, 2006, 2010, 2014	16
2	Ronaldo	Brazil	1998, 2002, 2006	15
3	Gerd Muller	West Germany	1970, 1974	14
4	Just Fontaine	France	1958	13
5	Pele	Brazil	1958, 1962, 1966, 1970	12
6	Jurgen Klinsmann	Germany	1990, 1994, 1998	11
=	Sandor Kocsis	Hungary	1954	11
8	Gabriel Batistuta	Argentina	1994, 1998, 2002	10
=	Teofilo Cubillas	Peru	1970, 1978	10
=	Grzegorz Lato	Poland	1974, 1978, 1982	10
=	Gary Lineker	England	1986, 1990	10
=	Thomas Muller	Germany	2010, 2014	10
=	Helmut Rahn	West Germany	1954, 1958	10

⚽ THE BRADLEY BUNCH

Michael Bradley's late equalizer for the United States, in their Group C 2-2 draw with Slovenia in June 2010, made him the first person to score a FIFA World Cup goal for a team coached by his own father – in this case, Bob Bradley.

⚽ MESSI MISSING OUT

Argentina's **Lionel Messi** is the only player to have recorded an assist in each of the last four FIFA World Cups. But not everything has gone his way. Messi has played 756 minutes of football in World Cup knockout stage matches without scoring a single goal. In the 2014 finals he captained Argentina to the final where they lost to Germany. Messi's consolation was to be awarded the golden ball as best player, selected by FIFA's technical study group.

PELE SO UNLUCKY

Pele would surely have been the all-time FIFA World Cup top scorer but for injuries. He was sidelined early in the 1962 finals, and again four years later. He scored six goals in Brazil's 1958 triumph, including two in the 5-2 final victory over Sweden. He also netted Brazil's 100th FIFA World Cup goal as they beat Italy 4-1 in the 1970 final.

MULLER'S SCORING HABIT

West Germany's **Gerd Muller** had the knack of scoring in important games. He struck the winner against England in the 1970 quarter-final and his two goals in extra-time against Italy almost carried his side to the final. Four years later, Muller's goal against Poland ensured that West Germany reached the final on home soil. Then he scored the winning goal against the Netherlands in the FIFA World Cup final. He also had a goal disallowed for offside – wrongly, as TV replays proved.

RONALDO SO CONSISTENT

Ronaldo was a consistent scorer in the three FIFA World Cup finals tournaments he played in. He netted four times in 1998, when they were runners-up to France, eight as Brazil won the 2002 tournament – including both goals in the final – and three more in 2006. He became the all-time top scorer when netting Brazil's opener in a 3-0 win over Ghana in the last-16 round at Dortmund on 27 June 2006. As a teenager, Ronaldo had been a member of Brazil's FIFA World Cup winning squad in the United States in 1994, but did not play.

KLINSMANN'S CONTRIBUTION

Jurgen Klinsmann has been one of the most influential personalities at the modern FIFA World Cup. He scored three goals when West Germany won the FIFA World Cup in 1990 and a further eight in 1994 and 1998. As team coach he then led Germany to third place in 2006, and the United States to the second round in 2014.

HIGH FIVES

Germany forwards **Thomas Muller** (in 2010 and 2014) and Miroslav Klose (2002 and 2006) are the only men to have scored five or more goals at successive FIFA World Cup finals. Muller's 10 goals came in only 13 matches, but he failed to score in three further appearances at the 2018 finals in Russia.

WHO SCORED THE FIRST HAT-TRICK?

For many years, Argentina's Guillermo Stabile was considered the first hat-trick scorer in the FIFA World Cup finals. He netted three in Argentina's 6-3 win over Mexico on 19 July 1930, but has since been superseded by Bert Patenaude of the United States. FIFA changed its records in November 2006, to acknowledge that Patenaude's treble two days earlier, in the Americans' 3-0 win over Paraguay, had been the tournament's first hat-trick.

FIFA WORLD CUP APPEARANCES

Rafael Marquez joined an elite club when he played for Mexico at the 2018 FIFA World Cup. Marquez, 39, was only the third player to appear in five tournaments after playing in 2002, 2006, 2010 and 2014. He was the second-oldest outfield player after England's 39-year-old Stanley Matthews in 1954. The other two five-finals stars were Mexico goalkeeper Antonio Carbajal (1950–66) and German midfielder Lothar Matthaus (1982–98). Goalkeeper Gianluigi Buffon was in Italy's squad at five World Cups but played in only four.

⚽ YOUNGEST AND OLDEST

Northern Ireland's Norman Whiteside is the youngest player in FIFA World Cup finals history, being just 17 years and 41 days when he started against Yugoslavia in 1982. The oldest player is Egypt goalkeeper Essam El-Hadary, who started against Saudi Arabia in 2018, aged 45 years and 161 days. The oldest outfield player is Cameroon's Roger Milla who was 42 years and 39 days in 1994.

CITY SLICKERS

Manchester City sent more players than any other club to the 2018 FIFA World Cup. Their 16 included one who collected a winner's medal, defender **Benjamin Mendy**. City were followed by Real Madrid (15 players) and Barcelona (14). Historically Italy's Juventus (128) have provided more players than any other club.

⚽ DOUBLE WINNERS

The following players have played on the winning side in two FIFA World Cup finals

Giovanni Ferrari (Italy), 1934, 1938
Giuseppe Meazza (Italy), 1934, 1938
Didi (Brazil), 1958, 1962
Garrincha (Brazil), 1958, 1962
Gilmar (Brazil), 1958, 1962
Vava (Brazil), 1958, 1962

Djalma Santos (Brazil), 1958, 1962
Nilton Santos (Brazil), 1958, 1962
Zagallo (Brazil), 1958, 1962
Zito (Brazil), 1958, 1962
Pele (Brazil), 1958, 1970
Cafu (Brazil), 1994, 2002

⚽ MOST APPEARANCES IN FIFA WORLD CUP FINALS

25 **Lothar Matthaus** (West Germany/Germany)
24 **Miroslav Klose** (Germany)
23 **Paolo Maldini** (Italy)
21 **Diego Maradona** (Argentina)
   Uwe Seeler (West Germany)
   Wladyslaw Zmuda (Poland)
20 **Cafu** (Brazil)
   Philipp Lahm (Germany)
   Grzegorz Lato (Poland)
   Javier Mascherano (Argentina)
   Bastian Schweinsteiger (Germany)

THE "DOUBLE" CHAMPIONS

Didier Deschamps joined Franz Beckenbauer and Mario Zagallo in the history books at the 2018 FIFA World Cup finals. Until France's victory in Russia under Deschamps, their 1998 winning captain, Zagallo and Beckenbauer had been the only men to win the World Cup as both player and manager. Zagallo was a left-winger in the Brazil teams which won the World Cup in both 1958 and 1962. He retired from playing in 1965, after scoring five goals in 33 international appearances. Five years later he took over at short notice from Joao Saldanha as Brazil manager and secured his third FIFA World Cup triumph at the 1970 final in Mexico. Beckenbauer played at those 1970 finals for West Germany whom he captained, as sweeper, to victory on home soil in 1974. Beckenbauer scored 14 goals in 103 appearances between 1965 and 1977. He was appointed national coach in 1984. Although his team lost to Argentina in the 1986 final, they took revenge in Italy four years later.

MOST FIFA WORLD CUP FINALS TOURNAMENTS

The following all played in at least four FIFA World Cup finals.

5 **Antonio Carbajal** (Mexico) 1950, 1954, 1958, 1962, 1966
  Lothar Matthaus (Germany) 1982, 1986, 1990, 1994, 1998
  Rafael Marquez (Mexico) 2002, 2006, 2010, 2014, 2018
4 **Gianluigi Buffon** (Italy) 2002, 2006, 2010, 2014
  Sami Al-Jaber (Saudi Arabia) 1994, 1998, 2002, 2006
  DaMarcus Beasley (United States) 2002, 2006, 2010, 2014
  Valon Behrami (Switzerland) 2006, 2010, 2014, 2018
  Giuseppe Bergomi (Italy) 1982, 1986, 1990, 1998
  Cafu (Brazil) 1994, 1998, 2002, 2006
  Tim Cahill (Australia) 2006, 2010, 2014, 2018
  Denis Caniza (Paraguay) 1998, 2002, 2006, 2010
  Fabio Cannavaro (Italy) 1998, 2002, 2006, 2010
  Iker Casillas (Spain) 2002, 2006, 2010, 2014
  Samuel Eto'o (Cameroon) 1998, 2002, 2010, 2014
  Andres Guardado (Mexico) 2006, 2010, 2014, 2018
  Thierry Henry (France) 1998, 2002, 2006, 2010
  Xavi Hernandez (Spain) 2002, 2006, 2010, 2014
  Hong Myung-Bo (South Korea) 1990, 1994, 1998, 2002
  Andres Iniesta (Spain) 2006, 2010, 2014, 2018
  Miroslav Klose (Germany) 2002, 2006, 2010, 2014
  Paolo Maldini (Italy) 1990, 1994, 1998, 2002
  Diego Maradona (Argentina) 1982, 1986, 1990, 1994
  Javier Mascherano (Argentina) 2006, 2010, 2014, 2018
  Lionel Messi (Argentina) 2006, 2010, 2014, 2018
  Pele (Brazil) 1958, 1962, 1966, 1970
  Sergio Ramos (Spain) 2006, 2010, 2014, 2018
  Gianni Rivera (Italy) 1962, 1966, 1970, 1974
  Pedro Rocha (Uruguay) 1962, 1966, 1970, 1974
  Cristiano Ronaldo (Portugal) 2006, 2010, 2014, 2018
  Djalma Santos (Brazil) 1954, 1958, 1962, 1966
  Karl-Heinz Schnellinger (W Germany) 1958, 1962, 1966, 1970
  Enzo Scifo (Belgium) 1986, 1990, 1994, 1998
  Uwe Seeler (W Germany) 1958, 1962, 1966, 1970
  Rigobert Song (Cameroon) 1994, 1998, 2002, 2010
  Franky Van Der Elst (Belgum) 1986, 1990, 1994, 1998
  Wladyslaw Zmuda (Poland) 1974, 1978, 1982, 1986
  Andoni Zubizarreta (Spain) 1986, 1990, 1994, 1998

EXTRA-TIME HISTORY

Aleksandr Erokhin, a Zenit St Petersburg midfielder, made history at the 2018 FIFA World Cup when he replaced clubmate Daler Kuziaev in extra-time in Russia's second round tie against Spain. It was Russia's fourth change. A rule amendment by FIFA's law-making International Board meant that teams could make a fourth substitution, but only in extra-time.

VARANE AT THE DOUBLE

Raphael Varane became the 11th player to clinch the double of success in the UEFA Champions League and FIFA World Cup when he anchored France's defence at the 2018 finals in Russia. Varane, born in Lille and a youth protege at Lens, joined Real Madrid in 2011, two years before making his senior debut for France. By the time he lined up at the 2018 FIFA World Cup, he had won 15 major club honours with Madrid. At the World Cup he played every minute in all seven of France's games including the final victory over Croatia.

SONG FAMILY GOES OFF KEY

In playing 17 minutes at the 2010 FIFA World Cup, Cameroon defender **Rigobert Song** became the first African to play in four finals tournaments – nine matches, across 16 years and nine days. He featured in 1994, 1998, 2002 and 2010 – Cameroon failed to qualify in 2006. He, and Colombia's Faryd Mondragon, share the fourth-longest FIFA World Cup career-spans, bettered only by Mexicans Antonio Carbajal (spanning 16 years, 25 days) and Hugo Sanchez (16 years, 17 days) and West Germany/Germany's Lothar Matthaus (16 years, 14 days). On the down side, Song was sent off twice at World Cups and cousin Alex Song was dismissed at the 2014 finals for elbowing Mario Mandzukic in a 4-0 loss to Croatia. Thus, the Song family is responsible for three of Cameroon's eight FIFA World Cup finals red cards.

MOST FIFA WORLD CUP FINALS MATCHES (BY POSITION)

Goalkeeper: Sepp Maier (West Germany, 18 matches) and Claudio Taffarel (Brazil, 18 matches)
Defence: Paolo Maldini (Italy, 23); Wladyslaw Zmuda (Poland, 21); Cafu (Brazil, 20); Philipp Lahm (Germany, 20)
Midfielders: Lothar Matthaus (W. Germany/Germany, 25); Bastian Schweinsteiger (Germany, 20); Javier Mascherano (Argentina, 20)
Forwards: Miroslav Klose (Germany, 24); Diego Maradona (Argentina, 21); Uwe Seeler (West Germany, 21); Grzegorz Lato (Poland, 20)

PROSINECKI'S SCORING RECORD

Robert Prosinecki is the only player to have scored for different countries in FIFA World Cup finals tournaments. He netted for Yugoslavia in their 4-1 win over the United Arab Emirates in the 1990 tournament. Eight years later, following the break-up of the old Yugoslavia, he scored for Croatia in their 3-0 group-game win over Jamaica, and then netted the first goal in his side's 2-1 third-place play-off victory over the Netherlands.

QUICKEST SUBSTITUTIONS

The three fastest substitutions in the history of the FIFA World Cup finals have all come in the fourth minute. In each case the player substituted was so seriously injured that he took no further part in the tournament: Steve Hodge came on for Bryan Robson in England's 0-0 draw with Morocco in 1986; Giuseppe Bergomi replaced Alessandro Nesta in Italy's 2-1 win over Austria in 1998; and Peter Crouch subbed for Michael Owen in England's 2-2 draw with Sweden in 2006.

PRIZE PROBLEM

Winning the FIFA Best Player award has not always proved a lucky omen for its proud bearers. The winner has never validated the award by winning the next World Cup and it was no different in 2018 as **Cristiano Ronaldo**, FIFA's 2017 choice as player of the year, and his Portugal team-mates, went out in the second round. His predecessor as world player, Lionel Messi of Argentina, had been on the losing side in the 2014 final. Messi was also the title-holder going into the 2010 World Cup but Argentina lost in the quarter-finals.

TIM'S HAIL AND FAREWELL

Tim Cahill became the first Australian to appear at four different FIFA World Cup finals when he appeared as a substitute against Peru in Russia in 2018. Cahill had played previously at the finals in 2006, 2010 and 2014. He is Australia's all-time leading scorer with 50 goals in 107 games and has scored the most goals (five) by any Australian in the World Cup.

LEADING CAPTAINS

Three players have each captained their teams in two FIFA World Cup finals – Diego Maradona of Argentina, Dunga of Brazil and West Germany's Karl-Heinz Rummenigge. Maradona lifted the trophy in 1986, but was a loser four years later. Dunga was the winning skipper in 1994, but was on the losing side in 1998. Rummenigge was a loser on both occasions, in 1982 and 1986. Maradona has made the most appearances as captain at the FIFA World Cup finals, leading out Argentina 16 times between 1986 and 1994.

FASTEST SENDINGS–OFF IN THE FIFA WORLD CUP FINALS

1 min Jose Batista (Uruguay) v Scotland, 1986
4 min Carlos Sanchez (Colombia) v Japan, 2018
8 min Giorgio Ferrini (Italy) v Chile, 1962
14 min Zeze Procopio (Brazil) v Czechoslovakia, 1938
19 min Mohammed Al Khlaiwi (Saudi Arabia) v France, 1998
Miguel Bossio (Uruguay) v Denmark, 1986
21 min Gianluca Pagliuca (Italy) v Rep of Ireland, 1994

FASTEST YELLOW CARDS IN THE FIFA WORLD CUP FINALS

1 min Jesus Gallardo (Mexico) v Sweden, 2018
Sergei Gorlukovich (Russia) v Sweden, 1994
Giampiero Marini (Italy) v Poland, 1982
2 min Jesus Arellano (Mexico) v Italy, 2002
Henri Camara (Senegal) v Uruguay, 2002
Michael Emenalo (Nigeria) v Italy, 1994
Humberto Suazo (Chile) v Switzerland, 2010
Mark van Bommel (Netherlands) v Port., 2006

SUPER SUBS IMPOSE THEIR WILL

Substitutes scored more goals in the Brazil 2014 FIFA World Cup than in any previous finals. Mario Gotze's goal in the final was the 32nd by a substitute, extending the record from the previous mark of 24 set in 2006 in Germany. Substitutes, two of them, were first permitted for the 1970 finals in Mexico, and it went up to three from 1998. The 1998 FIFA World Cup finals also saw the fastest goal by a substitute. Denmark's Ebbe Sand scored 16 seconds after coming on against Nigeria.

FIRST ELEVEN

In an age of squad numbers, **Brazil** may have pleased some traditionalists when fielding players wearing shirt numbers one to 11 in the starting line-ups for their first two games of the 2010 FIFA World Cup, against North Korea and the Ivory Coast. Kicking off for coach Dunga on each occasion were: 1 Julio Cesar, 2 Maicon, 3 Lucio, 4 Juan, 5 Felipe Melo, 6 Michel Bastos, 7 Elano, 8 Gilberto Silva, 9 Luis Fabiano, 10 Kaka and 11 Robinho. **the Netherlands** managed a similar starting structure for not only their second-round tie against Slovakia, but the final against Spain: 1 Maarten Stekelenburg, 2 Gregory van der Wiel, 3 Johnny Heitinga, 4 Joris Mathijsen, 5 Giovanni van Bronckhorst, 6 Mark van Bommel, 7 Dirk Kuyt, 8 Nigel de Jong, 9 Robin van Persie, 10 Wesley Sneijder and 11 Arjen Robben. Both Brazil and the Netherlands came close to the same feat when they met in the quarter-finals, though both featured a number 13 – Brazil's Dani Alves, in place of 7 Elano, and the Netherlands' Andre Ooijer instead of 4 Joris Mathijsen (Elano and Mathijsen were unavailable through injury).

YOUNGEST PLAYERS IN FIFA WORLD CUP FINAL

Pele (Brazil) – 17 years, 249 days, in 1958
Giuseppe Bergomi (Italy) – 18 years, 201 days, in 1982
Kylian Mbappe (France) – 19 years, 207 days, in 2018

OLDEST PLAYERS IN FIFA WORLD CUP FINAL

Dino Zoff (Italy) – 40 years, 133 days, in 1982
Gunnar Gren (Sweden) – 37 years, 241 days, in 1958
Jan Jongbloed (Netherlands) – 37 years, 212 days, in 1978
Nilton Santos (Brazil) – 37 years, 32 days, in 1962

PUZACH THE FIRST SUB

The first substitute in FIFA World Cup finals history was Anatoli Puzach of the Soviet Union. He replaced Viktor Serebrianikov at half-time of the Soviets' 0-0 draw with hosts Mexico on 31 May 1970. The 1970 tournament was the first in which substitutes were allowed, with two permitted for each side. FIFA increased this to three per team for the 1998 finals.

FOUR AND OUT

The most players sent off in one FIFA World Cup finals game is four. Costinha and Deco of Portugal and Khalid Boulahrouz and Gio van Bronckhorst of the Netherlands were sent off by Russian referee Valentin Ivanov in their second-round match in Germany in 2006.

CANIGGIA – SENT OFF, WHILE ON THE BENCH...

Claudio Caniggia of Argentina became the first player to be sent off from the substitutes' bench, during the match against Sweden in 2002. Caniggia was dismissed in first-half stoppage time for dissent towards UAE referee Ali Bujsaim. Caniggia carried on protesting after the referee warned him to keep quiet, so Bujsaim showed him a red card.

OH, BABIES!

Sweden's **Andreas Granqvist** and England's **Fabian Delph** took different approaches to fatherhood during the 2018 FIFA World Cup. Manchester City midfielder Delph flew home to welcome his new daughter before flying back to Russia to rejoin the England squad. Granqvist stayed at the finals while his wife Sofia gave birth to a daughter. She had insisted her husband stay with the team because "it's these World Cup moments that he dreamed about as a little boy."

GERMANY UNITED

Germany and West Germany are counted together in World Cup records because the Deutscher Fussball-Bund, founded in 1900, was the original governing body and the DFB was in charge of the national game before World War 2, during the East–West split and post-reunification. German sides have won the World Cup four times and appeared in the Final a record eight times. In 2014, match-deciding substitutes Andre Schurrle and Mario Gotze were the first players born in Germany since reunification to win the World Cup, while team-mate Toni Kroos was the only 2014 squad-member to have been born in what was East Germany. Kroos was also the first player from the former East Germany to win the World Cup.

UNBEATEN GOALKEEPERS IN THE FIFA WORLD CUP FINALS*

Walter Zenga (Italy)	517 minutes without conceding a goal, 1990
Peter Shilton (England)	502 minutes, 1986–90
Iker Casillas (Spain)	476 minutes, 2010–14
Sepp Maier (W Germany)	475 minutes, 1974–78
Gianluigi Buffon (Italy)	460 minutes, 2006
Emerson Leao (Brazil)	458 minutes, 1978
Gordon Banks (England)	442 minutes, 1966

* Pascal Zuberbuhler did not concede a goal in all 390 minutes played by Switzerland in the 2006 FIFA World Cup.

FIFA GOALKEEPING

KING HUGO THE FOURTH

Hugo Lloris became the fourth goalkeeper to captain his country to FIFA World Cup glory when France became champions for the second time in Russia in 2018. The Tottenham Hotspur keeper joined Italians Gianpiero Combi (1934) and Dino Zoff (1982) as well as Spain's Iker Casillas (2010). A mistake by Lloris on a back-pass in the final cost France their second goal, but they went on to beat Croatia 4-2. The final was Loris's 104th appearance in 10 years for France. The former Nice and Lyon keeper had been appointed national team captain in 2012.

NOT THINKING OUTSIDE THE BOX

Italy's Gianluca Pagliuca was the first goalkeeper to be sent off at a FIFA World Cup match – for handball outside his penalty area – against Norway in 1994. Despite sacrificing playmaker Roberto Baggio for goalkeeper Luca Marchegiani, Italy still won 1-0.

ITALY'S ELDER STATESMEN

Dino Zoff became both the oldest player and oldest captain to win the FIFA World Cup when Italy lifted the trophy in Spain in 1982. He was 40 years 133 days old. A predecessor as goalkeeper and captain of both Italy and Juventus, Gianpiero Combi, had led Italy to World Cup glory in 1934.

PICKFORD MOVES UP

Jordan Pickford was one of England's heroes when they finished fourth at the 2018 FIFA World Cup in Russia. The Everton goalkeeper had made his senior debut only the previous autumn when he excelled in a goalless friendly against Germany. In Russia he emerged triumphant from the biggest test of his career when his save from Colombia's Carlos Bacca helped England end a 28-year penalty shoot-out jinx. He was named man of the match in the subsequent 2-0 win over Sweden.

KEEPERS CAUGHT OUT

The 2018 FIFA World Cup proved a testing tournament for goalkeepers. Mistakes by **Willy Caballero** cost goals in Argentina's opening 1-1 draw against Iceland and the next game 3-0 defeat by Croatia. Uruguay's Fernando Muslera began well with three clean sheets but then misjudged a goal-bound shot from Antoine Griezmann in their quarter-final defeat by France. Even Germany's goalkeeper-captain Manuel Neuer had a tough time on returning to duty after a long injury lay-off. In the last group game, as Germany chased an equaliser against South Korea, Neuer was caught in the opposition half by a high-speed counter-attack which provided the Koreans' second goal.

NUMBER-ONE NUMBER ONES

The Lev Yashin Award was introduced in 1994 for the man voted best goalkeeper of the FIFA World Cup – though a goalkeeper was selected subsequently for an all-star team at the end of every tournament dating back to 1930. The all-star team was expanded from 11 to 23 players in 1998, allowing room for more than one goalkeeper, but returned to 11 players in 2010. Players who were picked for the all-star teams but missed out on the Lev Yashin Award were Paraguay's Jose Luis Chilavert in 1998, Turkey's Rustu Recber in 2002, and Germany's Jens Lehmann and Portugal's Ricardo in 2006. The first Lev Yashin Award was presented to Belgium's Michel Preud'homme, even though he only played four games, conceding four goals, at the 1994 competition – his side were edged out 3-2 by Germany in the second round. Legendary Soviet goalkeeper Lev Yashin, after whom the trophy was named, played in the 1958, 1962 and 1966 FIFA World Cups and was a member of his country's 1970 squad as third-choice keeper and assistant coach – although he was never chosen for a FIFA World Cup team of the tournament. From 2010 commercial priorities led to Yashin's name being dropped from the award and it was renamed the Golden Glove award.

OLIVER'S ARMS

Germany's **Oliver Kahn** is the only goalkeeper to have been voted FIFA's Player of the Tournament, winning the award at the 2002 FIFA World Cup – despite taking a share of the blame for Brazil's winning goals in the final.

RIGHT WAY FOR RICARDO

Spain's Ricardo Zamora became the first man to save a penalty in a FIFA World Cup finals match, stopping Valdemar de Brito's spot-kick for Brazil in 1934. Spain went on to win 3-1.

HOWARD'S WAY

Tim Howard wrote his name into the FIFA World Cup history books with his amazing performance in the United States' second round clash with Belgium in 2014. Howard registered 16 superb saves in defying wave upon wave of Belgian attacks. This was the most saves ever recorded in a FIFA World Cup tie since the statistic was first introduced in 1966. It was not enough, however: the United States lost a thriller of a match 2-1 after extra time.

LEADING FROM THE BACK

Belgium's Thibaut Courtois was awarded the Golden Glove as top goalkeeper at the 2018 FIFA World Cup. The 26-year-old produced a tournament-best 27 saves as the Red Devils finished a best-ever third. The 2-0 playoff win over England was his 65th international. Behind Courtois came Mexico's Guillermo Ochoa (25), Denmark's Kasper Schmeichel (21) and England's Jordan Pickford (17).

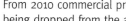

UNLUCKY BREAK

Goalkeeper Frantisek Planicka broke an arm during Czechoslovakia's 1938 second-round clash against Brazil, but played on, even though the game went to extra-time before ending in a 1-1 draw. Not surprisingly, given the extent of his injury, Planicka missed the replay two days later, which the Czechs lost 2-1, and the goalkeeper of the 1938 FIFA World Cup never added to his tally of 73 caps.

PLAYERS VOTED BEST GOALKEEPER OF THE TOURNAMENT

1930	Enrique Ballestrero (Uruguay)	1982	Dino Zoff (Italy)
1934	Ricardo Zamora (Spain)	1986	Harald Schumacher (West Germany)
1938	Frantisek Planicka (Czechoslovakia)	1990	Sergio Goycoechea (Argentina)
1950	Roque Maspoli (Uruguay)	1994	Michel Preud'homme (Belgium)
1954	Gyula Grosics (Hungary)	1998	Fabien Barthez (France)
1958	Harry Gregg (Northern Ireland)	2002	Oliver Kahn (Germany)
1962	Viliam Schrojf (Czechoslovakia)	2006	Gianluigi Buffon (Italy)
1966	Gordon Banks (England)	2010	Iker Casillas (Spain)
1970	Ladislao Mazurkiewicz (Uruguay)	2014	Manuel Neuer (Germany)
1974	Jan Tomaszewski (Poland)	2018	Thibaut Courtois (Belgium)
1978	Ubaldo Fillol (Argentina)		

BATTERING RAMON

Argentina's 6-0 win over Peru at the 1978 FIFA World Cup aroused suspicion because the hosts needed to win by four goals to reach the final at the expense of arch-rivals Brazil – and Peruvian goalkeeper Ramon Quiroga had been born in Argentina. He insisted, though, that his saves prevented the defeat from being even more embarrassingly emphatic. Earlier in the same tournament, Quiroga had been booked for a foul on Grzegorz Lato after running into the Polish half of the field.

END TO END STUFF

When Miroslav Klose raced on to a long ball from German team-mate **Manuel Neuer** to score against England in their 2010 FIFA World Cup second round tie, it made Neuer the first goalkeeper to directly set up a finals goal for 44 years. The last before then had been the Soviet Union's Anzor Kavazashvili, providing an assist for Valery Porkuyan's late winner against Chile in the 1966 group stage.

MORE AND MORA

Luis Ricardo Guevara Mora holds the unenviable record for most goals conceded in just one FIFA World Cup finals match. The 20-year-old had to pick the ball out of the net ten times in El Salvador's thrashing by Hungary in 1982 – and his team-mates managed only one goal of their own in reply. In this game he also set the record for being the youngest goalkeeper to participate in the FIFA World Cup finals.

TONY AWARD

United States goalkeeper **Tony Meola** left the national team after the 1994 FIFA World Cup because he wanted to switch sports and take up American football instead. He failed to make it in gridiron and returned to soccer, but did not play for his country again until 1999. He retired for a second time after reaching a century of international appearances and still holds the record for being the youngest FIFA World Cup captain, having worn the armband for the US's 5-1 defeat to Czechoslovakia in 1990, aged 21 years 316 days.

SWEDISH STALEMATE

Gilmar and Colin McDonald were the goalkeepers who made history at the 1958 FIFA World Cup in Sweden when first round group rivals Brazil and England fought out the first goalless draw in the history of the finals.

KEEPING THE FAITH

Switzerland's **Diego Benaglio** was the only goalkeeper to register a shot at the 2014 FIFA World Cup in Brazil. With the Swiss losing their second-round tie 1-0 to Argentina in Sao Paulo, he charged upfield at a corner. The ball fell loose to him in the penalty area, but his effort on goal was blocked. Benaglio's Swiss predecessor, at the 2006 finals, was equally unlucky. Pascal Zuberbuhler kept a clean sheet in all four of their matches, three in the group stage and a goalless draw with Ukraine in the second round. However the Swiss lost the resulting penalty shoot-out 3-0, despite Zuberbuhler saving Ukraine's first kick by Andriy Shevchenko.

TOP GOALS

1930	70	(3.89 per match)
1934	70	(4.12 per match)
1938	84	(4.67 per match)
1950	88	(4 per match)
1954	140	(5.38 per match)
1958	126	(3.6 per match)
1962	89	(2.78 per match)
1966	89	(2.78 per match)
1970	95	(2.97 per match)
1974	97	(2.55 per match)
1978	102	(2.68 per match)
1982	146	(2.81 per match)
1986	132	(2.54 per match)
1990	115	(2.21 per match)
1994	141	(2.71 per match)
1998	171	(2.67 per match)
2002	161	(2.52 per match)
2006	147	(2.3 per match)
2010	145	(2.27 per match)
2014	171	(2.67 per match)
2018	169	(2.64 per match)
Total	2,548	(2.83 per match)

THE PETER PRINCIPLE

Peter Shilton became the oldest FIFA World Cup captain when he led England for their 1990 third-place play-off against hosts Italy. He was 40 years and 292 days old as he made his 125th and final appearance for his country – though his day was spoiled by a 2-1 defeat, including a goalkeeping error that gifted Roberto Baggio Italy's opener. Shilton, born in Leicester on 18 September 1949, also played for England at the 1982 and 1986 tournaments. He became captain in Mexico in 1986 after Bryan Robson was ruled out of the tournament by injury and Ray Wilkins by suspension, and featured in one of the FIFA World Cup's all-time memorable moments, when he was out-jumped by Argentina's Diego Maradona for the infamous "Hand of God" goal. Shilton jointly holds the record for most FIFA World Cup clean sheets, with ten – along with France's Fabien Barthez, who played at the 1998, 2002 and 2006 tournaments. Both men made 17 FIFA World Cup finals appearances apiece.

TRADING PLACES

The first goalkeeper to be substituted at a FIFA World Cup was Romania's Stere Adamache, who was replaced by Rica Raducanu 27 minutes into a 3-2 defeat to Brazil in 1970. Romania were 2-0 down at the time.

THIRD TIME LUCKY

Steve Mandanda was given special consideration by France manager Didier Deschamps when he played in a goalless draw against Denmark in Moscow at the 2018 FIFA World Cup. Marseille keeper Mandanda had not enjoyed the best of luck as far as the World Cup was concerned. He made his France debut in 2008 and became first-choice but was replaced by Hugo Lloris and was a substitute for France's three matches at the 2010 World Cup in South Africa. Mandanda was selected for the 2014 finals but was forced to pull out before the finals through injury. In Russia Lloris was goalkeeper-captain but, with France qualified for the second round after two matches, Deschamps handed Mandanda his long-awaited finals debut in the last group game against Denmark.

HOW GOING DUTCH PAYS OFF

Argentina's Sergio Romero will never be forgotten in the Netherlands – for using the experience he gained there to put the Dutchmen out of the 2014 FIFA World Cup. Romero had been brought to Europe in 2007 by Louis Van Gaal when the Dutch master coach was boss of AZ Alkmaar. In 2011 Romero moved to Italy to play for Sampdoria. Then he fell out of favour with the Genoese club and was loaned to French club AS Monaco in August 2013. Romero was hardly a regular in Ligue 1 either, indeed he played only three league matches in the season leading up to the FIFA World Cup. However, he did remain the first-choice with Argentina coach Alejandro Sabella. Argentina won all their group matches and then Romero kept clean sheets in initial knockout victories over Switzerland and Belgium. When the semi-final went to penalties, Romero became a national hero, with match-winning saves from the Netherlands' Ron Vlaar and Wesley Sneijder. Romero said later he owed Van Gaal special thanks ... "for teaching me how to save penalties."

FIFA MANAGERS
WORLD CUP

BETTER LATE THAN NEVER

Zlatko Dalic proved at the 2018 FIFA World Cup that a pedigree of club success is not essential to succeed in the national team sphere. Dalic had been working in club football in Saudi Arabia and the United Arab Emirates before being selected to replace Ante Cacic when Croatia struggled in qualifying. Under Dalic they finished second in the group behind Iceland and reached Russia by defeating Greece in the playoffs. Dalic then varied his tactics masterfully to achieve three wins in the group stage plus two nerve-jangling victories on penalties and one in extra-time to take Croatia to their first final.

YOUNG JUAN, OLD OTTO

Juan Jose Tramutola is the youngest ever FIFA World Cup finals coach, leading Argentina to the 1930 final at the age of 27 years 267 days. The oldest manager in a finals was German **Otto Rehhagel**, aged 71 years 307 days when he led Greece in South Africa in 2010.

DREAM TO NIGHTMARE

Luiz Felipe Scolari quit as Brazil coach after the 2014 FIFA World Cup brought the worst defeat in their history, by 7-1 against Germany in the semi-finals, and then a 3-0 defeat to the Netherlands in the third-place play-off. However, he had won the FIFA World Cup with Brazil in 2002 and went on, with Portugal in 2006, to set an individual record of 11 successive wins at the finals.

PUFF DADDIES

The coaches of the two sides appearing at the 1978 FIFA World Cup final were such prolific smokers that an oversized ashtray was produced for Argentina's Cesar Luis Menotti and the Netherlands's Ernst Happel so they could share it on the touchline.

SOCCER SIX

Only one man has gone to six FIFA World Cups as coach: Brazilian **Carlos Alberto Parreira**, whose greatest moment came when he guided Brazil to the trophy for the fourth time in 1994. His second stint as Brazil coach was less successful – they fell in the quarter-finals in 2006. Parreira also led Kuwait (1982), the United Arab Emirates (1990), Saudi Arabia (1998) and hosts South Africa (2010) at the finals. He had stepped down as South Africa coach in April 2008, for family reasons, but returned late the following year. Parreira was once sacked midway through a FIFA World Cup. In 1998 he led Saudi Arabia for the first two of their three games – losing 1-0 to Denmark and 4-0 to France – before receiving his marching orders.

⚽ WAISTCOAT WONDER
England manager **Gareth Southgate** became an unlikely style icon at the 2018 World Cup by eschewing a suit or tracksuit and wearing a waistcoat during matches. Southgate was the first man to have represented England in semi-finals as both a player (UEFA Euro 1996) and a manager (Russia 2018).

CRASHING BORA
Only one tournament behind record-holder Carlos Alberto Parreira, **Bora Milutinovic** has coached at five different FIFA World Cups – with a different country each time, two of them being the hosts. As well as Mexico in 1986 and the United States in 1994, he led Costa Rica in 1990, Nigeria in 1998 and China in 2002. He reached the knockout stages with every country except China – who failed to score a single goal.

⚽ DIVIDED LOYALTIES
No coach has won the FIFA World Cup in charge of a foreign team, but several have faced their homeland. These include Jurgen Klinsmann, who played for Germany when they won the Cup in 1990 and then managed them to third-place in 2006. Klinsmann, who was German boss 2004–06, having already made his home in California, was appointed United States coach in 2011. In the 2014 FIFA World Cup, "Klinsi" and the US lost 1-0 in a group match to Germany, now led by his former assistant Joachim Low, whom he had appointed in 2004. In the 2018 semi-finals, Thierry Henry, a World Cup-winning player with France in 1998, found himself on the opposite – losing – side as Roberto Martinez's assistant coach with Belgium.

⚽ FIFA WORLD CUP–WINNING COACHES

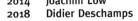

1930	Alberto Suppici
1934	Vittorio Pozzo
1938	Vittorio Pozzo
1950	Juan Lopez
1954	Sepp Herberger
1958	Vicente Feola
1962	Aymore Moreira
1966	Alf Ramsey
1970	Mario Zagallo
1974	Helmut Schon
1978	Cesar Luis Menotti
1982	Enzo Bearzot
1986	Carlos Bilardo
1990	Franz Beckenbauer
1994	Carlos Alberto Parreira
1998	Aime Jacquet
2002	Luiz Felipe Scolari
2006	Marcello Lippi
2010	Vicente del Bosque
2014	Joachim Low
2018	Didier Deschamps

⚽ SCHON SHINES
West Germany's **Helmut Schon** was coach for more FIFA World Cup matches than any other man – 25, across the 1966, 1970, 1974 and 1978 tournaments. He has also won the most games as a coach, 16 in all – including the 1974 final against the Netherlands. The 1974 tournament was third time lucky for Schon. He he had taken West Germany to second place in 1966 and to third in 1970. Before taking charge of the national side, Schon had worked as an assistant to Sepp Herberger, coach of West Germany's 1954 FIFA World Cup-winning team – Schon was coach of the then-independent Saarland regional side at the time. Dog-lover Schon, born in Dresden on 15 September 1915, scored 17 goals in 16 internationals for Germany between 1937 and 1941. He succeeded Herberger in 1964 and spent 14 years in charge of his country. He was the first coach to win both the FIFA World Cup (1974) and the European Championship (1972).

FIFA WORLD CUP DISCIPLINE

FIFA BITES BACK

Uruguay's **Luis Suarez** incurred a record instant FIFA sanction after biting Italy's Giorgio Chiellini during Uruguay's 1-0 win in the 2014 World Cup, a result that put them, and not the Azzurri, into the second round. Suarez missed the subsequent 2-0 defeat by Colombia because he had been banned from all football for four months, from international competition for nine games and fined 100,000 Swiss francs. It was not the first time Suarez had been in trouble at the FIFA World Cup finals, having been banned for one match at the 2010 finals after being dismissed for handball on the goal-line in a quarter-final against Ghana.

REPEAT OFFENDERS

France's **Zinedine Zidane** and Brazil's **Cafu** are both FIFA World Cup winners – and both notched up a record six FIFA World Cup cards, though Cafu escaped any reds, while Zidane was sent off twice. Most famously, Zidane was dismissed for headbutting Italy's Marco Materazzi in extra-time of the 2006 final in Berlin – the final match of the Frenchman's career. He had also been sent off during a first-round match against Saudi Arabia in 1998, but returned from suspension in time to help France win the trophy with a sensational two-goal performance in the final. The only other man to have been sent off twice at two different FIFA World Cups is Cameroon's Rigobert Song. When dismissed against Brazil in 1994, he became the FIFA World Cup's youngest red card offender – aged just 17 years and 358 days. He saw red for the second time against Chile in 1998.

NOT LEADING BY EXAMPLE

The first man to be sent off at a FIFA World Cup was Peru's Placido Galindo, at the first tournament in 1930 during a 3-1 defeat to Romania. Chilean referee Alberto Warnken dismissed the Peruvian captain for fighting.

ARGIE BARGEY

Argentina defender Pedro Monzon became the first player sent off in a World Cup final when he was dismissed in 1990 for a foul on West Germany's Jurgen Klinsmann. Monzon had been on the pitch only 20 minutes after coming on as a half-time substitute. Three minutes from full-time Mexican referee Edgardo Codesal reduced Argentina to nine men by dismissing Gustavo Dezotti after a skirmish with Jurgen Kohler. Marcel Desailly, of France in 1998, is the only member of a winning team to have been sent off in a World Cup final.

KEN'S CARD TRICK

English referee Ken Aston – who officiated at the 1962 FIFA World Cup – devised the idea of red and yellow cards while sitting in his car at traffic lights pondering discipline problems at the 1966 tournament. His card system was tested at the 1968 Olympics in Mexico City and then introduced at the FIFA World Cup Mexico 1970.

FIFA WORLD CUP RED CARDS, BY TOURNAMENT

1930	1
1934	1
1938	4
1950	0
1954	3
1958	3
1962	6
1966	5
1970	0
1974	5
1978	3
1982	5
1986	8
1990	16
1994	15
1998	22
2002	17
2006	28
2010	17
2014	10
2018	4

FINAL COUNT

England's Howard Webb set a record with one red card and 14 yellow in the 2010 FIFA World Cup Final between Spain and Netherlands. The previous 18 finals had featured 40 bookings and three dismissals between them. Webb's card total of 15 was nine more than the six shown by Brazil's Romualdo Arppi Filho in the 1986 final between Argentina (four) and Germany (two). Italy's Nicola Rizzoli showed four yellow cards (two each) when the same teams met in the 2014 FIFA World Cup Final.

SOLE CHANCE OF GLORY

India withdrew from the 1950 FIFA World Cup because some of their players wanted to play barefoot but FIFA insisted all players must wear football boots. India have not qualified for the tournament since.

BREAKING COVER

Zaire defender Mwepu Llunga was booked for running out of the wall and kicking the ball away as Brazil prepared to take a free-kick, at the 1974 FIFA World Cup. Romanian referee Nicolae Rainea ignored Llunga's pleas of innocence.

PLAYING IT FAIR

FIFA decided, at the 2018 World Cup, to use fair play as a tie-breaker in separating teams which had finished level on points, goal difference, goal scored, and mutual result. That led to an unreal end to Japan's last game against Poland when they refused to tackle to ensure they collected fewer yellow cards than Senegal – with whom they had drawn 2-2 – in the other group game. They finished level on points and goals, but Japan went into the second round while Senegal went home. The introduction of the VAR video referee system was credited with helping to reduce the number of red cards in the finals to four, the lowest total since 1978. No red cards were issued for violent conduct and only two were direct, Colombia's Carlos Sanchez (handball) in Group H against Japan and Switzerland's Michael Lang (professional foul) in the second round against Sweden. Germany's **Jerome Boateng** (against Sweden) and Russia's Igor Smonikov (against Uruguay) saw red after being shown two yellow cards each.

SIMUNIC'S TRIPLE CHANCE

In the 2006 FIFA World Cup, Croatia midfielder Josip Simunic played on against Australia – his country of birth – despite having been shown a second yellow card. English referee Graham Poll had forgotten the first booking, but Simunic was later sent off after being shown a third yellow card.

YELLOW MELO'S RED MIST

Felipe Melo's red card for stamping on Arjen Robben, in Brazil's 2010 FIFA World Cup quarter-final defeat to the Netherlands, meant Brazil have had more players sent off in FIFA World Cup history than any other team – one more than Argentina. Melo was Brazil's 11th dismissal, after Kaka had become the 10th in a first-round victory over the Ivory Coast. Melo could also have gone down as the first player ever to score an own goal and be sent off in the same FIFA World Cup match, but the first Dutch goal was later officially awarded to their own playmaker Wesley Sneijder.

THREE LIONS' THREE REDS

Ray Wilkins, David Beckham and Wayne Rooney are the only three England players to have been sent off at the FIFA World Cup. Wilkins was dismissed for a second yellow card in a group game against Morocco in 1986; Beckham incurred a straight red in the second round against Argentina in 1998; and Rooney also received a straight red against Portugal in the 2006 quarter-finals. All three matches ended in draws, but England lost penalty shoot-outs to Argentina and Portugal.

FIFA WORLD CUP ATTENDANCES

CAPACITY PLANNING

The **Lusail** World Cup stadium in Qatar, which will host the 2022 FIFA World Cup final, could record the biggest attendance for the competition climax since 1994. The planned capacity for Lusail, designed by Foster + Partners, is 86,250, which would exceed the final attendances recorded at Saint-Denis (1998), Yokohama (2002), Berlin (2006), Johannesburg (2010), Rio de Janeiro's Maracanã (2014) and Moscow (2018) – but not the 94,194 who saw Brazil play Italy at Pasadena's Rose Bowl in 1994. Initially Qatar's Supreme Committee for Delivery & Legacy proposed 12 new stadia, but this was later scaled back to eight. A number of these stadia are modular so they can be reduced in size or even dismantled altogether after the finals.

TWO'S COMPANY, 300'S A CROWD

The 300 people who were recorded as watching Romania beat Peru 3-1 in 1930 formed the FIFA World Cup finals' smallest attendance, with plenty of room for manoeuvre inside the Estadio Pocitos in Montevideo. A day earlier, ten times as many people are thought to have been there to watch France's 4-1 win over Mexico.

RUSH TO RUSSIA

FIFA claimed a near-perfect attendance rate at the 2018 World Cup finals after concern over empty seats at low-profile matches in some of the early group stage matches. Colin Smith, the world federation's chief competitions officer, reported an average 98 per cent capacity in the 12 stadia in the 11 Russian cities. The largest slice of the 2.4m tickets were bought by Russian fans (872,000), with the United States recording the greatest number of foreign sales (88,825). English ticket sales, normally amongst the highest in visiting nations, was a disappointing 10th overall – around 33,000 sales.

LUZHNIKI'S NEW LIFE

Moscow's **Luzhniki Stadium**, which staged seven matches at the 2018 FIFA World Cup, including the Opening Match and final, is one of sport's historic venues. Originally the Lenin Stadium, it was opened in 1956 as a multi-sport venue with a 100,000 capacity. Major events included the 1980 Olympic Games and it also hosted the finals of the UEFA Champions League in 2008 and the UEFA Cup in 1999. Recent redevelopment meant a 78,011 capacity in a football-specific stadium for the World Cup.

GENDER EQUALITY

Only two stadiums have hosted the finals of the FIFA World Cup for both men and women. The **Rose Bowl**, in Pasadena, California, was the venue for the men's final in 1994 – when Brazil beat Italy – and the women's showdown between the victorious US and China five years later, which was watched by 90,185 people. But Sweden's Rasunda Stadium, near Stockholm, just about got there first – though it endured a long wait between the men's final in 1958 and the women's in 1995. Both sets of American spectators got their money's worth, watching games that went into extra-time and which were settled on penalties.

FIFA WORLD CUP FINAL ATTENDANCES

Year	Attendance	Stadium	City
1930	93,000	Estadio Centenario	Montevideo
1934	45,000	Stadio Nazionale del PNF	Rome
1938	60,000	Stade Olympique de Colombes	Paris
1950	173,850	Estadio do Maracana	Rio de Janeiro
1954	60,000	Wankdorfstadion	Berne
1958	51,800	Rasunda Fotbollstadion	Solna
1962	68,679	Estadio Nacional	Santiago
1966	98,000	Wembley Stadium	London
1970	107,412	Estadio Azteca	Mexico City
1974	75,200	Olympiastadion	Munich
1978	71,483	Estadio Monumental	Buenos Aires
1982	90,000	Estadio Santiago Bernabeu	Madrid
1986	114,600	Estadio Azteca	Mexico City
1990	73,603	Stadio Olimpico	Rome
1994	94,194	Rose Bowl	Pasadena
1998	80,000	Stade de France	Paris
2002	69,029	International Stadium	Yokohama
2006	69,000	Olympiastadion	Berlin
2010	84,490	Soccer City	Johannesburg
2014	74,738	Maracana	Rio de Janeiro
2018	78,011	Luzhniki	Moscow

TOURNAMENT ATTENDANCES

Year	Total	Average
1930	434,500	24,139
1934	358,000	21,059
1938	376,000	20,889
1950	1,043,500	47,432
1954	889,500	34,212
1958	919,580	26,274
1962	899,074	28,096
1966	1,635,000	51,094
1970	1,603,975	50,124
1974	1,768,152	46,530
1978	1,546,151	40,688
1982	2,109,723	40,572
1986	2,393,331	46,026
1990	2,516,348	48,391
1994	3,587,538	68,991
1998	2,785,100	43,517
2002	2,705,197	42,269
2006	3,359,439	52,491
2010	3,178,856	49,670
2014	3,429,873	53,592
2018	3,031,768	47,371
TOTAL	**37,570,605**	**45,102**

MORBID MARACANA

The largest attendance for a FIFA World Cup match was at Rio de Janeiro's Maracana for the last clash of the 1950 tournament – though no one is quite sure how many were there. The final tally was officially given as 173,850, though some estimates suggest as many as 210,000 witnessed the host country's traumatic defeat. Tensions were so high at the final whistle, winning Uruguay captain Obdulio Varela was not awarded the trophy in a traditional manner, but had it surreptitiously nudged into his hands. FIFA president Jules Rimet described the crowd's overwhelming silence as "morbid, almost too difficult to bear". Uruguay's triumphant players barricaded themselves inside their dressing room for several hours before they judged it safe enough to emerge. However, at least Brazil did make it to Maracana in 1950. In the 2014 FIFA World Cup, as hosts again, Brazil played in Sao Paulo, Fortaleza, Brasilia and Belo Horizonte but, after losing in the semi-finals, ended up back in Brasilia for the third-place play-off instead of Maracana for the final.

FAN FESTS FIND FAVOUR

City centre **Fan Fests**, including giant television screens, food service and entertainment provision, proved more popular than ever at the 2018 FIFA World Cup in **Russia**. Fan Fests were organised in all 11 venue cities, though a proposal to extend the network to other cities was dropped. More than 7m fans visited the sites over the 31 days of the finals – an increase of 2m on the totals in Brazil in 2014. The concept was developed commercially after the success of open-air viewing sites organized in Germany in 2006.

ABSENT FRIENDS

Only 2,823 spectators turned up at the Rasunda Stadium in Stockholm to see Wales play Hungary in a first-round play-off match during the 1958 FIFA World Cup. More than 15,000 had attended the first game between the two sides, but boycotted the replay in tribute to executed Hungarian uprising leader Imre Nagy.

FIFA STADIUMS & HOSTS
WORLD CUP

BERLIN CALL

Despite later becoming the capital of a united Germany, then-divided Berlin only hosted three group games at the 1974 FIFA World Cup in West Germany – the host country's surprise loss to East Germany took place in Hamburg. An unexploded World War Two bomb was discovered beneath the seats at Berlin's Olympiastadion in 2002, by workers preparing the ground for the 2006 tournament. Germany, along with Brazil, had applied to host the tournament in 1942, before it was cancelled due to the outbreak of World War Two.

TWIN PEAKS

Six stadiums hold the distinction of having staged both the final of a FIFA World Cup and the summer Olympics athletics: Berlin's Olympiastadion (1936 Olympics, 2006 World Cup), Paris's Stade Colombes (1924 Olympics, 1938 World Cup), London's Wembley (1948 Olympics, 1966 World Cup), Rome's Stadio Olimpico (1960 Olympics, 1990 World Cup) and Munich's Olympiastadion (1972 Olympics, 1974 World Cup) and Moscow's Luzhniki Stadium (1980 Olympics, 2018 World Cup). The Estadio Azteca (Mexico City) and Rose Bowl (Pasadena) have hosted both World Cup finals as well as Olympic football gold medal games.

FUTURE PERFECT

The future of the FIFA World Cup depends more and more on neighbouring countries banding together to play host. **Gianni Infantino**, elected as FIFA president in 2016, has declared himself in favour of co-hosting as a means both to encourage more countries to share organization of the finals and to guard against the building of "white elephant" stadia. The United States, Mexico and Canada will host 2026 and a co-hosting bid for 2030 is planned by Uruguay, Argentina and Paraguay.

RIO'S MARIO

Most people know Brazil's largest stadium as the Maracana, named after the Rio neighbourhood and a small nearby river. But, since the mid-1960s, the official title has been "Estadio Mario Filho" after the influential sports journalist and editor who campaigned for the stadium's construction on that site.

TERRITORIAL GAINS

In 2022 Qatar will become the smallest country to stage the FIFA World Cup. The Gulf state, with a population of 2.6m, was awarded host rights by FIFA's executive committee in December 2010, on the same day that the 2018 finals were awarded to Russia. Qatar beat rival bids from the United States, Japan, South Korea and Australia. Concern over midsummer heat later led FIFA to switch the staging from June/July to November and December.

MEXICAN SAVE

Mexico was not the original choice to host the 1986 FIFA World Cup, but stepped in when Colombia withdrew in 1982 due to financial problems. Mexico held on to the staging rights despite suffering from an earthquake in September 1985 that left approximately 10,000 people dead, but which left the stadiums unscathed. FIFA kept faith in the country, and the **Azteca Stadium** went on to become the first venue to host two FIFA World Cup final matches – and Mexico the first country to stage two FIFA World Cups. The Azteca – formally named the "Estadio Guillermo Canedo", after a Mexican football official – was built in 1960 using 100,000 tonnes of concrete, four times as much as was needed for the old Wembley.

ARCHITECTS' PREROGATIVE

Distinctive and creative elements were added to the stadiums built especially for the 2010 FIFA World Cup in South Africa, including the giraffe-shaped towers at **Nelspruit's Mbombela stadium**, the 350-metre-long arch with its mobile viewing platform soaring above **Durban's main arena**, and the white "petals" shrouding the Nelson Mandela Bay stadium in Port Elizabeth.

UNSUCCESSFUL HOSTING BIDS

1930	Hungary, Italy, Netherlands, Spain, Sweden
1934	Sweden
1938	Argentina, Germany
1950	None
1954	None
1958	None
1962	Argentina, West Germany
1966	Spain, West Germany
1970	Argentina
1974	Spain
1978	Mexico
1982	West Germany
1986	Colombia*, Canada, USA
1990	England, Greece, USSR
1994	Brazil, Morocco
1998	Morocco, Switzerland
2002	Mexico
2006	Brazil, England, Morocco, South Africa
2010	Egypt, Libya/Tunisia, Morocco
2014	None
2018	England, Netherlands/Belgium, Spain/Portugal
2022	Australia, Japan, South Korea, USA
2026	Morocco

* Colombia won hosting rights for 1986 but later withdrew.

RATIONAL IN RUSSIA

Organizers of the 2018 FIFA World Cup in Russia tried to return to the "clusters" system of adjacent venues to ease travel, accommodation and logistical problems around the 11 host cities, thus reducing costs for fans. Two stadia were used in Moscow – Luzhniki and **Spartak**. The system was compromised, however, by the use of Ekaterinburg in the far eastern region of European Russia. The "clusters" concept had been abandoned by the French hosts for 1998. Michel Platini, president of the local organizing committee, preferred a rotation schedule so the top teams' matches could be spread all around the country.

THREE-WAY WINNERS

The FIFA World Cup finals in 2026 will make history twice over. Firstly, it will feature 48 teams – playing 80 matches – after the world federation decided to open up the finals to more national teams than the current 32 which competed in Russia in 2018. Secondly, staging the finals will be shared between three countries after the United States, Canada and Mexico were awarded host rights by FIFA Congress in Moscow in June 2018. The United 2026 bid beat its lone rival, Morocco, by 134 to 65. A shortlist of 23 candidate cities were named in the bid, which will be trimmed to 10 in the US and three each in Canada and Mexico. Canada and Mexico will host 10 matches each with the US the other 60, including all ties from the quarter-finals onward. Mexico staged the World Cup in 1970 and 1986 with the final in the **Estadio Azteca** on both occasions. The US played host in 1994, the final being in Pasadena's Rose Bowl, while Canada staged the Women's World Cup in 2015.

HOSTS WITH THE MOST

No other single-hosted FIFA World Cup has used as many venues as the 14 spread across Spain in 1982. The 2002 tournament was played at 20 different venues, but ten of these were in Japan and ten in co-host country South Korea.

FIFA WORLD CUP PENALTIES

FIFA WORLD CUP PENALTY SHOOT-OUTS

Year	Round	120-minute Score	Winners	Shoot-out Score
1982	Semi-final	West Germany 3 France 3	West Germany	5-4
1986	Quarter-final	West Germany 0 Mexico 0	West Germany	4-1
1986	Quarter-final	France 1 Brazil 1	France	4-3
1986	Quarter-final	Belgium 1 Spain 1	Belgium	5-4
1990	Second round	Republic of Ireland 0 Romania 0	Republic of Ireland	5-4
1990	Quarter-final	Argentina 0 Yugoslavia 0	Argentina	3-2
1990	Semi-final	Argentina 1 Italy 1	Argentina	4-3
1990	Semi-final	West Germany 1 England 1	West Germany	4-3
1994	Second round	Bulgaria 1 Mexico 1	Bulgaria	3-1
1994	Quarter-final	Sweden 2 Romania 2	Sweden	5-4
1994	Final	Brazil 0 Italy 0	Brazil	3-2
1998	Second round	Argentina 2 England 2	Argentina	4-3
1998	Quarter-final	France 0 Italy 0	France	4-3
1998	Semi-final	Brazil 1 Netherlands 1	Brazil	4-2
2002	Second round	Spain 1 Republic of Ireland 1	Spain	3-2
2002	Quarter-final	South Korea 0 Spain 0	South Korea	5-3
2006	Second round	Ukraine 0 Switzerland 0	Ukraine	3-0
2006	Quarter-final	Germany 1 Argentina 1	Germany	4-2
2006	Quarter-final	Portugal 0 England 0	Portugal	3-1
2006	Final	Italy 1 France 1	Italy	5-3
2010	Second round	Paraguay 0 Japan 0	Paraguay	5-3
2010	Quarter-final	Uruguay 1 Ghana 1	Uruguay	4-2
2014	Second round	Brazil 1 Chile 1	Brazil	3-2
2014	Second round	Costa Rica 1 Greece 1	Costa Rica	5-3
2014	Quarter-final	Netherlands 0 Costa Rica 0	Netherlands	4-3
2014	Semi-final	Argentina 0 Netherlands 0	Argentina	4-2
2018	Second round	Russia 1 Spain 1	Russia	4-3
2018	Second round	Croatia 1 Denmark 1	Croatia	3-2
2018	Second round	England 1 Colombia 1	England	4-3
2018	Quarter-final	Croatia 2 Russia 2	Croatia	4-3

BAGGIO OF DISHONOUR

Pity poor **Roberto Baggio**: the Italian maestro stepped up in three FIFA World Cup penalty shoot-outs, more than any other player – and has been a loser in every one. Most painfully, it was his shot over the bar that gifted Brazil the trophy at the end of the 1994 Final. But he had also ended on the losing side against Argentina in a 1990 semi-final and would do so again, against France in a 1998 quarter-final. At least, in 1990 and 1998, his own attempts were successful.

DOUBLE TROUBLE

Denmark's **Yussuf Poulsen**, at the 2018 FIFA World Cup, became the first player to concede two penalties in a single tournament since Serbia's Milan Dudic in 2006. In the teams' opening game, Poulsen fouled Christian Cueva, but the Peruvian fired his spot-kick over the bar and Poulsen made amends by scoring Denmark's winner, then received a yellow card in additional time. In the next game, he not only gave away a penalty against Australia but also collected another yellow card that ruled him out of the final group game, against France. Mile Jedinak scored the equalizer in 1-1 draw.

WOE FOR ASAMOAH

Ghana striker Asamoah Gyan is the only player to have missed two penalties during match-time at FIFA World Cups. He hit the post with a spot-kick against the Czech Republic during a group game at the 2006 tournament, then struck a shot against the bar with the final kick of extra-time in Ghana's 2010 quarter-final versus Uruguay. Had he scored then, Gyan would have given Ghana a 2–1 win – following Luis Suarez's goal-stopping handball on the goal-line – and a first African place in a FIFA World Cup semi-final. Despite such a traumatic miss, Gyan did then step up to take Ghana's first penalty in the shoot-out, again striking it high – but this time into the back of the net. His team still lost, though, 4–2 on penalties.

FRENCH KICKS

The first penalty shoot-out at a FIFA World Cup finals came in the 1982 semi-final in Seville between West Germany and France, when French takers Didier Six and **Maxime Bossis** were the unfortunate players to miss. The same two countries met in the semi-finals four years later – and West Germany again won, though in normal time, 2-0. The record for most shoot-outs is shared by the 1990 and 2006 tournaments, with four apiece. Both semi-finals in 1990 went to penalties, while the 2006 final was the second to be settled that manner – Italy beating France 5-3 after David Trezeguet struck the crossbar.

DANIJEL THE LION

At the 2018 FIFA World Cup in Russia, **Danijel Subasic** of Croatia became the second goalkeeper to save four penalties in shoot-outs in one tournament. The Monaco man saved three against Denmark in a second-round shoot-out and then another in Croatia's quarter-final victory over hosts Russia. Before Subasic the only other goalkeeper to have saved four kicks in shootouts in the same tournament had been Sergio Goycoechea of Argentina in the 1990 finals. Goycoechea saved two against Yugoslavia in the quarter-final and another two against Italy in the last four to book Argentina's final place. German goalkeeper Toni Schumacher had also saved four penalties in shoot-outs but he did it in two tournaments, saving two against France in the 1982 semi-final – the first-ever finals shootout – and then two more in West Germany's defeat of hosts Mexico in the 1986 quarter-final.

PENALTIES TAKE-OFF

A record 29 penalties were awarded at the 2018 FIFA World Cup in Russia. The sharp rise, from 13 in 2014, was down to the introduction of Video Assistant Referees (VAR). Seven penalties were missed or saved. Four players converted more than one. France's Antoine Griezmann and England's Harry Kane both scored three with two each by Sweden's Andreas Granqvist and Australia's Mile Jedinak.

PENALTY SHOOT-OUTS BY COUNTRY

5 Argentina (4 wins, 1 defeat)	1 Bulgaria (1 win)
4 Germany/West Germany (4 wins)	1 Paraguay (1 win)
4 Brazil (3 wins, 1 defeat)	1 Portugal (1 win)
4 France (2 wins, 2 defeats)	1 South Korea (1 win)
4 England (1 win, 3 defeats)	1 Sweden (1 win)
4 Italy (1 win, 3 defeats)	1 Ukraine (1 win)
4 Spain (1 win, 3 defeats)	1 Uruguay (1 win)
3 Netherlands (1 win, 2 defeats)	1 Yugoslavia (1 win)
2 Croatia (2 wins)	1 Chile (1 defeat)
2 Costa Rica (1 win, 1 defeat)	1 Colombia (1 defeat)
2 Republic of Ireland (1 win, 1 defeat)	1 Denmark (1 defeat)
2 Russia (1 win, 1 defeat)	1 Ghana (1 defeat)
2 Mexico (2 defeats)	1 Greece (1 defeat)
2 Romania (2 defeats)	1 Japan (1 defeat)
1 Belgium (1 win)	1 Switzerland (1 defeat)

GERMAN EFFICIENCY

Germany, or West Germany, have won all four of their FIFA World Cup penalty shoot-outs, more than any other team. Argentina also have four wins, but they have lost one – to Germany in the 2006 quarter-final. The German run began with a semi-final victory over France in 1982, when goalkeeper Harald Schumacher was the matchwinner, despite being lucky to stay on the pitch for a vicious extra-time foul on France's Patrick Battiston. West Germany also reached the 1990 final thanks to their shoot-out expertise, this time proving superior to England – as they similarly did in the 1996 European Championships semi-final. In that 2006 quarter-final, Germany's goalkeeper Jens Lehmann consulted a note predicting the direction the Argentine players were likely to shoot towards. The vital information was scribbled on a scrap of hotel notepaper by Germany's chief scout Urs Siegenthaler. The only German national team to lose a major tournament penalty shoot-out were the West Germans, who contested the 1976 UEFA European Championships final against Czechoslovakia – their first shoot-out experience, and clearly an effective lesson, because they have not lost a shoot-out since.

THE PLAYERS WHO MISSED IN SHOOT-OUTS

Argentina: Diego Maradona (1990), Pedro Troglio (1990), Hernan Crespo (1998), Roberto Ayala (2006), Esteban Cambiasso (2006)
Brazil: Socrates (1986), Julio Cesar (1986), Marcio Santos (1994), Willian (2014), Hulk (2014)
Bulgaria: Krassimir Balakov (1994)
Chile: Mauricio Pinilla (2014), Alexis Sanchez (2014), Gonzalo Jara (2014)
Colombia: Mateus Uribe, Carlos Bacca (2018)
Costa Rica: Bryan Ruiz (2014), Michael Umana (2014)
Croatia: Milan Badelj, Mateo Kovacic, Josip Pivaric (2018)
Denmark: Christian Eriksen, Lasse Schone, Nicolai Jorgensen (2018)
England: Stuart Pearce (1990), Chris Waddle (1990), Paul Ince (1998), David Batty (1998), Frank Lampard (2006), Steven Gerrard (2006), Jamie Carragher (2006); Jordan Henderson (2018)
France: Didier Six (1982), Maxime Bossis (1982), Michel Platini (1986), Bixente Lizarazu (1998), David Trezeguet (2006)
Germany/West Germany: Uli Stielike (1982)
Ghana: John Mensah (2010), Dominic Adiyiah (2010)
Greece: Theofanis Gekas (2014)
Italy: Roberto Donadoni (1990), Aldo Serena (1990), Franco Baresi (1994), Daniele Massaro (1994), Roberto Baggio (1994), Demetrio Albertini (1998), Luigi Di Biagio (1998)

Japan: Yuichi Komano (2010)
Mexico: Fernando Quirarte (1986), Raul Servin (1986), Alberto Garcia Aspe (1994), Marcelino Bernal (1994), Jorge Rodriguez (1994)
Netherlands: Phillip Cocu (1998), Ronald de Boer (1998), Ron Vlaar (2014), Wesley Sneijder (2014)
Portugal: Hugo Viana (2006), Petit (2006)
Republic of Ireland: Matt Holland (2002), David Connolly (2002), Kevin Kilbane (2002)
Romania: Daniel Timofte (1990), Dan Petrescu (1994), Miodrag Belodedici (1994)
Russia: Fedor Smolov, Mario Fernandes (2018)
Spain: Eloy (1986), Juanfran (2002), Juan Carlos Valeron (2002), Joaquin (2002); Iago Aspas, Koke (2018)
Sweden: Hakan Mild (1994)
Switzerland: Marco Streller (2006), Tranquillo Barnetta (2006), Ricardo Cabanas (2006)
Ukraine: Andriy Shevchenko (2006)
Uruguay: Maximiliano Pereira (2010)
Yugoslavia: Dragan Stojkovic (1990), Dragoljub Brnovic (1990), Faruk Hadzibegic (1990)

PART 3: UEFA EUROPEAN CHAMPIONSHIP

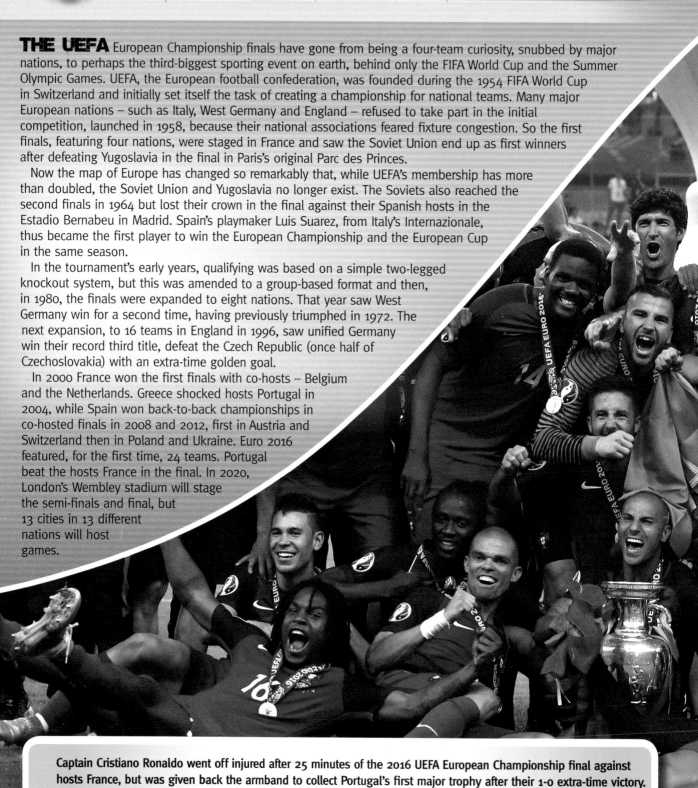

THE UEFA European Championship finals have gone from being a four-team curiosity, snubbed by major nations, to perhaps the third-biggest sporting event on earth, behind only the FIFA World Cup and the Summer Olympic Games. UEFA, the European football confederation, was founded during the 1954 FIFA World Cup in Switzerland and initially set itself the task of creating a championship for national teams. Many major European nations – such as Italy, West Germany and England – refused to take part in the initial competition, launched in 1958, because their national associations feared fixture congestion. So the first finals, featuring four nations, were staged in France and saw the Soviet Union end up as first winners after defeating Yugoslavia in the final in Paris's original Parc des Princes.

Now the map of Europe has changed so remarkably that, while UEFA's membership has more than doubled, the Soviet Union and Yugoslavia no longer exist. The Soviets also reached the second finals in 1964 but lost their crown in the final against their Spanish hosts in the Estadio Bernabeu in Madrid. Spain's playmaker Luis Suarez, from Italy's Internazionale, thus became the first player to win the European Championship and the European Cup in the same season.

In the tournament's early years, qualifying was based on a simple two-legged knockout system, but this was amended to a group-based format and then, in 1980, the finals were expanded to eight nations. That year saw West Germany win for a second time, having previously triumphed in 1972. The next expansion, to 16 teams in England in 1996, saw unified Germany win their record third title, defeat the Czech Republic (once half of Czechoslovakia) with an extra-time golden goal.

In 2000 France won the first finals with co-hosts – Belgium and the Netherlands. Greece shocked hosts Portugal in 2004, while Spain won back-to-back championships in co-hosted finals in 2008 and 2012, first in Austria and Switzerland then in Poland and Ukraine. Euro 2016 featured, for the first time, 24 teams. Portugal beat the hosts France in the final. In 2020, London's Wembley stadium will stage the semi-finals and final, but 13 cities in 13 different nations will host games.

Captain Cristiano Ronaldo went off injured after 25 minutes of the 2016 UEFA European Championship final against hosts France, but was given back the armband to collect Portugal's first major trophy after their 1-0 extra-time victory.

UEFA EUROPEAN CHAMPIONSHIP QUALIFIERS

The UEFA European Championship qualifying competition is now a huge event in its own right. For Euro 2016, 53 countries battled through a group stage to join hosts France, who qualified automatically. Times had changed since the 1960 competition when only 17 nations entered and were winnowed down by a two-leg knockout tournament. The 1968 tournament was the first for which a group stage was introduced with seven groups of four and one group of three. By 2014 UEFA had 54 members so the qualifying competition has had to grow to match that expansion. For Euro 2016 the top two in all nine groups and the third-placed team with the best record all qualified automatically. The remaining four spots were decided by two-legged play-offs between the eight other third-placed teams.

QUICK TURNOVER

Germany's **Joachim Low** was the only manager from the eight Euro 2008 quarter-finalists still in his job for the 2016 finals. Low guided Germany to the final that year in Austria and Switzerland and then to the semi-finals in Poland and Ukraine in 2012. Two years later, he further enhanced his reputation when Germany defeated Argentina in Rio de Janeiro's Maracana to win the 2014 FIFA World Cup in Brazil.

FONTAINE MAKES HISTORY JUST SO

Just Fontaine of France scored the first hat-trick in Euro history in the inaugural 1958-60 tournament. Fontaine, top scorer at the 1958 FIFA World Cup, hit three goals in France's 5-2 second-round win over Austria in Paris on 13 December 1959. France won the return 4-2 for a 9-4 aggregate win and went on to host the finals, at which they finished fourth.

IRISH VICTORY NOT ENOUGH

West Germany's 1-0 defeat by Northern Ireland in Hamburg on 11 November 1983 was their first-ever home loss in the qualifying competition, but their 2-1 win over Albania in Saarbrucken four days later enabled them to pip Northern Ireland on goal difference for a place in the 1984 finals.

ROCKING UP

Gibraltar became the most recent European Championship qualifying competition debutants when they played Poland in September 2014. UEFA had tightened their rules for admission to the federation, but the Gibraltar Football Association appealed to the Court of Arbitration for Sport and their 16-year legal battle ended in 2013, when the CAS asserted their right to join Europe's football family. UEFA decided, diplomatically, that Spain and Gibraltar would be kept apart in competition draws. There was no dream home competitive debut for the "Rock", as they suffered a 7-0 defeat by Poland in a match played in Faro in neighbouring Portugal. Tormentor-in-chief was Robert Lewandowski, who scored four times. Things got no easier for Gibraltar in their remaining matches as, despite scoring two goals, they conceded 57 in all, including another eight to Poland and seven more to both Germany and the Republic of Ireland.

GERMANS RUN UP 13

Germany's 13-0 win in San Marino on 6 September 2006 was the biggest victory margin in qualifying history. **Lukas Podolski** (4), Miroslav Klose (2), Bastian Schweinsteiger (2), Thomas Hitzlsperger (2), Michael Ballack, Manuel Friedrich and Bernd Schneider scored the goals. The previous biggest win was Spain's 12-1 rout of Malta in 1983.

GERMANY'S WEMBLEY WONDER NIGHT

West Germany's greatest-ever team announced their arrival at Wembley on 29 April 1972, when they beat England 3-1 in the first leg of the UEFA European Championship quarter-finals. Uli Hoeness, Gunter Netzer and Gerd Muller scored the goals. West Germany went on to win the trophy, beating the Soviet Union 3-0 in the final. Their team at Wembley was: Sepp Maier; Horst Hottges, Georg Schwarzenbeck, Franz Beckenbauer, Paul Breitner; Jurgen Grabowski, Herbert Wimmer, Gunter Netzer, Uli Hoeness; Sigi Held, Gerd Muller. Eight of them played in West Germany's 1974 FIFA World Cup final win over the Netherlands.

APPEARANCES IN THE FINALS TOURNAMENT

12	West Germany/Germany
11	Soviet Union/CIS/Russia
10	Spain
9	Czechoslovakia/Czech Republic
	England
	France
	Italy
	Netherlands
8	Denmark
7	Portugal
6	Sweden
5	Belgium
	Croatia
	Romania
	Yugoslavia
4	Greece
	Switzerland
	Turkey
3	Hungary
	Poland
	Republic of Ireland
2	Austria
	Bulgaria
	Scotland
	Ukraine
1	Albania
	Iceland
	Latvia
	Northern Ireland
	Norway
	Slovakia
	Slovenia
	Wales

Includes appearances as hosts/co-hosts.

PANCEV FORCED TO MISS OUT

Yugoslavia's **Darko Pancev** (born in Skopje on 7 September 1965) was top scorer in the qualifiers for Euro 1992 with ten goals. Yugoslavia topped qualifying Group Four, but they were banned from the finals because of their country's war in Bosnia, so Pancev never had the chance to shine. After the break-up of the Yugoslav federation, he went on to become the star player for the new nation of Macedonia.

ANDORRA, SAN MARINO STRUGGLE

Minnows Andorra and San Marino each have yet to win a European Championship qualifier. Andorra have lost all of their 50 games, with a goal difference of 11-149. San Marino, whose first-ever point came in a November 2014 0-0 draw with Estonia, have lost their other 65 matches. San Marino's goal difference is 7-289 and their -55 goal difference in 2008 qualifying is the worst ever.

DUTCH EDGE FIRST PLAY-OFF

The first-ever group qualifying play-off was held on 13 December 1995 at Liverpool's Anfield stadium when the Netherlands beat the Republic of Ireland 2-0 to clinch the final place at Euro 96. Patrick Kluivert scored both Dutch goals.

LEWANDOWSKI ON TERMS WITH HEALY

Poland's **Robert Lewandowski** was leading marksman in the UEFA Euro 2016 qualifying competition with 13 goals – to equal the mark set by Northern Ireland's **David Healy** in the Euro 2008 preliminaries. The difference was that, unlike the luckless Healy, Lewandowski's goals shot his team to the finals and extended a proud record. After being the Polish league's top scorer with Lech Poznan, he reached 100 goals in the German Bundesliga quicker than any non-German-born player, achieving the feat for Borussia Dortmund and then Bayern Munich. Lewandowski's qualifying goals saw him rise up to fifth in Poland's all-time scoring charts.

HOSTS ARE PLACED IN EURO 2016 QUALIFYING GROUP

France, as hosts, qualified automatically for the 2016 UEFA European Championship finals. However, they were included in the qualifying competition draw and were placed in Group I. They did not play competitive matches, but had friendlies against the team not in action during each round of games. France thus had home and away friendlies against the five Group I teams, Albania, Armenia, Denmark, Portugal and Serbia.

FANCY SEEING YOU AGAIN

When Spain and Italy met in the 2012 final it was the fourth time UEFA European Championship opponents had faced each other twice in the same tournament. Each time, it followed a first-round encounter. The Netherlands lost to the Soviet Union, then beat them in the final in 1988; Germany beat the Czech Republic twice at Euro 96, including the final; and Greece did the same to Portugal in 2004. Spain and Italy drew in Euro 2012's Group C, with Cesc Fabregas replying to Antonio Di Natale's opener for Italy. Their second showdown was rather less even.

THREE OFF AS CZECHS ADVANCE

Czechoslovakia's 3-1 semi-final win over the Netherlands in Zagreb, on 16 June 1976, featured a record three red cards. The Czechs' Jaroslav Pollak was dismissed for a second yellow card – a foul on Johan Neeskens – after an hour. Neeskens followed in the 76th minute for kicking Zdenek Nehoda. Wim van Hanegem became the second Dutchman dismissed, for dissent, after Nehoda scored the Czechs' second goal with six minutes of extra-time left.

DENMARK'S UNEXPECTED TRIUMPH

Denmark were unlikely winners of UEFA Euro 1992. They had not even expected to take part after finishing behind Yugoslavia in their qualifying group, but they were invited to complete the final eight when Yugoslavia were barred for security fears following the country's collapse. Goalkeeper **Peter Schmeichel** was their hero – in the semi-final shoot-out win over the Netherlands and again in the final against Germany, when goals by John Jensen and Kim Vilfort earned Denmark a 2-0 win.

GERMANY IN THE ASCENDANCY

In 56 years, the UEFA European Championship has grown to become arguably the most important international football tournament after the FIFA World Cup. Only 17 teams entered the first four-team tournament, won by the Soviet Union in 1960 – yet 53 took part in qualifying for the right to join hosts France in a newly expanded 24-team event in 2016. Germany (formerly West Germany) and Spain have each won the competition three times, though the Germans have played and won most matches (49 and 26, respectively), as well as scoring and conceding more goals (72 and 48) than any other nation. Defender Berti Vogts is the only man to win the tournament as a player (1972) and coach (1996), both with the Germans. Portugal's 2016 triumph, in their 35th UEFA European Championship finals match, means England have now played most tournament games (31) without ever managing to lift the trophy.

DOMENGHINI RESCUES ITALY

The most controversial goal in the history of the final came on 8 June 1968. Hosts Italy were trailing 1-0 to Yugoslavia with ten minutes left. The Yugoslavs seemed still to be organizing their wall when Angelo Domenghini curled a free-kick past goalkeeper Ilja Pantelic for the equalizer. Yugoslavia protested but the goal was allowed to stand. Italy won the only replay in finals history 2-0, two days later, with goals from Gigi Riva and Pietro Anastasi.

FRANCE BOAST PERFECT RECORD

France, on home soil in 1984, are the only side to win all their matches since the finals expanded beyond four teams. They won them without any shoot-outs, too, beating Denmark 1-0, Belgium 5-0 and Yugoslavia 3-2 in their group, Portugal 3-2 after extra-time in the semi-finals and Spain 2-0 in the final.

CZECHS WIN MOST EFFICIENT SHOOT-OUT

The most efficient penalty shoot-out in the finals was the third-place play-off between hosts Italy and Czechoslovakia, in Naples on 21 June 1980. The Czechs won 9-8, following a 1-1 draw. After eight successful spot-kicks each, Czech goalkeeper **Jaroslav Netolicka** saved Fulvio Collovati's kick. In 2016, there were also 18 penalties when Germany won their quarter-final against Italy, 6-5 at Bordeaux, with the last of Italy's four misses being by Matteo Darmian.

FRANCE STRIKE, WITHOUT STRIKERS

France still hold the record for the most goals scored by one team in a finals tournament, 14 in 1984. Yet only one of those goals was netted by a recognized striker – Bruno Bellone, who hit the second in their 2-0 final win over Spain. France's inspirational captain, Michel Platini, supplied most of the French firepower, scoring an incredible nine goals in five appearances. He hit hat-tricks against Belgium and Denmark and a last-gasp winner in the semi-final against Portugal. Midfielders Alain Giresse and Luis Fernandez chipped in with goals in the 5-0 win over Belgium. Defender Jean-Francois Domergue gave France the lead against Portugal in the semi-finals, and added another in extra-time after Jordao had put Portugal 2-1 ahead.

TOP TEAM SCORERS IN THE FINALS

1960	Yugoslavia	6
1964	Spain, Soviet Union, Hungary	4
1968	Italy	4
1972	West Germany	5
1976	West Germany	6
1980	West Germany	6
1984	France	14
1988	Netherlands	8
1992	Germany	7
1996	Germany	10
2000	France, Netherlands	13
2004	Czech Republic	9
2008	Spain	12
2012	Spain	12
2016	France	13

SPAIN REFUSE TO MEET SOVIETS

Political rivalries wrecked the planned clash between Spain and the Soviet Union in the 1960 quarter-finals. The fascist Spanish leader, General Francisco Franco, refused to allow Spain to go to the communist Soviet Union – and banned the Soviets from entering Spain. The Soviet Union were handed a walkover on the grounds that Spain had refused to play. Franco relented four years later, allowing the Soviets to come to Spain for the finals. He was spared the embarrassment of presenting the trophy to them, however, as Spain beat the Soviet Union 2-1 in the final.

UEFA EUROPEAN CHAMPIONSHIP WINNERS

3	West Germany/Germany (1972, 1980, 1996)
	Spain (1964, 2008, 2012)
2	France (1984, 2000)
1	Soviet Union (1960)
	Italy (1968)
	Czechoslovakia (1976)
	Netherlands (1988)
	Denmark (1992)
	Greece (2004)
	Portugal (2016)

SAME OLD SPAIN

Spain not only cruised their way to the largest winning margin of any UEFA European Championship final by trouncing Italy 4-0 in the climax to 2012 – they also became the first country to successfully defend the title. David Silva, **Jordi Alba** – with his first international goal – and substitutes Fernando Torres and Juan Mata got the goals in Kiev's Olympic Stadium on 1 July. Spain thus landed their third major trophy in a row, having won Euro 2008 and the 2010 FIFA World Cup.

BIGGEST WINS IN THE FINALS

Netherlands 6, Yugoslavia 1, 2000
France 5, Belgium 0, 1984
Denmark 5, Yugoslavia 0, 1984
Sweden 5, Bulgaria 0, 2004

TOSS FAVOURS HOSTS ITALY

Italy reached the 1968 final on home soil thanks to the toss of a coin. It was the only game in finals history decided in such fashion. Italy drew 0-0 against the Soviet Union after extra-time in Naples on 5 June 1968. The Soviet captain, Albert Shesternev, made the wrong call at the toss – so Italy reached the final where they beat Yugoslavia.

DELLAS TIMES IT RIGHT FOR GREECE

Greece scored the only "silver goal" victory in Euro history in a 2004 semi-final. (The silver goal rule meant that a team leading after the first period of extra-time won the match.) **Traianos Dellas** headed Greece's winner seconds before the end of the first period of extra-time against the Czech Republic in Porto on 1 July. Both golden goals and silver goals were abandoned for UEFA Euro 2008, and drawn knockout ties reverted to being decided over the full 30 minutes of extra-time, and penalties if necessary.

UEFA EUROPEAN CHAMPIONSHIP PLAYER RECORDS

SHEARER TALLY BOOSTS ENGLAND

Alan Shearer is the only Englishman to top the finals scoring chart. Shearer led ····● the scorers with five goals as England lost on penalties to Germany in the Euro 96 semi-final at Wembley. He netted against Switzerland, Scotland and the Netherlands (two) in the group and gave England a third-minute lead against the Germans. He added two more goals at Euro 2000 and now is behind only Michel Platini and Cristiano Ronaldo in the all-time list.

ILYIN GOAL MAKES HISTORY

Anatoly Ilyin of the Soviet Union scored the first goal in UEFA European Championship history when he netted after four minutes against Hungary on 29 September 1958. A crowd of 100,572 watched the Soviets win 3-1 in the Lenin Stadium, Moscow. The Soviet Union went on to win the first final, in 1960.

GOLDEN ONE–TOUCH

Spain striker Fernando Torres claimed the Golden Boot, despite scoring the same number of goals – three – as Italy's Mario Balotelli, Russia's Alan Dzagoev, Germany's Mario Gomez, Croatia's Mario Mandzukic and Portugal's Cristiano Ronaldo. The decision came down to number of assists – with Torres and Gomez level on one apiece – then amount of time played. The 92 minutes spent on the pitch by Torres, compared to Gomez, meant his contributions were deemed better value for the prize.

VONLANTHEN BEATS ROONEY RECORD

The youngest scorer in finals history was Switzerland midfielder **Johan Vonlanthen.** ······ He was 18 years 141 days when he netted in their 3-1 defeat by France on 21 June 2004. He beat the record set by England forward Wayne Rooney four days earlier. Rooney was 18 years 229 days when he scored the first goal in England's 3-0 win over the Swiss. Vonlanthen retired from football at the age of 26 in May 2012 due to a knee injury.

KIRICHENKO NETS QUICKEST GOAL

The fastest goal in the history of the finals was scored by Russia forward **Dmitri Kirichenko**. He netted after just 67 seconds to give his side the lead against Greece on 20 June 2004. Russia won 2-1, but Greece still qualified for the quarter-finals – and went on to become shock winners. The fastest goal in the final was Spain midfielder Jesus Pereda's sixth-minute strike in 1964, when Spain beat the Soviet Union 2-1. The latest opening goal was Eder's 109th-minute winner for Portugal against France in the 2016 final.

TREBLE TROUBLE

There has been no UEFA European Championship hat-trick since David Villa, for Spain v Russia in 2008 – only the tournament's eighth ever. The first came from West Germany substitute Dieter Muller, v Yugoslavia, in 1976. There were seven doubles in 2016: Antoine Griezmann (two), France, v Republic of Ireland and v Germany; Alvaro Morata, Spain, v Turkey; Romelu Lukaku, Belgium, v Republic of Ireland; Balazs Dzsudzsak, Hungary, v Portugal; Cristiano Ronaldo, Portugal, v Hungary; and Olivier Giroud, France, v Iceland.

TOP SCORERS IN FINALS HISTORY

1 Michel Platini (France)   9
= Cristiano Ronaldo (Portugal)
3 Alan Shearer (England)   7
4 Nuno Gomes (Portugal)   6
= Antoine Griezmann (France)
= Thierry Henry (France)
= Zlatan Ibrahimovic (Sweden)
= Patrick Kluivert (Netherlands)
= Wayne Rooney (England)
= Ruud van Nistelrooy (Netherlands)

BIERHOFF NETS FIRST "GOLDEN GOAL"

Germany's **Oliver Bierhoff** scored the first golden
goal in the history of the tournament when he hit the
winner against the Czech Republic in the Euro 96 final at
Wembley on 30 June. (The golden goal rule meant the first
team to score in extra-time won the match.) Bierhoff netted
in the fifth minute of extra-time. His shot from 20 yards
deflected off defender Michal Hornak and slipped through
goalkeeper Petr Kouba's fingers.

PONEDELNIK'S MONDAY MORNING FEELING

Striker Viktor Ponedelnik headed the Soviet Union's extra-time winner to beat
Yugoslavia 2-1 in the first final on 10 July 1960 – and sparked some famous headlines
in the Soviet media. The game in Paris kicked off at 10pm Moscow time on Sunday,
so it was Monday morning when Ponedelnik – whose name means "Monday" in
Russian – scored. He said: "When I scored, all the journalists wrote the headline
'Ponedelnik zabivayet v Ponedelnik' – 'Monday scores on Monday'." This goal, in the
113th minute, remains the latest ever in a European Championship/Nations Cup final.

MARCHING ORDERS

Only one man has been sent off in a UEFA European Championship
final: France defender Yvon Le Roux, who received a second yellow
card with five minutes remaining of his team's 2-0 triumph over Spain
in 1984. The most red cards were shown at Euro 2000, when the ten
dismissals included Romania's Gheorghe Hagi, Portugal's **Nuno Gomes**,
Italy's Gianluca Zambrotta and the Czech Republic's Radoslav Latal
who, having been sent off at Euro 96, is the only man to be dismissed
in two tournaments. At Euro 2016, there were only three red cards.

VASTIC THE OLDEST

The oldest scorer in finals history is Austria's Ivica Vastic.
He was 38 years and 257 days old when he equalized in
the 1-1 draw with Poland at UEFA Euro 2008.

TOP SCORERS IN THE FINALS

Year	Player	Goals
1960	Francois Heutte (France)	2
	Milan Galic (Yugoslavia)	
	Valentin Ivanov (Soviet Union)	
	Drazan Jerkovic (Yugoslavia)	
	Slava Metreveli (Soviet Union)	
	Viktor Ponedelnik (Soviet Union)	
1964	Ferenc Bene (Hungary)	2
	Dezso Novak (Hungary)	
	Jesus Pereda (Spain)	
1968	Dragan Dzajic (Yugoslavia)	2
1972	Gerd Muller (West Germany)	4
1976	Dieter Muller (West Germany)	4
1980	Klaus Allofs (West Germany)	3
1984	Michel Platini (France)	9
1988	Marco van Basten (Netherlands)	5
1992	Dennis Bergkamp (Netherlands)	3
	Tomas Brolin (Sweden)	
	Henrik Larsen (Denmark)	
	Karlheinz Riedle (Germany)	
1996	Alan Shearer (England)	5
2000	Patrick Kluivert (Netherlands)	5
	Savo Milosevic (Yugoslavia)	
2004	Milan Baros (Czech Republic)	5
2008	David Villa (Spain)	4
2012	Mario Balotelli (Italy)	3
	Alan Dzagoev (Russia)	
	Mario Gomez (Germany)	
	Mario Mandzukic (Croatia)	
	Cristiano Ronaldo (Portugal)	
	Fernando Torres (Spain)	
2016	Antoine Griezmann (France)	6

LOW CONQUERS ALMOST ALL

Germany coach Joachim Low holds the record for most UEFA European Championship matches and victories in charge. His side's shoot-out victory over Italy in a Euro 2016 quarter-final took him to 12 victories, before their 2-0 defeat to France in the semi-finals put him on 17 games across the 2008, 2012 and 2016 competitions.

NAMES ON THEIR SHIRTS

Players wore their names as well as their numbers on the back of their shirts for the first time at Euro 92. They had previously been identified only by numbers.

TAKE CLATT

In 2012, Pedro Proenca from Portugal achieved the double feat of refereeing the UEFA Champions League final between Chelsea and Bayern Munich and that summer's UEFA European Championship final between Spain and Italy. English referee Mark Clattenburg went one better in 2016: he did his homeland's FA Cup final between Manchester United and Crystal Palace and the UEFA Champions League final between Real Madrid and Atletico Madrid in May and the UEFA European Championship final between France and Portugal in July.

DOUBLING UP

The 2016 UEFA European Championship final between hosts France and eventual champions Portugal was the sixth to go to extra-time but the first to be goalless after 90 minutes, before Eder's 109th-minute winner – the latest opening goal in any Euros final.

RECORD EURO GOAL DROUGHT

Between **Xabi Alonso**'s added-time penalty in Spain's 2-0 quarter-final defeat of France and Mario Balotelli's 20th-minute semi-final strike for Italy in their 2-1 victory against Germany, Euro 2012's goalless spell lasted 260 minutes – a UEFA European Championship record.

ELLIS BLOWS THE WHISTLE

English referee **Arthur Ellis** took charge of the first UEFA European Championship final between the Soviet Union and Yugoslavia in 1960. Ellis had also refereed the first-ever European Cup final, between Real Madrid and Reims, four years earlier. After he retired from football, he became the "referee" on the British version of the Europe-wide game show *It's a Knock-out*.

GREEKS HAND ALBANIA WALKOVER

When Greece were drawn against Albania in the first round of the 1964 tournament, the Greeks immediately withdrew, handing Albania a 3-0 walkover win. The countries had technically been at war since 1940. The Greek government did not formally lift the state of war until 1987, although diplomatic relations were re-established in 1971.

FINALS HOSTS

1960	France
1964	Spain
1968	Italy
1972	Belgium
1976	Yugoslavia
1980	Italy
1984	France
1988	West Germany
1992	Sweden
1996	England
2000	Netherlands and Belgium
2004	Portugal
2008	Austria and Switzerland
2012	Poland and Ukraine
2016	France

HOSTS WITH (ALMOST) THE MOST

In 2000, Belgium and the Netherlands began the trend for dual hosting the UEFA European Championship finals – it was the first time the tournament was staged in more than one country. The opening game was Belgium's 2-1 win over Sweden in Brussels on 10 June, with the final in Rotterdam. Austria and Switzerland co-hosted Euro 2008, starting in Basel and climaxing in Vienna, before Poland and Ukraine teamed up in 2012. Warsaw staged the opening match and Kiev was the host city for the final.

SHARE AND SHARE ALIKE

Ten venues across France were used for the 2016 UEFA European Championship. This equalled the record set by Portugal in 2004, and was two more than the eight stadia which were used in the three shared tournaments (four in each country): Belgium and the Netherlands in 2000; Austria and Switzerland in 2008; and Poland and Ukraine in 2012. It will be all change for the finals in 2020, however, as, for the first time, the first round group stage and first two knock-out rounds will be played across 13 cities in 13 different countries. England has the honour of hosting both semi-finals and the final, with all three to be played at London's Wembley Stadium.

PEAKING EARLY

Just as at the 2012 UEFA European Championship, where the first-round game between England and Sweden in Kyiv attracted the tournament's highest official attendance (64,640), the Euro 2016 final between France and Portugal could not claim the event's biggest crowd. Instead, that honour went to the French hosts' 5-2 victory over Iceland in the quarter-finals, watched in the Stade de France by 76,833 spectators.

THE "ITALIAN JOB"

The 1968 finals in Italy were used as the backdrop to a famous English-language film – *The Italian Job*, starring Michael Caine – about a British gang who use the cover of the finals to stage a daring gold robbery in Turin. The film was released in England on 2 June 1969.

UEFA EUROPEAN CHAMPIONSHIP FINAL REFEREES

1960	Arthur Ellis (England)
1964	Arthur Holland (England)
1968	Gottfried Dienst (Switzerland)
	Replay: Jose Maria Ortiz de Mendibil (Spain)
1972	Ferdinand Marschall (Austria)
1976	Sergio Gonella (Italy)
1980	Nicolae Rainea (Romania)
1984	Vojtech Christov (Czechoslovakia)
1988	Michel Vautrot (France)
1992	Bruno Galler (Switzerland)
1996	Pierluigi Pairetto (Italy)
2000	Anders Frisk (Sweden)
2004	Markus Merk (Germany)
2008	Roberto Rosetti (Italy)
2012	Pedro Proenca (Portugal)
2016	Mark Clattenburg (England)

GOALS AREN'T EVERYTHING

The expanded, 24-team UEFA European Championship may have boasted more goals than any previous Euros – 108 in all. But these came at a rate of just 2.12 per game – the lowest since the 1996 UEFA European Championship's 2.06. Euro 2016's three own goals was another competition record – the unlucky players putting into their own nets were the Republic of Ireland's Ciaran Clark, Northern Ireland's Gareth McAuley and Iceland's Birkir Mar Saevarsson.

KEEPING IT CLEAN

Only three red cards were shown during Euro 2016 – to Albania captain **Lorik Cana**, Aleksandar Dragovic of Austria and the Republic of Ireland's Shane Duffy – which was the same tally as at each of the 2008 and 2012 UEFA European Championships. In contrast, twice as many players were sent off at the 2004 tournament. The final, however, saw ten yellow cards shown, the most ever shown in any UEFA European Championship match.

PART 4:
COPA AMERICA

THE WORLD'S OLDEST surviving international championship finds its rich history repeating itself even in a modern football world otherwise unrecognizable since the days when Uruguay won the inaugural South American Championship in 1916 – a time when much of the rest of the world was embroiled in the First World War.

Travel was an awkward, costly and time-consuming business for the first competitive nations of South America. The possibility of flying to Europe and back for even a single game was beyond officials' imagination. Hence the need for South America to organize itself and create its own early competitions.

The founding members of world federation FIFA, in 1904, had all been European. South American nations such as Brazil, Argentina and Uruguay were not slow in signing up but the opportunities for inter-continental competition were minimal.

The South Americans decided to organize their own international competitions, which led to the creation, in 1916, of the South American Championship. Four countries contested that opening tournament, hosts Argentina, Brazil, Chile and Uruguay, who were the inaugural winners. Fast forward 99 years, and 12 months after staging a spectacular FIFA World Cup in Brazil, South America was the venue for another high-class football extravaganza in the form of the 2015 Copa America.

Once again, the old masters of Brazil and Argentina missed out on the top prize as the hosts Chile, after 99 years of trying, landed the trophy for the first time in their history. Argentina lost on penalties, the same fate suffered by Brazil in the quarter-finals. The next "ordinary" Copa America is scheduled for Brazil in 2019, but a special Centenario celebration event was staged in 2016 – outside the continent, in the United States – in 2016. The event provided a sense of *déjà vu*, as Chile defeated Argentina on penalties for the second year running.

Chile's race to celebrate with Francisco Silva after he had scored the winning penalty of the shoot-out against Argentina in the final of the 2016 Copa America Centenario.

COPA AMERICA TEAM RECORDS

🔵 LITTLE NAPOLEON

In 1942, Ecuador and their goalkeeper Napoleon Medina conceded more goals in one tournament than any other team, when they let in 31 goals across six games – and six defeats. Three years later he and his team-mates finally managed to keep a clean sheet, in a goalless draw against Bolivia – but still managed to let in another 27 goals in their five other matches.

🔵 LUCK OF THE DRAW

Paraguay reached the 2011 final despite not winning a single game in normal play. Instead, they drew all three matches in the first-round group stage, then needed penalties to win their quarter-final against Brazil and semi-final versus Venezuela after both games ended goalless. Perhaps not surprisingly, their captain **Justo Villar** was voted the tournament's best goalkeeper.

COPA AMERICA WINNERS

1916	Uruguay (league format)
1917	Uruguay (league format)
1919	Brazil 1 Uruguay 0
1920	Uruguay (league format)
1921	Argentina (league format)
1922	Brazil 3 Paraguay 1
1923	Uruguay (league format)
1924	Uruguay (league format)
1925	Argentina (league format)
1926	Uruguay (league format)
1927	Argentina (league format)
1929	Argentina (league format)
1935	Uruguay (league format)
1937	Argentina 2 Brazil 0
1939	Peru (league format)
1941	Argentina (league format)
1942	Uruguay (league format)
1945	Argentina (league format)
1946	Argentina (league format)
1947	Argentina (league format)
1949	Brazil 7 Paraguay 0
1953	Paraguay 3 Brazil 2
1955	Argentina (league format)
1956	Uruguay (league format)
1957	Argentina (league format)
1959	Argentina (league format)
1959	Uruguay (league format)
1963	Bolivia (league format)
1967	Uruguay (league format)
1975	Peru 4 Colombia 1 (on aggregate, after three games)
1979	Paraguay 3 Chile 1 (on aggregate, after three games)
1983	Uruguay 3 Brazil 1 (on aggregate, after two games)
1987	Uruguay 1 Chile 0
1989	Brazil (league format)
1991	Argentina (league format)
1993	Argentina 2 Mexico 1
1995	Uruguay 1 Brazil 1 (Uruguay won 5-3 on penalties)
1997	Brazil 3 Bolivia 1
1999	Brazil 3 Uruguay 0
2001	Colombia 1 Mexico 0
2004	Brazil 2 Argentina 2 (Brazil won 4-2 on penalties)
2007	Brazil 3 Argentina 0
2011	Uruguay 3 Paraguay 0
2015	Chile 0 Argentina 0 (Chile won 4-1 on penalties)
2016	Chile 0 Argentina 0 (Chile won 4-2 on penalties)

🔵 HOSTING RIGHTS BY COUNTRY

Argentina	9	(1916, 1921, 1925, 1929, 1937, 1946, 1959, 1987, 2011)
Chile	7	(1920, 1926, 1941, 1945, 1955, 1991, 2015)
Uruguay	7	(1917, 1923, 1924, 1942, 1956, 1967, 1995)
Peru	6	(1927, 1935, 1939, 1953, 1957, 2004)
Brazil	4	(1919, 1922, 1949, 1989)
Ecuador	3	(1947, 1959, 1993)
Bolivia	2	(1963, 1997)
Paraguay	1	(1999)
Colombia	1	(2001)
Venezuela	1	(2007)
USA	1	(2016)

🔵 EXTRA TIME

The longest match in the history of the Copa America was the 1919 final between Brazil and Uruguay. It lasted 150 minutes, 90 minutes of regular time plus two extra-time periods of 30 minutes each.

🔵 HOW IT STARTED

The first South American "Championship of Nations", as it was then known, was held in Argentina from 2–17 July 1916, during the country's independence centenary commemorations. The tournament was won by Uruguay, who drew with Argentina in the last match of the tournament. It was an inauspicious beginning. The 16 July encounter had to be abandoned at 0-0 when fans invaded the pitch and set the wooden stands on fire. The match was continued at a different stadium the following day and still ended goalless ... but Uruguay ended up topping the mini-league table and were hailed the first champions. **Isabelino Gradin** was the inaugural tournament's top scorer. The event also saw the foundation of the South American federation CONMEBOL, which took place a week into the competition on 9 July 1916. From that point on the tournament was held every two years, though some tournaments are now considered to have been unofficial. There was, a three-year gap between the 2004 and 2007 tournaments, and the competition is now staged every four years instead.

SUB-STANDARD

During the 1953 Copa America, Peru were awarded a walkover win when Paraguay tried to make one more substitution than they were allowed. Would-be substitute Milner Ayala was so incensed, he kicked English referee Richard Maddison and was banned from football for three years. Yet Paraguay remained in the tournament and went on to beat Brazil in the final – minus, of course, the disgraced Ayala.

TARGET PRACTICE

Despite ending the 2016 Copa America Centenario as runners-up again, Argentina extended their records for most Copa America matches won, 119, and goals scored, 455 – the last two of which were two of which were struck by Gonzalo Higuain in a 4-0 victory over the USA in the 2016 Copa America Centenario semi-final in Houston. Argentina have also now lost more Copa America shoot-outs than any other side, five.

HISTORY MEN

The Copa America is the world's oldest surviving international football tournament, having been launched in 1916 when four nations entered: Argentina, Brazil, Chile and Uruguay. Bolivia, Colombia, Ecuador, Paraguay, Peru and Venezuela had all joined by 1967. In 1910, an unofficial South American championship was won by Argentina, who beat Uruguay 4-1 in the decider – though the final match had been delayed a day after rioting fans burnt down a stand at the Gimnasia stadium in Buenos Aires.

FALLEN ANGELS

Argentina's 1957 Copa America-winning forward trio of Humberto Maschio, Omar Sivori and Antonio Valentin Angelillo became known by the nickname "the angels with dirty faces". At least one of them scored in each of the side's six matches – Maschio finished with nine, Angelillo eight and Sivori three. Argentina's most convincing performance was an opening 8-2 win over Colombia, in which Argentina had scored four goals and missed a penalty within the first 25 minutes. The dazzling displays made Argentina, not eventual winners Brazil, favourites for the following year's FIFA World Cup. Before then, however, Maschio, Sivori and Angelillo had all been lured away to Europe by Italian clubs and the Argentine federation subsequently refused to pick them for the trip to Sweden for the FIFA World Cup. Sivori and Maschio ultimately made it to the FIFA World Cup, in 1962. However, to fury back home, they did so wearing not the light blue-and-white stripes of Argentina, but the Azzurri blue of their newly adopted Italy.

CONSISTENT COLOMBIANS

In 2001, Colombia, who went on to win the trophy for the first and only time in their history, became the only country to go through an entire Copa America campaign without conceding a single goal. They scored 11 themselves, more than half of them from six-goal tournament top scorer **Victor Aristazabal**. Keeping the clean sheets was goalkeeper Oscar Cordoba, who had previously spent much of his international career as back-up to the eccentric Rene Higuita. Just a month earlier, Cordoba had won the South American club championship, the Copa Libertadores, with Argentine side Boca Juniors.

TRIUMPHS BY COUNTRY

Uruguay 15 (1916, 1917, 1920, 1923, 1924, 1926, 1935, 1942, 1956, 1959, 1967, 1983, 1987, 1995, 2011)
Argentina 14 (1921, 1925, 1927, 1929, 1937, 1941, 1945, 1946, 1947, 1955, 1957, 1959, 1991, 1993)
Brazil 8 (1919, 1922, 1949, 1989, 1997, 1999, 2004, 2007)
Peru 2 (1939, 1975)
Paraguay 2 (1953, 1979)
Chile 2 (2015, 2016)
Bolivia 1 (1963)
Colombia 1 (2001)

MORE FROM MORENO

Argentina were not only responsible for the Copa America's biggest win, but also the tournament's highest-scoring game, when they put 12 past Ecuador in 1942 – to no reply. Jose Manuel Moreno's five strikes in that game included the 500th goal in the competition's history. Moreno, born in Buenos Aires on 3 August 1916, ended that tournament as joint top scorer with team-mate Herminio Masantonio – hitting seven goals. Both men ended their international careers with 19 goals for their country, though Moreno did so in 34 appearances – compared to Masantonio's 21. Masantonio scored four in the Ecuador thrashing.

JAMAICA STILL WAITING

To date, four teams have appeared in only one Copa America: Japan (1999), Honduras (2001), and Haiti and Panama (both 2016). Jamaica played in the Copa America for the second time in 2016, having played a year earlier too, but they are still to avoid defeat. They lost 1-0 to each of Uruguay, Paraguay and Argentina in 2015, and in 2016 lost 1-0 to Venezuela, 2-0 to Mexico and 3-0 to Uruguay. Their side included Wes Morgan, who had won a shock English Premier League title with Leiceser City, and skipper Adrian Mariappa, who had ended the season as an FA Cup runner-up for Crystal Palace. Mariappa was born in London to a Fijiian father and a mother with Jamaican parents.

FROG PRINCE

Chilean goalkeeper Sergio Livingstone holds the record for most Copa America appearances, with 34 games, across the 1941, 1942, 1945, 1947, 1949 and 1953 tournaments. Livingstone, nicknamed "The Frog", was voted player of the tournament in 1941 – becoming the first goalkeeper to win the award – and might have played even more Copa America matches had he not missed out on the 1946 competition. Livingstone, born in Santiago on 26 March 1920, spent almost his entire career in his home country – save for a season with Argentina's Racing Club in 1943–44. Overall, he made 52 appearances for Chile between 1941 and 1954, before retiring and becoming a popular TV journalist and commentator.

OVERALL TOP SCORERS

1	Norberto Mendez (Argentina)	17
=	Zizinho (Brazil)	17
3	Teodoro Fernandez (Peru)	15
=	Severino Varela (Uruguay)	15
5	Ademir (Brazil)	13
=	Jair da Rosa Pinto (Brazil)	13
=	Gabriel Batistuta (Argentina)	13
=	Jose Manuel Moreno (Argentina)	13
=	Hector Scarone (Uruguay)	13
10	Roberto Porta (Uruguay)	12
=	Angel Romano (Uruguay)	12

CHILE'S ILL FORTUNE

The first Copa America own goal was scored by Chile's Luis Garcia, giving Argentina a 1-0 win in 1917, in the second edition of the tournament. Even more unfortunately for Chile, Garcia's strike was the only goal by one of their players throughout the tournament – making Chile the first team to fail to score a single goal in a Copa America competition.

MOST GAMES PLAYED

1	Sergio Livingstone (Chile)	34
2	Zizinho (Brazil)	33
3	Leonel Alvarez (Colombia)	27
4	Carlos Valderrama (Colombia)	27
5	Javier Mascherano (Argentina)	26
6	Alex Aguinaga (Ecuador)	25
=	Claudio Taffarel (Brazil)	25
8	Teodoro Fernandez (Peru)	24
9	Angel Romano (Uruguay)	23
10	Djalma Santos (Brazil)	22
=	Claudio Suarez (Mexico)	22

REPEATING THE FEAT

Gabriel Batistuta is the only Argentinian to win the award twice as leading marksman at the Copa America. He made his *Albiceleste* debut only days before the 1991 event in which his six goals – including a crucial strike in the concluding match (it was a mini group as opposed to a final) victory over Colombia – earned a transfer from Boca Juniors to Fiorentina. Nicknamed "Batigol" in Italy, he was joint top scorer in 1995, with four goals, along with Mexico's Luis Garcia.

LIKE GRANDFATHER, LIKE FATHER, LIKE SON

Diego Forlan's two goals in the 2011 Copa America final helped Uruguay to a 3-0 victory over Paraguay and their record 15th South American championship. They also ensured he followed in family footsteps in lifting the trophy – his father **Pablo** was part of the Uruguay side who won in 1967, when his grandfather Juan Carlos Corazzo was the triumphant coach. Corazzo had previously managed Uruguay's winning team in 1959. The brace against Paraguay put the youngest Forlan level with Hector Scarone as Uruguay's all-time leading scorer, with 31 goals. Yet it was Forlan's strike partner Luis Suarez – opening goal-scorer in the final – who was voted best player of the 2011 tournament.

MAGIC ALEX

When Alex Aguinaga lined up for Ecuador against Uruguay in his country's opening game at the 2004 event, he became only the second man to take part in eight different Copa Americas – joining legendary Uruguayan goalscorer Angel Romano. Aguinaga, a midfielder born in Ibarra on 9 July 1969, played a total of 109 times for his country – 25 of them in the Copa America, a competition that yielded four of his 23 international goals. His Copa America career certainly began well: Ecuador went undefeated for his first four appearances, at the 1987 and 1989 events, but his luck had ran out by the time his Ecuador career was coming to an end: he lost his final seven Copa America matches.

START TO FINISH

Colombia playmaker Carlos Valderrama and defensive midfielder **Leonel Alvarez** played in all 27 of their country's Copa America matches between 1987 and 1995, winning ten, drawing ten and losing seven – including third-place finishes in 1987, 1993 and 1995. Valderrama's two Copa America goals came in his first and final appearances in the competition – in a 2-0 victory over Bolivia in 1987 and a 4-1 thrashing of the United States eight years later.

ED BOY

Two players have monopolized the Golden Boot prizes for top marksmen at recent Copa America tournaments. **Eduardo Vargas** ended the 2016 Copa America Centenario not only as a champion for the second successive year, but this time adding the Golden Boot to his own personal collection of honours – he won the same prize in 2015, albeit jointly with Peru's Paulo Guerrero who had himself clinched the Golden Boot outright at the previous tournament in 2011. Four of Vargas's six goals in 2016 came in Chile's 7-0 quarter-final trouncing of Mexico, making him only the 13th man to score at least four in one Copa America match. Vargas's other achievements for Chile include scoring in six consecutive internationals (nine goals) during 2013, beating the previous record of five shared by Carlos Caszely and Marcelo Salas.

FANTASTIC FIVES

Four players have scored five goals in one Copa America game: Hector Scarone in Uruguay's 6-0 win over Bolivia in 1926; Juan Marvezzi in Argentina's 6-1 win over Ecuador in 1941; Jose Manuel Moreno in Argentina's 12-0 win over Ecuador in 1942; and Evaristo de Macedo in Brazil's 9-0 win over Colombia in 1957.

LOW–KEY JOSE

The first-ever Copa America goal, in 1916, was scored by Jose Piendibene – setting Uruguay on the way to a 4-0 triumph over Chile. But he is not thought to have marked the moment with any great extravagance – Piendibene, renowned for his sense of fair play, made a point of not celebrating goals, to avoid offending his opponents.

PELE'S INSPIRATION

Brazilian forward **Zizinho** jointly holds the all-time goalscoring record for the Copa America, along with Argentina's Norberto Mendez. Both men struck 17 goals, Zizinho across six tournaments and Mendez three – including the 1945 and 1946 tournaments, which featured both men. Mendez was top scorer once and runner-up twice and won championship medals on all three occasions, while Zizinho's goals helped Brazil take the title only once, in 1949. Zizinho, Pele's footballing idol, would emerge from the 1950 FIFA World Cup as Brazil's top scorer and was also voted the tournament's best player – but was forever traumatized by the hosts' surprise defeat to Uruguay that cost Brazil the title.

AWAY WINNERS

Only four men have coached a country other than their native one to Copa America glory. The first was Englishman Jack Greenwell, with Peru in 1939. Brazilian Danilo Alvim was the second, with Bolivia in 1963 – against Brazil. History repeated itself in 2015 and 2016, when Argentina-born Jorge Sampaoli and then Juan Antonio Pizzi took Chile to Copa glory, both times beating Argentina in final penalty shoot-outs.

HOME COMFORTS

Uruguay have a unique record in remaining unbeaten in 38 Copa America games on home turf, all played in the country's capital Montevideo – comprising 31 wins, seven draws. The last tournament match they hosted was both a draw and a win – 1-1 against Brazil in 1995, with Uruguay emerging as champions, 5-3 on penalties after Fernando Alvez saved Tulio's penalty.

INVITED GUESTS

1993	Mexico (runners-up), United States
1995	Mexico, United States (fourth)
1997	Costa Rica, Mexico (third)
1999	Japan, Mexico (third)
2001	Costa Rica, Honduras (third), Mexico (runners-up)
2004	Costa Rica, Mexico
2007	Mexico (third), United States
2011	Costa Rica, Mexico
2015	Jamaica, Mexico
2016	Costa Rica, Haiti, Jamaica, Mexico, Panama, United States (hosts, fourth)

WRONG JUAN

It took 21 years, but Uruguay's Juan Emilio Piriz became the first Copa America player sent off, against Chile in 1937 – the first of 186 dismissals in the Copa (15 players and Ecuador coach Gustavo Quienteros saw red in 2016). Some 142 disgraced players have been shown red cards since FIFA introduced the card system in 1970.

MULTI-TASKING

Argentina's **Guillermo Stabile** not only holds the record for most Copa America triumphs as coach – he trounces all opposition. He led his country to the title on no fewer than six occasions – in 1941, 1945, 1946, 1947, 1955 and 1957. No other coach has lifted the trophy more than twice. Stabile coached Argentina from 1939 to 1960, having been appointed at the age of just 34. He lasted for 123 games in charge, winning 83 of them – and still managed to coach three clubs on the side at different times throughout his reign. He remained as Red Star Paris manager during his first year in the Argentina role, then led Argentine club Huracan for the next nine years – before leading domestic rivals Racing Club from 1949 to 1960. Stabile's Argentina may have, unusually, missed out on Copa America success in 1949, but that year brought the first of three Argentina league championships in a row for Stabile's Racing Club.

CAPTAIN CONSISTENT

Uruguay's 1930 World Cup-winning captain **Jose Nasazzi** is the only footballer to be voted player of the tournament at two different Copa America tournaments. Even more impressively, he achieved the feat 12 years apart – first taking the prize in 1923, then again in 1935. He was a Cup winner in 1923, 1924, 1926 and 1935. Nasazzi also captained Uruguay to victory in the 1924 and 1928 Olympic Games and in the 1930 World Cup.

KEEP COMING BACK

Hernan Dario Gomez coached Panama at the 2016 Copa American Centenario, making him only the third man to manage at six different Copa America tournaments. Close behind him is Oscar Washington Tabarez, who took charge of Uruguay at a fifth Copa America in 2016, having been in charge in 1989, 2007, 2011 and 2015. Dario Gomez previously led his native Colombia in 1995, 1997 and 2011, and Ecuador in 2001 and 2004. He is now level on tournaments with Guillermo Stabile, Argentina boss in 1941, 1945, 1946, 1947, 1955 and 1957, and Francisco Maturana who took Colombia to the finals in 1987, 1989, 1993 and 2001 and Ecuador in 1995 and 1997. Dario Gomez had been Maturana's assistant both at Colombian club Atletico Nacional and taking Colombia to third place at the 1987 Copa America. Stabile solely holds the record for managing most Copa America matches (44), followed by Chile's Luis Tirado (35), Paraguay's Manuel Fleitas Solich (33), Maturana (27), Tabarez (26) and Dario Gomez (23).

TROPHY-WINNING COACHES

6 Guillermo Stabile (Argentina 1941, 1945, 1946, 1947, 1955, 1957)

2 Alfio Basile (Argentina 1991, 1993)
Juan Carlos Corazzo (Uruguay 1959, 1967)
Ernesto Figoli (Uruguay 1920, 1926)

1 Jorge Pacheco and Alfredo Foglino (Uruguay 1916)
Ramon Platero (Uruguay 1917)
Pedro Calomino (Argentina 1921)
Lais (Brazil 1922)
Leonardo De Lucca (Uruguay 1923)
Ernesto Meliante (Uruguay 1924)
Americo Tesoriere (Argentina 1925)
Jose Lago Millon (Argentina 1927)
Francisco Olazar (Argentina 1929)
Raul V Blanco (Uruguay 1935)
Manuel Seoane (Argentina 1937)
Jack Greenwell (Peru 1939)
Pedro Cea (Uruguay 1942)
Flavio Costa (Brazil 1949)
Manuel Fleitas Solich (Paraguay 1953)
Hugo Bagnulo (Uruguay 1956)
Victorio Spinetto (Argentina 1959)
Danilo Alvim (Bolivia 1963)
Marcos Calderon (Peru 1975)
Ranulfo Miranda (Paraguay 1979)
Omar Borras (Uruguay 1983)
Roberto Fleitas (Uruguay 1987)
Sebastiao Lazaroni (Brazil 1989)
Hector Nunez (Uruguay 1995)
Mario Zagallo (Brazil 1997)
Wanderlei Luxemburgo (Brazil 1999)
Francisco Maturana (Colombia 2001)
Carlos Alberto Parreira (Brazil 2004)
Dunga (Brazil 2007)
Oscar Washington Tabarez (Uruguay 2011)
Jorge Sampaoli (Chile 2015)
Juan Antonio Pizzi (Chile 2016)

GOALS AT A PREMIUM

In terms of goals per game, the 2011 Copa America was the second tightest of all time – with only 54 strikes hitting the back of the net in 26 matches, an average of 2.08 per game. The 1922 tournament, in Brazil, saw fewer – 22 goals in 11 games, an average of two. Both competitions were a far cry from the prolific 1927 event in Peru, where 37 goals across six games averaged out at 6.17. The 91 goals in 2016 came at an average of 2.84 per match.

SEEING RED

Brazil may have the worst FIFA World Cup disciplinary record, but neighbours Uruguay assume that unenviable position in the Copa America. Uruguayan players have been sent off 32 times – the latest being **Matias Vecino** against Mexico in 2016 – followed by Peru and Argentina on 24 dismissals apiece, Brazil and Venezuela (20 each), Chile (18), Paraguay (14), Bolivia (13), Colombia and Ecuador (11 apiece), Mexico (ten), the United States (three), Costa Rica (two), and Honduras, Jamaica, Japan and Panama (one each).

MARKARIAN MAKES HIS MARK

The 2011 Copa America was not only a Uruguayan success story for the eventual champions, but also third-placed Peru's Uruguayan coach Sergio Markarian. Uruguay's winning manager Oscar Washington Tabarez had Markarian as his club coach at Bella Vista in the 1970s. Markarian could also claim some credit for Paraguay's runners-up finish, having been a successful and influential coach in that country during the 1980s, 1990s and early 21st century.

PART 5:
AFRICA CUP OF NATIONS

THE AFRICAN governing football confederation – Confederation Africaine de Football (or CAF) – is three years younger than UEFA, yet its cross-continental tournament, the Africa Cup of Nations, kicked off before the first European Championship. Formed on 8 February 1957, the CAF announced the first championship just three days later. Egypt's ultimate triumph in that inaugural tournament set an appropriate pattern – the "Pharaohs" have won a record seven titles and been runners-up twice, including in 2017 – but the competition has expanded and progressed remarkably since those early days.

Only three nations competed in 1957 (South Africa entered, but were expelled for political reasons), while 51 vied for the 15 qualification spots at the 2017 event, alongside already-seeded hosts Gabon who were staging the finals on their own for the first time – they had been co-hosts with Equatorial Guinea in 2012. The global prominence of the Africa Cup of Nations has also grown, especially when the spotlight fell on major African stars taking time off from European club duties every other January. But the African confederation has decided to switch the finals to June/July from 2019, when Cameroon is due to be the hosts, and they will be expanded to 24 teams.

Whatever the place in the calendar, the trophy – now in its third physical incarnation – will always be contested with vivacious skills and fierce local pride. More different countries have won the ACN than any other continental championship, with glory being shared among 14 separate nations – including Africa's largest three countries Sudan, Algeria and Congo DR, as well as mid-sized entrants such as 2017 champions Cameroon, Morocco, the Ivory Coast, winners in 2015, and early standard-setters Ghana, plus surprise 2012 victors Zambia.

Unusually, the 2010 Cup's preliminary rounds carried extra importance as they doubled for the qualifying competition for the subsequent World Cup in South Africa.

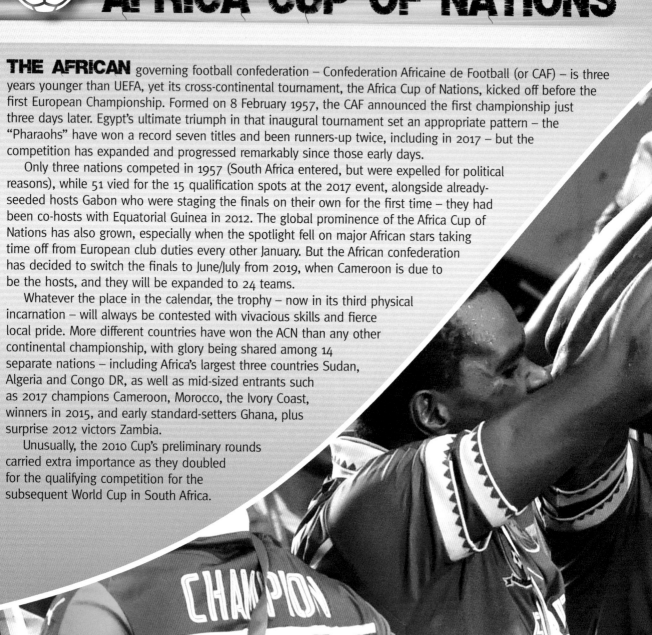

Cameroon, winners four times between 1984 and 2002, ended a 15-year wait for further Africa Cup of Nations glory with a 2-0 defeat of Egypt in the 2017 final at Stade de l'Amitie, Libreville, Gabon.

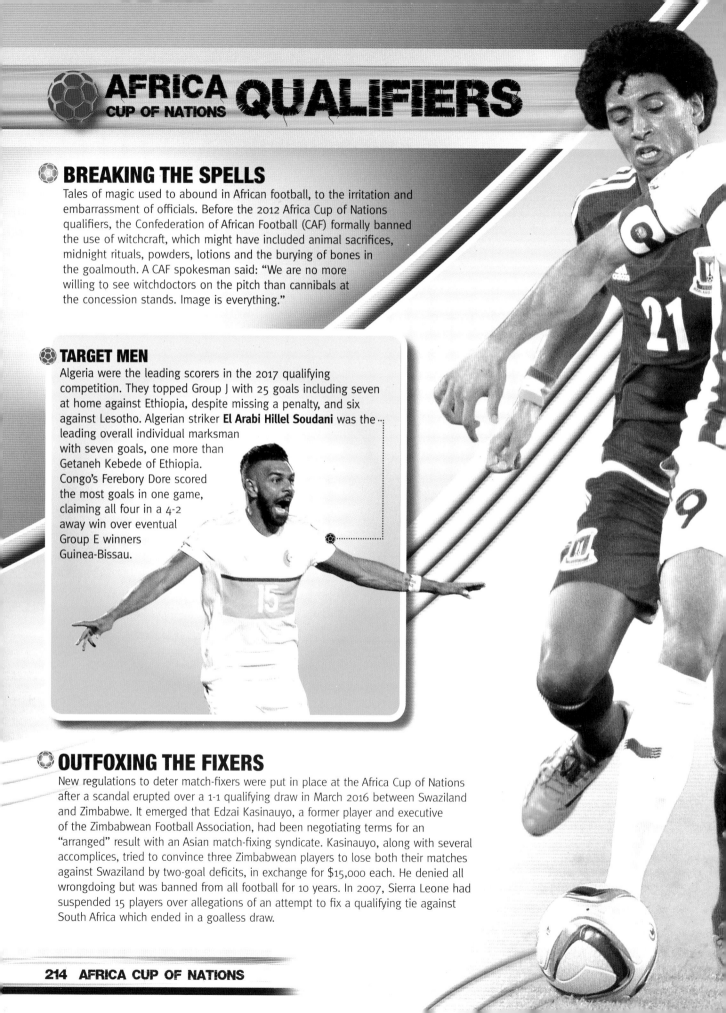

AFRICA CUP OF NATIONS QUALIFIERS

BREAKING THE SPELLS

Tales of magic used to abound in African football, to the irritation and embarrassment of officials. Before the 2012 Africa Cup of Nations qualifiers, the Confederation of African Football (CAF) formally banned the use of witchcraft, which might have included animal sacrifices, midnight rituals, powders, lotions and the burying of bones in the goalmouth. A CAF spokesman said: "We are no more willing to see witchdoctors on the pitch than cannibals at the concession stands. Image is everything."

TARGET MEN

Algeria were the leading scorers in the 2017 qualifying competition. They topped Group J with 25 goals including seven at home against Ethiopia, despite missing a penalty, and six against Lesotho. Algerian striker **El Arabi Hillel Soudani** was the leading overall individual marksman with seven goals, one more than Getaneh Kebede of Ethiopia. Congo's Ferebory Dore scored the most goals in one game, claiming all four in a 4-2 away win over eventual Group E winners Guinea-Bissau.

OUTFOXING THE FIXERS

New regulations to deter match-fixers were put in place at the Africa Cup of Nations after a scandal erupted over a 1-1 qualifying draw in March 2016 between Swaziland and Zimbabwe. It emerged that Edzai Kasinauyo, a former player and executive of the Zimbabwean Football Association, had been negotiating terms for an "arranged" result with an Asian match-fixing syndicate. Kasinauyo, along with several accomplices, tried to convince three Zimbabwean players to lose both their matches against Swaziland by two-goal deficits, in exchange for $15,000 each. He denied all wrongdoing but was banned from all football for 10 years. In 2007, Sierra Leone had suspended 15 players over allegations of an attempt to fix a qualifying tie against South Africa which ended in a goalless draw.

FEAST OR FAMINE

In 22 tournaments since 1976, Nigeria have been Africa Cup of Nations champions three times, beaten finalists on four occasions and finished third seven times; they have also qualified for five of the last six FIFA World Cups, 1994–2014. It has not been glory all the way, however, because – apart from winning in 2013 – Nigeria have failed to qualify for the other three AfCon finals since 2012. They had the misfortune in 2015–16, to be in same qualifying group as Egypt, Tanzania and Chad, but Chad withdrew during qualifying and it meant that only the group winners would make the finals and that place went to Egypt. Yet, simultaneously, Nigeria's juniors have been in outstanding form. The youngsters have won five World U-17 Cups including the last two staged, in 2013 and 2015.

CHIK KING

Tunisia midfielder **Yassine Chikhaoui** was quick off the mark to hit the first hat-trick of the 2017 qualifying campaign. He opened the scoring against Djibouti on 12 June 2015, with a ninth-minute penalty and had completed his treble within the first 23 minutes. Tunisia went on to win 8-1, matching their biggest previous winning margins from 7-0 victories over Togo in January 2000 and Malawi in March 2005.

UGANDA END 39 YEARS OF HURT

Uganda upset all the forecasts by reaching the finals for the first time since 1978 when they were runners-up to Ghana in qualification for 2017. Coach **Milutin Sredojevic** said: "The biggest power given to us in sport is the power of making people happy, it's a special, special feeling." Ugandan fans were not so happy after the finals when the Cranes finished bottom of Group D with only one point.

QUALIFYING TOURNAMENT HISTORY

There was no qualifying competition in either 1957 or 1959. The hosts or co-hosts (in 2000 and 2012) qualified automatically and defending champions did likewise until Egypt had to qualify for the 2008 competition. Some entrants failed to play any or all of their scheduled matches.

Year	Entries	Qualifiers
1962	6	2
1963	8	4
1965	13	4
1968	20	6
1970	18	6
1972	24	6
1974	27	6
1976	30	6
1978	24	6
1980	27	6
1982	34	6
1984	34	6
1986	32	6
1988	34	6
1990	33	6
1992	34	8
1994	37	8
1996	42	14
1998	34	14
2000	44	13
2002	49	14
2004	42	14
2006	51	14
2008	51	15
2010	53	15
2012	44	14
2013	46	15
2015	51	15
2017	51	15

GABON DOUBLE–TAKE

The 2017 tournament saw a new wrinkle in qualifying because finals hosts Gabon were included in the Group I mini-league. In fact, Gabon's matches were only friendlies, providing the hosts with guaranteed fixtures to aid preparations while the rest of Africa battled over qualifying points. This system had been used for hosts France during the qualifying tournament for UEFA Euro 2016.

AFRICA
CUP OF NATIONS
TEAM RECORDS

TEST OF ENDURANCE

The Ivory Coast have won the two highest-scoring penalty shoot-outs in full international history – they defeated Ghana 11-10 over 24 penalties in the 1992 Africa Cup of Nations final, and Cameroon 12-11, over the same number of kicks, in the quarter-finals of the 2006 Africa Cup of Nations.

GHANA AGAIN

Ghana's "Black Stars" became the first country to reach the final of four consecutive Africa Cup of Nations, lifting the trophy in 1963 and 1965 and finishing runners-up in 1968 and 1970. They have now reached nine finals in all – a tally Egypt matched in 2017. The two have also staged the finals four times each, though Ghana co-hosted once with Nigeria.

FROM TRAGEDY TO TRIUMPH

Zambia's unexpected glory at the 2012 African Cup of Nations was both fitting and poignant as the setting for their glory was just a few hundred metres from the scene of earlier calamity. The 2012 players spent the day before the final against **Ivory Coast** laying flowers in the sea in tribute to the 30 people killed when a plane crashed off the coast of Gabonese city Libreville on 27 April 1993. Victims that day included 18 Zambian internationals flying to Senegal for a FIFA World Cup qualifier. French coach Herve Renard dedicated the 2012 victory to the dead, after watching his side beat Ivory Coast 8-7 on penalties following a goalless draw after extra-time. Centre-back Stoppila Sunzu struck the decisive spot-kick, after Ivory Coast's Kolo Toure had his penalty saved by Kennedy Mweene and Gervinho blazed his over the bar. Both teams were competing in their third African Cup of Nations final, Ivory Coast having won in 1992 and lost in 2006, while Zambia had finished runners-up in 1974 and 1994. Zambia's success was the climactic surprise of a tournament that produced shocks when traditional powerhouses Egypt, Cameroon, Nigeria and South Africa all failed to even make the finals – then Senegal, Angola and Morocco were knocked out in the first round.

REIGNING PHARAOHS

Egypt dominate the Africa Cup of Nations records. They won the first tournament, in 1957, having been helped by a bye to the final when semi-final opponents South Africa were disqualified, and have emerged as champions another six times since – more than any other country. Their victories in the last three tournaments – 2006, 2008 and 2010 make them the only country to have lifted the trophy three times in a row. They have also appeared in a record 23 tournaments, one more than Ivory Coast and two more than Ghana. The Pharaohs have also played the most matches – 96 – one more than the Ghanaians and six more than Ivory Coast. Egypt have won 54 matches followed by Ghana (53), Nigeria (46), Cameroon (40) and Ivory Coast (39).

BAFANA BRILLIANCE

The Africa Cup of Nations has been won by its hosts on 11 separate occasions – including three times by Egypt and twice by Ghana. But perhaps the most surprising host-country triumph was South Africa's in 1996. The country had returned to international football only four years earlier, post-apartheid, when an 82nd-minute penalty by Theophilus "Doctor" Khumalo gave them a win over Cameroon on 7 July 1992. In February 1996, substitute Mark Williams scored both goals against Tunisia as South Africa won the Africa Cup of Nations trophy – lifted by white captain **Neil Tovey**, and handed over by the country's president Nelson Mandela, in Johannesburg's Soccer City stadium. South Africa were not even meant to be hosts, but stepped in for original choice Kenya who were stripped of staging rights after falling behind on new stadium-building.

GIMME GUINEA GIMME

Guinea equalled the record for biggest ever win at an African Cup of Nations when they beat Botswana 6-1 in a first-round match in 2012 – though both teams failed to make it out of Group D. Guinea were also only the third team to score six times in one match at a finals, following Egypt's 6-3 win over Nigeria in 1963 and Ivory Coast's 6-1 defeat of Ethiopia seven years later. The only other game to match the record-winning margin saw Guinea not as the victors but the victims, going down 5-0 to Ivory Coast in 2008.

EQUATORIAL DEBUTANTS

Equatorial Guinea took part in an Africa Cup of Nations finals for the first time in 2012, thanks to co-hosting the tournament with Gabon. Equatorial Guinea had never managed to qualify before while Gabon had reached the finals only four times previously. Botswana and Niger were the 2012 competition's other first-timers. The opening match of the 2012 competition was staged in Equatorial Guinea, in Bata, while the final was played in Gabonese city Libreville. The 2012 event was only the second to be shared between two host nations, after Ghana and Nigeria shared duties in 2000. Libya was awarded the right to host the Africa Cup of Nations, for a second time, in 2013, but turmoil in the country meant it was switched to South Africa, despite Nigeria initially being nominated as first reserve. Equatorial Guinea stepped in as solo hosts in 2015, replacing original choice Morocco. Libya withdrew as 2017 hosts, Gabon taking on the honour instead.

TOURNAMENT TRIUMPHS

7 **Egypt** (1957, 1959, 1986, 1998, 2006, 2008, 2010)
5 **Cameroon** (1984, 1988, 2000, 2002, 2017)
4 **Ghana** (1963, 1965, 1978, 1982)
3 **Nigeria** (1980, 1994, 2013)
2 **Ivory Coast** (1992, 2015)
  Zaire/Congo DR (1968, 1974)
1 **Algeria** (1990)
  Congo (1972)
  Ethiopia (1962)
  Morocco (1976)
  South Africa (1996)
  Sudan (1970)
  Tunisia (2004)
  Zambia (2012)

TOURNAMENT APPEARANCES

23 **Egypt**
22 **Ivory Coast**
21 **Ghana**
18 **Cameroon, DR Congo, Tunisia**
17 **Nigeria, Zambia, Algeria**
16 **Morocco**
14 **Senegal**
11 **Burkina Faso, Guinea**
10 **Ethiopia, Mali**
9 **South Africa**
8 **Sudan, Togo**
7 **Angola, Congo, Gabon**
6 **Uganda**
5 **Kenya**
4 **Mozambique**
3 **Benin, Libya, Zimbabwe**
2 **Cape Verde, Equatorial Guinea, Liberia, Malawi, Namibia, Niger, Sierra Leone**
1 **Botswana, Guinea-Bissau, Mauritius, Rwanda, Tanzania**

FOUR SHAME

Hosts **Angola** were responsible for perhaps the most dramatic collapse in Africa Cup of Nations history, when they threw away a four-goal lead in the opening match of the 2010 tournament. Even more embarrassingly, they were leading 4-0 against Mali with just 11 minutes left, in the capital Luanda's Estadio 11 de Novembro. Mali's final two goals, by Barcelona's Seydou Keita and Boulogne's Mustapha Yatabare, were scored deep into stoppage-time. Mali failed to make it through the first round, while Angola went out in the quarter-finals.

THE WAITING IS THE HARDEST PART

Some 15 of the 54 full members of the African football confederation have yet to appear in the finals of the Cup of Nations. The latest newcomers to join the party in Gabon were Guinea-Bissau. They shocked their hosts by forcing a 1-1 draw with Gabon in the Opening Match thanks to a stoppage-time equaliser from **Juary Soares**. They were then eliminated after defeats by Cameroon (2-1) and Burkina Faso (2-0). Still waiting to join the finals party are Burundi, Central African Republic, Chad, Comoros, Djibouti, Eritrea, Gambia, Lesotho, Madagascar, Mauritania, Sao Tome e Principe, Seychelles, Somalia, Swaziland and South Sudan – who made their qualifying debut only in 2015.

MANE SHOWS HOW MUCH HE MATTERS

The Africa Cup of Nations' cost to European clubs was illustrated perfectly after Senegal's **Sadio Mane** left Liverpool to play at the finals in Gabon in January 2017. Mane had first played in England with Senegal at the London 2012 Olympic Games and returned two years later to play in the Premier League with Southampton. In 2016 Liverpool bought him for £30m, making him, at the time, the most expensive ever African player. With Mane helping Senegal to the quarter-finals, Liverpool won only once in nine games. Mane, however, missed the crucial penalty as Senegal lost in a shootout to Ghana and he was carried, in tears, from the pitch. On his return to Liverpool, he scored twice as his club got back to winning form against title-rivals Tottenham Hotspur.

REVOLUTION #9

No player has scored more goals in one Africa Cup of Nations than Zaire's Ndaye Mulamba's nine during the 1974 tournament. Three months later he was sent off at the FIFA World Cup in West Germany, as his team crashed to a 9-0 defeat against Yugoslavia.

RECORD MEN

Cameroon's Rigobert Song and Egypt's Ahmed Hassan share the record for having appeared in eight Africa Cup of Nations finals, coincidentally the same consecutive ones between 1996 and 2010. Hassan was four times a champion (in 1998, 2006, 2008 and 2010) and Song twice (in 2000 and 2002).

PROLIFIC POKOU

Ivory Coast striker Laurent Pokou scored a record five goals in one Africa Cup of Nations match, as his side trounced Ethiopia 6-1 in the first round of the 1968 tournament. He finished top scorer at that tournament, and the following one – though ended both without a winners' medal. Only modern-day Cameroon star Samuel Eto'o has overtaken his overall Africa Cup of Nations tally of 14 goals.

OPENING GOAL

The first Africa Cup of Nations goal was a penalty scored by Egypt's Raafat Ateya in the 21st minute of their 2-1 semi-final win over Sudan in 1957. But his team-mate Mohamed Diab El-Attar would soon take over – he not only scored Egypt's second goal that day, but all four goals in the final against Ethiopia.

TOURNAMENT TOP SCORERS

Year	Player	Goals
1957	Mohamed Diab El-Attar (Egypt)	5
1959	Mahmoud Al-Gohari (Egypt)	3
1962	Abdelfatah Badawi (Egypt) Mengistu Worku (Ethiopia)	3
1963	Hassan El-Shazly (Egypt)	6
1965	Ben Acheampong (Ghana) Kofi Osei (Ghana) Eustache Mangle (Ivory Coast)	3
1968	Laurent Pokou (Ivory Coast)	6
1970	Laurent Pokou (Ivory Coast)	8
1972	Salif Keita (Mali)	5
1974	Ndaye Mulamba (Zaire)	9
1976	Keita Aliou Mamadou 'N'Jo Lea' (Guinea)	4
1978	Opoku Afriyie (Ghana) Segun Odegbami (Nigeria) Philip Omondi (Uganda)	3
1980	Khaled Al Abyad Labied (Morocco) Segun Odegbami (Nigeria)	3
1982	George Alhassan (Ghana)	4
1984	Taher Abouzaid (Egypt)	4
1986	Roger Milla (Cameroon)	4
1988	Gamal Abdelhamid (Egypt) Lakhdar Belloumi (Algeria) Roger Milla (Cameroon) Abdoulaye Traore (Ivory Coast)	2
1990	Djamel Menad (Algeria)	4
1992	Rashidi Yekini (Nigeria)	4
1994	Rashidi Yekini (Nigeria)	5
1996	Kalusha Bwalya (Zambia)	5
1998	Hossam Hassan (Egypt) Benni McCarthy (South Africa)	7
2000	Shaun Bartlett (South Africa)	5
2002	Julius Aghahowa (Nigeria) Patrick Mboma (Cameroon) Rene Salomon Olembe (Cameroon)	5
2004	Francileudo Santos (Tunisia) Frederic Kanoute (Mali) Patrick Mboma (Cameroon) Youssef Mokhtari (Morocco) Jay-Jay Okocha (Nigeria)	4
2006	Samuel Eto'o (Cameroon)	5
2008	Samuel Eto'o (Cameroon)	5
2010	Mohamed **Nagy 'Gedo'** (Egypt)	5
2012	Pierre-Emerick Aubameyang (Gabon) Cheick Diabate (Mali) Didier Drogba (Ivory Coast) Christopher Katongo (Zambia) Houssine Kharja (Morocco) Manucho (Tunisia) Emmanuel Mayuka (Zambia)	3
2013	Emmanuel Emenike (Nigeria) Mubarak Wakaso (Ghana)	4
2015	Ahmed Akaichi (Tunisia) Andre Ayew (Ghana) Javier Balboa (Equatorial Guinea) Thievy Bifouma (Congo) Dieumerci Mbokani (DR Congo)	3
2017	Junior Kabananga (DR Congo)	3

SIBLING HARMONY

Both teams in the final of the 2015 Africa Cup of Nations called upon a pair of brothers. Runners-up Ghana included Jordan and Andre Ayew, while Ivory Coast's champions were spearheaded by captain **Yaya Toure** and his centre-back brother Kolo. All four brothers took penalties in the 2015 final and scored, unlike in 2012, when the Ivory Coast were beaten in another penalty shoot-out, this time against Ghana. Yaya had been substituted in extra time, but Kolo missed in the 8-7 loss. Zambia's triumphant captain in 2012, player of the tournament Christian Katongo, had among his team-mates brother Felix – he came off the bench – and they both scored in that shoot-out. There is a history of siblings enjoying victory in the Africa Cup of Nations. In 1962, when Ethiopia won the trophy, denying Egypt a third title, they were captained by Luciano Vassalo, whose brother Italo scored the goal that gave Ethiopia a 3-2 extra-time lead in the final – they eventually won 4-2. In 1988 Francois Omam-Biyik and brother Andre Kana-Biyik helped Cameroon to win the tournament, though Francois was injured in the opening match.

SAM THE MAN

Cameroon's Samuel Eto'o, who made his full international debut – away to Costa Rica on 9 March 1997 – one day short of his 16th birthday, is the Africa Cup of Nations' all-time leading goalscorer. He was part of Cameroon's victorious teams in 2000 and 2002, but had to wait until 2008 to pass Laurent Pokou's 14-goal Africa Cup of Nations record. That year's competition took his overall tally to 16 goals – only for the former Real Madrid and Barcelona striker, now with Italy's Internazionale, to add another two in 2010. In 2005, Eto'o became the first player to be named African Footballer of the Year three years running. He also won an Olympic Games gold medal with Cameroon in 2000 and the UEFA Champions League three times, with Barcelona in 2006 and 2009 – scoring in both finals – and Inter in 2010.

YO, YOBO

Nigeria's **Joseph Yobo** was brought on as a substitute to the fans' acclaim in the closing minutes of the Green Eagles' victory over Burkina Faso in the 2013 Africa Cup of Nations final in Johannesburg. As captain, the one-time Marseille and Everton defender then had the honour of lifting the trophy. Yobo retired from international football in 2014, have made a record 101 appearances in his 13-year career.

AFRICA CUP OF NATIONS ALL-TIME TOP SCORERS

1	Samuel Eto'o (Cameroon)	18
2	Laurent Pokou (Ivory Coast)	14
3	Rashidi Yekini (Nigeria)	13
4	Hassan El-Shazly (Egypt)	12
5	Didier Drogba (Ivory Coast)	11
=	Hossam Hassan (Egypt)	11
=	Patrick Mboma (Cameroon)	11
8	Kalusha Bwalya (Zambia)	10
=	Ndaye Mulamba (Zaire)	10
=	Francileudo Santos (Tunisia)	10
=	Joel Tiehi (Ivory Coast)	10
=	Mengistu Worku (Ethiopia)	10

NO HASSLE FOR HASSAN

Egypt's **Ahmed Hassan** not only became the first footballer to play in the final of four different Africa Cup of Nations in 2010 – he also became the first to collect his fourth winners' medal. Earlier in the same tournament, his appearance in the quarter-final against Cameroon gave him his 170th cap – an Egyptian record. Hassan marked the game with three goals – one in his own net and two past Cameroon goalkeeper Carlos Kameni – although one appeared not to cross the line.

AFRICA CUP OF NATIONS — OTHER RECORDS

AFRICA CUP OF NATIONS: FINALS

1957	(Host country: Sudan) Egypt 4 Ethiopia 0
1959	(Egypt) Egypt 2 Sudan 1
1962	(Ethiopia) Ethiopia 4 Egypt 2 (aet)
1963	(Ghana) Ghana 3 Sudan 0
1965	(Tunisia) Ghana 3 Tunisia 2 (aet)
1968	(Ethiopia) Zaire/Congo DR 1 Ghana 0
1970	(Sudan) Sudan 1 Ghana 0
1972	(Cameroon) Congo 3 Mali 2
1974	(Egypt) Zaire/Congo DR 2 Zambia 2
	Replay: Zaire/Congo DR 2 Zambia 0
1976	(Ethiopia) Morocco 1 Guinea 1 (Morocco win mini-league system)
1978	(Ghana) Ghana 2 Uganda 0
1980	(Nigeria) Nigeria 3 Algeria 0
1982	(Libya) Ghana 1 Libya 1 (aet; Ghana win 7-6 on penalties)
1984	(Ivory Coast) Cameroon 3 Nigeria 1
1986	(Egypt) Egypt 0 Cameroon 0 (aet; Egypt win 5-4 on penalties)
1988	(Morocco) Cameroon 1 Nigeria 0
1990	(Algeria) Algeria 1 Nigeria 0
1992	(Senegal) Ivory Coast 0 Ghana 0 (aet; Ivory Coast win 11-10 on penalties)
1994	(Tunisia) Nigeria 2 Zambia 1
1996	(South Africa) South Africa 2 Tunisia 0
1998	(Burkina Faso) Egypt 2 South Africa 0
2000	(Ghana & Nigeria) Cameroon 2 Nigeria 2 (aet; Cameroon win 4-3 on penalties)
2002	(Mali) Cameroon 0 Senegal 0 (aet; Cameroon win 3-2 on penalties)
2004	(Tunisia) Tunisia 2 Morocco 1
2006	(Egypt) Egypt 0 Ivory Coast 0 (aet; Egypt win 4-2 on penalties)
2008	(Ghana) Egypt 1 Cameroon 0
2010	(Angola) Egypt 1 Ghana 0
2012	(Gabon & Equatrorial Guinea) Zambia 0 Ivory Coast 0 (aet; Zambia 8-7 on pens)
2013	(South Africa) Nigeria 1 Burkina Faso 0
2015	(Equatorial Guinea) Ivory Coast 0 Ghana 0 (aet; Ivory Coast 9-8 on pens)
2017	(Gabon) Cameroon 2 Egypt 1

RENARD REDEEMED

In 2015, Frenchman **Herve Renard** became the first coach to win the Africa Cup of Nations with two different countries. This time he was in charge of Ivory Coast as they defeated Ghana on penalties. Three years earlier, Renard's Zambia had defeated the Ivorians, also on spot-kicks, in what was his second spell as national coach. He had resigned in 2010 to become Angola's coach, and his return was not universally welcomed in Zambia. All was forgiven when his team won their first Africa Cup of Nations. Renard's celebrations included carrying on to the pitch injured defender Joseph Musonda, who had limped off after ten minutes of the final. He also handed his winner's medal to Kalusha Bwalya, probably Zambia's greatest ever player. Bwalya later coached Zambia but, by the time of the 2012 final, he was president of the country's football association.

GEDO BLASTER

Egypt's hero in 2010 was Mohamed Nagy, better known by his nickname "Gedo" – Egyptian Arabic for "Grandpa". He scored the only goal of the final, against Ghana, his fifth of the tournament, giving him the Golden Boot. Yet he did all this without starting a single game. He had to settle for coming on as a substitute in all six of Egypt's matches, playing a total of 135 minutes in all. Gedo – born in Damanhur on 3 October 1984 – made his international debut only two months earlier, and had played only two friendlies for Egypt before the tournament proper.

TOGO'S TRAGIC FATE

Togo were the victims of tragedy shortly before the 2010 Africa Cup of Nations kicked off – followed by expulsion from the event. The team's bus was fired on by Angolan militants three days before their first scheduled match, killing three people: the team's assistant coach, press officer and bus driver. The team returned home to Togo for three days of national mourning, and were then thrown out of the competition by the CAF as punishment for missing their opening game against Ghana. Togo were later expelled from the 2012 and 2014 competitions, but this sanction was overturned on appeal in May 2010.

UNFINISHED BUSINESS

Beware – if you go to see Nigeria play Tunisia, you may not get the full 90 minutes. Nigeria were awarded third place at the 1978 Africa Cup of Nations after the Tunisian team walked off after 42 minutes of their play-off, with the score at 1-1. They were protesting about refereeing decisions, but thus granted Nigeria a 2-0 victory by default. Oddly enough, it had been Nigeria walking off when the two teams met in the second leg of a qualifier for the 1962 tournament. Their action came when Tunisia equalized after 65 minutes. The punishment was a 2-0 win in Tunisia's favour – putting them 3-2 ahead on aggregate.

MAURITANIA MANIA

Mauritania made unwanted Africa Cup of Nations history by having five players sent off during a qualifier away to Cape Verde in June 2003, forcing the match to be abandoned. The hosts were leading 3-0 at the time and that stood as the final result.

BIG BOSS KESHI LEAVES MARK ON AFRICAN FOOTBALL

Stephen Keshi – known to admiring fans as "Big Boss" – became only the second man to win the Africa Cup of Nations as both player and manager, when leading Nigeria to the title in 2013. He previously lifted the trophy as captain in 1994. The Nigerian football association had its grudging faith in Keshi vindicated in 2013. Keshi, who returned in glory as their 19th manager in 19 years, died in 2016. Before Keshi the only man to have won the cup both as a player and manager was Egypt's Mahmoud Al-Gohary – top scorer in 1959 and in charge 39 years later. Hassan Shehata, striker when Egypt finished third in 1970, then won a record-breaking three times as his country's coach.

OFF TARGET

The 2017 tournament in Gabon was the second-lowest-scoring Nations Cup of all time with an average of a mere 2.06 goals per game. This was a drop from 2.12 in 2015 and "better" only than the nadir of 1.59 in 2002. Runners-up Egypt failed to score more than one goal in all of their games.

RECENT AFRICA CUP OF NATIONS–WINNING COACHES

1988	Claude Le Roy (Cameroon)
1990	Abdelhamid Kermali (Algeria)
1992	Yeo Martial (Ivory Coast)
1994	Clemens Westerhof (Nigeria)
1996	Clive Barker (South Africa)
1998	Mahmoud El-Gohary (Egypt)
2000	Pierre Lechantre (Cameroon)
2002	Winfried Schafer (Cameroon)
2004	Roger Lemerre (Tunisia)
2006	Hassan Shehata (Egypt)
2008	Hassan Shehata (Egypt)
2010	Hassan Shehata (Egypt)
2012	Herve Renard (Zambia)
2013	Stephen Keshi (Nigeria)
2015	Herve Renard (Ivory Coast)
2017	Hugo Broos (Cameroon)

ATAK ATTACKS

South Sudan won an international for the first time on 5 September 2015, when midfielder Atak Lual got the only goal of a 2017 Africa Cup of Nations qualifier against Equatorial Guinea. The game was played at South Sudan's national stadium in Juba. South Sudan had initially gained independence as a country in 2011, receiving CAF admission in February 2012 and FIFA status three months later. They drew their first official international, 2-2 against Uganda on 10 July 2012, but their winless run continued with one more draw and ten defeats before that success against Equatorial Guinea.

MISSING THE POINT

The absences of Cameroon, Nigeria and reigning champions Egypt from the 2012 African Cup of Nations were surprising – though each could at least comfort themselves on not missing out in quite such embarrassing circumstances as South Africa. They appeared happy to play out a goalless draw with Sierra Leone in their final qualifier, believing that would be enough to go through – and greeted the final whistle with celebrations on the pitch. But they were mistaken in thinking goal difference would be used to separate teams level on points in their group, with Niger qualifying instead thanks to a better head-to-head record. South Africa's distraught coach Pitso Mosimane admitted misinterpreting the rules and deliberately targeting his side's tactics towards a draw. The South African football association initially appealed against elimination, claiming goal difference should be the decider – but ultimately decided not to pursue the matter.

MISSING A (HAT-)TRICK

The last of the Africa Cup of Nations' 15 hat-tricks was scored back in 2008, by **Soufiane Alloudi** in the opening half-hour of Morocco's 5-1 first-round win over Namibia. Only Egypt's Hassan El-Shazly has hit two trebles: his first came in a 6-3 first-round victory over Nigeria in 1963; he repeated the feat, six years later, in a 3-1 victory over Ivory Coast in the third-place play-off.

PART 6:
OTHER FIFA TOURNAMENTS

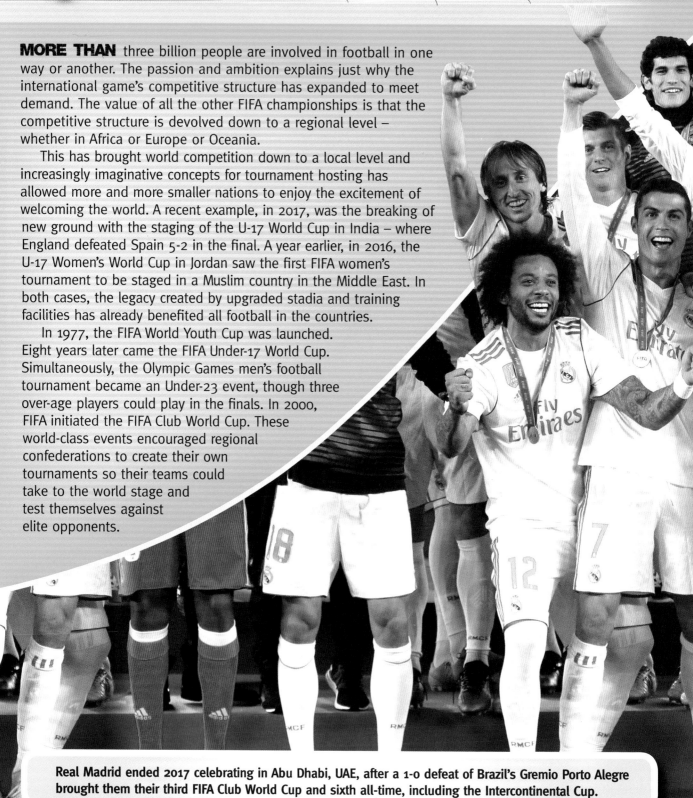

MORE THAN three billion people are involved in football in one way or another. The passion and ambition explains just why the international game's competitive structure has expanded to meet demand. The value of all the other FIFA championships is that the competitive structure is devolved down to a regional level – whether in Africa or Europe or Oceania.

This has brought world competition down to a local level and increasingly imaginative concepts for tournament hosting has allowed more and more smaller nations to enjoy the excitement of welcoming the world. A recent example, in 2017, was the breaking of new ground with the staging of the U-17 World Cup in India – where England defeated Spain 5-2 in the final. A year earlier, in 2016, the U-17 Women's World Cup in Jordan saw the first FIFA women's tournament to be staged in a Muslim country in the Middle East. In both cases, the legacy created by upgraded stadia and training facilities has already benefited all football in the countries.

In 1977, the FIFA World Youth Cup was launched. Eight years later came the FIFA Under-17 World Cup. Simultaneously, the Olympic Games men's football tournament became an Under-23 event, though three over-age players could play in the finals. In 2000, FIFA initiated the FIFA Club World Cup. These world-class events encouraged regional confederations to create their own tournaments so their teams could take to the world stage and test themselves against elite opponents.

Real Madrid ended 2017 celebrating in Abu Dhabi, UAE, after a 1-0 defeat of Brazil's Gremio Porto Alegre brought them their third FIFA Club World Cup and sixth all-time, including the Intercontinental Cup.

FIFA U-20 WORLD CUP

First staged in 1977 in Tunisia and known as the FIFA Youth World Championship until 2005, the FIFA U-20 World Cup is the world championship for footballers under the age of 20. It has featured some of the game's most notable names. Staged in alternate years, the tournament's most successful team has been Argentina, who have lifted the trophy on six occasions.

HISTORY BOYS

England celebrated their first world crown since 1966 when the Under-20s triumphed in South Korea in 2017. They defeated Venezuela 1-0 in the final in Suwon, thanks to a 34th-minute goal from Everton's Dominic Calvert-Lewin. Both teams hit the post during the game and Newcastle goalkeeper Freddie Woodman was England's other hero, saving a 75th-minute penalty from Adalberto Penaranda, who, ironically, was on the books of English Premier League club Watford. Woodman took the award as the tournament's top keeper while Dominic Solanke was voted best player. England manager Paul Simpson was born on 26 July 1966, four days before England's World Cup victory.

SUPER SUB

The Soviet Union became the first winners of the FIFA Under-20 World Cup when they beat hosts Mexico 9-8 on penalties after a 2-2 draw in the 1977 final. Their shoot-out hero was substitute goalkeeper Yuri Sivuha, who had replaced Aleksandre Novikov during extra-time. It remains the only time the Soviet Union won the event, though their striker **Oleg Salenko**, a future 1994 FIFA World Cup Golden Boot winner, took the top scorer award in 1989, with five goals. Two years later, fellow Soviet Sergei Sherbakov also finished top scorer, also with five goals, although his full international career was less successful. He played only twice for Ukraine before injuries suffered in a car accident in 1993 left him in a wheelchair.

DOMINANT DOMINIC

Ghana became the first African country to lift the trophy when they upset Brazil in the 2009 final – despite playing 83 of the 120 minutes with just 10 men, following Daniel Addo's red card. The final finished goalless, one of only two games in which **Dominic Adiyiah** failed to score. He ended the tournament as top scorer with eight goals and also won the Golden Ball prize for best player. Immediately afterwards a further reward was a transfer from Norway's Fredrikstad to Italy's AC Milan. The Silver Ball went to Brazil's Alex Teixeira, even though it was his missed penalty, when the final shoot-out went to sudden death, which handed Ghana victory.

LISBON LIONS

In 1991, **Portugal** became the first hosts to win the tournament with a team that became known as the country's "Golden Generation", featuring Luis Figo, Rui Costa, Joao Pinto, Abel Xavier and Jorge Costa. Portugal's winning squad was coached by Carlos Queiroz, who would later manage the full national side twice, with spells in charge at Real Madrid and as assistant at Manchester United in between. Their penalty shoot-out win over Brazil in the final was played at Benfica's iconic Estadio da Luz in the capital Lisbon. In 2001, Argentina became the second team to lift the trophy on home territory.

SAVIOUR SAVIOLA

Javier Saviola has scored more goals in one FIFA Under-20 World Cup than any other player – he managed 11 in seven games at the 2001 competition, as his side Argentina went on to beat Ghana in the final, with Saviola scoring his team's three unanswered goals. Saviola, born on 11 December 1981 in Buenos Aires, was playing for River Plate at the time but joined Barcelona for £15 million not long afterwards – before later signing for the Spanish side's arch-rivals Real Madrid. When Pele picked his 125 "greatest living footballers" for FIFA in March 2004, 22-year-old Saviola was the youngest player on the list.

OSCAR WINNING

Only one player has scored a hat-trick in the final of a FIFA Under-20 World Cup: Brazilian midfielder Oscar, who hit all his side's goals in their 3-2 triumph over Portugal to claim the latest trophy in August 2011. He was further rewarded by making his senior Brazil debut the following month, against Argentina. They were actually Oscar's first goals of the tournament staged in Colombia, with the Golden Shoe going to his team-mate Henrique for five goals in the preceding six matches – including the 200th goal in FIFA Under-20 World Cup history, in a 3-0 first-round victory over Austria.

CAPTAIN MARVELS

Two men have lifted both the FIFA Under-20 World Cup and the FIFA World Cup as captain: Brazil's Dunga (in 1983 and 1994) and Argentina's Diego Maradona (in 1979 and 1986). Many had expected Maradona to make Argentina's full squad for the 1978 FIFA World Cup but he missed out on selection. He showed his potential by being voted best player at the 1979 youth tournament in Japan.

TOURNAMENT HOSTS AND FINAL RESULTS

1977	(Host: Tunisia) USSR 2 Mexico 2 (aet: USSR win 9-8 on penalties)
1979	(Japan) Argentina 3 USSR 1
1981	(Australia) West Germany 4 Qatar 0
1983	(Mexico) Brazil 1 Argentina 0
1985	(USSR) Brazil 1 Spain 0 (aet)
1987	(Chile) Yugoslavia 1 West Germany 1 (aet: Yugoslavia win 5-4 on penalties)
1989	(Saudi Arabia) Portugal 2 Nigeria 0
1991	(Portugal) Portugal 0 Brazil 0 (aet: Portugal win 4-2 on penalties)
1993	(Australia) Brazil 2 Ghana 1
1995	(Qatar) Argentina 2 Brazil 0
1997	(Malaysia) Argentina 2 Uruguay 1
1999	(Nigeria) Spain 4 Japan 0
2001	(Argentina) Argentina 3 Ghana 0
2003	(United Arab Emirates) Brazil 1 Spain 0
2005	(Holland) Argentina 2 Nigeria 1
2007	(Canada) Argentina 2 Czech Republic 1
2009	(Egypt) Ghana 0 Brazil 0 (aet: Ghana win 4-3 on penalties)
2011	(Colombia) Brazil 3 Portugal 2 (aet)
2013	(Turkey) France 0, Uruguay 0 (aet: France win 4-1 on penalties)
2015	(New Zealand) Serbia 2, Brazil 1 (aet)
2017	(South Korea) England 1 Venezuela 0

WHAT A MESSI

Lionel Messi was the star of the show for Argentina in 2005, and not just for scoring both his country's goals in the final – both from the penalty spot. He achieved a hat-trick by not only winning the Golden Boot for top scorer and Golden Shoe for best player, but also by captaining his side to the title. This feat was emulated two years later by compatriot Sergio Aguero, who scored once in the final against the Czech Republic, before team-mate Mauro Zarate struck a late winner. Four other men have finished as both top scorer and as the tournament's best player (as voted by journalists) – Brazil's Geovani in 1983, Argentina's Javier Saviola in 2001, Dominic Adiyiah of Ghana in 2009 and another Brazilian, Henrique, in 2011.

TOURNAMENT TOP SCORERS

1977	Guina (Brazil)	4
1979	Ramon Diaz (Argentina)	8
1981	Ralf Loose (West Germany), Roland Wohlfarth (West Germany), Taher Amer (Egypt), Mark Koussas (Argentina)	4
1983	Geovani (Brazil)	6
1985	Gerson (Brazil), Balalo (Brazil), Muller (Brazil), Alberto Garcia Aspe (Mexico), Monday Odiaka (Nigeria), Fernando Gomez (Spain), Sebastian Losada (Spain)	3
1987	Marcel Witeczek (West Germany)	7
1989	Oleg Salenko (USSR)	5
1991	Sergei Sherbakov (USSR)	5
1993	Ante Milicic (Australia), Adriano (Brazil), Gian (Brazil), Henry Zambrano (Colombia), Vicente Nieto (Mexico), Chris Faklaris (USA)	3
1995	Joseba Etxeberria (Spain)	7
1997	Adailton Martins Bolzan (Brazil)	10
1999	Mahamadou Dissa (Mali), Pablo (Spain)	5
2001	Javier Saviola (Argentina)	11
2003	Fernando Cavenaghi (Argentina), Dudu (Brazil), Daisuke Sakata (Japan), Eddie Johnson (USA)	4
2005	Lionel Messi (Argentina)	6
2007	Sergio Aguero (Argentina)	7
2009	Dominic Adiyiah (Ghana)	8
2011	Henrique (Brazil)	5
2013	Ebenezer Assifuah (Ghana)	6
2015	Viktor Kovalenko (Ukraine)	5
	Bence Mervo (Hungary)	5
2017	Riccardo Orsolini (Italy)	5

SERBIA TAKE HEART

Serbia won their first major FIFA prize defeating favourites Brazil 2-1 after extra time in the final of the 2015 FIFA U-20 World Cup. They were guided to success in Auckland, New Zealand, by the commanding displays of the event's top goalkeeper in captain **Predrag Rajkovic** and powerful Sergej Milinkovic in midfield. The team lived up to their motto of "one team with one heart". They were taken to extra time in all four knockout matches and beat Brazil with a goal from Nemanja Maksimovic two minutes from the end of extra time. Stanisa Mandic gave Serbia a 70th-minute lead, only for substitute Andreas Pereira to equalize three minutes later. A penalty shoot-out seemed likely until Maksimovic struck in the 118th minute.

FIFA U-17 WORLD CUP

First staged in China in 1985, when it was known as the FIFA Under-16 World Championship, the age limit was adjusted from 16 to 17 in 1991 and the tournament has been labelled the FIFA U-17 World Cup ever since 2007. Chile hosted the 2015 finals and reigning champions Nigeria were winners for a record-extending fifth time – they have also been runners-up three times. England won their first U-17 World Cup in India in 2017.

TAKING WING

Nigeria's youth side, the "Golden Eaglets", became the first African nation to win a FIFA tournament when they triumphed at the inaugural Under-16 FIFA World Cup in 1985 (it became an Under-17 event in 1991). Their opening goal in the final against West Germany was scored by striker Jonathan Akpoborie, who would go on to play for German clubs Stuttgart and Wolfsburg.

ENGLAND'S GLORY

England won their first world U-17 title in the most thrilling way possible by hitting back from two goals down to beat Spain 5-2 in the 2017 final in Kolkata, India. They were the second successive England age-group team, after the U-20s' victory in South Korea, to become world champions. Liverpool's **Rhian Brewster** led the recovery with a goal just before half-time, after Spain had hit England twice on the break through Sergio Gomez. Brewster ended the tournament as the Golden Boot winner with hat-tricks in the quarter- and semi-finals. His strike in the final was his eighth goal in the competition. Manager Steve Cooper's team thus avenged their defeat in the European finals. Phil Foden, also of England, received the Golden Ball as the tournament's top player.

GOALS FLO

The first player to win both the Golden Ball and the Golden Shoe at the FIFA U-17 World Cup was French striker **Florent Sinama-Pongolle**. His nine goals in 2001 set a tournament record for one player. His tally included two hat-tricks in the opening round. Unlike Cesc Fabregas, two years later, Sinama-Pongolle ended the final on the winning side. The team goalscoring record is held by Spain, who struck 22 times on their way to third place in 1997. Sinama-Pongolle's scoring record was equalled in 2011 by Ivory Coast striker Souleymane Coulibaly. While Sinama-Pongolle needed six matches, the young Ivorian managed his in just four games but his team only reached the second round – though he earned a transfer from Italy's Siena to English Premier League club Tottenham Hotspur not long afterwards.

SEOUL SURVIVOR

The final of the 2007 tournament was the first to be hosted by a former FIFA World Cup venue – the 68,476-capacity Seoul FIFA World Cup Stadium in South Korea's capital, which had been built for the 2002 FIFA World Cup. The game was watched by a crowd of 36,125, a tournament record. The 2007 event was the first to feature 24 teams instead of 16, and was won by Nigeria – after Spain missed all three of their spot-kicks in a penalty shoot-out.

GOOD AND BAD BOY BOJAN

Barcelona star **Bojan Krkic** quickly went from hero to villain in the final moments of Spain's semi-final victory over Ghana in 2007 – he scored his team's winner with four minutes of extra-time remaining, but was then sent off for a second yellow-card offence just before the final whistle. His expulsion meant he was suspended for the final, which Spain lost on penalties to Nigeria.

GOLDEN HAUL

West Germany's Marcel Witeczek is the only person to finish top scorer at both a FIFA Under-16 World Championship and the Under-20 version of the event. The Polish-born striker hit eight goals at the 1985 Under-16 tournament, followed by seven more at the Under-20 championship two years later. Brazil's Adriano – a different Adriano to the one who later played for the senior side and Serie A club Internazionale – came closest to equalling the feat: he won the Golden Shoe, for top scorer, after scoring four goals at the 1991 FIFA Under-17 World Cup, then the Golden Ball, for best player, at the Under-20 event in 1993.

LITTLE ITALY

The 1991 tournament was originally scheduled to take place in Ecuador, but a cholera outbreak in the country meant it was switched to Italy instead – though played in much smaller venues than those that had been used for the previous year's senior FIFA World Cup in the country. The 1991 tournament was the first to be open to Under-17s – the first three had been known as the FIFA U-16 World Cup.

TOURNAMENT TOP SCORERS

Year	Player	Goals
1985	Marcel Witeczek (West Germany)	8
1987	Moussa Traore (Ivory Coast)	5
	Yuri Nikiforov (USSR)	5
1989	Khaled Jasem (Bahrain)	3
	Fode Camara (Guinea)	3
	Gil (Portugal)	3
	Tulipa (Portugal)	3
	Khalid Al Roaihi (Saudi Arabia)	3
1991	Adriano (Brazil)	4
1993	Wilson Oruma (Nigeria)	6
1995	Daniel Allsopp (Australia)	5
	Mohamed Al Kathiri (Oman)	5
1997	David (Spain)	7
1999	Ishmael Addo (Ghana)	7
2001	Florent Sinama-Pongolle (France)	9
2003	Carlos Hidalgo (Colombia)	5
	Manuel Curto (Portugal)	5
	Cesc Fabregas (Spain)	5
2005	Carlos Vela (Mexico)	5
2007	Macauley Chrisantus (Nigeria)	7
2009	Borja (Spain)	5
	Sani Emmanuel (Nigeria)	5
	Sebastian Gallegos (Uruguay)	5
	Haris Seferovic (Switzerland)	5
2011	Souleymane Coulibaly (Ivory Coast)	9
2013	**Valmir Berisha** (Sweden)	7
2015	Victor Osimhen (Nigeria)	10
2017	Rhian Brewster (England)	8

HIGH–FLYING EAGLETS

In 2013, remarkably, the teams that finished first, second and third, respectively in Group F, ended the tournament in that order. Nigeria's Golden Eaglets won in fine style to complete a memorable year in which the seniors won the African Cup of Nations and qualified for the FIFA World Cup finals. The unbeaten juniors crushed Mexico 3-0 in the final. In addition star forward Kelechi Iheanacho was named best player and Dele Alampasu top goalkeeper. Sweden, thanks in part to top-scorer Valmir Berisha (seven goals), finished third in their first-ever appearance in the finals.

GOMEZ AT HOME

Mexico became the first host country to lift the FIFA U-17 World Cup trophy on home soil, when they beat Uruguay 2-0 in the final in the Azteca Stadium in Mexico City in July 2011. The Golden Ball award for the tournament's best player went to Mexican winger **Julio Gomez**, whose brace against Germany in the semi-final including a spectacular bicycle-kick for the last-minute winner – though he played only ten minutes of the final, as a substitute, after picking up an injury in the previous game.

INDIAN OUTREACH

International football broke through another barrier when India played host to the world game for the first time, staging the 2017 FIFA U-17 World Cup. Despite foreign perceptions of Indian sports fans as caring about only cricket and hockey, a record 1.3 million fans attended the matches in New Delhi, Goa, Guwahati, Kochi, Mumbai and Kolkata, which staged the final where England defeated Spain 5-2. This exceeded the 1.2m fans in China in 1985 and was more than double the attendance at the 2015 finals in Chile. FIFA tournaments boss Jaime Yarza hailed it as a "fantastic tournament", while Indian officials immediately announced an intention to bid for the U-20 tournament.

HOSTS AND FINAL RESULTS
(Host country)

1985	(China) Nigeria 2 West Germany 0
1987	(Canada) USSR 1 Nigeria 1 (aet: USSR win 4-2 on penalties)
1989	(Scotland) Saudi Arabia 2 Scotland 2 (aet: Saudi Arabia win 5-4 on penalties)
1991	(Italy) Ghana 1 Spain 0
1993	(Japan) Nigeria 2 Ghana 1
1995	(Ecuador) Ghana 3 Brazil 2
1997	(Egypt) Brazil 2 Ghana 1
1999	(New Zealand) Brazil 0 Australia 0 (aet: Brazil win 8-7 on penalties)
2001	(Trinidad & Tobago) France 3 Nigeria 0
2003	(Finland) Brazil 1 Spain 0
2005	(Peru) Mexico 3 Brazil 0
2007	(South Korea) Nigeria 0 Spain 0 (aet: Nigeria win 3-0 on penalties)
2009	(Nigeria) Switzerland 1 Nigeria 0
2011	(Mexico) Mexico 2 Uruguay 0
2013	(United Arab Emirates) Nigeria 3 Mexico 0
2015	(Chile) Nigeria 2 Mali 0
2017	(India) England 5 Spain 2

FIFA CONFEDERATIONS CUP

The FIFA Confederations Cup has assumed numerous guises over the years. In 1992 and 1995 it was played in Saudi Arabia and featured a collection of continental champions. From 1997 to 2003 FIFA staged a tournament every two years. The tournament was played in its current format for the first time in Germany in 2005. It is now celebrated throughout the football world as the Championship of Champions.

OVERALL TOP SCORERS

1	Cuauhtemoc Blanco (Mexico)	9
=	Ronaldinho (Brazil)	9
3	Fernando Torres (Spain)	8
4	Romario (Brazil)	7
=	Adriano (Brazil)	7
6	Marzouk Al-Otaibi (Saudi Arabia)	6
=	David Villa (Spain)	6
8	Alex (Brazil)	5
=	John Aloisi (Australia)	5
=	Luis Fabiano (Brazil)	5
=	Fred (Brazil)	5
=	Vladimir Smicer (Czech Republic)	5
=	Robert Pires (France)	5

TREBLE DEUTSCH

Germany's first FIFA Confederations Cup triumph in 2017 – they beat Chile 1-0 in the final – completed a remarkable treble. In 2014 coach Joachim Low's men won the FIFA World Cup for the fourth time and, as world champions, qualified for the 2017 Confederations Cup in Russia. Two days before the final in St Petersburg, Germany's under-21s won the European title in Poland. Borussia Monchengladbach striker **Lars Stindl** scored the only goal of the final, just as he had done against the same opponents in a group game when it ended as a 1-1 draw.

TOURNAMENT TOP SCORERS

1992	Gabriel Batistuta (Argentina), Bruce Murray (USA) 2
1995	Luis Garcia (Mexico) 3
1997	Romario (Brazil) 7
1999	Ronaldinho (Brazil), Cuauhtemoc Blanco (Mexico), Marzouq Al-Otaibi (Saudi Arabia) 6
2001	Shaun Murphy (Australia), Eric Carriere (France), Robert Pires (France), Patrick Vieira (France), Sylvain Wiltord (France), Takayuki Suzuki (Japan), Hwang Sun-Hong (South Korea) 2
2003	Thierry Henry (France) 4
2005	Adriano (Brazil) 5
2009	Luis Fabiano (Brazil) 5
2013	Fernando Torres (Spain) 5 Fred (Brazil) 5
2017	Leon Goretzka (Germany) 3 Lars Stindl (Germany) 3 Timo Werner (Germany) 3

FIT FOR A KING

Before being rebranded as the FIFA Confederations Cup, a tournament bringing together the continental champions of the world was known as the King Fahd Cup and was hosted in Saudi Arabia. Copa America holders Argentina reached both finals, beating their hosts in the first in 1992 thanks to goals by Leonardo Rodriguez, Claudio Caniggia and Diego Simeone. Only four teams took part in the 1992 event, with the United States and the Ivory Coast also represented, but world champions Germany and European champions Holland did not participate. In 1995, a six-team version was won by European champions Denmark. The current eight-team format, with two groups and knockout semi-finals, was adopted in 2005.

TON-UP SUPERSTARS

Andrea Pirlo and Diego Forlan both celebrated their 100th international appearance at the 2013 Confederations Cup. Italy playmaker Pirlo scored the *Azzurri*'s first goal in their opening 2-1 win over Mexico in Maracana. Forlan marked his own achievement (becoming the first Uruguayan to reach 100 caps) by hitting a brilliant left-footed drive which proved the decisive goal in a 2-1 victory over Nigeria.

NO STOPPING NEYMAR

The 2013 Confederations Cup crowned a memorable six months for Brazilian striker Neymar. In January he had been voted South American Footballer of the Year for the second successive year and in June he agreed to leave Santos and take up a five-year contract with Spanish champions Barcelona. In one of his farewell appearances in Brazil, Neymar da Silva Santos Junior struck the first goal of the Confederations Cup in only the third minute of the tournament's opening match against Japan. Neymar scored in each of Brazil's group matches and then again in the defeat of Spain in the final.

HIGH-TECH INSURANCE

FIFA used the 2017 Confederations Cup as a high-visibility trial for the experimental video refereeing system. Referees' chairman Pierluigi Collina reported six game-changing mistakes had been corrected in the 16 matches. Controversy concerned mainly the time taken to reach video decisions. The 2013 tournament in Brazil had seen goal-line technology used for the first time in a FIFA tournament.

BURSTING A SOUTH SEA BUBBLE

Minnows Tahiti suffered the heaviest defeat in Confederations Cup history when they crashed 10-0 to Spain in the 2013 tournament in Brazil. The South Pacific part-timers – including an accountant, a carpenter and a teacher – were not too upset, however. None of them had ever even dreamed of playing in the legendary Maracana or against the world and European champions and now they had done both in one match. The Oceania champions also conceded a cup record 24 goals in their three games, with Jonathan Tehau scoring their historic single goal, against Nigeria, in return. The defeat by Spain equalled the Cup's largest single-match aggregate: in 1999, Brazil thrashed Saudi Arabia 8-2.

BRILLIANT BRAZIL

Brazil's 3-0 demolition of world and European champions Spain in the 2013 final in Maracana enhanced their historical command of the Confederations Cup. Their 12th consecutive win in the competition saw Luiz Felipe Scolari's men become the first nation to land the Cup three times in a row. They scored at least three goals in each of their title match victories and are the competition's only four-times champions. Brazil set a standard off the pitch as well: record ticket sales generated a 16-match aggregate attendance of 804,659 for an average of 50,291 per game. The 68 goals averaged out at 4.25 per match, the most prolific marksmanship over the last six competitions.

CLINT MAKES AMERICA'S DAY

The United States' surprise run to the 2009 final included a shock semi-final win over Spain that ended the European champions' long unbeaten run. Heading into the match, Spain had won a record 15 international matches in a row – and gone 35 successive games unbeaten, a tally shared with Brazil. But their hopes of extending their run to 36 matches were ruined by goals from US striker Jozy Altidore and winger **Clint Dempsey**. The result put the Americans into the final of a FIFA men's senior competition for the first time.

SHARED SADNESS

The 2003 FIFA Confederations Cup was overshadowed by the tragic death of Cameroon's 28-year-old midfielder **Marc-Vivien Foe**, who collapsed on the Lyon pitch after suffering a heart attack 73 minutes into his country's semi-final win against Colombia. After Thierry Henry scored France's golden-goal winner against Cameroon in the final, he dedicated his goal to Foe, who played much of his club career in the French championship. When the trophy was presented at the Stade de France in Paris, it was jointly lifted by the captains of both teams – Marcel Desailly for France and Rigobert Song for Cameroon.

FIFA CONFEDERATIONS CUP HOSTS AND FINAL RESULTS

1997	(Host country: Saudi Arabia) Brazil 6 Argentina 0
1999	(Mexico) Mexico 4 Brazil 3
2001	(South Korea and Japan) France 1 Japan 0
2003	(France) France 1 Cameroon 0 (aet: France win on golden goal)
2005	(Germany) Brazil 4 Argentina 1
2009	(South Africa) Brazil 3 United States 2
2013	(Brazil) Brazil 3 Spain 0
2017	(Russia) Germany 1 Chile 0

FIFA CLUB WORLD CUP

As is the case with the FIFA Confederations Cup, the FIFA Club World Cup has been played in several different formats since 1960, when Real Madrid defeated Penarol. In its current guise, the competition pits the champion clubs from all six continents against each other. It has been staged on an annual basis, mostly in Japan from 2005, apart from two hostings in Abu Dhabi and in 2013 and 2014 in Morocco.

CORINTHIAN SPIRIT

Corinthians of Sao Paulo are the last Brazilian club – the last South American outfit – to have won the FIFA Club World. In 2012 Peruvian striker Paulo Guerrero scored the only goal of their semi-final victory over Egypt's Al-Ahly, and repeated the feat in the final against England's Chelsea. The Corinthians line-up included goalkeeper and player-of-the-tournament **Cassio**, as well as Danilo and Fabio Santos, a pair who had both won the tournament with Sao Paulo seven years earlier. Defeat for the European champions prevented Chelsea manager Rafael Benitez – Internazionale's winning coach in 2010 – from equalling former Barcelona boss Pep Guardiola in winning the tournament in its current guise twice. Real Madrid coach Zinedine Zidane did match Guardiola, winning in both 2016 and 2017.

WINNERS BY COUNTRY*

- 10 Brazil, Spain
- 9 Argentina, Italy
- 6 Uruguay
- 4 Germany
- 3 Netherlands
- 2 Portugal, England
- 1 Paraguay, Yugoslavia

Includes Intercontinental Cup

MOROCCO GO–AHEAD

Morocco staged the December 2014 tournament for a second successive year, despite having just withdrawn from hosting the following month's Africa Cup of Nations because of fears of the spread of the ebola virus. Organizers were happy to go ahead with the FIFA competition because none of the clubs taking part came from nations struggling to contain the disease.

THE REIGN OF SPAIN

Spain has dominated the FIFA Club World Cup since 2009. Between them current champions Real Madrid and Barcelona have won six of the last nine finals. Barcelona launched the era of Spanish supremacy by defeating Estudiantes de La Plata from Argentina, 2-1 after extra time, on goals from Pedro and Lionel Messi. They won again in 2015, while **Cristiano Ronaldo**'s Madrid triumphed three times in four years in 2014, 2016 and 2017 in three different host nations: Morocco, Japan and the UAE. Madrid have won the world title a record six times.

SIX APPEAL

Barcelona's triumph in 2009 made them the first club to lift six different major trophies in one calendar year: the FIFA Club World Cup, the UEFA Champions League, the UEFA European Super Cup, and a Spanish hat-trick of La Liga, Copa del Rey and Super Cup. This made their trophy cabinet one cup heavier than Liverpool's in 2001, when Gerard Houllier's men won the FA Cup, League Cup and Charity Shield in England and the UEFA Cup and Super Cup in Europe.

VETERAN IVAN

New Zealand's Auckland City were one of the surprises of the 2014 FIFA Club World Cup, spearheaded by 38-year-old **Ivan Vacelich** who won the bronze award for third best player at the tournament. Only Real Madrid's Sergio Ramos and Cristiano Ronaldo finished ahead of him. Auckland City finished third, the highest finish for a club from Oceania. They beat Cruz Azul on penalties, after a 1-1 draw in the third-place play-off.

SWITCHING SYSTEMS

From 1960 until 1968, the two-team Intercontinental Cup was settled, not on aggregate scores but by using a system of two points for a win and one for a draw. This meant a third, deciding match was needed in 1961, 1963, 1964 and 1967, when Racing of Argentina beat Celtic 1-0 in a bad-tempered play-off in Montevideo. From 1980 until 2004, the annual event was a single match staged in Japan before it was swallowed up in FIFA's expanded Club World Cup.

FIGURE OF EIGHT

Manchester United's 5-3 win over Gamba Osaka in the semi-final of the FIFA Club World Cup in 2008 was the highest-scoring single game in the history of the competition in all its forms – bettering the 5-2 victory over Benfica by a Santos team featuring Pele in 1962. Even more amazingly, all but two of the goals in the Manchester United–Gamba game were scored in the final 16 minutes, plus stoppage-time. United were leading 2-0 with 74 minutes gone, before a burst of goals – including two by substitute Wayne Rooney – at both ends. Manchester United became the first team to score five goals in the FIFA Club World Cup's revised format.

LONG-DISTANCE, LONG-RUNNING RIVALRY

The precursor to the modern FIFA Club World Cup was the Intercontinental Cup, also known informally as the World Club Cup and/ or the Europe–South America Cup, which pitted the champions of Europe and South America against each other. Representatives of UEFA and CONMEBOL contested the event from 1960 to 2004, but now all continental federations send at least one club to an expanded Club World Cup organized and endorsed by the world federation, FIFA. The original final, in 1960, was between Spain's Real Madrid and Uruguay's Penarol. After a goalless draw in the rain in Montevideo, Real triumphed 5-1 at their own stadium in Madrid – including three goals scored in the first eight minutes, two of them by Ferenc Puskas. The two clubs are among five sharing the record for Intercontinental Cup triumphs, with three victories apiece – the others being Argentina's Boca Juniors, Uruguay's Nacional and AC Milan of Italy. Milan were the first of the five clubs to add a FIFA Club World Cup to their tally, as the championship was first contested in 2000 (in Brazil) before it was swallowed up by the Intercontinental Cup and was instituted on an annual basis. Since then Real Madrid have won the FIFA crown three times.

THE HISTORY MEN

Several attempts to stage world club events preceded the formal start in 1960. In 1887 Scottish Cup holders Hibernian claimed the honour after beating Preston North End, then English amateur club West Auckland Town won a trophy donated by Sir Thomas Lipton in 1909 and 1922 against opposition from Italy, Germany and Switzerland. Meanwhile, Palmeiras of Brazil still press claims for recognition of a 1951 victory in an international club tournament in Rio de Janeiro.

AFRICAN DOUBLE

In 2010, for the first time in the overall event's history, a club not from Europe or South America contested the final. African champions TP Mazembe from the Democratic Republic of Congo defeated Internacional of Brazil 2-0 in the semi-finals before losing 3-0 to Italy's Internazionale. Mazembe achieved their surprise progress despite missing star striker and captain Tresor Mputu through suspension. In 2013, in Morocco, home favourite Raja Casablanca became the second African club to reach the final before losing 2-0 to Bayern Munich. A third non-European club followed up in Japan in 2016 when Kashima Antlers took Real Madrid to extra time before losing 4-2.

FIFA CLUB WORLD CUP FINALS (2000–17)

2000 Corinthians (Brazil) 0
Vasco da Gama (Brazil) 0
(aet: Corinthians win 4-3 on penalties)
2005 Sao Paulo (Brazil) 1 Liverpool (England) 0
2006 Internacional (Brazil) 1 Barcelona (Spain) 0
2007 AC Milan (Italy) 4 Boca Juniors (Argentina) 2
2008 Manchester United (England) 1
LDU Quito (Ecuador) 0
2009 Barcelona (Spain) 2
Estudiantes (Argentina) 1 (aet)
2010 Internazionale (Italy) 3
TP Mazembe (DR Congo) 0
2011 Barcelona (Spain) 4 Santos (Brazil) 0
2012 Corinthians (Brazil) 1 Chelsea (England) 0
2013 Bayern Munich (Germany) 2
Raja Casablanca (Morocco) 0
2014 Real Madrid (Spain) 2
San Lorenzo (Argentina) 0
2015 Barcelona (Spain) 3
River Plate (Argentina) 0
2016 **Real Madrid (Spain) 4**
Kashima Antlers (Japan) 2 (aet)
2017 Real Madrid (Spain) 1 Gremio (Brazil) 0

OVERALL WORLD CLUB CHAMPIONS (1960–2017*)

6 wins: Real Madrid, Spain (1960, 1998, 2002, 2014, 2016, 2017)

4 wins: AC Milan, Italy (1969, 1989, 1990, 2007)

3 wins: Penarol, Uruguay (1961, 1966, 1982); Internazionale, Italy (1964, 1965, 2010); Nacional, Uruguay (1971, 1980, 1988); Bayern Munich, West Germany/Germany (1976, 2001, 2013); Boca Juniors, Argentina (1977, 2000, 2003); Sao Paulo, Brazil (1992, 1993, 2005); Barcelona, Spain (2009, 2011, 2015)

2 wins: Santos, Brazil (1962, 1963); Ajax, Netherlands (1972, 1995); Independiente, Argentina (1973, 1984); Juventus, Italy (1985, 1996); Porto, Portugal (1987, 2004); Manchester United, England (1999, 2008); Corinthians, Brazil (2000, 2012)

1 win: Racing Club, Argentina (1967); Estudiantes, Argentina (1968); Feyenoord, Netherlands (1970); Atletico de Madrid, Spain (1974); Olimpia Asuncion, Paraguay (1979); Flamengo, Brazil (1981); Gremio, Brazil (1983); River Plate, Argentina (1986); Red Star Belgrade, Yugoslavia (1991); Velez Sarsfield, Argentina (1994); Borussia Dortmund, Germany (1997); Internacional, Brazil (2006)

* = not contested in 1975 and 1978

MEN'S OLYMPIC FOOTBALL TOURNAMENT

First played at the 1900 Olympic Games in Paris, although not recognized by FIFA as an official tournament until London 1908, the men's Olympic football tournament was played in strict accordance with the Games' strong amateur tradition until 1984, when pros were allowed to play. The competition is now an Under-23 event – with allowance for three over-age players – to give rising stars the chance of major tournament experience. Since World War 2, however, no Olympic champions have won the FIFA World Cup within 10 years.

CZECH OUT

The climax of the 1920 Olympic Games tournament is the only time a major international football final has been abandoned. Czechoslovakia's players walked off the pitch minutes before half-time, in protest at the decisions made by 65-year-old English referee John Lewis – including the dismissal of Czech player Karel Steiner. Belgium, who were 2-0 up at the time, were awarded the victory, before Spain beat Holland 3-1 in a play-off for silver.

MEN'S OLYMPIC FOOTBALL FINALS

1896 Not played
1900 (Paris, France)
Gold: Upton Park FC (GB) Silver: USFSA XI (France) Bronze: Universite Libre de Bruxelles (Belgium) (only two exhibition matches played)
1904 (St Louis, US)
Gold: Galt FC (Canada) Silver: Christian Brothers College (US) Bronze: St Rose Parish (US) (only five exhibition matches played)
1908 (London, England)
Great Britain 2 Denmark 0 (Bronze: Netherlands)
1912 (Stockholm, Sweden)
Great Britain 4 Denmark 2 (Bronze: Netherlands)
1916 Not played
1920 (Antwerp, Belgium) Belgium 2 Czechoslovakia 0
(Gold: Belgium, Silver: Spain, Bronze: Netherlands)
1924 (Paris, France)
Uruguay 3 Switzerland 0 (Bronze: Sweden)
1928 (Amsterdam, Netherlands)
Uruguay 1 Argentina 1; Uruguay 2 Argentina 1 (Bronze: Italy)
1932 Not played
1936 (Berlin, Germany) Italy 2 Austria 1 (aet) (Bronze: Norway)
1940 Not played
1944 Not played
1948 (London, England) Sweden 3 Yugoslavia 1 (Bronze: Denmark)
1952 (Helsinki, Finland) Hungary 2 Yugoslavia 0 (Bronze: Sweden)
1956 (Melbourne, Australia) USSR 1 Yugoslavia 0 (Bronze: Bulgaria)
1960 (Rome, Italy) Yugoslavia 3 Denmark 1 (Bronze: Hungary)
1964 (Tokyo, Japan) Hungary 2 Czechoslovakia 1 (Bronze: Germany)
1968 (Mexico City, Mexico) Hungary 4 Bulgaria 1 (Bronze: Japan)
1972 (Munich, West Germany) Poland 2 Hungary 1 (Bronze: USSR/East Germany)
1976 (Montreal, Canada) East Germany 3 Poland 1 (Bronze: USSR)
1980 (Moscow, USSR) Czechoslovakia 1 East Germany 0 (Bronze: USSR)
1984 (Los Angeles, USA) France 2 Brazil 0 (Bronze: Yugoslavia)
1988 (Seoul, South Korea) USSR 2 Brazil 1 (Bronze: West Germany)
1992 (Barcelona, Spain) Spain 3 Poland 2 (Bronze: Ghana)
1996 (Atlanta, USA) Nigeria 3 Argentina 2 (Bronze: Brazil)
2000 (Sydney, Australia) **Cameroon** 2 Spain 2
(Cameroon win 5-3 on penalties) (Bronze: Chile)
2004 (Athens, Greece) Argentina 1 Paraguay 0 (Bronze: Italy)
2008 (Beijing, China) **Argentina 1** Nigeria 0 (Bronze: Brazil)
2012 (London, England) Mexico 2 Brazil 1 (Bronze: South Korea)
2016 (Rio de Janeiro, Brazil): Brazil 1 Germany 1
Brazil 5-4 on penalties after extra time (Bronze: Nigeria)

BARCELONA BOUND

Future Barcelona team-mates Samuel Eto'o and Xavi scored penalties for opposing sides in 2000, when Cameroon and Spain contested the first Olympic final to be settled by a shoot-out. Ivan Amaya was the only player to miss, handing Cameroon gold.

NEYMAR'S CROWNING GLORY

Soccer is usually a sideshow at the Olympic Games but, in 2016, it took centre stage in football-mad Rio de Janeiro. Host Brazil's bid to make amends for three final failures and win gold for the first time succeeded as they defeated World Cup winners Germany in the final. Two years earlier, at Belo Horizonte, Brazil had been routed 7-1 by the Germans, so the nerves were even more acute. The 2016 gold medal game, like the 2014 World Cup final, was played at the Maracana stadium. After 120 minutes, the score was 1-1, Neymar's first half goal being cancelled out by Max Meyer after an hour. It meant that penalties would decide the men's gold medal for only the second time. After the first eight kicks were all scored, Weverton saved from Nils Petersen. It was left to Brazil's superstar skipper Neymar to make history and he duly beat Timo Horn to win Brazil's first Olympic football gold medal.

BLOC PARTY

Eastern European countries dominated the Olympic Games football competitions from 1948 to 1980, when professional players were officially banned from taking part. Teams comprising so-called "state amateurs" from the Eastern Bloc took 23 of the 27 medals available during those years.

AFRICAN AMBITION

Ghana became the first African country to win an Olympic football medal, picking up bronze in 1992, but Nigeria went even better four years later by claiming the continent's first Olympic football gold medal – thanks to Emmanuel Amunike's stoppage-time winner against Argentina. Nigeria's triumph came as a huge surprise to many – especially as their rival teams included such future world stars as Brazil's Ronaldo and Roberto Carlos, Argentina's Hernan Crespo and Roberto Ayala, Italy's Fabio Cannavaro and Gianluigi Buffon, and France's Robert Pires and Patrick Vieira. Future FIFA World Cup or UEFA European Championship winners to have played at Summer Olympics include France's Michel Platini and Patrick Battiston (at the Montreal Games in 1976); West Germany's Andreas Brehme and Brazil's Dunga (Los Angeles, 1984); Brazil's Taffarel, Bebeto and Romario and West Germany's Jurgen Klinsmann (Seoul, 1988); France's Vieira, Pires and Sylvain Wiltord, Italy's Cannavaro, Buffon and Alessandro Nesta, and Brazil's Roberto Carlos, Rivaldo and Ronaldo (Atlanta, 1996); Italy's Gianluca Zambrotta and Spain's Xavi, Carles Puyol and Joan Capdevila (Sydney, 2000); and Italy's Daniele De Rossi, Andrea Pirlo and Alberto Gilardino and Portugal's Cristiano Ronaldo and Bruno Alves (Athens, 2004).

LAPPING IT UP

Until London 2012, Uruguay had a perfect Olympic football record. They won gold on the first two occasions they took part (1924 and 1928). Those Games were seen as a world championship and helped prompt FIFA into organizing the first World Cup in 1930 – also won by Uruguay, who included 1924 and 1928 gold medallists Jose Nasazzi, Jose Andrade and **Hector Scarone** (right) in their squad. Uruguay's 1924 champions are thought to have pioneered the lap of honour.

LONDON CALLING

Mexico were the unexpected winners when Wembley Stadium became the first venue to stage two men's Olympic Games football finals as part of London 2012. The old stadium hosted the showpiece game when England's capital held the Olympics in 1948 and London is also now the only city to stage three separate summer Olympics, though the football final back in 1908 was played at White City. **Oribe Peralta** scored both goals as Mexico – managed by Luis Tena, the senior team's assistant coach – defeated Brazil 2-1 in the 2012 final at the renovated venue. A late reply by Hulk was little consolation for the highly-fancied South Americans, though Brazil's Leandro Damiao did end as six-goal top scorer. London 2012 matches were shared with cities away from the English capital, including Hampden Park in Glasgow, Old Trafford in Manchester, St James' Park in Newcastle and the City of Coventry Stadium. A united British team competed in the Olympic finals for the first time since 1960, featuring English Premier League stars such as Ryan Giggs and Craig Bellamy.

PART 7:
WOMEN'S FOOTBALL

ORGANISED WOMEN'S FOOTBALL has taken vast steps since it was banned in England by The Football Association in 1921. The latest high-profile demonstration of its popular modern surge was the Dutch victory as hosts in the UEFA Women's European Championship in 2017.

More than 30 million women now play football across the globe and social media bubbled over in excitement when Lieke Martens helped inspire the Netherlands to a victory which ended Germany's six-title monopoly of the European crown. Europe will provide a focus for the women's game again in 2019 when France hosts the ever-more-popular FIFA Women's World Cup.

Such progress is long overdue considering the time wasted along the way. Although women's football was recorded in England more than a century ago, The Football Association banned it in 1921. That led to the creation of an independent women's association with a cup competition of its own.

Women's football developed simultaneously elsewhere and the surge of interest ultimately led, in the early 1980s, to the first formal European Championships and, in 1988, to a FIFA invitational tournament in Chinese Taipei.

FIFA launched an inaugural world championship in 1991, which was won by the US to establish their claim to primacy in the game. The Americans duly hosted the next FIFA Women's World Cup, which saw a record crowd of 90,185 celebrate their shoot-out victory over China in the final in Pasadena. They underlined their No.1 status by winning the first women's football gold medal at the Olympic Games in 1996, taking silver in 2000 and gold again in 2004, 2008 and 2012.

FIFA set up a world youth championship in 2002, initially for players aged Under-19, later amended to Under-20, and added an Under-17 event to the international calendar in 2008. Women's football, once considered a fleeting sporting fashion, is here to stay.

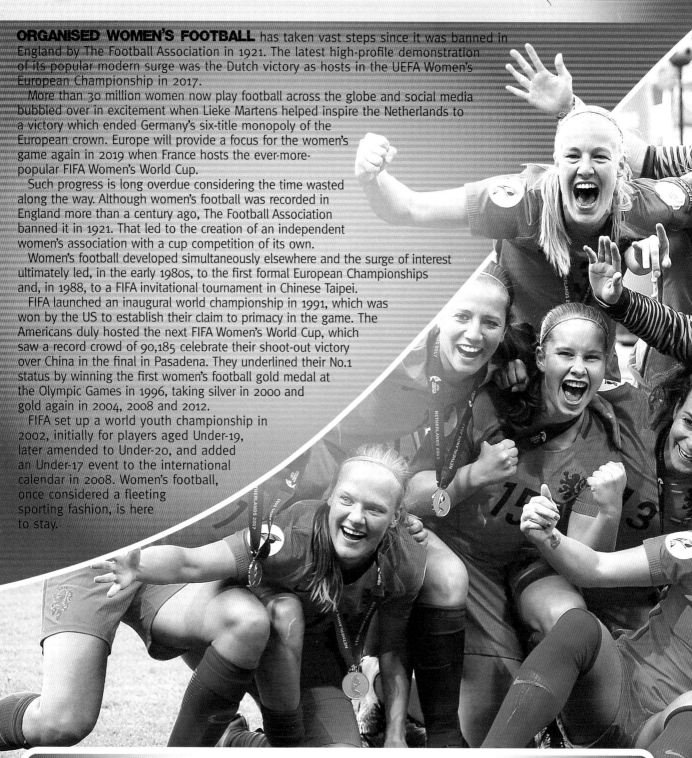

The Dutch hosts enjoy that winning feeling after defeating Denmark 4-2 to land the UEFA Women's Championship crown on home soil in Enschede.

FIFA WOMEN'S WORLD CUP

The first FIFA Women's World Cup finals were held in China in 1991. Twelve teams, divided into three groups of four, took part, with the top two in each group, plus the two "best losers" going through to the knockout quarter-finals. The tournament was expanded in 1999 to include 16 teams in four groups. There was further expansion in 2015, with Canada as hosts, to 24 teams in six groups of four, with the top two plus four best third-placed teams reaching the knockout second round.

HAVELANGE'S DREAM COMES TRUE

The FIFA Women's World Cup was the brainchild of former FIFA president João Havelange. The tournament began as an experimental competition in 1991 and has expanded in size and importance ever since. The success of the 1999 finals in the United States was a turning point for the tournament, which now attracts big crowds and worldwide TV coverage. The USA and Norway – countries in which football (soccer) is one of the most popular girls' sports – dominated the early competitions. The Americans won the inaugural competition and the 1999 tournament. Norway lifted the trophy in 1995. Germany became the dominant force in the new century, winning the trophy in 2003 and retaining it in 2007. The recent emergence of challengers such as Brazil, China and Sweden underlined the worldwide spread and appeal of the women's game.

PITCH PERFECT

There was controversy ahead of the 2015 finals over the decision to play all ties on artificial turf. FIFA and the Canadian organisers justified this on the grounds of climatic challenges and the need for a metaphorical level playing field. Goal-line technology was also employed for the first time.

US CELEBRATE FIRST ACHIEVEMENT

The USA's victory in the inaugural FIFA Women's World Cup in 1991 made them the first USA team to win a world football title. The USA men's best performance came when they reached the semi-finals in 1930, losing 6-1 to Argentina.

ASIA MAJORS

Japan's women became the country's first football side to claim a FIFA world title when they upset the odds to win the 2011 FIFA Women's World Cup, beating favourites USA 3-1 on penalties after a 2-2 draw. Player of the tournament Homare Sawa had levelled the scores with just three minutes of extra-time remaining, before **Saki Kumagai** struck the winning spot-kick in the shoot-out. Japan had failed to win in the two teams' previous 25 meetings, losing 22 and drawing three. The Japanese women's previous best FIFA World Cup performance had been reaching the quarter-finals in 1995. The 2011 generation's triumph was all the more moving, as they dedicated the victory to victims of the devastating tsunami that had struck Japan in March that year.

FIFA WOMEN'S WORLD CUP FINALS

Year	Venue	Winners	Runners-up	Score
1991	Ghuangzhou	USA	Norway	2-1
1995	Stockholm	Norway	Germany	2-0
1999	Los Angeles	USA	China	0-0
USA won 5-4 in penalty shoot-out				
2003	Los Angeles	Germany	Sweden	2-1 (aet)
2007	Shanghai	Germany	Brazil	2-0
2011	Frankfurt	Japan	USA	2-2 (aet)
Japan won 3-1 in penalty shoot-out				
2015	Vancouver	USA	Japan	5-2

THIRD–PLACE PLAY–OFF MATCHES

Year	Venue	Winners	Losers	Score
1991	Guangzhou	Sweden	Germany	4-0
1995	Gavle	USA	China	2-0
1999	Los Angeles	Brazil	Norway	0-0
Brazil won 5-4 in penalty shoot-out				
2003	Los Angeles	USA	Canada	3-1
2007	Shanghai	USA	Norway	4-1
2011	Sinsheim	Sweden	France	2-1
2015	Montreal	England	Germany	1-0

FOUR GAIN DOUBLE MEDALS

Four of the USA's 1991 winners were in the team that beat China on penalties in the 1999 final: **Mia Hamm** (left), Michelle Akers, Kristine Lilly and Julie Foudy.

WINNERS KEEP SQUAD TOGETHER

Six Germany players appeared in their 2003 and 2007 final wins: **Kerstin Stegemann**, Birgit Prinz, Renate Lingor, Ariane Hingst and Kerstin Garefrekes started both games, while Martina Muller came on as a substitute both times.

GERMANS SET DEFENSIVE RECORD

In 2007, Germany became the first team to make a successful defence of the FIFA Women's World Cup. They also set another record. They went through the tournament – six games and 540 minutes – without conceding a single goal. As a result, their goalkeeper Nadine Angerer overhauled Italy keeper Walter Zenga's record of 517 minutes unbeaten in the 1990 men's finals. The last player to score against the Germans had been Sweden's **Hanna Ljungberg** in the 41st minute of the 2003 final. The run ended when Christine Sinclair of Cananda scored after 82 minutes of Germany's opening game in 2011.

SPANISH REBELLION

Spain's FIFA Women's World Cup finals debut quickly turned sour. They won only one point from their three group games in Canada in 2015 and were eliminated. On returning home, the players blamed veteran coach Ignacio Quereda, citing insufficient preparation for the cooler climate, lack of warm-up friendlies and poor analysis of opponents. They concluded: "We need a change. We have conveyed this to the coach and his staff."

CANADA'S RECORD TURNOUT

Canada's enthusiasm for the 2015 FIFA Women's World Cup broke many records. The total attendance of 1,353,506 was the best for any FIFA women's competition, beating the previous Women's World Cup total of 1,194,215, set in the USA in 1999 (albeit from 20 more matches). The 54,027 who watched the hosts play England in the quarter-finals in Vancouver was a Canadian record for a women's game and one of seven matches to top 50,000 fans.

TOP TEAMS

Country	Winners	Runners-up	Third
USA	3	1	3
Germany	2	1	-
Norway	1	1	1
Japan	1	1	-
Brazil	-	1	1
Sweden	-	1	2
China	-	1	-
England	-	-	1

TOP TEAM SCORERS

1991:	USA	25
1995:	Norway	23
1999:	China	19
2003:	Germany	25
2007:	Germany	21
2011:	USA	13
2015:	Germany	20

TOP ALL-TIME TEAM SCORERS

1	USA	112
2	Germany	111
3	Norway	86
4	Brazil	59
=	Sweden	59

THE FIRST GAME

The first-ever game in the FIFA Women's World Cup finals was hosts China's 4-0 win over Norway at Guangzhou on 16 November 1991. A 65,000 crowd watched the game.

THE REGULAR EIGHT

Eight teams have played in all six finals tournaments – Brazil, China, Germany, Japan, Nigeria, Norway, Sweden and the United States.

NORWAY POST LONGEST WIN RUN

Norway, winners in 1995, hold the record for the most consecutive matchtime wins in the finals – ten. Their run started with an 8-0 win over Nigeria on 6 June 1995 and continued until 30 June 1999 when they beat Sweden 3-1 in the quarter-finals. It ended when they lost 5-0 to China in the semi-finals on 4 July.

UNBEATEN CHINA SENT HOME

In 1999, China became the only team to go through the finals without losing a match, yet go home empty-handed. The Chinese won their group games, 2-1 against Sweden, 7-0 against Ghana and 3-1 against Australia. They beat Russia 2-0 in the quarter-finals and Norway 5-0 in the semi-finals, but they lost on penalties to the USA in the final after a 0-0 draw. In 2011, Japan became the first team to lift the trophy despite losing a match in the first-round – as had runners-up the USA.

FIFTEEN ON TARGET FOR NORWAY

Norway hold the record for scoring in the most consecutive games – 15. They began their sequence with a 4-0 win over New Zealand on 19 November 1991 and ended it with a 3-1 win over Sweden in the quarter-finals on 30 June 1999.

HAT-TRICKS AT THE DOUBLE

Germany are the only team to have twice scored double figures in a game at the finals. The first time was an 11-0 thrashing of Argentina in Shanghai in the 2007 finals, when Birgit Prinz and Sandra Smisek both scored hat-tricks. Then, in Canada in 2015, the Germans crushed Ivory Coast 10-0 in the first round with trebles for strikers Celia Sasic and Anja Mittag.

THE LOWEST CROWD...

The lowest attendance for any match at the finals came on 8 June 1995, when only 250 spectators watched the 3-3 draw between Canada and Nigeria at Helsingborg.

AMERICANS BANK ON LLOYD

Carli Lloyd was the runaway winner of the Golden Ball as star player of the 2015 World Cup finals. She crowned a decade of international football by scoring a hat-trick in the 5-2 defeat of Japan in the final. Best of all was the hat-trick goal which Lloyd struck from the halfway line. Amazingly, this goal was the United States' fourth of the final and the match was only 16 minutes old. Previously she had helped the US finish third and runners-up at the 2007 and 2011 Women's World Cups respectively. The 33-year-old had also scored the gold medal-winning goals in the finals of both the 2008 and 2012 Olympic Games.

QUICKEST RED AND YELLOW

The record for the fastest red card is held by Australia's Alicia Ferguson, who was sent off in the second minute of their 3-1 defeat by China in New York on 26 June 1999. North Korea's Ri Hyang Ok received the quickest yellow card, in the first minute of their 2-1 defeat by Nigeria in Los Angeles on 20 June 1999.

THE FASTEST GOAL

Lena Videkull of Sweden netted the fastest goal in finals history when she scored after 30 seconds in their 8-0 win over Japan at Foshan on 19 November 1991. Canada's **Melissa Tancredi** struck the second-fastest goal – after 37 seconds – in their 2-2 draw with Australia in Chengdu on 20 September 2007.

PRINZ SEIZES FINALS CHANCE

In 2007, Birgit Prinz became the first player to appear in three FIFA Women's World Cup finals. She was also the youngest player to appear in a FIFA Women's World Cup final. The Germany forward was 17 years 336 days when she started in the 2-0 defeat by Norway in 1995. Team-mate Sandra Smisek was just 14 days older. The oldest finalist was Sweden's Kristin Bengtsson, who was 33 years 273 days when her side lost to Germany in the 2003 final.

HOT SHOT AKERS SETS THE STANDARD

US forward Michelle Akers (born in Santa Clara on 1 February 1966) hold the record for the most goals scored in a single finals tournament – ten in 1991. She also set a record for the most goals scored in one match, with five in the USA's 7-0 quarter-final win over Taiwan at Foshan on 24 November 1991. Akers grabbed both goals in the USA's 2-1 victory in the final, including their 78th-minute winner. Judges voted her as FIFA's Women's Player of the 20th Century.

THE FASTEST SUBSTITUTIONS

The fastest substitutions in finals history were both timed at six minutes. Taiwan's defender Liu Hsiu Mei was subbed by reserve goalkeeper Li Chyn Hong in their 2-0 win over Nigeria in Jiangmen on 21 November 1991. Li replaced No. 1 keeper Lin Hui Fang, who had been sent off. Therese Lundin subbed for the injured Hanna Ljungberg, also after six minutes, in Sweden's 2-0 win over Ghana at Chicago on 26 June 1999.

DANILOVA THE YOUNGEST SCORER

The youngest scorer at the finals was Russia's Elena Danilova. She was 16 years 96 days when she scored her country's only goal in the 2003 quarter-final against Germany at Portland on 2 October. The Germans scored seven in reply.

MORACE HITS FIRST HAT-TRICK

Carolina Morace of Italy scored the first hat-trick in finals history when she netted the last three goals in Italy's 5-0 win over Taiwan at Jiangmen on 17 November 1991.

ENGLAND'S GLORY IN CANADA

England flew home from Canada after finishing third in their most successful Women's World Cup. Coach Mark Sampson, who replaced Hope Powell after a disappointing 2013 European Championship, saw his team stutter in their opening game, losing 1-0 to France. They recovered to beat Mexico and Colombia, both times 2-1, to finish group runners-up and reach the knockout stage. That 2-1 scoreline remained the theme as England beat Norway and then hosts Canada by that score to reach their first-ever FIFA Women's World Cup semi-final, **Lucy Bronze** scoring the decisive second goal in both games. But the semi-final ended tearfully in a 2-1 extra-time defeat by holders Japan. Laura Bassett settled it inadvertently with an own goal two minutes into added time at the end of the second half. England recovered morale magnificently to beat European champions Germany 1-0 for third place with a Fara Williams penalty in the second period of extra-time deciding the bronze medal. Sampson compared his team with the World Cup-winning men of 1966, saying: "Moments from 1966 like the Hurst hat-trick, the Moore tackle – these players will be remembered forever for this tournament. I really hope, in 50 or 60 years, people mark this team as legends of the country."

FIFA WOMEN'S WORLD CUP
PLAYER OF THE TOURNAMENT

Year	Venue	Winner
1991	China	Carin Jennings (USA)
1995	Sweden	Hege Riise (Norway)
1999	USA	Sun Wen (China)
2003	USA	Birgit Prinz (Germany)
2007	China	Marta (Brazil)
2011	Germany	Homare Sawa (Japan)
2015	Canada	Carli Lloyd (USA)

FIFA WOMEN'S WORLD CUP FINALS TOP SCORER

1991	Michelle Akers (USA)	10
1995	Ann-Kristin Aarones (Norway)	6
1999	Sissi (Brazil)	7
2003	Birgit Prinz (Germany)	7
2007	Marta (Brazil)	7
2011	Homare Sawa (Japan)	5
2015	Celia Sasic (Germany)	6
	Carli Llloyd (USA)	6

ALL–TIME TOP SCORERS

1	Marta (Brazil)	15
2	Birgit Prinz (Germany)	14
=	Abby Wambach (USA)	14
4	Michelle Akers (USA)	12
5	Sun Wen (China)	11
=	Bettina Wiegmann (Germany)	11
7	Ann-Kristin Aarones (Norway)	10
=	Heidi Mohr (Germany)	10
9	Linda Medalen (Norway)	9
=	Hege Riise (Norway)	9
=	Christine Sinclair	9

FIFA WOMEN'S WORLD CUP WINNING CAPTAINS

1991	April Heinrichs (USA)
1995	Heidi Store (Norway)
1999	Carla Overbeck (USA)
2003	Bettina Wiegmann (Germany)
2007	Birgit Prinz (Germany)
2011	Homare Sawa (Japan)
2015	Christie Rampone (USA)

MOST FINALS APPEARANCES (BY GAMES)

1	Kristine Lilly (USA)	30
2	Abby Wambach (USA)	25
3	Formiga (Brazil)	24
=	Julie Foudy (USA)	24
=	Birgit Prinz (Germany)	24
=	Homare Sawa (Japan)	24
7	Joy Fawcett (USA)	23
=	Mia Hamm (USA)	23
9	Bente Nordby (Norway)	22
=	Hege Riise (Norway)	22
=	Bettina Wiegmann (Germany)	22

TEAM PLAYERS

Only six players have been named in the tournament all-star teams at two separate FIFA Women's World Cups: China's Wang Liping, Germany's Bettina Wiegmann, Brazil's Marta, Japan's Aya Miyama and the USA's Shannon Boxx and Hope Solo. In both 2007 and 2011, all-star squads were chosen, but FIFA reverted to 11 players in 2015.

US RECORD AUDIENCE

The United States' FIFA Women's World Cup 2015 defeat of Japan was the most-watched football match – men or women – in US history. Fox Sports registered almost 23 million viewers, an increase of 77 percent compared with the 2011 final between the same teams. Telemundo recorded its Spanish-language audience at 1.27 million viewers.

LAST-DITCH FIRST

Japan's 2011 success was bittersweet at the last for defender **Azuza Iwashimizu**, whose red card in stoppage-time of extra-time against the USA made her the first player to be sent off in a FIFA Women's World Cup final. Her punishment was for a foul on American attacker Alex Morgan, just minutes after Japan had equalised at 2-2.

THE FIRST SENDING OFF

Taiwan goalkeeper Lin Hui Fang was the first player to be sent off in finals history. She was red-carded after six minutes of Taiwan's 2-0 win over Nigeria in Jiangmen on 21 November 1991.

SUN RATTLES THE MEN

In 1999, Shanghai-born **Sun Wen** became the first woman player ever to be nominated for the Asian Footballer of the Year award, following her performances in China's run to the 1999 FIFA Women's World Cup final. Three years later, she won the Internet poll for FIFA's Women's Player of the 20th Century.

UEFA WOMEN'S EUROPEAN CHAMPIONSHIP

⚽ ORANGE FEVER LIGHTS UP EUROPE

Hosts Netherlands celebrated victory in the European women's championship for the first time in their history in 2017 by defeating Denmark 4-2 to the delight of a capacity, orange-bedecked crowd in Enschede. Some 13 members of the 23-strong Dutch squad brought to the party their experience of playing with foreign clubs – notably goalkeeper Sari van Veenendaal and centre-forward **Vivianne Miedema** (both Arsenal), midfielder Jackie Groenen (Frankfurt) and the tournament's finest player in Barcelona left winger Lieke Martens. Head coach Sarina Wiegman's team won all three group games without conceding a goal ahead of the Danes, whom they beat 1-0 first time around. Miedema scored once in each of the subsequent knockout victories over Sweden and England then two in the final triumph over Denmark.

⚽ END OF AN ERA FOR GERMANS

Germany's 2-1 defeat by Denmark in the quarter-finals of UEFA Euro 2017 ended an astonishing run of success featuring six successive titles won since 1995. Their exit was a bad start to a new job for head coach Steffi Jones, who had succeeded title-winning specialist Silvia Neid in 2016. Neid appeared an impossible act to match. She had been a European champion three times as a player and twice as coach as well as being voted FIFA Women's Coach of the Year on three occasions.

⚽ THE ALL–TIME CHAMPIONS

Number	Country	(years)
8	Germany	(1989, 1991, 1995, 1997, 2001, 2005, 2009, 2013)
2	Norway	(1987, 1993)
1	Netherlands	(2017)
=	Sweden	(1984)

HOSTS AND FINALS

Year	(host)	Final
1984	(no host/two legs)	Sweden bt England 1-0, 0-1 (4-3 on pens)
1987	(Norway)	Norway 2 Sweden 1
1989	(W Germany)	W Germany 4, Norway 1
1991	(Denmark)	Germany 3 Norway 1 (after extra time)
1993	(Italy)	Norway 1 Italy 0
1995	(Germany)	Germany 3 Sweden 2
1997	(Norway/Sweden)	Germany 2 Italy 0
2001	(Germany)	Germany 1 Sweden 0 golden goal after extra time)
2005	(England)	Germany 3 Norway 1
2009	(Finland)	Germany 6 England 2
2013	(Sweden)	Germany 1 Norway 0
2017	(Netherlands)	Netherlands 4 Denmark 2

⚽ NADIM'S LONG JOURNEY TO STARDOM

Forward **Nadia Nadim** grabbed the spotlight from even experienced team-mate Pernille Harder as Denmark reached the Euro women's final for the first time after five previous semi-final exits. Nadim, her mother and sisters had fled a war-torn Afghanistan in 2000 when she was only 11. They sought refugee status in Denmark, where Nadim began playing football for Aalborg. Her talent prompted the Danish federation to obtain a special regulatory exemption from FIFA so she could play for her adopted country. Her starring role at Euro 2017, where she opened the scoring against the Netherlands in the final, prompted a transfer to Manchester City in the FA Women's Super League.

RECORD–BREAKING EUROS

The 2017 UEFA Women's European Championship set all sorts of records for European federation UEFA. The total aggregate attendance of 240,045 was a record exceeding the 216,888 in 2013. Away from the stadia, the total television audience hit 165m for a final screened in 80 countries. Youngest player at UEFA Euro 2017 was Russia's 17-year-old midfielder Viktoriya Shkoda from the southern city of Krasnodar while the oldest was the 37-year-old Norwegian goalkeeper **Ingrid Hjelmseth**. The German women's Bundesliga provided the most players (61) followed by the English club game (41). Wolfsburg were the top club in being represented by 14 players – albeit "only" five in the German squad – followed by Barcelona and European champions Lyon with 12 each.

BEST PLAYERS

Year	Best player (Country)
1984	Pia Sundhage (Sweden)
1987	Heidi Store (Norway)
1989	Doris Fitschen (W Germany)
1991	Silvia Neid (Germany)
1993	Hege Riise (Norway)
1995	Birgit Prinz (Germany)
1997	Carolina Morace (Italy)
2001	Hanna Ljungberg (Sweden)
2005	Anne Makinen (Finland)
2009	Inka Grings (Germany)
2013	Nadine Angerer (Germany)
2017	Lieke Martens (Netherlands)

STEP UP FOR STEINHAUS

One of the most high-profile personalities at the 2017 finals was not a player but Bibiana Steinhaus, the German referee. Steinhaus, a police commander from Hanover, learned shortly before the finals that she had become the first woman official promoted to referee matches in the men's Bundesliga. This was 10 years after she had become the first female referee in German professional football in the lower divisions. Highlights in the women's game included the final of the 2011 World Cup and then the gold medal match at the London 2012 Olympic Games. Six weeks before UEFA Euro 2017, she refereed the UEFA Women's Champions League Final between Lyon and Paris Saint-Germain.

RECORD ATTENDANCES

Attendance	Result	Venue, match
41,301	Germany 1 Norway 0	(Stockholm, 2013 final)
29,092	England 3 Finland 2	(Manchester City, 2005 group)
28,182	Netherlands 4, Denmark 2	(Enschede, 2017 final)
27,093	Netherlands 3, England 0	(Enschede, 2017 semi-final)
25,694	England 0, Sweden 1	(Blackburn, 2005 group)
21,731	Netherlands 1, Norway 0	(Utrecht, 2017 group)
21,105	Germany 3, Norway 1	(Blackburn, 2005 final)
21,000	West Germany 4, Norway 1	(Osnabruck, 1989 final)
18,000	Germany 1, Sweden 0	(Ulm, 2001 group)
16,608	Sweden 0, Germany 1	(Gothenburg, 2013 semi-final)

TOURNAMENT LEADING SCORERS

Tournament	Leading Scorers	Total
1984	Pia Sundhage (Sweden)	3
1987	Trude Stendal (Norway)	3
1989	Sissel Grude (Norway)	2
=	Ursula Lohn (Germany)	2
1991	Heidi Mohr (Germany)	4
1993	Susan Mackensie (Denmark)	2
1995	Lena Videkull (Sweden)	3
1997	Carolina Morace (Italy)	4
=	Marianne Pettersen (Norway)	4
=	Angelique Roujas (France)	4
2001	Claudia Müller (Germany)	3
=	Sandra Smisek (Germany)	3
2005	Inka Grings (Germany)	4
2009	Inka Grings (Germany)	6
2013	Lotta Schelin (Sweden)	5
2017	Jodie Taylor (England)	5

TAYLOR MAKES HISTORY FOR ENGLAND

England centre-forward **Jodie Taylor** enjoyed a sensational campaign at the 2017 finals of the Women's European Championship. She started with a hat-trick in a 6-0 thrashing of Scotland and followed up against Spain and in the quarter-final defeat of France to become the first England player to finish as the tournament's top scorer. Taylor's treble was the first at the finals in two decades. Her five-goal haul for the Lionesses was one short of the record set by Germany's Inka Grings in 2009.

Taylor, who had played for 12 clubs in five countries before exploding at Euro 2017, was only the third player ever to score a hat-trick in the women's Euro.

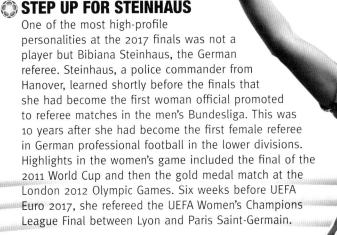

OTHER WOMEN'S TOURNAMENTS

MAGNIFICENT MARTA

Brazil superstar Marta finished with an Olympic women's silver medal in both 2004 and 2008 but missed out on home turf in 2016 when the Canarinha lost the bronze medal play-off to Canada. Her consolation was in becoming, with a total of 15 goals, the all-time leading scorer in Olympic women's football, one more than Germany's Birgit Prinz.

WOMEN'S OLYMPIC FINALS

Year	Venue	Winners	Runners-up	Score
1996	Atlanta	USA	China	2-1
2000	Sydney	Norway	USA	3-2
		Norway won with a golden goal		
2004	Athens	USA	Brazil	2-1 (aet)
2008	Beijing	USA	Brazil	1-0 (aet)
2012	London	USA	Japan	2-1
2016	Rio de Janeiro	Germany	Sweden	2-1

BRONZE MEDAL PLAY–OFFS

Year	Venue	Winners	Losers	Score
1996	Atlanta	Norway	Brazil	2-0
2000	Sydney	Germany	Brazil	2-0
2004	Athens	Germany	Sweden	1-0
2008	Beijing	Germany	Japan	2-0
2012	London	Canada	France	1-0
2016	Sao Paulo	Canada	Brazil	2-1

MEDALLISTS

Country	Gold	Silver	Bronze
USA	4	1	–
Germany	1	–	3
Norway	1	–	1
Brazil	–	2	–
China	–	1	–
Japan	–	1	–
Sweden	–	1	–
Canada	–	–	2

WOMEN'S OLYMPIC TEAM TOP SCORERS

1996:	Norway	12
2000:	USA	9
2004:	Brazil	15
2008:	USA	12
2012:	USA	16
2016:	Germany	14

WOMEN'S OLYMPIC INDIVIDUAL TOP SCORERS

1996:	Ann-Kristin Aarones (Norway)	
	Linda Medalen (Norway)	
	Pretinha (Brazil)	4
2000:	Sun Wen (China)	4
2004:	Cristiane (Brazil)	
	Birgit Prinz (Germany)	5
2008:	Cristiane (Brazil)	5
2012:	Christine Sinclair (Canada)	6
2016:	Melanie Behringer (Germany)	5

CRISTIANE'S TREBLE DOUBLE

Brazil's **Cristiane** is the only player to score two hat-tricks in FIFA Olympic history. She scored three in a 7-0 win over hosts Greece in 2004 and repeated the feat in a 3-1 win over Nigeria at Beijing 2008. Birgit Prinz (four goals for Germany against China in 2004) and Christine Sinclair (for Canada against the USA in 2012) are the only others to net Olympic hat-tricks.

GERMANS CHALK UP BIGGEST WIN

Germany hold the record for the biggest win in the Olympic finals. They beat China 8-0 at Patras on 11 August 2004, with Birgit Prinz scoring four times. The Germans' other goals came from Pia Wunderlich, Renate Lingor, Conny Pohlers and Martina Muller. Yet, in a major surprise, Germany failed to qualify for the women's football tournament at the 2012 Olympic Games in London. The 2011 FIFA Women's World Cup was used as UEFA's qualifiers, meaning beaten quarter-finalists Germany fell short. Semi-finalists Sweden – including their most-capped player Therese Sjogran – and France, whose stars include midfielder Louisa Necib, went through to the 2012 event instead.

HOSTS WITH THE MOST

The FIFA Under-20 Women's World Cup is held every two years, in contrast to the four-yearly senior contest. Since 2010, the younger players' event has been staged by the same nation one year before they host the FIFA Women's World Cup. In 2014, Canada became the first country to host the Under-20 tournament twice, having previously done so in 2002 – while Germany emerged as the second three-times champions, emulating the USA. In 2016 the finals were staged in Papua Guinea, a late replacement after original host South Africa withdrew. North Korea won the tournament for a second time, defeating France 3-1 in the final. The 113 goals in the finals matched the competition's record with Chile 2008. In March 2015, the world governing body FIFA in keeping with their policy, awarded the U-20 finals in 2018 to France, hosts-in-waiting of the 2019 FIFA Women's World Cup finals.

LATE STARTS, LATE FINISHING

American Carli Lloyd is one of the greatest players in Olympic women's football history. In Beijing in 2008 she struck the winning goal for the USA against Brazil and, four years later in London, scored both goals in their 2-1 victory over Japan. Other memorable moments from London 2012 included Alex Morgan's winner for the USA against Canada in the semi-final – she made it 4-3 three minutes into stoppage-time at the end of extra-time, the latest goal in Olympic history. Hosts Great Britain fielded a team for the first time and although they finished top of their first round group with a perfect three wins from three, without conceding a goal, they were beaten 2-0 by Canada in the quarter-final and missed out on a medal.

JAPAN'S DOUBLE JOY

Japan clinched the AFC Asian Women's Cup title for the first time in 2014, when the tournament was staged in Vietnam. Defender **Azusa Iwashimizu** not only scored the winner in extra-time stoppage-time in the semi-final against China, but also struck the only goal of the final against Australia – some solace for her red card in the 2011 FIFA Women's World Cup final. Also in 2014, Japan won the FIFA Under-17 Women's World Cup for the first time, beating Spain 2-0 in the final in Costa Rica and seeing five-goal Hina Sugita voted best player. North Korea beat the USA 2-1 in the inaugural final in New Zealand in 2008, before South Korea beat Japan on penalties following a 3-3 draw in the climax to the tournament in Trinidad and Tobago two years later. France goalkeeper Romane Bruneau was the heroine of another shoot-out in the 2012 final in Azerbaijan, decisively saving two spot-kicks after a 1-1 draw with North Korea.

US DOMINATE OLYMPIC GOLDS

The USA have dominated the Olympics since women's football was introduced at the 1996 Games in Atlanta. They have won four gold medals and secured silver in 2000. Rio 2016 was the first time the USA were not among the medals as they lost a quarter-final shootout against Sweden. The tournament has grown rapidly in popularity with a 52,432 crowd watching the 2016 gold medal match between Germany and Sweden in Rio's Maracana Stadium despite the absence of hosts Brazil. In the meantime, FIFA has added two junior age-group tournaments worldwide. The FIFA U-20 Women's World Cup was staged for the first time in 2000 and the first edition of the Under-17 event followed in 2008. Once more, the USA have been prominent, though there is now a strong challenge from North Korea, winners of both competitions in 2016.

FIFA U-20 WOMEN'S WORLD CUP

FINALS

Year	Venue	Winner	Runners-up	Score
2002	Edmonton	USA	Canada	1-0 (aet)
2004	Bangkok	Germany	Chile	2-0
2006	Moscow	North Korea	China	5-0
2008	Santiago	USA	North Korea	2-1
2010	Bielefeld	Germany	Nigeria	2-0
2012	Tokyo	USA	Germany	1-0
2014	Montreal	Germany	Nigeria	1-0 (aet)
2016	Port Moresby (PNG)	North Korea	France	3-1

TOP SCORERS

2002	Christine Sinclair (Canada)	10
2004	Brittany Timko (Canada)	7
2006	Ma Xiaoxu (China),	
	Kim Song Hui (North Korea)	5
2008	Sydney Leroux (USA)	5
2010	Alexandra Popp (Germany)	10
2012	Kim Un-Hwa (Japan)	7
2014	Asisat Oshoala (Nigeria)	7
2016	Stina Blackstenius (Sweden)	5
	Gabi Nunes (Portugal)	5
	Mami Ueno (Japan)	5

FIFA U-17 WOMEN'S WORLD CUP

FINALS

Year	Venue	Winner	Runners-up	Score
2008	Auckland	North Korea	USA	2-1 (aet)
2010	Port of Spain	South Korea	Japan	3-3 (aet)
	(South Korea won 5-4 on penalties)			
2012	Baku	France	North Korea	1-1 (aet)
	(France won 7-6 on penalties)			
2014	San Jose (CR)	Japan	Spain	2-0
2016	Amman	North Korea	Japan	0-0
	(North Korea won 5-4 on penalties)			

TOP SCORERS

2008	Dzsenifer Marozsan (Germany)	6
2010	Yeo Min-Ji (South Korea)	8
2012	Ri Un-Sim (North Korea)	8
2014	Deyna Castellanos (Venezuela)	6
	Gabriela Garcia (Venezuela)	6
2016	Lorena Navarro (Spain)	8

SILVIA'S GOLDEN GOODBYE

Germany maintained a remarkable sequence in women's football when they beat Sweden 2-1 to claim 2016 gold in Rio de Janeiro. After two Women's World Cups and eight European Championship victories this was their first Olympic success and a perfect climax to coach Silvia Neid's career in her last match after 11 years in charge. In addition Germany's Melanie Behringer was the tournament's five-goal leading scorer.

SINCLAIR HITS FIVE

Christine Sinclair of Canada and Alexandra Popp of Germany share the record for most goals scored in a single FIFA Under-20 Women's World Cup. Each struck 10, Sinclair in 2002 and Popp eight years later. Sinclair also holds the record for the most goals in one game. She netted five in Canada's 6-2 quarter-final win over England at Edmonton on 25 August 2002. But Popp is the only player to score in all of her country's six games at a tournament. Only Sinclair and Popp have won both the Golden Ball for best player and Golden Shoe for top scorer. Sinclair finished the 2012 Olympics as six-goal top-scorer in the women's football tournament. Her tally included a hat-trick – in vain – in Canada's 4-3 semi-final defeat to the US.

APPENDIX 1: FIFA AWARDS

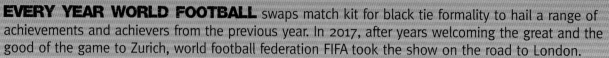

EVERY YEAR WORLD FOOTBALL swaps match kit for black tie formality to hail a range of achievements and achievers from the previous year. In 2017, after years welcoming the great and the good of the game to Zurich, world football federation FIFA took the show on the road to London.

The world federation had launched its own World Player and associated awards in 1990. Between 2010 and 2015, the main award had been shared with the Ballon d'Or, launched by the Paris magazine, *France Football*, in the mid-1950s.

In 2016 the FIFA and *France Football* awards separated, the latter reclaiming sole rights to the Ballon d'Or, while FIFA stepped out with a new title. Hence the rebranding of the FIFA prize-giving as The Best awards for the outstanding team and individual achievements of the year.

The voters of both FIFA and *France Football* still concurred that the outstanding player of 2017, as of 2016, had been Cristiano Ronaldo of Portugal and Real Madrid. London magazine *World Soccer*, which has been running its own world player poll since 1982, made it three-way agreement. Five times FIFA's top player, Argentina and Barcelona's Lionel Messi, was again runner-up to Ronaldo, with Neymar of Brazil and Paris Saint-Germain third.

FIFA's Best Woman player was the brilliant Dutch left-winger Lieke Martens, after her performances in the host Netherlands' triumph at the UEFA European Women's Championship. Runner-up was the USA's 2016 winner Carli Lloyd, with Deyna Castellanos of Venezuela third.

A real all-star team: the FIFA FIFPro World11 2017, selected by more than 45,000 of their fellow players from around the world, take to the stage at The Best FIFA Football Awards in London.

FIFA PLAYER OF THE YEAR 2017

CRISTIANO RONALDO

Cristiano Ronaldo Real Madrid's Portugal superstar, won world federation FIFA's annual prize as Best Player for the second year in succession at a star-studded spectacular at the London Palladium. He collected 43.16 per cent of the vote, ahead of Argentina and Barcelona's Lionel Messi (19.25 per cent) and Brazil's Neymar (6.97 per cent). Ronaldo was also one of six Real Madrid players selected in the FIFPro Team of the Year while club boss Zinedine Zidane was named Coach of the Year.

Ronaldo was presented with his award by Diego Maradona and his Brazilian namesake. He had always been clear favourite for the world player prize after inspiring Madrid's triumphs in the UEFA Champions League and Spain's La Liga in 2016–17. He had scored 44 goals for club and country to that point in late 2017, including a decisive double in the Champions League Final defeat of Juventus in June as Madrid retained the trophy – the first club to achieve this since the competition was rebranded in 1992 – and became European champions for a record-extending 12th time.

Ronaldo said: "Thank you a lot, guys, for voting for me. I must give a mention to Leo and Neymar for being here. Real Madrid supporters, my teammates, coach, president all support me all through the year so I have to say thank you to them.

"We are in England for this event for the first time and I win consecutive awards so I'm really glad, it's a great moment for me. FIFA give the opportunity to fans, and I know I have fans all over the world (so) thanks for the support, I appreciate it ... I'm so happy. Thank you very much."

Messi, FIFA's top player in 2015, came to the Gala having scored 50 goals for Barcelona and Argentina thus far in 2017. Neymar, who had become the world's most expensive player when he left Barcelona for Paris Saint-Germain in the summer for 222m, had 25 goals to his name for club and country. All three had played key roles in their countries' success in qualifying for the 2018 FIFA World Cup finals in Russia.

In fourth place was veteran Italy and Juventus goalkeeper, Gianluigi Buffon, who receive the inaugual Best FIFA Goalkeeper award.

PREVIOUS WINNERS

1991 Lothar Matthaus **(Germany)**
1992 Marco van Basten **(Netherlands)**
1993 Roberto Baggio **(Italy)**
1994 Romario **(Brazil)**
1995 George Weah **(Liberia)**
1996 Ronaldo **(Brazil)**
1997 Ronaldo **(Brazil)**
1998 Zinedine Zidane **(France)**
1999 Rivaldo **(Brazil)**
2000 Zinedine Zidane **(France)**
2001 Luis Figo **(Portugal)**
2002 Ronaldo **(Brazil)**
2003 Zinedine Zidane **(France)**
2004 Ronaldinho **(Brazil)**
2005 Ronaldinho **(Brazil)**
2006 Fabio Cannavaro **(Italy)**
2007 Kaka **(Brazil)**
2008 Cristiano Ronaldo **(Portugal)**
2009 Lionel Messi **(Argentina)**
2010 Lionel Messi **(Argentina)**
2011 Lionel Messi **(Argentina)**
2012 Lionel Messi **(Argentina)**
2013 Cristiano Ronaldo **(Portugal)**
2014 Cristiano Ronaldo **(Portugal)**
2015 Lionel Messi **(Argentina)**
2016 Cristiano Ronaldo **(Portugal)**

LIEKE MARTENS

Lieke Martens became only the second player to break the long monopoly of Brazil, Germany and the United States of the FIFA Best Women's Player prize-winners at the world football federation's annual gala, staged in England for the first time. The Netherlands and Barcelona left-winger collected 21.72 per cent of the vote to beat the 2015 and 2016 winner Carli Lloyd (16.28 per cent) and the US-based Venezuelan starlet Deyna Castellanos (11.69 per cent).

"This is simply incredible," said 24-year-old Martens, who was accompanied in the honours list by her Dutch national team boss Sarina Wiegman, winner of the Best Women's Coach award. The Women's Player of the Year award was created in 2001 and the only previous occasion when an "outsider" had taken the prize was in 2011 when Japan's Women's World Cup-winning Homare Sawa was honoured.

The award completed a clean sweep of prizes for Martens. Previously she had been voted Women's Player of the Year by European federation UEFA on the back of her inspirational performances at the UEFA European Women's Championship – she won that top player prize too. Martens scored three goals and contributed one assist as the tournament's Dutch hosts won the European crown for the first time. It was the first trophy won by a Dutch senior team since their men triumphed at Euro 88 in Germany.

Martens was born and raised in Bergen, northern Netherlands, made her women's Eredivisie debut at 16 with Heerenveen, and was four-goal joint-top scorer with the Netherlands under-19 at the European age-group championship. She moved to VVV Venlo and Standard Femina de Liege in Belgium before making her senior national team debut in 2011. Further club transfers followed to Duisburg in Germany, and Swedish clubs Gothenburg then Rosengard of Malmo. Her performances at the Women's Euros earned another move, this time to Barcelona.

In 2015, Martens scored the Netherlands' first ever goal in the FIFA Women's World Cup in Canada before raising her game still further at the UEFA Euro 2017.

PREVIOUS WINNERS

2001	Mia Hamm **(United States)**
2002	Mia Hamm **(United States)**
2003	Birgit Prinz **(Germany)**
2004	Birgit Prinz **(Germany)**
2005	Birgit Prinz **(Germany)**
2006	Marta **(Brazil)**
2007	Marta **(Brazil)**
2008	Marta **(Brazil)**
2009	Marta **(Brazil)**
2010	Marta **(Brazil)**
2011	Homare Sawa **(Japan)**
2012	Abby Wambach **(United States)**
2013	Nadine Angerer **(Germany)**
2014	Nadine Kessler **(Germany)**
2015	Carli Lloyd **(United States)**
2016	Carli Lloyd **(United States)**

OTHER FIFA AWARDS

Zinedine Zidane became the first individual to win both player and manager awards when he was hailed as Best Coach of the Year at the annual FIFA Gala in London. The world football federation had celebrated the Frenchman as the best player in 1998, 2000 and 2003, and now he was rewarded for his outstanding achievements in the technical area after guiding Real Madrid to success in the UEFA Champions League, the UEFA Super Cup and Spain's La Liga. Zidane was accompanied on the stage by Best Player Cristiano Ronaldo, also from Real Madrid, and four team-mates who were named in the Team of the Year as selected by the worldwide membership of the international players' union FIFPro.

Zidane was the first coach to win back-to-back Champions League titles as Madrid beat Juventus in the 2017 final in Cardiff. Juventus' Massimiliano Allegri and Chelsea's Antonio Conte had also been shortlisted for the award.

Gianluigi Buffon was voted Goalkeeper of the Year, at the age of 39, after helping Juve to a sixth consecutive Serie A title and managing to go 600 Champions League minutes without conceding a goal.

Two awards were voted for directly by football fans from all around the world via FIFA.com. In the Puskas Goal of the Year section Arsenal's Olivier Giroud won with 36.17 per cent of the 792,062 votes for his "scorpion kick" for the Gunners against Crystal Palace. Other contenders had been Venezuela's Deyna Castellanos and South African goalkeeper Oscarine Masuluke.

Celtic supporters received 55.92 per cent of votes for the fans' award and were commended for the 360-degree card displayed around Celtic Park during their final Scottish Premier League match, celebrating the 50th anniversary of the club's European Champions Cup triumph in 1967.

The fair play prize went to Togo's **Francis Kone** of Zbrojovla Brno, who had performed life-saving first aid on an opponent – Bohemians 1905's goalkeeper Martin Berkovec – during a Czech League game in February.

FIFA Awards 2017

Men's Best Player: Cristiano Ronaldo (Portugal, Real Madrid)
Women's Best Player: Lieke Martens (Netherlands, Barcelona)
Goalkeeper of the Year: Gianluigi Buffon (Italy, Juventus)
Men's Best Coach: Zinedine Zidane (Real Madrid)
Women's Best Coach: Sarina Wiegman (Netherlands)
FIFA Ferenc Puskas Award (outstanding goal): Olivier Giroud (France, Arsenal) ··················
Fair Play Award: Francis Kone (Togo, FC Zbrojovka Brno)
Fans Award: Celtic
FIFA FIFPro World 11: Gianluigi Buffon (Italy, Juventus); Dani Alves (Brazil, Juventus/ Paris Saint-Germain), Leonardo Bonucci (Italy, Juventus/Milan), Sergio Ramos (Spain, Real Madrid), Marcelo (Brazil, Real Madrid); Andres Iniesta (Spain, Barcelona), Toni Kroos (Germany, Real Madrid), Luka Modric (Croatia, Real Madrid); Cristiano Ronaldo (Portugal, Real Madrid), Lionel Messi (Argentina, Barcelona), Neymar (Brazil, Barcelona/Paris Saint-Germain).

1991
Fair Play award: Real Federacion Espanola de Futbol (Spanish FA), Jorginho (Brazil)

1992
Fair Play award: Union Royale Belge des Societes de Football Association

1993
Fair Play award: Nandor Hidgekuti (Hungary)*, Football Association of Zambia
Top Team of the Year: Germany
Best Mover of the Year: Colombia
award presented posthumously

1994
Top Team of the Year: Brazil
Best Mover of the Year: Croatia

1995
Fair Play award: Jacques Glassmann (France)
Top Team of the Year: Brazil
Best Mover of the Year: Jamaica

1996
Fair Play award: George Weah (Liberia)
Top Team of the Year: Brazil
Best Mover of the Year: South Africa

1997
Fair Play award: Irish spectators at the FIFA World Cup preliminary match versus Belgium, Jozef Zovinec (Slovak amateur player), Julie Foudy (United States)
Top Team of the Year: Brazil
Best Mover of the Year: Yugoslavia

1998
Fair Play award: National associations of Iran, the United States and Northern Ireland
Top Team of the Year: Brazil
Best Mover of the Year: Croatia

1999
Fair Play award: New Zealand football community
Top Team of the Year: Brazil
Best Mover of the Year: Slovenia

2000
Fair Play award: Lucas Radebe (South Africa)
Top Team of the Year: Holland
Best Mover of the Year: Nigeria

2001
Presidential award Marvin Lee (Trinidad)*
Fair Play award: Paolo Di Canio (Italy)
Top Team of the Year: Honduras
Best Mover of the Year: Costa Rica
award presented posthumously

2002
Presidential award: Parminder Nagra (England)
Fair Play award: Football communities of Japan and Korea Republic
Top Team of the Year: Brazil
Best Mover of the Year: Senegal

2003
Presidential award: Iraqi football community
Fair Play award: Fans of Celtic FC (Scotland)
Top Team of the Year: Brazil
Best Mover of the Year: Bahrain

2004
Presidential award: Haiti
Fair Play award: Confederacao Brasileira de Futebol
Top Team of the Year: Brazil
Best Mover of the Year: China PR
Interactive World Player: Thiago Carrico de Azevedo (Brazil)

2005
Presidential award: Anders Frisk (Sweden)
Fair Play award: Football community of Iquitos (Peru)
Top Team of the Year: Brazil
Best Mover of the Year: Ghana
Interactive World Player: Chris Bullard (England)

2006
Presidential award: Giacinto Facchetti (Italy)*
Fair Play award: Fans of the 2006 FIFA World Cup
Top Team of the Year: Brazil
Best Mover of the Year: Italy
Interactive World Player: Andries Smit (Holland)
award presented posthumously

2007
Presidential award: Pele (Brazil)
Fair Play award: FC Barcelona (Spain)
Top Team of the Year: Argentina
Best Mover of the Year: Mozambique

2008
Presidential award: Women's football (presented to the United States women's team)
Fair Play award: Armenia, Turkey
Development award: Palestine
Interactive World Player: Alfonso Ramos (Spain)
Top Team of the Year: Spain
Best Mover of the Year: Spain

2009
Presidential award: Queen Rania Al Abdullah of Jordan [co-chair of 1Goal: Education for All]
Fair Play Award: Sir Bobby Robson (England)*
Development prize: Chinese Football Association
Interactive World Player: Bruce Grannec (France)
Top Team of the Year: Spain
FIFA Ferenc Puskas Award (outstanding goal): Cristiano Ronaldo, Manchester United v FC Porto
award presented posthumously

2010
Coach of the Year (men): Jose Mourinho (Internazionale, then Real Madrid)
Coach of the Year (women): Silvia Neid (Germany women)
FIFA Ferenc Puskas Award (outstanding goal): Hamit Altintop, Turkey v Kazakhstan
Presidential award: Archbishop Desmond Tutu, South Africa
Fair Play Award: Haiti Under-17 women's team

2011
Coach of the Year (men): Pep Guardiola (Barcelona)
Coach of the Year (women): Norio Sasaki (Japan women)
FIFA Ferenc Puskas Award (outstanding goal): Neymar, Santos v Flamengo
Presidential award: Sir Alex Ferguson, Manchester United
Fair Play award: Japan Football Association

2012
Coach of the Year (men): Vicente Del Bosque (Spain)
Coach of the Year (women): Pia Sundhage (Sweden)
FIFA Ferenc Puskas Award (outstanding goal): Miroslav Stoch, Fenerbahce v Genclerbirligi
Presidential: Franz Beckenbauer (Germany)
Fair Play award: Uzbekistan Football Federation

2013
Coach of the Year (men): Jupp Heynckes (Bayern Munich)
Coach of the Year (women): Silvia Neid (Germany)
FIFA Ferenc Puskas Award (outstanding goal): Zlatan Ibrahimovic, Sweden v England
Presidential: Jacques Rogge (Honorary President, IOC)
Fair Play award: Afghanistan Football Federation

2014
Coach of the Year (men): Joachim Low (Germany)
Coach of the Year (women): Ralf Kellerman (Germany, Wolfsburg)
FIFA Ferenc Puskas Award (outstanding goal): James Rodriguez, Colombia v Uruguay
Presidential: Hiroshi Kagawa (Japanese journalist)
Fair Play Award: FIFA World Cup volunteers

2015
Coach of the Year (men): Luis Enrique (Barcelona)
Coach of the Year (women): Jill Ellis (United States)
FIFA Ferenc Puskas Award (outstanding goal): Wendell Lira (Goianesia, Brazil)
Fair Play: All football organizations assisting refugees

2016
Men's Best Coach: Claudio Ranieri (Leicester City)
Women's Best Coach: Silvia Neid (Germany)
FIFA Ferenc Puskas Award (outstanding goal): Mohd Faiz Subri (Malaysia, Penang FA)
Fair Play: Atletico Nacional (Colombia)
Fan Award: Borussia Dortmund & Liverpool supporters
Outstanding career: Falcao [Alessandro Rosa Vieira] (Brazil, futsal)

APPENDIX 2: FIFA/COCA-COLA WORLD RANKINGS

FIFA introduced a world ranking system in December 1992 to provide a monthly statistical analysis of the rise and fall of the fortunes of all the world game's national teams in men's football. Placings are computed on results in what are termed international A games and consider match status, goals scored, strength of opposition and regional balance. The rankings are important, having sometimes been used as a form-guide guide by FIFA for draws of international competitions. A short break in publication accompanied the 2018 FIFA World Cup when the system was refined to adjust anomalies concerning the assessment of friendly matches. The women's world rankings, introduced in 2003, are published on a quarterly basis.

Russia ranked 70th in the FIFA World Rankings entering the 2018 FIFA World Cup but the tournament hosts defied their lowest position of all 32 finalists and went all the way to the quarter-finals.

FIFA MEN'S WORLD RANKINGS 2018

Germany went into the 2018 FIFA World Cup finals on top of the FIFA World Ranking after the 2017–18 season. Coach Joachim Low's men had qualified easily for their defence in Russia. The rankings made it clear they would face a major challenge, but their group stage exit was still a shock.

The ranking system provides a regular statistical insight into the rise and fall of all FIFA member national teams, from giants to minnows. Placings are based on computer-based comparisons of match results, goals scored, strength of opposition, regional balance and competition status. A significant reshuffle in the rankings will be seen in autumn 2018 after an adjustment to the computerized system itself.

RANKINGS (as at June 2018)

Pos.	Country	Pts	(+/-)
1	Germany	1558	0
2	Brazil	1431	0
3	Belgium	1298	0
4	Portugal	1274	0
5	Argentina	1241	0
6	Switzerland	1199	0
7	France	1198	0
8	Poland	1183	+2
9	Chile	1135	0
10	Spain	1126	−2
11	Peru	1125	0
12	Denmark	1051	0
12	England	1051	+1
14	Uruguay	1018	+3
15	Mexico	989	0
16	Colombia	986	0
17	Netherlands	981	+2
18	Wales	953	+3
19	Italy	951	+1
20	Croatia	945	−2
21	Tunisia	910	−7
22	Iceland	908	0
23	Costa Rica	884	+2
24	Sweden	880	−1
25	United States	873	−1
26	Austria	845	0
27	Senegal	838	+1
28	Slovakia	804	+1
29	Northern Ireland	803	−2
30	Romania	782	+2
31	Rep. Ireland	777	0
32	Paraguay	773	0
33	Venezuela	755	+6
34	Serbia	751	+1
35	Ukraine	733	−5
36	Australia	718	+4

Pos.	Country	Pts	(+/-)
37	Iran	708	−1
38	Turkey	706	−1
38	Congo DR	706	0
40	Bosnia & Herzegovina	693	+1
41	Morocco	686	+1
42	Scotland	660	−8
43	Montenegro	652	+0
44	Greece	650	0
45	Egypt	649	+1
46	Czech Republic	641	−1
47	Ghana	624	+3
48	Nigeria	618	−1
49	Bulgaria	614	+4
49	Cameroon	614	+1
51	Hungary	612	−2
52	Burkina Faso	604	+2
53	Norway	596	−5
54	Jamaica	588	−2
55	Panama	571	0
56	Slovenia	558	+9
57	Korea Republic	544	+4
58	Albania	538	−2
59	Bolivia	536	−2
60	Ecuador	524	+3
61	Japan	521	−1
62	Honduras	503	−3
63	Finland	486	−1
64	Mali	484	+3
65	Cape Verde Islands	478	−7
66	Algeria	474	−2
67	Saudi Arabia	465	0
68	Cote d'Ivoire	463	+1
68	Guinea	463	+2
70	Russia	457	−4
71	FYR Macedonia	451	+6
72	El Salvador	442	+13

Pos.	Country	Pts	(+/-)
73	Syria	440	+3
74	South Africa	428	−2
75	China PR	423	−2
76	Zambia	420	+2
77	United Arab Emirates	418	+4
78	Belarus	417	+1
79	Lebanon	411	+3
79	Canada	411	+1
81	Curaçao	408	−10
82	Uganda	403	−8
83	Congo	393	+6
84	Oman	391	+3
85	Gabon	390	+5
85	Luxembourg	390	−2
87	Cyprus	384	−1
88	Benin	379	−4
89	Iraq	377	+2
90	Faroe Islands	376	+3
91	Trinidad & Tobago	370	+1
92	Kyrgyz Republic	363	−17
93	Israel	362	+5
94	Estonia	359	−1
95	Uzbekistan	354	−7
96	Georgia	352	−1
97	India	350	0
98	Qatar	348	+3
99	Palestine	347	−3
100	Armenia	338	−2
101	Libya	336	−1
102	Vietnam	334	0
103	Niger	323	+6
104	Haiti	322	+4
105	Azerbaijan	321	+21
106	Madagascar	308	+8
107	Mauritania	304	−2
108	Korea DPR	303	+2

France entered the 2018 FIFA World Cup seventh in the FIFA World Rankings, but the performances of **Antoine Griezmann** and his team-mates, as *Les Bleus* won the trophy, ensured they will soon be much higher.

Roberto Martinez oversaw Belgium's run to a best-ever FIFA World Cup third place in 2018, which matched the nation's position in the FIFA World Rankings entering the finals.

Pos.	Country	Pts	(+/-)
108	Central African Republic	303	+7
110	Jordan	296	+8
111	Sierra Leone	292	−8
112	Kenya	291	−1
113	Bahrain	289	+3
114	Mozambique	282	−8
115	Philippines	280	−4
116	Namibia	277	−9
117	Kazakhstan	273	0
118	Zimbabwe	265	−5
119	Tajikistan	264	+1
120	New Zealand	256	+13
121	Guinea-Bissau	255	−17
122	Thailand	248	0
123	Malawi	247	−4
123	Chinese Taipei	247	−2
125	Togo	241	+3
126	Lithuania	239	+7
126	Antigua & Barbuda	239	−2
128	Sudan	232	−2
129	Latvia	230	+10
130	Turkmenistan	229	−2
130	Andorra	229	+2
132	Nicaragua	228	+4
133	Yemen	227	−9
134	Swaziland	222	−3
135	St Kitts & Nevis	218	−5
136	Rwanda	216	−13
137	Angola	209	+1
138	Myanmar	206	−3
139	Botswana	205	+3
140	Tanzania	200	−3
141	Kosovo	197	+11
142	Hong Kong	195	+2
143	Equatorial Guinea	190	+2

Pos.	Country	Pts	(+/-)
143	Solomon Islands	190	+10
145	Afghanistan	188	−5
146	Guatemala	180	−5
147	Lesotho	175	+3
148	Burundi	174	−2
149	Comoros	172	−7
150	Maldives	171	−2
151	Ethiopia	166	−5
152	Dominican Republic	162	−3
153	Suriname	154	+1
154	New Caledonia	150	+2
155	Mauritius	140	+6
156	South Sudan	132	+1
157	Tahiti	130	+5
158	Liberia	129	−7
159	Kuwait	128	+1
160	Barbados	127	−2
161	Nepal	118	+3
162	Vanuatu	117	−7
163	Belize	115	+6
164	Indonesia	111	0
165	Fiji	104	+2
166	Cambodia	103	+4
166	Papua New Guinea	103	+14
168	Grenada	102	−5
169	Singapore	99	+3
170	St Lucia	95	+4
171	Malaysia	93	0
172	Gambia	92	+3
173	St Vincent & the Grenadines	89	+3
173	Puerto Rico	89	−14
175	Chad	88	−7
175	Moldova	88	−2
177	Dominica	86	0
178	Bermuda	82	0

Pos.	Country	Pts	(+/-)
178	Laos	82	+1
180	Liechtenstein	80	+1
181	Cuba	75	+1
182	Guyana	73	−18
183	Bhutan	68	+1
184	Malta	65	+1
185	Macau	60	+1
186	Mongolia	51	+2
186	São Tomé e Príncipe	51	+1
188	Seychelles	48	+6
188	Aruba	48	−6
190	Guam	45	−1
190	Timor-Leste	45	0
192	American Samoa	38	−1
192	Cook Islands	38	−1
194	Bangladesh	35	+3
195	Gibraltar	34	+1
195	Brunei Darussalam	34	0
197	Djibouti	32	+1
197	Samoa	32	−6
199	US Virgin Islands	18	0
200	Sri Lanka	17	0
201	Pakistan	10	+2
202	Cayman Islands	8	+2
203	San Marino	8	+2
204	British Virgin Islands	4	+2
204	Montserrat	4	−4
206	Turks & Caicos Islands	0	−4
206	Anguilla	0	+1
206	Bahamas	0	+1
206	Eritrea	0	+1
206	Somalia	0	+1
206	Tonga	0	+1

** Teams inactive for more than four years do not appear on the table.

FIFA WOMEN'S WORLD RANKINGS 2018

The significance of the world rankings is bound to increase in the run-up to the 2019 FIFA Women's World Cup finals in France. While the power of the United States remained evident from the charts, the threat of a significant European challenge was underlined by the ranking pursuit led by Germany, France, England and the 2017 European champions from the Netherlands.

The ranking system provides a regular statistical insight into the rise and fall of all FIFA member national teams, from giants to minnows. Placings are based on computer-based comparisons of match results, goals scored, strength of opposition, regional balance and competition status. Unlike the men's rankings, these come out four times a year.

Alex Morgan scored 13 goals for the United States in 2017–18, ensuring her nation continued to dominate the FIFA Women's World Rankings throughout the season.

RANKINGS (as at June 2018)

Pos.	Country	Pts	(+/-)
1	United States	2114	0
2	Germany	2049	+1
3	France	2032	+2
4	England	2026	-2
5	Canada	2009	-1
6	Japan	1988	+5
7	Brazil	1985	+1
8	Australia	1979	-2
9	Netherlands	1977	-2
10	Korea DPR	1955	0
11	Sweden	1941	-2
12	Spain	1911	0
13	Denmark	1903	0
14	Norway	1887	0
15	Korea Republic	1881	+1
16	Italy	1870	-1
17	China PR	1867	0
18	Switzerland	1861	0
19	Iceland	1823	0
20	New Zealand	1810	0
21	Scotland	1801	+1
22	Austria	1794	-1
23	Belgium	1773	0
24	Ukraine	1731	+3
25	Mexico	1724	0
26	Colombia	1722	-2
27	Russia	1702	-1
28	Thailand	1684	+2
29	Wales	1679	+5
30	Finland	1678	-2
31	Rep. Ireland	1664	-2
32	Czech Republic	1648	+1
33	Costa Rica	1645	-1

Pos.	Country	Pts	(+/-)
34	Portugal	1644	+2
35	Argentina	1633	+2
36	Poland	1629	-5
37	Vietnam	1623	-2
38	Nigeria	1607	0
39	Chile	1594	+1
40	Romania	1567	-1
41	Uzbekistan	1557	0
42	Chinese Taipei	1553	0
43	Serbia	1545	0
44	Myanmar	1539	-1
45	Hungary	1537	0
46	Ghana	1503	0
46	Slovakia	1503	+1
48	Cameroon	1494	0
48	Paraguay	1494	+2
50	Trinidad and Tobago	1473	-2
51	South Africa	1447	+2
52	Belarus	1431	+1
53	Croatia	1425	-1
54	Slovenia	1423	+8
55	Equatorial Guinea	1421	0
56	Northern Ireland	1419	0
57	Jordan	1413	-6
58	Iran	1411	0
58	Venezuela	1411	+6
60	India	1409	-1
61	Turkey	1403	+2
62	Ecuador	1393	+56
63	Israel	1392	-4
64	Peru	1380	-5
65	Greece	1374	+1
66	Bosnia & Herzegovina	1373	-9

Pos.	Country	Pts	(+/-)
67	Haiti	1367	+51
68	Côte d'Ivoire	1363	-3
69	Azerbaijan	1360	-2
70	Kazakhstan	1353	0
71	Jamaica	1348	+47
72	Uruguay	1347	-4
73	Philippines	1342	-1
74	Bulgaria	1340	-5
75	Albania	1325	0
76	Hong Kong	1323	-5
77	Indonesia	1316	+41
78	Morocco	1304	-5
79	Algeria	1294	+39
80	Bahrain	1278	-3
81	Faroe Islands	1272	-7
82	Senegal	1245	-3
83	Malaysia	1244	-3
83	Guyana	1244	+35
85	Cuba	1241	+33
86	Mali	1232	-4
86	Bolivia	1232	-2
88	United Arab Emirates	1230	-7
89	Moldova	1228	-4
90	Montenegro	1220	-4
90	Estonia	1220	-8
92	Latvia	1209	-5
93	Zimbabwe	1201	-5
94	Congo	1196	+24
95	Malta	1190	-6
96	Palestine	1181	-6
97	Lithuania	1180	-6
98	Dominican Republic	1169	+20
99	Puerto Rico	1166	+19

The form of 2017 Women's World Player of the Year **Lieke Martens** helped the Netherlands win the UEFA Women's European Championship and lifted the Dutch to ninth in the FIFA Women's World Rankings.

Pos.	Country	Pts	(+/–)
100	Georgia	1145	–8
101	Singapore	1137	–8
102	Nepal	1136	–8
103	Ethiopia	1132	+15
104	Luxembourg	1125	–9
105	Cyprus	1120	–9
106	Suriname	1113	+12
107	Burkina Faso	1062	–10
108	Zambia	1044	–10
109	Kosovo	1022	–10
110	Tajikistan	1018	–9
111	Namibia	1008	–11
112	Bangladesh	1003	–10
113	St Lucia	992	+5
114	St Kitts and Nevis	989	+4
115	Bermuda	984	+3
115	Barbados	984	+3
117	Sri Lanka	971	–14
118	Tanzania	967	0
119	Maldives	958	–15
120	St Vincent and the Grenadines	956	–2
121	Syria	921	–16
122	Dominica	913	–4
123	Kenya	912	–15
124	Grenada	892	–6
125	Afghanistan	884	–19
126	US Virgin Islands	874	–8
127	Iraq	873	–20
128	Mozambique	865	–19
129	Lesotho	858	–18
130	Malawi	842	–20
131	Uganda	829	–13

Pos.	Country	Pts	(+/–)
132	Swaziland	812	–20
133	Antigua and Barbuda	798	–15
134	Bhutan	771	–21
135	Curaçao	752	–17
136	Andorra	748	–22
137	Botswana	746	–22
138	Aruba	742	–20
139	Madagascar	693	–23
140	Mauritius	358	–23
**	Papua New Guinea	1473	–23
**	Panama	1363	–23
**	Tunisia	1313	–23
**	Guatemala	1297	–23
**	Fiji	1292	–23
**	Guam	1282	–65
**	Laos	1273	–23
**	Tonga	1258	–23
**	Egypt	1256	–63
**	New Caledonia	1252	–23
**	Tahiti	1238	–23
**	El Salvador	1198	–23
**	Benin	1187	–23
**	Cook Islands	1185	–23
*	Gambia	1183	0
**	Honduras	1152	–23
**	Solomon Islands	1144	–23
**	Vanuatu	1139	–23
**	Samoa	1138	–23
**	Angola	1134	–23
**	Kyrgyz Republic	1134	–23
**	Sierra Leone	1132	–23
**	Congo DR	1132	–23
**	Armenia	1104	–23

Pos.	Country	Pts	(+/–)
**	Guinea	1077	–23
**	American Samoa	1075	–23
**	Nicaragua	1073	–23
**	FYR Macedonia	1069	–23
**	Eritrea	1060	–23
*	Central African Rep.	1056	0
**	Gabon	1052	–23
**	Timor–Leste	991	–23
*	Togo*	962	–23
**	Lebanon	949	–23
**	Guinea–Bissau	927	–23
**	Pakistan	926	–23
**	Rwanda	908	–23
*	Niger	891	–23
**	Liberia	877	–23
**	Kuwait	870	–23
**	British Virgin Islands	867	–23
**	Qatar	864	–23
**	Cayman Islands	849	–23
*	Comoros	837	–23
**	Belize	825	–23
*	Macau	824	–23
*	Libya	761	–23
*	Turks and Caicos Islands	704	–23
*	Anguilla	697	0
**	Burundi	519	–23

* Listing and points are provisional as nation has not played five matches against officially ranked teams.

** Inactive for more than 18 months and therefore not ranked. Points total was last one when officially ranked.

PICTURE CREDITS

The publishers would like to thank the following sources for their kind permission to reproduce the pictures in this book. The page numbers for each of the photographs are listed below, giving the page on which they appear in the book and any location indicator (C-centre, T-top, B-bottom, L-left, R-right).

Alamy: /Paul Fearn 61L

Getty Images: 165TL; /2010 Qatar 2022: 188R; /AFP: 53C, 84C, 108B, 121TL, 121BL, 167BR, 175L, 198BR, 208BL, 210L; /Suhaimi Abdullah: 137R; /Luis Acosta/AFP: 102TL, 110TR; /Fatih Aktas/Anadolu Agency: 125BR; /Nelson Almeida/AFP: 189L; /Vanderlei Almeida/AFP: 164BR; /Anadolu Agency: 47BL, 87BR, 182BL, 214C; /Odd Andersen/AFP: 33R, 187TR; /Mladen Antonov/AFP: 132-133, 190TR; /The Asahi Shimbun: 18BL; /Matthew Ashton/Corbis: 57C, 77TL, 103B, 155TL; /Matthew Ashton – AMA: 49TR, 178TL, 179BR, 222-223; /Anthony Au-Yeung/LatinContent: 160TL; /Gokhan Balci/Anadolu Agency: 124C, 127C; /Scott Barbour: 134BL; /Steve Bardens: 40T; /Dennis Barnard/Fox Photos: 105TL; /Lars Baron: 58BL, 194-195, 230BR, 238BR, 252; /Robbie Jay Barratt – AMA: 20C, 92C, 96C, 111C, 122-123, 148-149, 179BC; /Juan Barreto/AFP: 118T; /Bruno Barros/DPI/NurPhoto: 246TL; /Farouk Batiche/AFP: 126TL, 165B; /James Bayliss – AMA: 4BR; /Robyn Beck/AFP: 185TR; /Sandra Behne/Bongarts: 138BL; /Bentley Archive/Popperfoto: 76L, 173BR; /Martin Bernetti/AFP: 84TR; /Gunnar Berning/Bongarts: 181BL; /Bongarts: 36L, 171BL; /Shaun Botterill: 19BL, 20T, 59BL, 130TR, 182C, 184BR, 191TR, 192R, 200BR; /Cris Bouroncle/AFP: 224T; /Gabriel Bouys/AFP: 42BL, 129B; /Michael Bradley: 134C; /Chris Brunskill: 16BL, 89BR, 104BL, 107B, 159TL, 166T, 170TR, 174BR; /Clive Brunskill: 113L; /Simon Bruty: 17TR, 118BR; /Andy Buchanan/AFP: 80BL; /Rodrigo Buendia/AFP: 101BL; /Martin Bureau/AFP: 203; /Eric Cabanis/AFP: 162R; /Jose Cabezas/AFP: 160TR; /Giuseppe Cacace/AFP: 35T; /David Cannon: 18L, 53BR, 72BR, 104TR; /Stephane Cardinale/Corbis: 10-11; /Jean Catuffe: 23TR, 47TL, 61BR; /Central Press: 75BL; /Central Press/Hulton Archive: 60BR; /Andre Chaco/FotoArena/LatinContent: 187BL; /Graham Chadwick: 72TR; /Stanley Chou: 243L; /Matteo Ciambelli/NurPhoto: 33TL, 57TL, 120B, 154BR; /Robert Cianflone: 79T, 81L, 116T, 178C; /Timothy A Clary/AFP: 155BR; /Tim Clayton/Corbis: 204-205; /Thomas Coex/AFP: 59T; /Fabrice Coffrini/AFP: 136, 184BL; /Chris Cole: 182TR; /Phil Cole: 55BR; /Yuri Cortez/AFP: 26TR, 46L; /Vinicius Costa: 124TR; /Kevin C Cox: 171TR; /Benjamin Cremel/AFP: 138TR; /Philippe Crochet/Photonews: 163R; /Charlie Crowhurst: 154L; /Jonathan Daniel: 102R; /Anesh Debiky/Gallo Images: 221TL; /Stephane de Sakutin/AFP: 191TL; /Carl de Souza/AFP: 177TR; /Adrian Dennis/AFP: 181TR, 200TR; /Philippe Desmazes/AFP: 129C, 140BR; /Khaled Desouki/AFP: 219TL, 219BL, 221C; /Valeriano di Domenico: 160BR; /Anthony Dibon/Icon Sport: 100BL; /Kevork Djansezian: 153C; /Denis Doyle: 43BR; /Stephen Dunn: 128BR; /Johannes Eisele/AFP: 5BL, 52C; /Paul Ellis/AFP: 27C; /Elsa: 180BL; /Alfredo Estrella/AFP: 150BL; /Paul Faith/AFP: 63C; /Jonathan Ferrey: 55TR; /Franck Fife/AFP: 21BR, 119BR, 156-157, 159BR, 180BR, 202TR, 216TC; /Julian Finney: 35BL, 52TL, 111T, 118L, 193; /Stu Forster: 51BL, 91BL, 103TL; /Foto Olimpik/NurPhoto: 162B; /Stuart Franklin: 111BL, 175B, 228L; /Romeo Gacad/AFP: 56C; /Daniel Garcia/AFP: 115TR; /Lluis Gene/AFP: 37TR; /Paul Gilham: 130C, 233TL; /Georges Gobet/AFP: 57BR; /Sergio Goya/AFP: 206C; /Mark Graham/AFP: 140L; /Otto Greule Jr: 152TR; /Laurence Griffiths: 29TL, 74TR, 77C, 168T, 172TR, 174L; /Alex Grimm: 47BR, 67TR, 227R; /Jeff Gross: 154TR; /Haraldur Gudjonsson/AFP: 161B; /Gianluigi Guercia/AFP: 218B; /Jack Guez/AFP: 98-99; /Valery Hache/AFP: 60L; /Joe Klamar/AFP: 55L, 65TR; /Christof Koepsel: 229C; /Mark Kolbe: 135TL, 135C; /Ozan Kose/AFP: 78B, 127TR; /Patrick Kovarik/AFP: 95C; /Kirill Kudryavtsev/AFP: 74B; /Isaac Lawrence/AFP: 144TL; /Nolwenn Le Gouic/Icon Sport: 86L; /David Leah: 179TL; /David Lean/Mexsport: 150TR; /Christopher Lee: 80TR; /Bryn Lennon: 70TR; /Francisco Leong/AFP: 24TR; /Matthew Lewis: 66TR; /Christian Liewig/Corbis: 214-215, 219R; /Alex Livesey: 5TL, 48TR, 56TR, 63TR, 83TL, 85C, 88TR, 90C, 141BR, 173TR, 184TL, 225BR; /Marco Luzzani: 31TR; /MB Media: 30BR; /Ian MacNicol: 16L, 52BL, 71BL, 95BL, 197BR, 253; /Pierre-Philippe Marcou/AFP: 44TL, 128TL; /Nigel Marple: 147C; /Hunter Martin/LatinContent: 113TR; /Angel Martinez/Real Madrid: 231; /Joosep Martinson: 158; /Clive Mason: 26L, 121TR, 129TL, 169BL; /Stephen McCarthy/Sportsfile: 71BR; /Jamie McDonald: 54BR, 60TR, 70C, 82TR, 227BL; /Chris McGrath: 101TR, 184TR; /Anatoly Medved/Icon Sportswire: 66B; /Marty Melville/AFP: 147T; /Buda Mendes: 226C; /Alex Menendez/LatinContent: 106BL; /Craig Mercer/CameraSport: 49BR; /Philippe Merle/AFP: 121R; /Aris Messinis/AFP: 200L; /Aurelien Meunier: 153BL; /Daniel Mihailescu/AFP: 73BC; /Douglas Miller/Keystone: 128L; /Sandra Montanez: 239T, 249; /Filippo Monteforte/AFP: 69BR; /Dean Mouhtaropoulos: 38T, 44B, 135TR, 247TR; /Peter Muhly/AFP: 70BR, 94B, 97TR, 197L; /Dan Mullan: 68B, 169R; /Paul Murphy: 247BL; /Hoang Dinh Nam/AFP: 152C; /Francois Nel: 112R; /Alexander Nemenov/AFP: 8-9, 75C; /Oleg Nikishin: 189BL; /Armend Nimani/AFP: 93BR; /Fayez Nureldine/AFP: 142BL; /NurPhoto: 29R, 217BR; /Kiyoshi Ota: 137BL; /Cem Ozdel/Anadolu Agency: 105TR; /Jeff Pachoud/AFP: 199C; /Ulrik Pedersen/Action Plus: 12TR; /Valerio Pennicino: 120TL; /Doug Pensinger: 14BR; /Frank Peters/Bongarts: 65L; /Sandro Pereyra/LatinContent: 117BL; /Hannah Peters: 146TR; /Ryan Pierse: 92BL, 178B; /Jan Pitman/Bongarts: 186TR; /Hrvoje Polan/AFP: 50C; /Joern Pollex: 28R; /Popperfoto: 15TL, 25L, 26BR, 28BL, 31C, 52BR, 62BL, 82C, 108L, 113B, 131L, 139L, 142R, 143T, 145B, 152BR, 163BR, 171BR, 173L, 198BL, 202B, 209BL, 210BR, 232BL; /Mike Powell: 188L; /Savo Prelevic/AFP: 97B; /Craig Prentis: 151TR; /Adam Pretty: 107TR; /Quality Sport Images: 23BR; /Ben Radford: 71C, 109C, 137T; /David Ramos: 185TL; /Michael Regan: 2, 13TR, 13B, 43TL, 88B, 91T, 250-251; /Kyle Rivas: 153TR; /Rafa Rivas/AFP: 45R; /Rolls Press/Popperfoto: 15B, 33B, 106TR; /Quinn Rooney: 116R, 243B; /Clive Rose: 5BR, 79BL, 89BL, 166R, 186BL, 191BL; /Martin Rose: 21C, 25TR; /Martin Rose/Bongarts: 87TR, 92BR; /David Rosenblum/Icon Sportswire: 255TL; /Evaristo Sa/AFP: 115R; /Karim Sahib/AFP: 230TR; /Jewel Samad/AFP: 69TR, 159BL; /Issouf Sanogo/AFP: 126BL, 130L, 131TR, 212-213; /Genia Savilov/AFP: 67L; /Sakis Savvides/AFP: 59R; /Rich Schultz: 211TL; /Abdelhak Senna/AFP: 220, 221BR; /Lefty Shivambu/Gallo Images: 216TR, 219C; /Torsten Silz/AFP: 175TR; /Christophe Simon/AFP: 22R, 83R; /Patrick Smith: 168BL, 242C; /Javier Soriano/AFP: 167L, 199B, 201BR; /Erwin Spek/Soccrates: 5L; /Jamie Squire: 124BR, 125TL; /Michael Steele: 51T, 82BL, 108TR; /Srdjan Stevanovic: 79R; /Patrik Stollarz/Bongarts: 94R; /Graham Stuart/AFP: 76TR; /Chris Szagola/LatinContent: 209TR; /TF-Images: 167TR, 176BL, 183BL, 241C; /Mehdi Taamallah/NurPhoto: 180C; /Justin Tallis/AFP: 215BL; /Trond Tandberg: 65B; /Bob Thomas: 16TR, 27R, 32TL, 32BL, 32BR, 37B, 38BR, 54L, 62TR, 63BL, 67BR, 68TR, 70BL, 90TR, 90BR, 102BR, 103C, 104BR, 109R, 112BL, 117BR, 119L, 125TR, 139BR, 186C, 190B, 192BR, 197TR; /Bob Thomas/Popperfoto: 46TR, 72C, 96BL, 114C, 114B; /Mark Thompson: 64TR, 216BR; /John Thys/AFP: 95R, 240TL; /ullstein bild: 61TR, 78C; /Pius Utomi Ekpei/AFP: 217TR; /VCG: 90BL, 139TR, 144BR; /VI Images: 4TR, 24B, 37TL, 40BR, 41TL, 73BL, 74C, 75TL, 76C, 100BR, 234-235, 241BR; /Robert van den Brugge/AFP: 48BL; /Manan Vatsyayana/AFP: 151BR; /Eric Verhoeven/Soccrates: 39R, 255TR; /Claudio Villa: 34B, 96BR; /Claudio Villa/Grazia Neri: 34TL; /Visionhaus/Corbis: 218L; /Hector Vivas: 110BL, 191R; /Friedemann Vogel: 236C; /Ian Walton: 39BL, 81TR; /Lakruwan Wanniarachchi/AFP: 143B, 160BL; /Koji Watanabe: 232TR; /Dave Winter/Icon Sport: 54C; /Maxim Zmeyev/AFP: 7

PA Images: 78TR, 208BR, 233TR; /ABACA Press: 169TL; /AP: 170BL; /Matthew Ashton: 39TL, 107C, 146BL; /Greg Baker/AP: 237BL; /Jon Buckle: 239BR; /Roberto Candia/AP: 237TL; /Barry Coombs: 58TR; /Malcolm Croft: 163TL; /Claudio Cruz/AP: 228C; /DPA: 22L, 27TL, 134TR, 135BR, 166BL; /Adam Davy: 236B; /Sean Dempsey: 25BR; /Paulo Duarte/AP: 68C; /Dominic Favre/AP: 84B; /Michel Gouverneur/Reporter: 226BL; /Intime Sports/AP: 58C; /Lee Jin-Man/AP: 238TR; /Ross Kinnaird: 209C; /Tony Marshall: 34L, 86B, 106TL, 171TL, 207TR, 225TL, 228TR, 229TR; /Cathal McNaughton: 12C; /Phil O'Brien: 30BL; /Panoramic: 226R; /Natacha Pisarenko/AP: 210C; /Peter Robinson: 35BR, 36TR, 62C, 66L, 76BR, 100L, 183TR, 224BL, 224BR; /S&G and Barratts: 17B, 180TR; /SMG: 77TT; /Ariel Schalit/AP: 126R; /Murad Sezer/AP: 23C; /Sven Simon: 106BR; /Neal Simpson: 73TR, 85BR, 208T; /Michael Sohn/AP: 242TR; /Jon Super/AP: 237TR; /Topham Picturepoint: 83BL, 94TL; /John Walton: 93TR, 103TR; /Witters: 185B

Wikimedia Commons: 64L, 204BR

Every effort has been made to acknowledge correctly and contact the source and/or copyright holder of each picture and Carlton Books Limited apologises for any unintentional errors or omissions that will be corrected in future editions of this book.

ABOUT THE AUTHOR

Keir Radnedge has been covering football for more than 50 years. He has written countless books on the subject, from tournament guides to comprehensive encyclopedias, aimed at all ages. His journalism career included the *Daily Mail* for 20 years, as well as the *Guardian* and other national newspapers and magazines in the UK and abroad. He is a former editor of *World Soccer*, generally recognized as the premier English-language magazine on global football. In addition to his writing, Keir has been a regular foreign football analyst for all UK broadcasters. He scripted official films of the early World Cups and is chairman of the football commission of AIPS, the international sports journalists' association.

ACKNOWLEDGEMENTS

Special thanks to Aidan Radnedge for support and assistance and an incomparable insight into the most intriguing corners of the world game.